D1615089

HAUNTED TEXTS
Studies in Pre-Raphaelitism

HAUNTED TEXTS
Studies in Pre-Raphaelitism
in Honour of William E. Fredeman

Edited by David Latham

UNIVERSITY OF TORONTO PRESS
Toronto Buffalo London

© University of Toronto Press Incorporated 2003
Toronto Buffalo London
Printed in Canada

ISBN 0-8020-3662-7

∞

Printed on acid-free paper

National Library of Canada Cataloguing in Publication

Haunted texts : studies in Pre-Raphaelitism in honour of
William E. Fredeman / edited by David Latham.

Includes bibliographical references and index.
ISBN 0-8020-3662-7

1. Pre-Raphaelitism – Great Britain.   2. Arts, British – 19th century.
I. Fredeman, William E. (William Evan), 1928–1999
II. Latham, David, 1951–

NX543.H39 2003   700′.941′09034   C2003-901711-7

University of Toronto Press acknowledges the financial assistance to its
publishing program of the Canada Council for the Arts and the
Ontario Arts Council.

University of Toronto Press acknowledges the financial support for its
publishing activities of the Government of Canada through the Book
Publishing Industry Development Program (BPIDP).

Contents

Preface   vii

1 Haunted Texts: The Invention of Pre-Raphaelite Studies   1
DAVID LATHAM

2 A Commentary on Some of Rossetti's Translations from Dante   35
JEROME MCGANN

3 Rossetti's Elegy for Masculine Desire: Seduction and Loss
in the *House of Life*   53
E. WARWICK SLINN

4 William Michael Rossetti and the Making of
Christina Rossetti's Reputation   71
ROGER PEATTIE

5 'Slight Channels': Arthur Hughes
and the Illustration of Children's Books   91
CAROLYN HARES-STRYKER

6 'Reading Aright' the Politcal Texts of Morris's
Textiles and Wallpapers   119
DAVID LATHAM

Contents

7 Whistler/Swinburne: 'Before the Mirror'   135

J. HILLIS MILLER

8 Scheherazade's 'Special Artist': Illustrations by
Arthur Boyd Houghton for *The Thousand and One Nights*   145

ALLAN LIFE

9 Sartorial Obsessions: Beardsley and Masquerade   177

LORRAINE JANZEN KOOISTRA

10 W.E.F.: Question Marks, Exclamation Points, and Asterisks   197

IRA B. NADEL

11 The Great Pre-Raphaelite Paper Chase: A Retrospective   211

WILLIAM E. FREDEMAN

12 William E. Fredeman: A Checklist of Publications   237

DAVID LATHAM

Contributors   247

Bibliography   249

Index   263

Illustrations follow p. 118

Preface

When William E. Fredeman began his study of Pre-Raphaelitism in the 1950s it was a subject dismissed as unfashionable and undefinable. Since then, Pre-Raphaelitism has emerged from the margins of nineteenth-century art and literature to the vanguard of interdisciplinary studies. The term that denotes the Pre-Raphaelite, Aesthetic, and Decadent movement in art, culture, and literature, however, has remained as undefinable as ever. *Haunted Texts* attempts to meet the challenge of defining and illustrating the full spectrum of Pre-Raphaelitism.

Much of the difficulty in defining the movement arises from the confusion propogated by the artists and writers themselves. Walter Crane defined Pre-Raphaelitism as 'primitive and archaic on one side; it was modern and realistic on another, and again, on another, romantic, poetic, and mystic, or again, wholly devoted to the ideals of decorative beauty' (*Ideals in Art*, 14). Crane is breathless in his qualifications for good reason. Figures as disparate as Christina Rossetti and Dante Rossetti, William Morris and Oscar Wilde, Walter Pater and Aubrey Beardsley all understood that they were charting a paradigmatic shift for the creative arts, one that positions creativity at the intersection between a reflexive discourse for an Art-for-Art's sake ideology and a communal discourse for an Arts-and-Crafts ideology. The result is a fusion of such seeming opposites as aesthetics and politics, the spiritual and the sexual, an ethereal symbolism and an earthly verisimilitude. Walter Pater epitomized this convergence of incongruities as 'the desire of beauty quickened by the sense of death' ('Poems by William Morris,' 309). Such jarring juxtapositions create a Möbius Strip of romance and reality that leaves the Pre-Raphaelite sensibility haunted by the abyss between the ideal of heaven and the reality of hell.

Crane's series of abstractions might be more aptly replaced by some concrete images of Pre-Raphaelitism. In various ways, Pre-Raphaelite art and literature emerge as haunted texts from the cellars and attics of Camelot. Not the moats and turrets of Camelot: such Gothic imagery is not specifically Pre-Raphaelite because moats, turrets, and Camelot belong together. And not the cradles and coffins of Camelot: cradles and coffins are simply the opposite ends of the same concept. But attics and cellars are appropriate images because they conflict with Camelot as concrete images of the real in juxtaposition with the ideal. William Michael Rossetti pinpointed this essence as the 'intimate intertexture of a spiritual sense with a material form' (*Dante Gabriel Rossetti as Designer and Writer*, 127). The conventional notion of Camelot is the heavenly ideal of the round table and spring blossoms. The Pre-Raphaelite sensibility is found not in this conventional Camelot but in that 'intimate intertexture' of its attics and cellars. It brings together the romance of the past with the sordid buried beneath; it brings together the romantic, autumnal nostalgia we hold for our dreams and desires preserved in the attic with the dark, sordid secrets we bury in the cellar in our effort to escape their consequences. Fusing together the realism of the attic/cellar with the idealism of Camelot is the paradoxical essence of Pre-Raphaelitism.

This Pre-Raphaelite principle of the 'intimate intertexture' brings together not the apples and oranges that Crane's all-inclusive definition applies to. Rather, we find it in the erotic prayer of an angel. We find it in the image of Guenevere and Launcelot reaching to kiss across the tomb of Arthur. If we were to extend the Pre-Raphaelite sensibility into our own century we might find it in the slippage that results from the intertexture of apples and iMacs, and from the intertexture of the self-description of Dante Rossetti transcribing 'Jenny' from his worm-holed manuscript exhumed from the coffin of Elizabeth Siddal in Highgate Cemetery and the enterprise of Jerome McGann creating an on-line hypertext edition of Rossetti's art and literature that is enabling scholars to study the entire Rossetti canon from their laptops.

Working with the diverse range of Pre-Raphaelite poetry, painting, decorative arts, book illustration, and political prose, the ten contributors to *Haunted Texts* pursue a variety of critical strategies. They study the bibliographical issues of archival research concerning the personal letters and diaries of the Rossetti family; the technological issues that challenge conventional methods of scholarship; the gender issues concerning constructions of identity derived from the changing conceptions of love, desire, anxiety, and brotherhood; and the interdisciplinary cultural issues that transgress the borders of high art and popular culture. William E. Fredeman devoted much of his career to establishing a critical foundation that would enable future scholars to define their understanding of the complexity of Pre-Raphaelitism. *Haunted Texts* pays tribute to Professor Fredeman in its pursuit of his mission.

I first met 'Dick' Fredeman at a conference in Montreal in 1980 when I was a graduate student. Spotting my name-tag in a crowd, he grabbed me by the arm and marched me to a cafeteria, explaining that he had been hoping to meet me. He sat me down and proceeded with vigour and zeal to advise me about pursuing an academic career. Two days later he handed me an original Rossetti drawing of Jane Morris. He had rolled it into a cardboard tube and asked me to deliver it to a Toronto art gallery for an appraisal. He was thinking of selling the drawing in order to finance the construction of a swimming pool in his back garden. I had met the embodiment of that 'intimate intertexture,' that convergence of incongruities, the Pre-Raphaelite grotesque. In our subsequent meetings and correspondence, it was always a pleasure to work with Dick. And as a young editor I was always surprised to hear his relief and delight when he received my approval of his work.

I welcome the opportunity to express my gratitude for the honour of editing this tribute to Dick's indispensable scholarship. I thank Carolyn Hares-Stryker, Lorraine Janzen Kooistra, Allan Life, Jerome McGann, Hillis Miller, Ira Nadel, Roger Peattie, and Warwick Slinn for making this collection a worthy tribute. I thank Jane Cowan and Betty Coley Fredeman for their generous support and guidance in helping with its publication. I am also grateful for the assistance of Kristen Pederson and Barbara Porter of the University of Toronto Press, and Professor William Whitla of York University and Gianna Wichelow of the William Morris Society. As always, I thank Sheila Latham for her assistance as a librarian at York University, for her interest as a fellow admirer of the Pre-Raphaelites, and for her patience as my wife.

1
Haunted Texts:
The Invention of Pre-Raphaelite Studies

David Latham

I

A movement begun in 1848 by three young British artists who pursued the paradoxical practice of presenting a literary subject in a naturalistic setting with a decorative style, Pre-Raphaelitism is now used as a term to denote the Victorian aesthetic movement that led to the socialism of William Morris and the Arts and Crafts guilds and to the decadence of Oscar Wilde and the Rhymers' Club. The last romantics, the last lovers of beauty, rebel youths haunted by the Gothic ruins of lost mythologies, they were also the first proponents of a disciplined art for art's sake. The Pre-Raphaelite elevation of art as a creed to worship and embody would inspire eulogies of prose flights throughout the otherwise disaffected century that followed their demise. Arthur Symons and W.B. Yeats, two writers who had outlived their *fin-de-siècle* colleagues in London, looked back at the turn of their century with an elegiac sense of the finality of what was lost. Symons concluded in an essay entitled 'The Decay of Craftsmanship in England' (1903) that 'it is certain that we have outlived the age of the craftsman, the age in which beauty was the natural attendant on use' (125). When Yeats visited Ezra Pound in Italy in 1929, they read together 'with great wonder' the poems of Morris's *Defence of Guenevere*, leaving Yeats sinking afterwards to a despondent conclusion: 'I have come to fear the world's last great poetic period is over' (*Letters*, 2 March 1929). The wonder experienced by Yeats with Pound lends greater poignance to Yeats's nostalgia for the aesthetic community of his youth: 'I was in all things Pre-Raphaelite ... We were all Pre-Raphaelites then' (*Autobiographies*, 141).

That their pervasive sense of degeneration from an idealized past led the Pre-Raphaelites to an inevitable fall from idealism to nostalgia is conveyed in the lament by Ford Madox Hueffer (Ford Madox Ford) in 1911:

> And we, the young men with long necks, long, fair hair, protruding blue eyes, and red ties, or the young maidens in our blue curtain serge with our round shoulders, our necks made as long as possible to remember Rossetti drawings, uttered with rapt expression long sentences about the social revolution that was just around the corner. We thought we were beautiful, we thought we were very beautiful; but Pre-Raphaelitism is dead, aestheticism is dead. Poor William Morris is very dead, too, and the age when poetry was marketable is most dead of all. It is dead, all dead, and that beautiful vision, the social revolution, has vanished ...
>
> What has become of the young men with their long necks and red ties? What has become of all the young maidens with the round shoulders, the dresses of curtain serge, and the amber necklaces? ... Where are all the adorers of the pre-Raphaelites? (qtd. in Fredeman, *Pre-Raphaelitism*, xx)

The recent revival of scholarly interest in and popular adoration for 'all things Pre-Raphaelite' owes its academic appeal to the interdisciplinary nature of the subject – to the interest in cultural studies and the relationship between image and text. It owes its more popular appeal to the interest in the Arts and Crafts aesthetic in a variety of forms, from ceramics to stained glass, from pottery in shops to poetry in hand-printed books. Hueffer, Yeats, and Symons could not have foreseen how a revolutionary movement begun by young rebels would become by the turn of the next century the subject of an upscale market-interest for the richest people from the counterculture world of the 1960s: Roger Daltry of The Who, Paul McCartney of the Beatles, Jimmy Page of Led Zeppelin, and Elton John purchase Pre-Raphaelite art and Morris & Co. crafts. Andrew Lloyd Webber outbids the Huntington and Pierpont Morgan libraries for Pre-Raphaelite art and manuscripts. J. Paul Getty, Jr., lives in the former home of Dante Rossetti on Cheyne Walk in Chelsea. In Hole's hit song 'Celebrity Skin,' Courtney Love sings from sonnet XCVII of *The House of Life*: 'Look in[to] my face; my name is Might-have-been.'

But when William E. Fredeman selected Hueffer's lament as the epigraph for his *Pre-Raphaelitism: A Bibliocritical Study* (1965), interest in the Pre-Raphaelites had long since reached its nadir. Fredeman intended to resurrect their works by facilitating the retrieval of its original nineteenth-century documents in a manner eerily parallel to Dante Rossetti's exhuming the manuscripts of his poems from his wife's coffin eight years after her death. Rossetti's letters alert us to the macabre condition of some of these documents: 'The poem Jenny which is the one I want most has got a great worm-hole right through every page of it. I could not examine it much, as the greater part still sticks together ... It has a dreadful smell, partly no doubt the disinfectants, but the doctor says there is nothing dangerous' (*Letters*, 2:753; 14 October 1869).

The title of this collection of essays, *Haunted Texts*, recalls not only the notion of exhumation and resurrection but also the Pre-Raphaelite way of seeing the present through prefigurations from the past and the eternal through the concrete details of mythology. The image of the haunted text is introduced by Jerome McGann in his insightful articulation of the effects of Dante Rossetti's interest in prefiguration, 'where the present world is regularly impinged upon by forces from the past and spirits of the dead ... where we glimpse living spirits appearing as premonitions of the past.' McGann's image is appropriate for the title of this book because it describes the essence of Pre-Raphaelitism in general and these eleven essays in particular. First, the image suggests how the Pre-Raphaelite attention to natural detail is employed to create a spiritualized naturalism wherein the heightened details from nature are treated as if they were prefigurations of the spiritual realm. This interest in typology has been recognized as a central Pre-Raphaelite concern since John Everett Millais exhibited *Christ in the House of His Parents*, which ignited the critical furore that catapulted the young Pre-Raphaelites to notoriety in 1850. The untitled painting was accompanied by a verse from Zachariah 13:6: 'And one shall say unto him, What are these wounds in thine hands? Then he shall answer, Those with which I was wounded in the house of my friends.' Millais thus foregrounded the typological vision of his art: the text of the Old Testament prefigures the text of the New, and the Christ child's injury in the carpenter's shop prefigures His crucifixion. What angered such critics as Charles Dickens was that in meticulous attention to each naturalistic detail, Millais portrayed Mary not as the divine madonna but as 'a kneeling woman,' vile in her commonness (*Household Words*, 15 June 1850) and showed Christ not as an educated noble, the aristocratic son of God, but as a common labourer, a mere apprentice among the working class. When Dante Rossetti accompanied his watercolour *The Passover of the Holy Family: Gathering the Bitter Herbs* (1855-6) with a sonnet, he pinpointed the pivotal significance of each incidental moment of our lives: 'Here meet together the prefiguring day / And the day prefigured.' By the end of the decade the typological practice was well understood: 'Great religious painters hitherto have striven to attain their aim through idealization ... by making the picture *unearthly*, it was sought to make it divine. With the Pre-Raphaelites the reverse; their principle is realization: in showing us as truly as possible *the real*, we are to behold the wonder of the divine' (S, G.U., 64).

Subverting this aspiration toward the eternal is the Pre-Raphaelite concern with the pervasive sense of loss through the mutable moment that arises from what Walter Pater epitomized as 'the desire of beauty quickened by the sense of death' ('Poems by William Morris,' 309). The haunted spirit arising from this sense of loss was recognized as a central Pre-Raphaelite concern by John Lucas Tupper in the third issue of *The Germ*: 'All things of the past come down to us with some poetry about them' (March 1850, 120). The first full volume of Pre-Raphaelite poetry – William Morris's *The Defence of Guenevere, and Other Poems* (1858) – is set not only in the medieval age, but moreover in an autumnal age wherein each character is haunted by their own irretrievable experience of a paradise lost. The poems present these characters, whether old or young, not in the midst of action or introspection, but recollecting aloud to others the scenes from their past. Details of love said to be 'all gone now' remain alive as haunting memories passed on to others:

> Ah! sometimes like an idle dream
> > That hinders true life overmuch,
> Sometimes like a lost heaven, these seem. ('Old Love,' 69-71)

Framed with singers and story-tellers, with old men's memories and young women's dreams, lives can be turned into legends and visions into chronicles. A pair of skeletons found in the overgrown grass stirs the teller of the tale 'Concerning Geffray Teste Noire' to read the story behind the bones until he no longer sees 'the small white bones that lay upon the flowers / But evermore ... saw the lady' – the untold story of her face, her eyes, her mouth, her kiss, her passion:

> I saw you kissing once, like a curved sword
> > That bites with all its edge, did your lips lie,
> Curled gently, slowly, long time could afford
> > For caught-up breathings; like a dying sigh

> They gather'd up their lines and went away,
> > And still kept twitching with a sort of smile,
> As likely to be weeping presently. (173-9)

The villainous Geffray is merely incidental as the imagined lives of the lovers become a 'true' tale to tell John Froissart who 'knoweth not this tale just past' (191). But the poem appears to foreground the irony that it is a dramatic monologue addressed to a young auditor on the slight chance that he may meet Froissart since he 'may well' happen to pass through Froissart's hometown. Froissart's *Chronicles* immortalize the notorious Geffray Teste Noire with no concern for resurrecting the lives of his anonymous victims.

Years later, Morris would define romance as 'the capacity for a true conception of history, a power of making the past part of the present' ('Address at the Twelfth Annual Meeting' [1889], 146). Thus romance, for Morris, was a dream of the ideal. Edward Burne-Jones could make this ideal sound like a celestial art far removed from life: 'I mean by a picture a beautiful romantic dream of something that never was, never will be – in a light better than any light that ever shone – in a land no one can define or remember, only desire (and then I wake up with the waking of Brynhild)' (qtd. in Harrison and Waters, 157). More tenuous than Tennyson's Camelot – 'built / To music, therefore never built at all, / And therefore built forever' ('Gareth and Lynette,' 272-4), the Pre-Raphaelite's golden realm of dream and desire exists only within the framework of a brazen reality ever-ready to intrude. Burne-Jones describes the creative sensibility of the Pre-Raphaelite artist in terms that embody the instability of their art:

> All by river's side I came back in a delirium of joy the land was so enchanted with bright colours, blue and purple in the sky, shot over with a dust of golden shower, and in the water a mirror'd counterpart, ruffled by a light west wind – and in my mind pictures of the old days, the abbey, and long processions of the faithful, banners of the cross, copes and crosiers, gay knights and ladies by the river bank, hawking-parties and all the pageantry of the golden age – it made me feel so wild and mad that I had to throw stones into the water to break the dream.
>
> I get frightened of indulging now in dreams, so vivid that they seem recollections rather than imaginations, but they seldom last more than half-an-hour; and the sound of earthly bells in the distance, and presently the wreathing of steam upon the trees where the railway runs, call me back to the years I cannot convince myself I am living in. (qtd. in Harrison and Waters, 15-16)

It is this abyss between the romantic ideal and the physical reality that haunts the work of the Pre-Raphaelites.

Second, the image of the haunted text is appropriate to the following essays inspired by William E. Fredeman, the self-acknowledged 'inventor' of Pre-Raphaelite studies. As tributes to the scholar who retrieved the subject forty years ago since it had fallen out of fashion at the end of the nineteenth century, these essays respond to the directions Fredeman set in motion and now point to the new trends for subsequent scholarship in the twenty-first century. The essays cover a wide range of Pre-Raphaelite topics: poetry, painting, decorative arts, book illustration, and political revolution. We may better understand how each of these topics are associated with Pre-Raphaelitism if we review his career and then construct a definition of the term Fredeman himself resisted defining.

II

'He is one of only three persons who have stirred a biographical impulse in me,' Robert Frost said, revealing his fascination with Thomas B. Mosher, the pirate publisher of American fine letter-press editions of Pre-Raphaelite literature (qtd. in Bishop, 434). Subsequently, the most interesting account of Mosher's career was written by the doyen of Pre-Raphaelite studies, Professor William E. Fredeman. If the lives of the American poet and the Canadian professor had crossed paths, Frost would surely have found Fredeman an equally fascinating subject. For Fredeman was not only the author of scholarly research on Dante Gabriel Rossetti, William Michael Rossetti, and Alfred Tennyson, but also the self-acknowledged inventor of the whole field of Pre-Raphaelite studies whose breathless accounts of his discoveries of archival treasures suggest an air of the opportunistic pirate but bear the essence of the discerning scholar and monastic preservationist.

In a confessional letter written to his friend and colleague John Stasny, Fredeman spoke of his effort to overcome the essential disintegration of his life:

My life, from infancy, has been so fragmented (familiarly, geographically, and nuptially), – orphanage, childhood in Little Rock; boarding school in Tennessee and Paris; Arkansas; navy; college; teaching in Oklahoma City; graduate school at OU; Vancouver, England, &c – that continuity has proved virtually impossible. Distance is a great divide and correspondence is a poor substitute for propinquity in buttressing friendships ... With yesterday distantly behind me, today less than satisfying, and tomorrows relentlessly diminishing, I'm afraid my resiliency, the spring and stretch that once characterized me may fast be abating. (qtd. in Stasny, iii)

Some might quibble about the alleged abatement in his spring and stretch. But more to the point is Stasny's encapsulating response to a scholar who succeeded in constructing a larger-than-life personality equal to the subjects of his scholarship: 'The introspection, which seems almost preternaturally Victorian and a real plot summary of a Dickensian or Meredithian novel or maybe a variation on a Gilbert and Sullivan 'I-am-an-orphan-boy' theme, is the essential Fredeman. He was not merely a Victorian scholar; he was a Victorian epitome' (Stasny, iii).

A recent news survey provides a fitting embellishment for the literary paradigm: Pine Bluff, Arkansas, scored in the 1999 U.S. survey as the least desirable urban community to inhabit in the United States. This was Fredeman's birthplace in 1928. After his removal from his home by children's authorities, he was raised in an orphanage until the age of six when he was adopted in Little Rock by an ambitious entrepreneur and her husband, an army officer. Though his new parents renamed him William Evan Fredeman, the child steadfastly answered only to his original name, Dick, the name he used informally throughout his life. And though his mother was a Christian Scientist, she had him educated at private military and Benedictine schools. Following his matriculation, he served in the U.S. Nay and then graduated with a B.A. from Hendrix College, Arkansas, at the age of 19. He joined the U.S. Army reserve, earning the rank of lieutenant by the end of the Korean War and taught high school while earning an M.A. in 1950 and a Ph.D. in 1956 at the University of Oklahoma, where he completed his dissertation, 'The Pre-Raphaelites and Their Critics: A Tentative Approach toward the Aesthetics of Pre-Raphaelitism,' despite the opposition of his committee who 'did not regard Pre-Raphaelitism as a bona fide area of research' (Lanigan, 5-6).

He found geographical stability when he moved to Canada in 1956 to join the English Department at the University of British Columbia. He remained there for forty years, with a home in the posh University Endowment Lands overlooking the Pacific Ocean. Within a year of his arrival, he discovered his first treasure trove of literary manuscripts and began the lifelong pursuit of collections that would transform the undergraduate library into a major research centre for Pre-Raphaelite scholarship. Fredeman's written account of the dealings involved with his first discovery there in Vancouver in 1957 reads with all the suspenseful twists and turns of a tragic cliff hanger: his account of coming across the name of Sir John Simeon in the Vancouver telephone directory, enquiring if this Sir John was related to Tennyson's neighbour on the Isle of Wight; learning that the descendant owned a cache of 300 letters from such eminent Victorians as

Tennyson, Browning, Rossetti, Hunt, and Woolner; cataloguing them for his university library to purchase; and meeting with the chief librarian only to be told 'in no uncertain terms that UBC's was *not* a research library,' and of at last reluctantly arranging their sale through Cecil Lang to the University of Syracuse for $750. The tension and disappointment are relieved only by the promised sequel: 'Later coups, however, would more than compensate for this initial failure' ('Scholarly Resources,' 204).

In 1963, his 'next encounter with the library bureaucracy was more successful.' Having crawled through an attic door at the top of a ladder in a Scottish castle, he discovered the Penkill Papers, 'a kind of mini-Malahide that altered the entire course of [his] future research' ('Scholarly Resources,' 211). The new chief librarian, Basil Stuart-Stubbs, understood the value of what Fredeman had found locked away in an attic trunk in Penkill Castle, the retreat of William Bell Scott and Alice Boyd. Hidden and henceforth forgotten since Alice's death in 1897 were Scott's notebooks, a scrapbook of drafts of his poems, an early draft of his *Autobiographical Notes*, and photographs of family, friends, and sites; there also were 550 letters between Scott and Alice Boyd, along with Alice's day-diaries from 1859 to 1897, which document not only Scott's relationship with Alice, but also Dante Gabriel Rossetti's relationship with Jane Morris; manuscript drafts of poems by D.G. Rossetti, Edmund Gosse, and W.J. Linton; and 67 letters from Arthur Hughes written over a number of years to keep Scott and Boyd abreast of current news about their fellow Pre-Raphaelites.

Fredeman met Helen Rossetti Angeli in 1963, and their subsequent friendship led to the acquisition in 1966 of a still much larger collection for the UBC library: the Angeli-Dennis Papers. Helen was the second daughter of William Michael Rossetti, and because she outlived her siblings as her father had outlived his, she had acquired all of the family manuscripts. And what an extended Pre-Raphaelite family it was: with William Michael Rossetti marrying Ford Madox Brown's daughter, Lucy, the family correspondence included the Ford Madox Brown family as well as the whole Rossetti family. The collection's 20,000 manuscripts include William Michael Rossetti's diaries (1867-68, 1876-1913), drafts for his critical essays and for his *Democratic Sonnets*, and 'roughly 5,000 incoming and well over 1,000 outgoing letters exchanged with a wide range of Victorian writers and artists, including 107 incoming letters relating to *The Germ* from the PRBs and their associates' ('Scholarly Resources,' 209); 818 outgoing letters from Dante Gabriel Rossetti and over 1,000 incoming letters to him; over 500 outgoing letters from Christina Rossetti; 1,600 letters to and from Lucy Brown Rossetti; over 300 letters to and from Ford

Madox Brown; the manuscript of Oliver Brown's 'The Black Swan,' the early draft of his published novel *Gabriel Denver* (1873); 50 letters from Dante Gabriel's godfather, the geologist Charles Lyell; and letters and an 1816 journal by the author of *The Vampire*, John Polidori, who was the Rossettis' uncle and Byron's physician. All in the family.

A third collection of manuscripts, the Leathart Papers, Fredeman acquired in 1968 from the grandson of James Leathart, the Pre-Raphaelite art patron from Newcastle. The collection is composed of 450 letters from the artists whose work Leathart admired and collected: Ford Madox Brown, with 95 letters; Edward Burne-Jones, with 15; Arthur Hughes, with 14; Holman Hunt, with 9; Albert Moore, with 15; D.G. Rossetti, with 49; William Bell Scott, with 146; and Simeon Solomon, with 10. Fredeman identifies these important letters as forming 'one of the few extant archives of a Victorian patron' ('Scholarly Resources,' 213).

Fredeman's fourth major acquisition – the Norman Colbeck collection of printed books, a 'magnificent collection of nineteenth-century and Edwardian poetry and Belles Lettres' – was one that complements the manuscript holdings. 'With Colbeck, UBC became overnight the Number Two repository for Pre-Raphaelite material on the continent, next to Princeton' ('Scholarly Resources,' 214). The arrangements that led to the Bournemouth bookseller's donation required the single-minded determination and the accommodating hospitality that typified Dick Fredeman: his meeting Colbeck at a Lytton Strachey booksale in 1966, his plotting a creative formula with the new UBC Librarian for government financial assistan ce, their establishing a curatorial position for Colbeck to catalogue the collection and publish the two-volume catalogue, and his welcoming the shy bookseller who had rarely left Bournmouth for more than a day's rail trip to now share Dick's home in Canada for the first year. Colbeck would later describe his life as 'divided into two unequal halves: pre- and post-Fredeman' (Fredeman, 'Great Paper Chase,' 224).

These collections rooted the orphan, who had never lived in the same place for more than five years, in a familiar home surrounded by his scholarly interests. He had created a place to work and a place to welcome other like-minded scholars. Having established 'Vancouver as a "must-see" on the scholarly Baedeker trail' ('Great Paper Chase,' 222), Fredeman enjoyed serving as more than a tour guide. He generously invited Pre-Raphaelite enthusiasts to his home where in the kitchen he would share their interests as he cooked dinner and then made his home available for them to pursue their studies with his personal collection of Pre-Raphaelite material.

The vast archival collections he secured for his university as well as his own personal collections were the natural by-product of the research for his first book: *Pre-Raphaelitism: A Bibliocritical Study* (1965). A reviewer in the *Times Literary Supplement* was dismissive,[1] recognizing that the book was 'beautifully produced and undoubtedly will prove useful as a reference book; but it should be consulted with a certain amount of caution.' Complaining that 'chit-chat takes the place of collation,' the reviewer was sceptical about its scope: 'The thin ice over which Mr. Fredeman skates with agility and exuberance creaks ominously, when he omits primary sources or lists them as haphazardly as the repositories of material to which he succeeded in gaining access: was every attic scaled personally in, say, the Isle of Man, and every crocket box explored on the Border?' ('Rossetti and the Rest,' 836). But, as the overwhelming range and depth of its scholarship was gradually recognized, the book became the Pre-Raphaelite bible. Cecil Lang identifies it as 'the one indispensable book ... that has made it possible to study Pre-Raphaelitism systematically. Its usefulness, as anyone who has tried to work the field Before Fredeman will recognize, cannot be overemphasized, and nineteenth-century scholarship will always be in his debt' (497).

The interdisciplinary nature of a field that includes painting, poetry, and printing required Fredeman to work with bibliographical material 'with which little has been previously done' and to navigate his way 'through a wilderness hitherto virtually uncharted' (*Pre-Raphaelitism*, vii; 41). He divided the study into five sections, beginning with a commentary that outlines 'the shifting critical attitudes toward the movement,' followed by a four-part bibliography that starts with an unconventional section that surveys the major art and manuscript collections (at university libraries as well as the homes of private collectors), the exhibitions mounted over the years, and the auction sales and booksellers' catalogues. The second part of the bibliography is divided into two sections: the first includes thirteen subsections on Dante Gabriel Rossetti and the second has sections for each of the thirty-one other Pre-Raphaelite associates and affiliates. The third part of the bibliography continues with critical works about the Pre-Raphaelite movement, and the fourth part concludes with a bibliography of Pre-Raphaelite book and periodical illustrations.

In his introductory commentary section, Fredeman describes Pre-Raphaelite scholarship as clustering 'around five salient dates': 1851 (Ruskin's defence of the artists, a defence that foregrounded Ruskin's own interests and thereby overemphasized the mimetic notion of the Pre-Raphaelites' fidelity to nature); 1857 (the annus mirabilis, when eight artists collaborated on the Oxford Union frescoes and then nine artists were part of a London exhibition of Pre-Raphaelite art); 1882 (the death of Dante Rossetti); 1928 (the centenary of Dante Rossetti's birth); and 1948 (the centenary of the founding of the Pre-Raphaelite Brotherhood). These 'five salient dates' are disproportionately Dante-centric. Indeed, to a lesser degree the whole bibliography is too Dante-centric. Citing Rossetti as the leader of the movement, Fredeman explained that the bibliographies are intended to be 'comprehensive' for Dante Rossetti, but are 'intentionally selective' for the other thirty-one Pre-Raphaelites, contending that 'to offer full coverage for such writers as Christina Rossetti, Ruskin, Patmore, Morris, and Swinburne would require a separate volume for each' (*Pre-Raphaelitism*, 89). The explanation is only marginally less strained than Holman Hunt's attempt to place Hunt himself at the centre of the original pleiad of James Collinson, William Holman Hunt, John Everett Millais, D.G. Rossetti, William Michael Rossetti, Frederic George Stephens, and Thomas Woolner. I would guess instead that Fredeman began his study with Dante Rossetti and that once he had applied his rigorously thorough scholarly skills to his subject, he realized that he could not practically apply the same rigour to the other thirty-one men and women he associated with Pre-Raphaelitism. He thus employed Dante Rossetti as the exemplary model for scholarly thoroughness. The other thirty-one Pre-Raphaelites provide not only a rich range of contemporaries for contextualizing Rossetti, but also a smorgasbord of samples for other scholars to pursue with the same effort Fredeman practised with Rossetti. His pithy biocritical accounts of the more obscure of the thirty-one others were intended to be starting points for critical enquiry, but they remain unsurpassed as the standard assessments.

What Fredeman could not likely have guessed during this early research is that his five Dante-centric dates would soon be revised by other scholars according to a more accurately Fredeman-centric scale, with Cecil Lang recognizing the year 1965 as the single pivotal date for dividing Pre-Raphaelite scholarship into the two eras of B.F. and A.F.: *before* Fredeman and *after* Fredeman (497). Many who met Fredeman after the publication of his Pre-Raphaelite bible no doubt agreed with Malcolm Warner's admission that it was 'like meeting Moses' (Fredeman, 'Great Paper Chase,' 211). Fredeman corrected this impression by identifying William Michael Rossetti as the real Moses and himself as the Sorcerer's Apprentice (212). William Michael Rossetti is 'the critic-amanuensis and self-appointed apostle-historian' of the Pre-Raphaelites (Fredeman, *Pre-Raphaelitism*, 27, 28). Still, we cannot turn to William Michael Rossetti for a definition of Pre-Raphaelitism, though he does offer one:

The bond of union among the Members of the Brotherhood was really and simply this: 1, To have genuine ideas to express; 2, to study Nature attentively, so as to know how to express them; 3, to sympathize with what is direct and serious and heartfelt in previous art, to the exclusion of what is conventional and self-parading and learned by rote; and 4, and most indispensable of all, to produce thoroughly good pictures and statues. (qtd in Lang, xxii)

As Cecil Lang complains, Rossetti's definition is not so much false as worthless: 'The same claims could be made for virtually any serious painter in the whole history of western art before the twentieth century' (xxii). Citing a number of 'seeming and actual inconsistencies in their working aesthetic,' centring on the 'unreconciled contradiction between the mimetic – "follow nature" – and the expressive – "fidelity to inner experience" – theories of art' (*Pre-Raphaelitism*, 3), Fredeman refuses to make the same mistake as Rossetti. He resists proposing a clear definition of Pre-Raphaelitism, preferring instead to examine 'the shifting critical attitudes toward the movement' (*Pre-Raphaelitism*, vii). He not only provides an historic review of the critical reception clustered around his selected focal points of his five dates, but also presents his commentary as an invitation to approach the archives of manuscripts and the canon of criticism as the necessary prerequisite for serious students to mediate their own way through the 'shifting critical attitudes.' To resolve the dynamic tensions of Pre-Raphaelitism for the construction of a limited definition would be to oversimplify the term just as John Ruskin had done in the first sustained critical commentary on the Pre-Raphaelites: *Pre-Raphaelitism: By the Author of 'Modern Painters'* (1851). Instead, with his four updates, Fredeman has contributed five major surveys of Pre-Raphaelite scholarship: *Pre-Raphaelitism: A Bibliocritical Study* (1965), 'The Pre-Raphaelites' (1968), 'Pre-Raphaelitism Revisited: or, Dr. Frankenstein Reprograms the Monster' (1988), 'The Great Pre-Raphaelite Paper Chase: A Retrospective' (1995), and 'Scholarly Resources: The Pre-Raphaelites in Canada' (1998).

Why has a definition remained so elusive? Dante Gabriel Rossetti was less helpful than his brother. When asked if he were the 'Pre-Raphaelite Rossetti,' Dante Gabriel replied: 'Madam, I am not an "ite" of any kind; I am a painter' (qtd. in Sharp, 71). Cecil Lang confesses that 'Pre-Raphaelitism, though we cannot do without it, is meaningless as a literary term.' It has 'never been satisfactorily defined either as a literary or pictorial term. Obviously, the components of the term itself have no meaning at all in poetry, and except for drawing attention to a state of mind, very little relevance to actual practice in painting' (xi; xxii). Having set down these inhibiting precautions, Lang ventures ever so warily beyond William Michael Rossetti's platitudes: Pre-Raphaelitism 'had a certain utility in literary history but does not belong to criticism ... If, however, it is to be used as a strictly critical term, it has to mean something like "visualized poetry of fantasy" or "fantasy crossed with realism"' (xxvi). Its essential principle is paradoxical: 'Pre-Raphaelitism strives, impossibly, to accept and reject [philosophical dualism] simultaneously: matter and spirit are not quite different and not quite identical, they are "the same and not the same." Pre-Raphaelite fantasy affirms the dichotomy, Pre-Raphaelite particularity repudiates it' (xxvii).

To pursue Lang's suggestions further we should first contextualize Pre-Raphaelitism as a historical term and then identify its characteristics as a critical term. Fredeman quotes Max Beerbohm to suggest how the flame of Pre-Raphaelitism could ignite passion and inspire poetry: '"In the days of deep, smug, thick, rich, drab, industrial complacency," Pre-Raphaelitism itself shone ... "with the ambiguous light of a red torch somewhere in a dense fog"' (*Pre-Raphaelitism*, 5). In reaction to the oppressive fog of industry, with its regimentation of labour for the mass production of cheap commodities, and its desperate squalor amidst ostentatious luxury, the Pre-Raphaelites offered new approaches to painting and to poetry, to the decorative arts and to the politicization of society. In the following paragraphs, I shall briefly outline the characteristics of Pre-Raphaelite painting and poetry, and follow their development towards decadence, towards the Arts and Crafts, and towards socialism.

III

Pre-Raphaelitism began in Britain with the term first being associated in 1848 with a brotherhood centred on three painters: William Holman Hunt, John Everett Millais, and Dante Gabriel Rossetti. Rossetti had apprenticed himself to Ford Madox Brown, an independent-minded artist influenced by an unfashionably pious group of German naturalists known as the Nazarenes who had rejected the classical manner of the art academies in Munich and Vienna. Because their pre-Renaissance style was well suited to the architecture of the Gothic Revival, the Nazarene Peter von Cornelius was employed as an adviser for frescos and decorative details for the new Houses of Parliament designed by Charles Barry and Augustus Pugin. The young Ford Madox Brown submitted designs for murals in the Queen's Robe Room. The enthusiasm for a medieval-style brotherhood of

painters originated with Brown's pupil Rossetti. The name of the brotherhood originated with the two other founders. Holman Hunt explained
how the term was first used as a label for Hunt and Millais in 1847 after their
stubborn dispute with their fellow students at the Royal Academy over the
alleged perfection of Raphael's grand manner:

> We did not bow down to the chorus of the blind, for when we advanced
> our judgment on 'The Transfiguration' we condemned it for its grandiose
> disregard of the simplicity of truth, the pompous posturing ... and the
> unspiritual attitudinising. In our final estimation this picture was a signal
> step in the decadence of Italian art. When we had advanced this opinion
> to other students, they as a *reductio ad absurdum* had said, 'Then you are
> Pre-Raphaelite.' Referring to this as we worked side by side, Millais and I
> laughingly agreed that the designation must be accepted. (Hunt, I:100-1)

They might have labelled themselves more accurately as 'Pre-
Reynoldsians,' since their rebellion was directed more against Reynolds's
Discourses than Raphael's art. Joshua Reynolds had derived his rules of style
from his study of Raphael. Though his eighteenth-century contemporary
Thomas Gainsborough was the first to disprove these rules (by showing
that the colour blue need not be considered inappropriate for the foreground of a composition), the Royal Academy adopted the *Discourses* as the
paradigm for its students. As Laurence Housman succinctly explained, 'art
was a coffin in which Raphael lay embalmed. Therefore, in order not to
remain mutes at a funeral, the men of the new movement had to become
Pre-Raphaelites; get rid, not of the living Raphael, but of his corpse' (6).
Rejecting the enforcement of such pre-determined rules, seven artists and
critics formed the original Pre-Raphaelite Brotherhood, and two years later
formalized their assault with the short-lived magazine *The Germ: Thoughts
towards Nature in Poetry, Literature, and Art* (with four issues in January,
February, March, and May 1850).

William Michael Rossetti attempted to explain the Pre-Raphaelite
agenda: '"Thoughts towards nature" indicated accurately enough the pre-
dominant conception of the Pre-Raphaelite Brotherhood, that the artist,
whether painter or writer, ought to be bent upon defining and expressing
his own thoughts, and that these ought to be based upon a direct study of
Nature, and harmonized with her manifestations' (W.M. Rossetti, *The Germ*,
9-10). Such vagueness invited John Ruskin's influential but misguided
defence (and led him to consider himself as a Pre-Raphaelite – 'We PRBs
must do better for you,' he wrote to Tennyson regarding the Moxon illus-

trated edition [24 July 1857]). In his preface to *Pre-Raphaelitism* (1851), Ruskin recalls his 'advice to the young artists of England' offered in the first volume of his *Modern Painters*: 'They should go to nature in all single-ness of heart, and walk with her laboriously and trustingly, having no other thought but how best to penetrate her meaning; rejecting nothing, select-ing nothing, and scorning nothing.' Now that his advice has been 'at last carried out, to the very letter, by a group of men who, for their reward, have been assailed with the most scurrilous abuse,' he feels duty-bound 'to contradict the directly false statements which have been made respecting their works' (*Works*, XII:339).

Ruskin's emphasis on a 'loving fidelity to the thing studied,' without 'fanciful or ornamental modifications,' went unchallenged until William Morris articulated his understanding of the three principles that charac-terize Pre-Raphaelitism in 1891. In his 'Address on the Collection of Paintings of the Pre-Raphaelite School,' Morris identifies the movement as a 'revolt against Academicism' and describes its naturalistic, narrative, and ornamental principles: 'Besides the mere presentment of naturalistic facts, they aimed ... at the conscientious presentment of incident ... telling some kind of story to the beholder.' Moreover, a Pre-Raphaelite painting ought to be 'something more than a representation of nature and teller of a tale ... It ought to be ornamental' (Morris, *AWS*, I:300-2). Morris's portrait of *La Belle Iseult* epitomizes this paradoxical presentation of a literary sub-ject in a naturalistic setting with a decorative style: an Arthurian heroine stands before her rumpled bed-sheets and cluttered dressing table, tying the belt around her embroidered gown, whose pattern is complemented by the surrounding tapestries. J.E. Millais's *Ophelia* is equally exemplary: Shakespeare's character is clothed in a floral-patterned gown, half-sub-merged in water, and enshrouded by willows and water-reeds whose every leaf and blade is depicted with the same meticulous detail as her drowned body.

The attempt to integrate these three paradoxical principles turns Pre-Raphaelite art into the haunted text. First, the narrative is not a sentimen-tal story but usually a moral dilemma or a dramatic moment of crisis. Secondly, the naturalistic element vivifies and intensifies the scene by making the figures real before our eyes, not as part of an idealized compo-sition but as part of our own ordinary experience. And thirdly, the decora-tive element monumentalises the moment by eternalizing the mundane verisimilitude of trivial detail into the ordered pattern of a fictional frame-work, what Pater recognized as an art based on art.

Even paintings that seem to lack the dialectical tension of balancing the

three paradoxical principles of the literary narrative, the mimetic naturalism, and the stylized ornament can still convey the tension of the haunted
text. Dante Rossetti's watercolour of *Arthur's Tomb* has none of the Pre-
Raphaelite attention to meticulous naturalistic detail. But its literary figures from Malory – Launcelot reaching over the tomb of Arthur in his effort
to kiss the repentant Guenevere – and the decorative effects of the grass,
foliage, and tree trunk are complemented by the relief that decorates the
side of the tomb with a chivalric text that prefigures and anticipates the
love, sin, death, and redemption captured in this dramatically charged
moment. The two scenes come together as the foliage of an unseen orchard tree casts its serpentine shadows on the grass and fallen apples in
the foreground at the left, while the orchard tree in the foreground at the
right casts its shadow as a cross over the round table of Camelot depicted on
the tomb. The scene is intensified by Morris in his poem on the same
subject, with his favourite preposition – 'across' – exploited as a momen-
tary crucifixion image,[2] as Guenevere agonizes over her desire to kiss the
lips of Launcelot 'across my husband's head' ('King Arthur's Tomb,' 209).
The kiss as a social vision, drawing separate souls together, is thwarted by
the imprint of these typological shadows that leave love haunted. Thus,
though Rossetti's watercolour ignores the technical aspects of verisimilitude, it still epitomizes the Pre-Raphaelite fixation with the conflict between the ideal and the real, between heaven and hell, 'between Christ
and a rival lover' (Pater, 'Poems,' 301).

    With figures from medieval tales and Shakespeare's plays, from the
poetry of Keats and Tennyson, the Pre-Raphaelites made the literary
appear at once real and ornamental. Henry James extended this conflation
of the literary and the living to his meeting with Morris's wife and model,
Jane Morris: 'She haunts me still. A figure cut out of a missal ... an apparition of fearful and wonderful intensity. It's hard to say whether she's a
grand synthesis of all the Pre-Raphaelite pictures ever made – or they a
'keen analysis' of her – whether she's an original or a copy' (*Letters of Henry
James*, 1:16; 10 March 1869). The 'missal-like intensity of Pre-Raphaelitism'
(Sketchley, 15), the minute details and bright, jarring colours, marked a
startling deviation from the Academy's rules for the harmonious relationships of ideal forms. Evelyn Waugh summarized the Pre-Raphaelite dis-
taste for 'Sir Sloshua's' *Discourses*: academy conventions dictated that the
composition on the canvas must form an 'S' or a triangle; the laws of
chiaroscuro required that the darkness-to-light ratio be three to one. The
surface was then 'toned' with varnish. 'Viewed obliquely the design was
usually invisible in a sheen of reflected light. At the right angle it achieved

a certain mellow harmony that went well with dining-room mahogany and roast mutton' (Waugh, 24).

Ruskin was the first to praise the prevalence of sunlight as a distinguishing quality in Pre-Raphaelite art: 'Their system of light and shade is exactly as the Sun's; which is, I believe, likely to outlast that of the Renaissance, however brilliant' (*Works*, XII:357). A year later, William Michael Rossetti noted that Holman Hunt's *Hireling Shepherd* conveyed a 'feeling of the country – its sunny shadow-varied openness – such as I do not remember to have seen ever before so completely expressed' (*Spectator*, 15 May 1852, 472). Frederic George Stephens singled out this attention to sunlight 'as an entirely new thing in art' (19). To replace chiaroscuro with sunlight, the Pre-Raphaelites moved their easels outdoors. But a more technical matter distinguishes their canvases. In striving to convey the effect of frescos, they experimented with the technique of painting on a white-primed canvas, adding the brightest colours to a still-wet white base, lending such vibrancy to mistletoe green, duck's-egg blue, and the rose-amber of the pomegranate flower.

That the Pre-Raphaelites moved outside to paint in the daylight, sunlight, or moonlight is not immediately obvious since so many of their paintings feature enclosures. Figures in the foreground often appear before a wall, with the distant background visible only through a window, a doorway, or beyond the top of the wall. As Ruskin appropriately observed, 'The painter of interiors feels like a caged bird, unless he can throw a window open, or set the door ajar' (*Works*, IV:82). Elizabeth Siddal's paintings both exemplify these partial enclosures and offer an interesting contrast to her poetry. While her poems convey the comfort found in grave-like beds of tall, bending grass, her paintings depict the structural enclosures that protect such virgins as the Lady of Shalott, Lady Clare, Madeline from *Eve of St Agnes*, May Margaret from *Clerk Saunders*, and the Holy Family from full engagement with life and death in the world beyond their windows. Why her paintings anticipate the expulsion from the womb of innocence, but her poems plead for a release from the tomb of experience, is a Swinburnean question for pondering, one that may have led William Fredeman to confess his temptation 'to say that Elizabeth Siddal was, after all, the only Pre-Raphaelite' (*Pre-Raphaelitism*, 210).

Siddal is often depicted as the possessed object of the male gaze so devastatingly critiqued by Christina Rossetti's 'In an Artist's Studio': 'One face looks out from all his canvases ... He feeds upon her face by day and night, / And she with true kind eyes looks back on him ... Not as she is, but as she fills his dream' (1, 9-10, 14). Christina's sonnet can be compared with two of her brother Dante's poems: 'The Portrait' – 'This is her picture as she was ... I gaze until she seems to stir' (1, 5) – and another 'Portrait,' sonnet X of *The House of Life* – 'Let all men note / That in all years (O Love thy gift is this!) / They that would look on her must come to me' (12-14). But unlike Robert Browning's last duchess, Siddal was not confined to another artist's canvas. Siddal speaks out with her own poems and paintings, moving beyond the patriarchal constructions observed by the young Yeats: 'The heroines of all the neo romantic London poets, namely Swinburne, Morris, Rossetti – and their satelites ... are essentially men's heroines with no separate life of their own' (*Letters*, 1:30; 1 August 1887). The feminist perspective that informs poems like 'Love and Hate' (the alleged cruel mistress spurns her unfaithful, guilt-ridden seeker of grace) and 'Dead Love' (consoling his rejected beloved, the speaker reveals his callousness as a smug rationalizer of the way of the world) also informs paintings like *Sir Patrick Spens* (the drunken king's order as it affects not the sailors, lords, and ladies but the sailors' wives and children). Ruskin considered Siddal among the five geniuses he had met: 'These geniuses are all alike, little and big. I have known five of them – Turner, Watts, Millais, Rossetti, and this girl' (*Works*, 36:217). Christina Rossetti's image of Siddal as the victim of a vampiric gaze should be more than tempered by Violet Hunt's image of Siddal as the creative artist: 'She worked up her poems ... inserting and erasing ... altering and re-altering them: urgently Pre-Raphaelite in her attempt to get the one lonely word, because it is the only one, and the little intimate detail amid the rhetoric which will bring the situation before us' (65).

IV

A most simplistic response to the interdisciplinary nature of Pre-Raphaelitism has persisted right from the start, with the criticism that followed the publication of the first Pre-Raphaelite poems in *The Germ*. A reviewer praised Dante Rossetti's poem 'My Sister's Sleep,' concluding that 'a poet's tongue told what an artist's eye has seen' (Cox, 94). Coventry Patmore similarly described the sculptor Thomas Woolner's two poems in *The Germ* as 'sculpturesque.' It has thus long been a critical commonplace to observe that the Pre-Raphaelites painted their poems and wrote their paintings.

Walter Pater wrote the first profound analysis of Pre-Raphaelite poetry. In his review of William Morris's dramatic lyrics and narrative tales, he recognized a new kind of poetry, an art based on art, which he was to call 'Aesthetic poetry':

This poetry is neither a mere reproduction of Greek or medieval life or poetry, nor a disguised reflex of modern sentiment. The atmosphere on which its effect depends belongs to no actual form of life or simple poetry. Greek poetry, medieval or modern poetry, projects above the realities of its time a world in which the forms of things are transfigured. Of that world this new poetry takes possession, and sublimates beyond it another still fainter and more spectral, which is literally an artificial or 'earthly paradise.' ('Poems,' 300)

Allusive and elusive, the 'still fainter and more spectral realm' of an art based on art is layered with irreconcilable readings. Not so much warring versions of reality requiring resolution, the haunted text invites complementary rather than competitive readings. Truth for the Pre-Raphaelite is neither Ruskin's faithful copy of a tuft of grass nor Oscar Wilde's dismissive shrug that 'in matters of art, it is one's last mood' (*Intentions*, 8:194). Truth for the Pre-Raphaelite is the variety of possibilities suspended among different readings.

Dante Rossetti's 'The Blessed Damozel' is an exemplary text. Though Rossetti suggested that he was rewriting Poe's 'The Raven,' his poem may equally be read as a rewriting of Tennyson's 'Mariana,' as the Damozel waits wearily with similar words: 'I wish that he were come to me / For he will come ... All this is when he comes' ('The Blessed Damozel,' 67-8; 135). Rossetti's poem may be about the erotic desires of a love-sick angel in heaven or about the projections of a self-obsessed man on earth; evidence abounds for both. The earth-bound lover betrays his own assertions when he recognizes the feeling of her hair on his face as only the fall of dead leaves:

> Surely she leaned o'er me – her hair
>   Fell all about my face ...
> Nothing: the autumn fall of leaves. (21-3)

He hears her speak only after his self-convincing rhetorical pleas:

> (Ah sweet! Even now, in that bird's song,
>   Strove not her accents there,
> Fain to be harkened? When those bells
>   Possessed the mid-day air,
> Strove not her steps to reach my side
>   Down all the echoing stair.) (61-6)

To fortify his prayers for death, he has to project an image of her waiting for him, calling for him, praying for him to join her. But the punctuation suggests three levels of narration: the earthbound lover within parentheses and the heavenbound beloved within quotation marks are distinguished from an omniscient narrator describing a celestial, angelic presence reaching down toward a scarcely believing earthly mortal. To dismiss the poem as a morbid projection is to miss the power of its tenuous evocation of a yearning love, the power of its vision of a lover on earth who sees not the flight of the heavenly angels, but his beloved's smile, who hears not the heavenly chorus of stars, but his beloved's tears:

> (I saw her smile.) But soon their path
>   Was vague in distant spheres:
> And then she cast her arms along
>   The golden barriers,
> And laid her face between her hands,
>   And wept. (I heard her tears.) (139-44)

Over the years, off and on, a relationship drifts into focus, as a heavenly figure leans out to reach for her earthly lover, until the paths of their distant spheres drift still again apart.

In addition to the non-mimetic, self-reflexive quality of Pre-Raphaelite poetry, Pater identifies the jarring juxtapositions that define the literary nature of the grotesque as a second characteristic. In the lyrics of *The Defence of Guenevere* (1858), Morris recreates the medieval mind torn between mystic religion in the cloister and mystic passion in the chateau, between 'Christ and a rival lover.' In the narrative tales of *Jason* (1867) and *The Earthly Paradise* (1868-70), he signals a revolt against the dreamlight of complex and subtle interests explored in *The Defence* to the daylight of elementary passions, revitalizing the Hellenism of Chaucer rather than Homer: 'Hellenism relieved against the sorrow of the middle age forms the chief motive of *The Earthly Paradise* ... the desire of beauty quickened by the sense of death' ('Poems,' 308-9)

In his essay on Dante Rossetti, Pater identifies the grotesque union of such opposites as the sacred and the sexual as an exhibition of sincerity. What Robert Buchanan had attacked as 'fleshly' in the poetry of Rossetti (*Contemporary Review*, 18 [October 1871]), Pater elegantly explains is the sincere, definite, and sensible imagery that characterizes the literary 'grotesque':

A perfect sincerity, taking effect in the deliberate use of the most direct and unconventional expression, for the conveyance of a poetic sense which recognized no conventional standard of what poetry was called upon to be ... One of the peculiarities of 'The Blessed Damozel' was a definiteness of sensible imagery, which seemed almost grotesque to some, and was strange, above all, in a theme so profoundly visionary. The gold bar of heaven from which she leaned, her hair yellow like ripe corn, are but examples of a general treatment, as naively detailed as the pictures of those early painters contemporary with Dante, who has shown a similar care for minute and definite imagery in his verse. (*Appreciations*, 206-7)

Couched within comparisons with Dante, Pater's explanation here of the grotesque points to a key distinction of Pre-Raphaelite poetry. The Pre-Raphaelites dispense with the borders of decorum that even Shakespeare resisted transgressing. Decorum in art demands that coarse issues are reserved for low characters, such as Juliet's nurse. But Pater recognizes that Rossetti's treatment of an erotic angel, sexually frustrated, is distinguished by perfect sincerity. Sincere passion is not simply ruing a month's separation from a lover, nor chivalrically dying for a lover; it is the all-consuming passion a damozel feels for her beloved, despite her ten years experiencing the divine bliss of heaven.

The Pre-Raphaelite's concern for the literary grotesque is founded upon the principle that 'material loveliness formed the great undeniable reality of things' (Pater, *Appreciations*, 213). When the painter and poet William Bell Scott located the seed of the flower of Pre-Raphaelitism in photography, he may have been thinking of painting, but his point is perhaps more relevant to poetry. Reviewers of Morris's *The Defence of Guenevere* praised this first volume of Pre-Raphaelite poetry for its 'loving elaboration of every minute detail' (Garnett, 226), for the '"conscientious rendering of the actual" in its minutest details' (*Tablet*, 266), though the reviewer for *Saturday Review* found the microscopic attention to 'every stain on every leaf' as extravagant and grotesque (206), no doubt recognizing its assault on the neo-classical paradigm as articulated by Samuel Johnson: 'The business of the poet ... is to examine, not the individual, but the species; to remark general properties and large appearances; he does not number the streaks of the tulip, or describe the different shades in the verdure of the forest. He ... must neglect the minuter discriminations' (*Rasselas*, XVI: ch. 10, 43-44).

As in Pre-Raphaelite painting, wherein minute details are not selected and arranged in a uniform pattern from a singular perspective, the Pre-

Raphaelite poets could depict individual details as independent of their context. Equally vivid details from nature, from walled gardens, from paintings of flowers (as in a shield depicting 'two red roses across the moon') could be combined in a union of verisimilitude and symbolism to create a spiritualized naturalism. William Michael Rossetti perceptively identified this Kantian union as the 'intimate intertexture of a spiritualized sense with a material form' (*Dante Gabriel Rossetti*, 127). The artifice of vivid details applied to fictional figures from the past produces two opposing effects. From one direction, the rendering of medieval matter in a modern manner challenges the Victorian faith in progress by making the fictional and the historical appear real and contemporary, thereby eternalizing the primitive. From the other direction, this 'inimate intertexture' of a spiritualized naturalism transfigures life into the visionary realm of art. As Pater observed in his description of the new poetry, dream and vision create a decorative and mythological world of an art based on art. Lured by its fictional figures to remain immersed in this aesthetic sphere, we know full well the fragility of the vision within the walled garden and the inevitability of our awakening beyond its walls. 'Vagrants in paradise' is the haunting epithet the poet Bliss Carman provides for this phenomenon.

The mutable moment is a defining Pre-Raphaelite concern. For Dante Rossetti, the sonnet was not only 'a moment's monument,' but, as Pater recognized, 'to him, life is a crisis at every moment' (*Appreciations*, 211). Much of Christina Rossetti's poetry is concerned with the passed-over moment, the moment of life that passed by unseized. For William Morris, the mutable moment arises from 'the desire of beauty quickened by the sense of death.' And for Walter Pater, life must be lived by experiencing the intensity of each individual moment. By focusing on every moment, we can experience 'a quickened, multiplied consciousness. Of this wisdom, the poetic passion, the desire of beauty, the love of art for art's sake, has most; for art comes to you professing frankly to give nothing but the highest quality to your moments as they pass, and simply for those moments' sake' ('Poems,' 312).

Pre-Raphaelite poetry is thus characterized by its choice of genre – ballads, songs, and sonnets; by its literary characters from medieval tales and popular ballads; by its jarring juxtaposition of vivid details that produce grotesque transgressions of decorum through an indeterminate focus that shifts between the spiritual and the sensual; and by its concern with the mutable moment that arises from 'the desire of beauty, quickened by the sense of death' and that leads to a pervading sense of degeneration from an idealized past.

Keats's 'La Belle Dame Sans Merci' and Tennyson's 'Mariana' and 'The Lady of Shalott' pre-date the Pre-Raphaelite movement, but they exemplify its poetry. The reviewer who considered Morris to be 'Rossetti *plus* Browning' (Garnett, 227) may have had such poems as Robert Browning's 'Two in the Campagna' in mind. Browning's speaker searches to trace his fleeting thought:

> First it left
> The yellowing fennel, run to seed
> There, branching from the brickwork's cleft,
> Some old tomb's ruin: yonder weed
> Took up the floating weft,
>
> Where one small orange cup amassed
> Five beetles – blind and green they grope
> Among the honey-meal. (11-18)

Another early reviewer, noting the similarity between Tennyson and the Pre-Raphaelite poetry of Morris, nevertheless found a significant difference in their aesthetic vision: 'The Laureate's "Lady of Shalott," that strange dream, which however beautiful, quaint, and touching it be, quivers on the furthest verge of Dream-land to which sane Fancy can penetrate, has been "the point of departure" for Mr. Morris' (Chorley, 427). The decorative artifice of Pre-Raphaelite poetry depends upon a self-reflexive, art-for-art's-sake ideology that was, for some Victorians, too far removed from their own lives.

V

Pre-Raphaelitism in poetry and painting developed in two directions from its original impulse. One direction arose from its pursuit of beauty, the other from its revolt against Academic convention. The first was concerned solely with an artistic revolution, while the second ultimately envisioned a social revolution.

The pursuit of beauty encouraged the elitist notion of the autonomy of art and the need for the artist to remain aloof from society. It led to the art for art's sake creed of Aestheticism, first articulated by Algernon Swinburne in his review of Baudelaire (1862) and later enshrined by Pater with his eloquent prescription for attaining the 'multiplied consciousness' that aesthetic experiences provide. It is traceable from Dante Rossetti and

Edward Burne-Jones, whose lack of interest in society epitomizes the Aestheticism prevalent from the 1850s through the 1870s, to Swinburne and Whistler, whose defiant contempt for society led them to attack and shock it, and culminates in the Decadence of Wilde and Beardsley in the *fin-de-siècle* 1890s.

In defining the Decadence of the Rhymers' Club (from Ernest Dowson to a young W.B. Yeats), Arthur Symons explained that its ideal was 'to fix the last fine shade, the quintessence of things; to fix it fleetingly; to be a disembodied voice, and yet the voice of a human soul' ('Decadent Movement,' 1893). The epigrams of Wilde's preface to *The Picture of Dorian Gray* provide the pivotal text for the transition between Aestheticism and Decadence; the human-sized sunflower and a musical stage caricature provide the image in art and the style of life that epitomize the aesthetic and decadent directions of Pre-Raphaelitism. As a caricature of the Pre-Raphaelite aesthete, Reginald Bunthorne of Gilbert and Sullivan's operetta *Patience* is, by 1881, an easily recognizable target of fun for the general public to sing of: 'Though the Philistines may jostle, you will rank as an apostle in the high aesthetic band, / If you walk down Piccadilly with a poppy or a lily in your medieval hand.'

While the revolt against Academicism led some to this pursuit of rarefied beauty, others pursued an anti-elitist democratization of art. But for a new paradigm of art to displace the old one, a socialist revolution would have to overturn the old order. That Pre-Raphaelitism would lead in this direction was not at all apparent. Beginning as an English nationalist movement, Pre-Raphaelitism was a rebellion against not only academicism but also against classicism, wherein the historic and literary models the English studied were Greek and Roman. Classical sophistication was replaced by a primitivist interest in the medieval heritage of British mythology. This Pre-Raphaelite interest in national origins is too often misconstrued as an indulgence, a nostalgic escape from the industrial horrors of the urban present to the beauty and innocence of a rural past (Spender, 32-3). Such works as Dante Rossetti's *Found* (1854-81) may be a source of this misconception, as Rossetti depicts a peasant from a medieval farm finding his strayed beloved corrupted in the modern city. However, the Pre-Raphaelite interest in the past was very much integral to the emerging national pride in the Victorian present. As citizens of the commercial centre of the world, the young Pre-Raphaelites understood that if England was to assert itself as the cultural centre of the world – the successor of the imperial centres of Greece and Rome – then the English would need to mine and cultivate their own heritage.

The young Ford Madox Brown, inspired by a trip to Rome in 1845, was determined to provide his homeland with an equivalent to the literary and artistic heritage he had found so glorified in Italy. In place of Dante and Giotto, he undertook for his subject the canonization of English literature, a subject considered unworthy for academic study in a university. *The Seeds and Fruits of English Poetry,* begun in 1845 and completed in two versions (1851 and 1853), presents a medieval triptych formed by Gothic arches richly hung with decorative foliage. The outer panels depict the inheritors of Chaucer's legacy from Spenser and Shakespeare to Burns and Byron. The central panel is the focus of the first completed version of the painting: *Geoffrey Chaucer Reading the 'Legend of Custance' to Edward III and His Court, at the Palace of Sheen, on the Anniversary of the Black Prince's Forty-Fifth Birthday.* Against a background formed by an archway glimpse of fertile farmland aglow in the sunshine, the busy foreground is filled on this festive occasion with courtiers, knights, and jesters, all captivated by the reading of poetry: Geoffrey Chaucer delivering from the secular pulpit tales that serve as a new native scripture, thereby challenging the supremacy of both classical and biblical mythology. Following Brown's example, Dante Rossetti, Elizabeth Siddal, William Morris, Edward Burne-Jones, and others would turn to Malory and the border ballads for stories of Galahad and Guenevere, Clerk Saunders and Sir Patrick Spens as inspiration for their art and poetry.

Hence, during the height of imperial expansion, the Victorians in Britain were rediscovering their own pre-colonial springs: the Arthurian mythology which, when first introduced by Tennyson, was criticized as 'a forgotten cycle of fables which never attained the dignity or substance of mythology' (Sterling, 400). A few years earlier, in 1833 Samuel Coleridge had been more insistent: 'As to Arthur, you could not by any means make a poem on him national to Englishmen. What have we to do with him' (*Works,* 14:441). It was Tennyson and the Pre-Raphaelites who created a national mythology for Britain by so thoroughly foregrounding what had been marginalized since Spenser.

Cultural nationalism led the more radical Pre-Raphaelites to political socialism through an unlikely channel: the sociological readings of art by the essentially conservative John Ruskin. Some of the same Pre-Raphaelites who served in the militia in the 1850s to protect Britain from a feared French invasion[3] were to shift their identities from the role of patriotic preservationists to that of socialist revolutionaries who sought to change our daily lives by eliminating the distinction between work and art. Raymond Williams explains how the concept of 'art' was gradually reduced in relevance from its original designation for a wide range of skills from mathematics to angling. It was not until the eighteenth century that the newly founded Royal Academy excluded engraving from the ranks of art and introduced the hierarchical distinction between artist and artisan, 'the latter being specialized to "skilled manual work" without "intellectual" or "imaginative" or "creative" purposes' (Williams, 41).

Ruskin articulated the consequences of this new hegemony in 'The Nature of Gothic' chapter of his *Stones of Venice* (1853). He argues that such distinctions between the artistic genius of the blueprint designer and the manual labour of the craftsman who carries out the vision lead to the degradation of both the artist and the art. Ruskin presents the asymmetrical, irregular imperfections of the Gothic style as exemplifying the independence of the craftsman freed from an enslaved conformity to the symmetrical uniformity of the Classical style. The ideal artist carves his own Gothic gargoyle, while the slave copies identical Corinthian columns. For Ruskin, the designer and the craftworker must be one and the same, so that spiritual contemplation and common daily experience are inseparable.

Praising 'The Nature of Gothic' as 'one of the few necessary utterances of the century,' William Morris developed from it the principles of the Arts and Crafts Movement, which were intended to unify art and work. As Morris explains, 'art is the expression of man's pleasure in labour' ('Preface' to *Nature of Gothic*, 367). Without such pleasure in our work, beauty cannot be restored to our productions, and we shall continue to toil and live in pain. Thus Morris was not simply arguing for a restoration of the equality of what had become known as the greater and lesser arts, and for the useful and the ornamental to be united; rather, he believed that for art to survive, civilization must change. He became a dedicated socialist, lecturing tirelessly from trade union halls to Hyde Park corner, campaigning for a socialist revolution that would save civilization by making art an integral and intrinsic part of life.

The Pre-Raphaelite movement that began in the late 1840s with a group of young rebels intent on revolutionizing art and literature had become, in the 1880s, a movement intent on revolutionizing life, with Morris adding a radicalized ideology to Ruskinian aesthetics and Marxist economics. According to Morris, art cannot continue to be marginalized as the exclusive culture of an elite class. Art must not only be essential to the life of everyone, but, as the expression of our joy in living, art must also change from being a way of life for a few to becoming the essential way of all our lives.

VI

The essays on Pre-Raphaelitism that follow are by colleagues, former students, and editorial associates of William E. Fredeman. When he assumed the editorship of the *Journal of Pre-Raphaelite Studies* in 1987, he respectfully devoted the first issue as a festschrift to the founding editor, Francis Golffing. We now, in turn, pay tribute to Professor Fredeman with essays that pursue his own earliest interests in the poetry of Dante Rossetti, in the archival research with letters and diaries of the Rossetti family, in the interdisciplinary work of William Morris, in the interdisciplinary relation between image and text, and in the reassessment of previously overlooked artists and their work. From these starting points the essays pursue technological issues that challenge conventional methods of scholarship; gender issues concerning constructions of identity through the changing conceptions of brotherhood, love, desire, anxiety, or theatrical subversion; interdisciplinary cultural issues that transgress the borders between high art and popular culture, between aesthetics and politics.

Jerome McGann and E. Warwick Slinn both note the importance of Dante Rossetti's *Early Italian Poets* (1861), a neglected book they consider integral to an understanding of the canon of the figure Fredeman considered to be the dominant leader of the Pre-Raphaelite movement. The book is Rossetti's first, containing not what we might consider original poetry, not the major poems retrieved from the coffin of his wife, but a selection of his translations. In McGann's important essay, we learn that Rossetti's influential theory of translation elevated translations to the level of original poetry. McGann informs us that Rossetti's theory and practice of translation became the dominant mode for twentieth-century translators, since Ezra Pound derived his influential theory 'straight out of Rossetti's prefatory commentary to his 1861 book.' Rossetti's prescriptions in *The Early Italian Poets* are cultural/aesthetic. Distinguishing 'faithful' from 'literal' translation, Rossetti erased the old distinction between '"original" poetry and verse "translation."' On the other hand, he bound translation 'to an obligation of close metrical equivalence.' This prescription included adhering to rhyme schemes that were difficult in English, while developing 'accentual equivalences for syllabic Italian measures.'

Seventeen of Rossetti's translations are studied as examples of his cultural/aesthetic theories put into practice. McGann explains how Rossetti secularizes Dante's *Vita Nuova* by summoning Dante rather than God and by pursuing cultural rather than religious redemption. Moreover, these translations demonstrate how deeply his reading of Dante's autobiography informs the life of Rossetti's whole work. McGann pinpoints the essence of Rossetti's artistry in a single but complex image: 'Figural palimpsest is perhaps Rossetti's central poetic (and artistic) device.' The effacement of an older text to be written over with a newer text means that Rossetti's poetry 'is replete with haunted texts, where the present world is regularly impinged upon by forces from the past and spirits of the dead.'

E. Warwick Slinn pursues the implications of Fredeman's 1965 analysis of Dante Rossetti's *The House of Life* as 'fundamentally elegiac,' with the word 'change' as its central focus. Slinn suggests that the subject Rossetti elegizes is the loss of masculine desire. Learning the structure of desire and sorrow from the medieval poets he translated for *The Early Italian Poets*, Rossetti 'internalizes the process that the Italian sonneteers rendered external,' turning the desired woman into an abstraction of signs. Beginning the sonnet sequence with a proposition about the power of poetry – how the sonnet can make a monument of the fleeting moment and thereby substantiate the insubstantial – Rossetti internalizes the structure of seduction, elevates the power of the male speaker, and reveals how male lyricism 'displays itself as an act of ideological absorption and self-enclosure.' As the sequence progresses, 'poet and reader become increasingly lost in a work of insubstantial allure.' Elegizing the 'self "severed"' from the lost literary tradition and patriarchal ideal of courtly love structures, Rossetti deomonstrates that these structures are no less outmoded for sustaining male identity and idealism than they proved to be for Elizabeth Barrett Browning and Christina Rossetti. With McGann articulating the theoretical essence of Rossetti's Pre-Raphaelite artistry and Slinn conveying and explaining the sensual power and purpose of Rossetti's fleshly poetry, these two essays stand together as seminal studies of the profound range and sensational intensity of Dante Rossetti's work.

Roger Peattie's essay on William Michael Rossetti's promotion of Christian Rossetti's career – a proprietary laying of his sister's ghost – is based on Peattie's study of the diaries and letters from the archival collections Fredeman acquired for the University of British Columbia Library. In assuming the role of official historian of the Pre-Raphaelite movement and of the careers of his sister Christina and brother Dante, William Michael wrote, compiled, or edited forty books between 1881 and 1911; consequently, he has been depicted as exploiting the reputations of his more talented siblings. The charge is unfair, as Peattie argues, for a number of reasons. First, William Michael had for years provided financial support for the extended Rossetti family, support that allowed Christina to pursue her vocation as a poet and allowed Dante to pursue his art studies. Second, he recognized that his privileged position as an original member of the Pre-Raphaelite Brotherhood and an intimate member of a talented family placed him at the centre of Victorian culture; he thus felt a responsibility to provide for posterity a thorough documentation of the Pre-Raphaelite movement. The preserved letters and diaries suggest that he remained honest and fair in his dealings. After Christina's death in December 1894 – the same time as William Michael retired from the Inland Revenue Office – he recorded in his diary during the next year his daily 'involvement in the literary and journalistic response to Christina's death': encouraging obituary notices, advising biographers, and improving her publisher's book designs. His impatience with Mackenzie Bell suggests that William exercised discriminating taste in promoting Christina's career. As her editor, he employed some questionable editorial procedures – conjectural emendations, retitling, regularizing the metre, and arranging the poems by subject divisions. But these methods were not uncommon in the nineteenth century, and they are the same procedures he practised with his editions of Blake, Shelley, Whitman, and Dante Rossetti.

David Latham turns to one of Fredeman's earliest and long-term interests: William Morris. He reviews Morris's theories of art and politics in order to reconcile the apparent contradictions in Morris's career and he centres his discussion on the integral relationship between Morris's conception of the decorative arts and his commitment to socialist revolution. Observing the succession of careers that Morris mastered in leaps and bounds, from theology, architecture, and painting to poetry and the decorative arts, until he 'crossed the river of fire' to commit himself to political action, Latham contends that Morris's development as an artist followed a remarkably consistent vision. By critiquing the relation between work and rest, Morris reveals how this consistency begins with the most fundamental level of our daily lives. Defining art as the expression of our 'pleasure in labour,' he consequently understood that what art required was 'not an evolutionary re-*routing* toward a new direction, but a revolutionary upheaval and ultimate re-*rooting* in a newly prepared ground.' Morris thus yearned for the cleansing flood of a new barbarism to bring an end to civilization: 'The arts have got to die, what is left of them, before they can be re-born.' By making art central to our daily lives, we can overturn the hierarchical relation between fine art and decorative art. A comparison of his theory and practice using such examples as his *Strawberry Thief* and *Honeysuckle* designs for chintzes and the *Trellis* and *Jasmine* designs for wallpapers suggests how Morris's interests in wallpaper and the walled garden are fully integrated with his paradisal vision of a revolutionary social order. The essay proposes the first analysis of wallpapers and woven textiles as texts that can be read in the manner that Ruskin reads stones and Morris reads the modes and matrices of cultural production.

J. Hillis Miller explores the implications of the new epoch of the Internet. The digital revolution – the shift from a manuscript and print culture to the new communications technologies of a digital culture – is part of the second industrial revolution that began in the mid-nineteenth century: the shift from a commodity-based economy to an information-based economy. By changing the means of preservation and dissemination of information, the digital revolution is creating a new cyberspace sensibility that threatens to destroy literature and literary study. The multimedia nature of Pre-Raphaelite art and literature sets Pre-Raphaelite studies at the vanguard of this paradigmatic shift. Miller discusses the relationship between Swinburne's poem 'Before the Mirror' and Whistler's painting *Symphony in White No. 2: The Little White Girl* as exemplifying revolutionary trends in scholarship. The Internet encourages such multimedia studies but also, by setting the painting and poem alongside each other on the computer screen, it encourages 'thinking of the poem and painting as a single unit made of manifold doublings, mirrorings, and enigmatic echoings.' Though each work on its own presents 'a provocative and enigmatic series of doublings,' together they form a 'double work of art, each illustrating or interpreting the other.' Essentially, both works raise 'the unanswerable question of priority of original and mirrored copy.'

Carolyn Hares-Stryker, Allan Life, and Lorraine Janzen Kooistra focus on Fredeman's interests in the relation between image and text. Hares-Stryker discusses Arthur Hughes's illustrations for children books. Practising the progressive ideological agenda for children's literature outlined by Ruskin and Dickens, Hughes appeared to 'favour pixiedust over clear Christian morals,' preferring to exemplify in his illustrations sweetness and innocence rather than dogmatic preaching and didactic satire. Hughes's illustrations for George MacDonald's *At the Back of the North Wind* and *The Princess and the Goblin* complement MacDonald's moral allegories through the Pre-Raphaelite manner of making their mysticism visible. Though critics often identify the unbound hair of Pre-Raphaelite women as a symbol of the seductive power of feminine sexuality, Hughes depicts the Godiva-like hair of the North Wind as the perfect aesthetic symbol: not threatening the innocence of the young boy but maternally powerful and supernaturally beautiful – 'a new and alluring divinity for an age of shaken faith.' Hughes displays his versatility by complementing with an equal subtlety the much darker *Tom Brown's School Days*, illustrating its evangelical sermon of English nationalism by conveying the notion of joyful brotherhood, respect for authority, and the mature unity of body, mind, and spirit. For Christina Rossetti's *Sing-Song*, Hughes alleviates the text's pervasive morbidity by pairing his illustrations of pain and sorrow on the verso with serene illustrations of closure through Christian affirmation on the recto. But in his illustrations for her *Speaking Likenesses*, Hughes reflects the full anxiety of the disturbing sexuality and violence of Rossetti's text. Only his concluding illustration departs from Rossetti's textual disruptions as Hughes manages to return to those 'slight channels' of innocence by comforting us with the reassuring images of a happy ending.

Following Fredeman's prescription that 'the art and actions of the past require constant reassessment,' a prescription that led Fredeman to revive scholarly interest in neglected writers and artists, Allan Life rescues the graphic art of Arthur Boyd Houghton from unjust neglect. Despite praise from such contemporaries as William Michael Rossetti, Laurence Housman, and Vincent Van Gogh, Houghton has long since fallen into obscurity. Life's analysis of Houghton's illustrations for *The Thousand and One Nights* reveals the artistry of a major draftsman responding with a sophisticated visual sensibility to the different levels of the verbal text. Subtle details in his designs suggest the complex relationship between Scheherezade and the Sultan. Some of these designs invite Freudian interpretations similar to Bruno Bettelheim's psychoanalytical readings of fairy tales. With careful attention to the cultural differences between Arabia and India, Life analyzes symbols of the feminine and masculine and finds beneath the dialectics of union and division the artist's 'faith in the reality of love between a woman and a man, and the power of that love' to provide 'mutual realization' and to thereby 'change the world.'

Aubrey Beardsley's commitment to challenging the conventional hierarchical distinctions between high and low art was very different from William Morris's. Lorraine Janzen Kooistra begins her study of Beardsley by examining how his work can be arbitrarily categorized as high art whose eroticism is sanctioned by cultural institutions and consequently protected from philistine censure or as low art likely to be charged as pornography. Kooistra shifts the focus from the erotic content of Beardsley's illustrations in order to understand the more significant 'performative aspects' underlying 'an art obsessed with dress, undress, and the liminal states in between.' Beardsley is interested in the theatrical masquerade as a means to challenge the hierarchical male/female division on which 'late-Victorian patriarchal society was founded.' By illustrating how we clothe our identities as artificially constructed masquerades, Beardsley 'challenges us to move beyond the limitations' of conventional gender categories 'to a liminal third space.' His frontispiece for *Salome* is 'a cultural sign subject to interpretation.' Capitalizing on the transgressive behaviour of the *fin de siecle* effeminate young man and masculine New Woman, Beardsley permitted the subject to inhabit different positions simultaneously and thereby 'disrupted fixed notions of personal identity.'

Ira B. Nadel provides a personal portrait of Dick Fredeman from his special vantage point as a colleague in the English Department at the University of British Columbia, as the co-editor of *The Journal of Pre-Raphaelite and Aesthetic Studies*, and as co-editor of two multi-volume reference collections. Nadel depicts the author of 36-page book reviews and 100-page articles as approaching his work with the 'attention of a medieval scribe and the enthusiasm of a graduate student.' His review of Fredeman's scrupulous scholarship is followed by a reminiscent tour of his campus home as a centre for Pre-Raphaelite industry, congenial hospitality, and eccentric antiquarianism.

A visit to the home of an elderly William Michael Rossetti, who had long outlived his Pre-Raphaelite contemporaries, was described by a twentieth-century visitor as a haunting experience: the 'muffled rooms ... [of] the old house ... with its portraits by D.G. Rossetti, its Japanese prints, its china and its cabinets ... As soon as one set foot over the threshold, one felt transported not merely in atmosphere but in time itself. An indescribable sensation, as if one had escaped into some other world' (Curle, 79).[4] If crossing William Michael's threshold could summon the realm of spectres from a bygone age, there was no aura of nostalgia associated with Dick's home. Its walls were lined with inner and outer rows of books shelved from floor to ceiling; its library tables were piled with first editions, original manuscripts, and Rossetti drawings, and with new books for review and new essays submitted by scholars for editorial assessment. Dick worked in the midst of a home that bustled with students and editorial assistants at work on the journal or the Rossetti letters, and with scholars visiting to consult his collection to complete their own work. He'd review the day's work with zest, advice, and jokes in the kitchen while chopping okra for the frying pan and preparing chantilly potatoes for the oven.

Haunted Texts concludes with 'The Great Pre-Raphaelite Paper Chase,' Fredeman's own lively account of his career as a scholarly detective, adventurous pirate, and archive conservationist of Pre-Raphaelite treasures. As a personal introduction to the sleuthing leg-work of scholarship as well as to the family descendants of the original Pre-Raphaelites, it is an eyewitness account that surpasses with verve and flair those of William Michael Rossetti. Since completing his dissertation in 1956 when his topic was considered an unworthy field for research, he continued to file for the rest of the century a 'systematic watching brief' as Pre-Raphaelitism gradually reached its current status as a 'growth industry' supporting a 'bullish' market. The 'Checklist' of Fredeman's publications provides an index to his contributions in all areas of Pre-Raphaelitism, to which future generations of scholars will remain forever indebted.

NOTES

1   Fredeman identifies the anonymous reviewer of his book as Lady Mander ('Great Pre-Raphaelite Paper Chase,' 217).
2   For other linguistic crucifixion images, compare 'The Haystack in the Floods,' as Robert and Jehane first fear 'what might betide / When the roads cross'd' (18-19) and then envision their 'wretched end' when 'they saw across the only way / That Judas, Godmar' (33-4).
3   The Pre-Raphaelite members of the Artists Rifle Corps in 1859, all volunteers, included Ford Madox Brown, Burne-Jones, Holman Hunt, Millais, Morris, Val Prinsep, Dante Rossetti, Simeon Solomon, Roddy Stanhope, and Algernon Swinburne! Fredeman's account of their militia experience includes such examples as Hunt forever losing parts of his disassembled rifle, Morris confusing his right from his left during close order drill, 'invariably begg[ing] pardon of the comrade whom he found himself facing,' Rossetti having to question and quarrel over the reason for every command, and Brown shooting his own dog 'the first time he was set to target practice' ('Visionary Vanities,' 10).
4   Roger Peattie drew my attention to Richard Curle's memorable description of William Michael Rossetti's home.

2

A Commentary on Some of
Rossetti's Translations from Dante

Jerome McGann

Overshadowed by the spectacular character and success of his 1870 volume
of *Poems*, Dante Gabriel Rossetti's first book, *The Early Italian Poets* (1861), is
at least as impressive, and was easily as influential, as his more celebrated
book of 'original' poetry. Like the latter, however, Rossetti's great book of
translations – the adjective does not overstate the case, as I hope to show
here – fell into obscurity with the coming of the Modernist movement. The
travesty of that anamnesis is only now becoming clear.

So much of the lost historical record has to be recovered. The case of
Rossetti's book of translations is particularly salient, however, because
without it Ezra Pound's work would probably not have been possible.
Pound's theory of translation – which dominated ideas about translation in
the twentieth century – is drawn straight out of Rossetti's prefatory commentary to his 1861 book. More significant than that, the project of the
Cantos – or at least its initiating ideas as articulated in Pound's early essays
and put into practice in the first thirty cantos – translates that theory of
translation into an entire poetic program – the now famous 'poem including history.' In *A Draft of XXX Cantos* (1930), that history is largely aesthetic
and cultural – in the important sense that cultural work is taken as norma-
tive for Pound's ideas about social order.

Rossetti was never much impassioned with ideas of social redemption,
and while he worked closely with Ruskin for a number of crucial years, he
turned more inward as he grew older. That biographical trajectory has
helped us forget the Poundian connection – a connection usefully recalled when we read Rossetti's *The Early Italian Poets*.

Rossetti's informing ideas about translating poetry are not difficult to recover. They are exceedingly interesting. First of all is the rule that 'a good poem shall not be turned into a bad one' by the translator (*EIP*, viii). This thought follows from the more general cultural/aesthetic prescription that 'the only true motive for putting poetry into a fresh language must be to endow a fresh nation, as far as possible, with one more possession of beauty' (viii).

From that premise Rossetti draws his distinction between 'literal' and 'faithful' translation (*EIP*, viii) and his erasure of another (more common) distinction between 'original' poetry and verse 'translation.' In one remarkable act of aesthetic thought (and practice), Rossetti leaps back across his Romantic inheritance to recover certain key ideas all but abandoned after the death of Pope. Rossetti's translations will be in verse forms that aspire to match the aesthetic resources that were their initial source and inspiration.

Rossetti adds a further interesting requirement to the pursuit of that aspiration. Though the verse translations were freed from an obligation to strict semantic 'literality,' they were bound to an obligation of close metrical equivalence. This obligation was in many ways a far more demanding one. In the particular case of the poetry Rossetti was choosing to translate, it meant (a) finding accentual equivalences for syllabic Italian measures and (b) adhering closely to rhyme schemes that would be difficult in English.

The result would prove astonishing – one of the greatest works of translation in the language precisely because it is a book of *poetry*.

The character of Rossetti's poems can best be shown, I think, through a series of attentive readings. These readings will make up the second part of my essay. I have chosen a selection of the poems in Rossetti's translation of Dante's *Vita Nuova* partly because of the excellence of Rossetti's models and partly because the intellectual integrity of Dante's autobiography throws into sharp relief Rossetti's own aesthetic intelligence.

Before embarking on these readings, a brief comment on Dante's *Vita Nuova* may be helpful. The story it tells is a recollective reconstruction, written between 1292 and 1295, of events that occurred earlier – between 1274, when Dante first saw Beatrice, and 1290, when she died. The *Vita Nuova*'s account connects the writing of certain poems with specific events, but we know, as Rossetti knew, that the poems in the book were not all written, originally, as part of the narrative in which they are placed. Dante sometimes applies poems to events in his narrative that were written for different reasons and under other circumstances than those given in the story. That kind of appropriation is germane to Dante's project, which argues – and seeks to demonstrate – the operation of a prevenient spiritual order in Dante's life. His personal history is shadowed by divine purposes and agency, a microcosm of the general economy of grace that Dante sees pervading human time.

Rossetti was attracted to Dante's project exactly because it draws a relation between poetic practice and historical agency. The *Vita Nuova* argues that poetry, properly executed, can co-operate with the divine economy that pervades historical events – indeed, it can escape the quotidian order to participate directly in this transhistorical order. Rossetti's translations, in that frame of reference, are second-order acts of poetic 'co-operation.' They are much closer to ritual acts of magic than they are to Romantic acts of self-expression. (Compare Rossetti's translation of the Paolo and Francesca episode in the *Commedia* with Byron's.) The magical purpose is to call back from the dead the power – Rossetti called it the 'beauty' – of Dante's poetry. Thus, the focus of the summons made by Rossetti's 1861 collection is Dante and his poetic contemporaries, not God, just as the ultimate object is not religious but cultural redemption. When Rossetti translates Dante and the associated poetry that informs and reveals the shape of Dante's work, his action is a cultic one, a secular *Imitatio Christi*. The striking early painting *Dantis Amor* is a clear iconic figuration of the purpose Rossetti has in mind.

II

Rossetti's general and programmatic approach to his book of translations is strikingly expressed in the sonnet 'Guido, an image of my lady dwells' (*EIP*, 333). Cavalcanti wrote his original sonnet to Guido Orlandi ('Una figura della donna mia'). It is one of his most irreverent and even anti-religious works and so stands out as an odd choice for Rossetti.

The sonnet refers to a celebrated episode recorded in the chronicles of Florence for 3 July 1292: the report of great miracles effected through a painting of the Virgin in the church of San Michele d'Orto. Especially interesting is how well Rossetti replicates the spirit of Cavalcanti's witty sonnet. Both original and translation work by reserve and implication, and Rossetti manages his imitation by departing from a literal strictness at certain key points – for example, in the opening quatrain. (Rossetti's rhyme scheme also varies from the original, but – as he regularly does in his translations – he chooses another scheme equally characteristic of the works he is translating.)

For my purposes, however, the crucial passage is lines 13-14, where

Rossetti manages a coded reference to the PRB, the Pre-Raphaelite 'Brethren,' as they called themselves, who created a stir and gained public notice by their admiration of early Italian painting. Rossetti thus introduces a whole range of meaning into his sonnet that is not present in Cavalcanti – although it remains true to the original in a Victorian fashion. Rossetti's reserved wit becomes a sign of the polemical aggression concealed in the PR Brethren's appeal to humble pictorial models painted by 'pictores ignoti,' the 'Lesser Brethren' who came before and set an example for the PRB program. Rossetti's prose note to these lines, equally reserved, nonetheless makes the point obliquely: 'The Franciscans, in profession of deeper poverty and humility than belonged to other Orders, called themselves *Fratres minores*.'

The sonnet shows in a most dramatic way Rossetti's determination to aim for a 'faithful' rather than a 'literal' rendering, to translate his twelfth- and thirteenth-century models into current terms. That procedure governs the entire volume and especially its centrepiece, the translation of Dante's *Vita Nuova*.

The subject calls for an extensive treatment, but here I shall simply indicate how Rossetti's ideas play out in several of the poetical works that organize Dante's autobiography. Rossetti's translations of these poems function within a 'performative' aesthetic whereby the act of translational rendering resurrects, as it were, the vital life of the original poetry. Implicit in the procedure is a very Victorian argument about the 'nature' of poetry. It distinctly recalls Arnold's general program, but it brings one crucial new element: for Rossetti, the transmission of an imaginative inheritance is most effectively managed through a reciprocating imaginative (= poetical) act. The fact that Rossetti's aesthetic manifesto, 'Hand and Soul,' was written as a work of 'fiction' is very much to the point of both his critical and his artistic views.

1. 'To every heart which the sweet pain doth move' (*EIP*, 227-8)

This sonnet is the first poem in the *Vita Nuova* and thus a determinative work. Composed early, circa 1283, before Dante conceived the *Vita Nuova*, it functions as a singular prophetic moment in Dante's autobiography because of that historical / biographical fact. The poem opens the sequence of imbedded poems and so announces, both within and prior to Dante's book of memory, the imperative presence of Love in his life. When Dante places it in the *Vita Nuova*, its orbit of relevance expands drastically. The sonnet was 'answered' by several of Dante's friends and acquaintances, as Rossetti's immediately succeeding note to the text indicates, but placed as it is in the autobiography, the sonnet is effectively being answered and reinterpreted by Dante himself.

Rossetti exploits that original Dantean situation in his poem, which now stands, as a translation, in an analogous relation to nineteenth-century English readers. Dante's sonnet had a second birth in his own life, and that fact is reflected in Rossetti's rendering, where we encounter it in yet another 'new life.' Rossetti's poem is thus an index of a kind of mystery needing 'true interpretation and kind thought' from Rossetti's contemporaries who try to make contact with sources of poetic inspiration. Dante's friends answered his sonnet with responsive interpretive sonnets, and Rossetti's work functions in an analogous way for his contemporary readers and poets. The structure of thought is precisely what Pound will follow in his translational approach to the cultural heritage he sought to recover.

Rossetti's translation exhibits some of his typical transformations, starting with the slight alteration of the sestet's rhyme scheme. Also, lines 3, 6-7 ('Wake and keep watch, the third was almost nought / When Love was shown me with such terrors fraught'), and 12 all make notable semantic departures from Dante's text. The octave variances, which expand Dante's thought beyond the literal Italian, seem clear attempts to render tonal qualities in the original – a certain decorous formality that pervades and indeed distinguishes Dante's style.

2. 'A day agone as I rode sullenly' (*EIP*, 236-7)

Dante's prose prelude to this sonnet is so explicit in its details that one might well wonder why he wrote the sonnet at all. But the verse is more than a concentrated reprisal of the prose; it comes in the text as a riddle poem quite like the opening sonnet ('To every heart which the sweet pain doth move'). Both are prophetic of the mysterious agency of Love, who is directing Dante's life in ways that he cannot always understand and that often bring pain and sorrow. So the poem's cryptic style cuts back across the lucid prose to suggest the presence of some secret level of meaning in the recorded events. The striking difference between the way the prose and the verse treat the disappearance of Love throws the uncanny character of the poetry into sharp relief.

The quality of Rossetti's translations is illustrated here in the way he 'rhymes' the first and the final lines through the repetition of the word 'gone.' The word immediately draws attention in line 1 because of the auditional play in the first three words (recalling certain similar effects in

Keats: for instance, 'Not to the sensual ear, but more endear'd'). With line 14, the word comes back to us in what Italian poets would call a *rima equivoca*. The move is important in this case because of the striking *rima equivoca* that Dante introduces into his original sonnet (it comes in lines 10 and 13). Because this metrical device is so distinctively Italian rather than English, Rossetti's move 'translates' it into an index or quasi-symbolic sign in his poem. It means to suggest that Dante's poem lives on, literally, in Rossetti's Victorian reprisal.

3. 'All my thoughts always speak to me of Love' (*EIP*, 244-5)

The translation is as poetically successful as it is semantically free. Rossetti makes some fine turns on the Italian original – for instance in the opening six lines or even more spectacularly in line 11: 'And lose myself in amorous wanderings.' Special note should be made of the opening four words and that typical Rossettian move coming in the relation All/always (compare the opening of 'A day agone, as I rode sullenly'). In this case, the wit gains special force because of the thematic importance of the word 'ways' so cunningly half-hidden from the eye.

The last two lines recall Beatrice's displeasure with Dante and her denial of her salutation: 'Unto mine enemy I needs must pray, / My lady Pity, for the help she brings.' But the paradoxical idea of Lady Pity as 'mine enemy' is thematically important and suggests further meanings in Dante's text. Rossetti chooses the safest path here: a fairly literal translation.

4. 'Even as the others mock, thou mockest me' (*EIP*, 247-8)

This is another fairly free translation, as line 2 emphasizes, though it is exact in its imitation of the rhyme scheme and – with the exception of line 14 – it follows the sense of the original closely. Rossetti's source text for line 14, Fraticelli, reads 'de' discacciati' where the authorized reading is 'de li scacciati.' Although Fraticelli leads Rossetti away from Dante's striking final *figura*, his poem's faithfulness to its variant source produces its own special excellence.

The central action of the poem, which comes in the sestet, carries an indirect allusion to 'A day agone, as I rode sullenly,' where Love disappears into some secret place within Dante himself. The 'rout' of Dante's senses here thus leaves behind a remarkably ambiguous apparition of the poet – the 'figura nova' ('strange semblances') of line 3 and line 12 ('This makes my face to change / Into another's'). Dante's face is disfigured by his sorrow, but this 'disfigurement' itself conceals the secret presence of the god of Love in him. I suppose it scarcely needs remarking that, in the context, terms like 'strange semblances' and 'disfigurement' carry important, purely aesthetic, resonances.

The repetition of the word 'face' in lines 4 and 12 is clearly deliberate. In both cases, the translation deviates from the original text, and the deviance signals Rossetti's effort to make his poem expose an important but inexplicit subject in the original sonnet: that Dante's facial 'disfigurement' nonetheless, and paradoxically, mirrors the (Love) splendour reflected in Beatrice's 'fair' face. That disfiguration then becomes an oblique index of the relation between Dante's poetry and its inspiring sources. And when this whole poetical dynamic falls into Rossetti's hands, it undergoes a further disfiguration, with Rossetti's sonnet adopting a pose of modesty before *its* inspiring source, Dante's verse.

5. 'At whiles (yea oftentimes) I muse over' (*EIP*, 251-2)

This work completes the sequence of four highly 'personal' sonnets in the *Vita Nuova* that began with 'All my thoughts always speak to me of Love.' The translation, more free at the literal level than most, is quite stunning in its interpretive boldness and clarity.

Everything in the original hinges on the 'spirto vivo solamente' (line 7), Dante's brilliant wordplay echoing 'la mente' in line 1. The prose introduction underscores and prepares the reader for this key 'pensero che parlava di questa donna' – specifically, in fact, Dante's own verse and the thought of writing of Beatrice in verse. We shall see in the next poem, the great canzone 'Donne ch' avete intelletto d'amore,' how this sonnet's commitment to intellectual reflection prepares for the breakthrough to the canzone, where Dante discovers what is involved in writing a love poetry that has transcended the subjectivity of its passion.

Rossetti's understanding of this poetical drama could scarcely be more clearly or more remarkably rendered than it is in this sonnet. It suffices to point to lines 6 and 10, and particularly to the words 'sign' and 'art,' which have no explicit equivalents in the Italian original. To translate this way is not merely to execute a sharp interpretation of Dante's sonnet, it is to incarnate Dante's 'spirto vivo' – what he will shortly reveal as 'intelletto d'amore' – as the poetical act itself. For Dante, this act is bound up with a Christian scheme of redemption as it was reworked through the tradition of courtly love. For Rossetti, however, the act is wholly modern and wholly secular. At this stage of Rossetti's work, the act involves a devotion to art *per se.* Later, however, that aesthetic devotion will be joined to the pursuit of erotic intensity.

The translation is also interesting for its metrical procedure. Line 1's final four syllables are not only startling, they make a signature for Rossetti's various efforts to flatten the effect of English stress-based verse. Line 6 marks another notable moment. Its ten single-syllable words take the breath from the English iambic line: 'So that of all my life is left no sign.' This device appears all over Rossetti's translations, and it is especially notable because of its variance from the Italian originals, where multisyllabic words abound. Rossetti saw clearly that the way to secure an imitation of Italian rhythm was to approach the rhythm of the English line through a multiplicity of short words and ground the rhythm in words of one syllable. Pater's sense of Rossetti's stylistic innovations comes from his recognition of this set of 'flattening' metrical procedures.

6. 'Ladies that have intelligence in love' (*EIP*, 255-7)

The original canzone is perhaps altogether beyond the reach of poetic equivalence or emulation, but Rossetti's poem is nonetheless a brilliant work in its own right. Dante's severe and passionate modesty toward his subject gets transformed into Rossetti's act of aesthetic repetition where Dante's poetry stands to Rossetti as Beatrice had stood to Dante.

It is important to keep in mind the immediate context of the canzone, its place in the *Vita Nuova* and, in particular, its relation to the preceding series of sonnets. The elaborate *divisio* following the canzone underscores the importance Dante attached to the work and its stylistic features; and that *divisio* reaches back to the prose passage introducing the canzone, where Dante lays down his formula for a poetry of praise that lifts the Guinizzellian tradition to this new level. The key moment in that passage comes when Dante says (in Rossetti's words), 'I declare that my tongue spake as though by its own impulse' ('dico che mia lingua parlò quasi come per se stessa mossa'). The remark conceals a crucial play on the word 'lingua,' which signifies Dante's own speech as well as his 'mother tongue.' We are being given an explicit introduction to a sweet new style, Dante's poetry 'in seconda persona' – the latter phrase in fact also involving a wordplay that signals the nonsubjective ground of Dante's 'personal' poetry. The god of Love, according to this representation of the matter, authorizes Dante's verse.

In writing this way in his nineteenth-century post-Romantic context, Rossetti is making very much the same argument about poetry that is implicit in Browning's dramatic monologues. Rossetti's translation involves a similar act of poetic ventriloquism; nor should we be at all surprised at how greatly Rossetti admired Browning's work. At the same time, we want to see the distinct turn taken in Rossetti's translational approach to the issue of poetic objectivity. Browning's dramatic monologues have few resources for involving his subjectivity directly in the poetic action. In contrast, moving at the problem through a translational model, Rossetti immediately opens the possibility of an art of the 'inner standing-point,' as he called it,[1] whereby the Romantic first person can be objectively introduced into his or her own poetic field. The importance of this move for the subsequent history of English poetry cannot be too strongly emphasized.

7. 'Love and the gentle heart are one same thing' (*EIP*, 260)

The sonnet explicates the ideas – which is also to say, the practice – of the great canzone preceding it in the autobiography, 'Ladies that have intelligence in love.' Once again, the inventive excellence of Rossetti's translation leaps to our attention. As Rossetti's note to the poem indicates, Dante's sonnet references Guinizzelli's famous canzone, also translated by Rossetti, 'Within the gentle heart Love shelters him' (*EIP*, 24-6). Rossetti's wit is especially striking right after the poem references Guinizzelli in line 2. The translation of line 3 ('Each, of itself, would be such life in death') stands out because it seems to have departed so far from Dante's Italian ('E così senza l'un l'altro esser osa'). But Rossetti is matching Dante's Italian allusion with his own English reference – most immediately, of course, to Coleridge and to the Romantic tradition of the organic poetical imagination. Indeed, Dante's (and Rossetti's) argument for the intimate relation of form and matter (see Dante's *divisio* for this sonnet) has no force unless the 'power [sustaining that relation] translates itself into act.' That prose explanation from the *divisio* involves its own remarkable act of translation, for the Italian source of 'translates itself' is 'si riduce.' We know that Rossetti asked his brother William to translate the work's prose divisions for him, but one wonders who is responsible for this trenchant linguistic moment.[2]

8. 'Canst thou indeed be he that still would sing' (*EIP*, 265)

The fine wit of Dante's opening lines is difficult to see in Rossetti's translation, and difficult to render in any: 'Se' tu colui, ch' hai trattato sovente / Di nostra donna' instantiates the style of writing 'in seconda persona' by making the verb in the subordinate clause agree with 'tu' rather than with 'colui.' The question is addressed to the preceding sonnet in the *Vita Nuova*, which is paired with this work. It asks the paired sonnet if it (or its voice?) is the same person (so to speak) as the one who addressed the ladies in the canzone 'Ladies that have intelligence in love.' Simply to ask that question in this way is to force readers to attend to the stylistic and rhetorical program being constructed in these striking poems. That Rossetti is fully aware of what is happening in his source texts can hardly be doubted. As in so many of the translations, his consciousness comes most clearly to view when he departs from literal translation: in this case, for example, in line 4: 'Thy visage might another witness bring.' The elaborate construction, not in Dante, carries the suggestion that 'another witness' might be this very sonnet, which is the sympathetic mirror of its paired sonnet spoken by the ambiguous 'tu colui.' The mistranslation – for it is that – in lines 5-6 ('And wherefore is thy grief so sore a thing / That grieving thou mak'st others dolorous') underscores Rossetti's purpose here.

9. 'I felt a spirit of love begin to stir' (*EIP*, 275)

In both Dante and Rossetti this sonnet focuses on the issue of prefiguration. The biblical context is very strong in Dante's poem, as is evident in the prose introduction where Dante quotes Matthew 33:13. The famous New Testament passage gets subtly reinforced in the sonnet itself, line 6 ('And in his speech he laugh'd and laugh'd again'), which carries an oblique allusion to Sarah's prophetic laugh when the Lord promises that she will bear a child (Genesis 18:12-15). Dante's wit turns his own sonnet into a *figura* of this prefigurative rhetoric in several ways. Most apparent is the backward reference to the opening sonnet of the autobiography, where the key image of the heart was associated with an image of Love weeping. (In this case, because Love is laughing, Dante 'scarce knew him' [4]). The various word plays on the names also function in this prefigurative rhetoric, most especially in the case of 'Primavera / Spring' (13); but the prose discussion of the names 'Giovanna' and 'Giovanni' announces the poem's purposes in the most explicit way. The general point is that Dante has a vision of a series of signs that forecast the coming of a life of love.

Throughout his translation Rossetti gives a distinctively aesthetic reading of his source texts and the case is no different here – indeed, that way of reading is never more apparent than it is in this sonnet. So Rossetti turns Dante's sonnet into a sign, or sign-constellation, that prefigures a second coming of the poetic imagination. In this reading, the pronoun 'I' simultaneously references Dante and Rossetti, and its latter reference forces one to see a corresponding mutation in the reference of the figure of Love, who now also signifies Dante. Rossetti's decision to translate 'la mente' as 'my memory' (12) flags his purpose, for the word recalls – in this strongly recollective moment – the 'book of my memory' where the autobiography opened its narrative.

Though not specifically signalled in Rossetti's translation, this sonnet is one of the poems that were clearly written before Dante conceived the *Vita Nuova*. That fact about the poem supplies yet another level of prefiguration to the original text, as it did for the opening sonnet of Dante's autobiography. In his major original work, *The House of Life*, Rossetti regularly takes poems written at one period and in one context and reworks them for new meanings by later putting them in different contexts. His model for doing so was almost certainly derived from Dante and from what he learned about Dante's poetic practices when he was translating the work of his Italian precursor.

10. 'My lady looks so gentle and so pure' (*EIP*, 280-1)

This sonnet forms a pair with the next sonnet in the *Vita Nuova*. As the prose of chapters XXV and XXVI of the autobiography indicates, both sonnets are consciously written – Dante's words are 'con ragione' and 'avendo ... ragionamento' – to illustrate and *perform* the aesthetic program Dante sets forth in his prose. This is the program by which figurative and rhetorical language that is not strictly 'realistic' is cultivated in order to suggest transphenomenal ideas and orders of truth. So in this sonnet Beatrice seems 'a creature sent from Heaven to stay / On earth, and show a miracle' (7-8). Even more dramatically, Beatrice's spiritual power is such that she inspires a poetry – this very poem, in fact – whose operations are essentially unexpressed and unapparent. This is a mute sonnet – it 'has nought to say' ('ogne lingua deven tremando muta,' 3) – because its deep 'ragione' functions beyond the order of physical expression. The argument is sealed in the sonnet's last two lines, where Dante plays on the words 'spirito' and 'Sospira' to intimate an immaterial level of erotic response.

As usual in Rossetti, this poetic economy is given a distinctive aesthetic turn in the translation. The effect is especially clear in the final three lines, where Rossetti shows himself quite aware of the transhistorical power of Dante's poetry:

> And from between her lips there seems to move
> A soothing spirit that is full of love,
>   Saying for ever to the soul, 'O sigh!'

The translation consciously echoes Shelley's 'Life of Life' lyric in *Prometheus Unbound* (II.5.48-71, especially 48-9: 'Life of Life! thy lips enkindle / With their love the breath between them'), which is itself a conscious recollection of this passage in Dante. Rossetti's 'for ever' (14), which is not in his source, nonetheless captures perfectly, even performatively, the 'spirit' of Dante's poetical argument.

11. 'Whatever while the thought comes over me' (*EIP*, 293)

The theme of confusion, so dramatically begun in the sonnet preceding this text, 'Stay with me now and listen to my sighs,' is indexed in both poems as a problem of language and poetical technique. As the prose introduction explicitly shows, this poem locates Dante searching uncertainly for an adequate form of expression. The text's 'occasional' character is extreme and in this respect emphasizes how arrested Dante's life has become, an exact equivalent of the *sola civitas* of Chapter XXVIII.

The central event in this truncated canzone is purely textual – the angel reference in line 24. Initially, it appears simply to recapitulate a now familiar figural theme in the story. But immediately after Dante writes this stanza – according to the story being told here – the textual angels reappear in another medium and as if through an agency beyond Dante's conscious purposes. The import of the famous incident narrated in Chapter XXXIV, of Dante caught drawing an angel by some unexpected Florentine visitors, lies concealed and anticipated in this interrupted canzone.

In his prose introduction, Dante discusses the work in terms of two imaginary speakers, Beatrice's brother (the first stanza) and himself (the second). But in the larger poetical context, one sees another speaker concealed in the text – another messenger, another angel, Beatrice herself, who now seems to be guiding the life-actions of a traumatized Dante.

The remarkable presentation of a secret spiritual ministry in Dante's life acquires a nineteenth-century Rossettian equivalence that seems to me scarcely less astonishing. The equation will remain invisible, however, if one's attention is too narrowly focused – just as one won't see Beatrice's secret messaging if one stays within the text of Dante's incomplete canzone. The Rossettian 'translation' becomes apparent as soon as Rossetti's New

Life is viewed in terms of its three textual/historical states: the late 1840s (when it was written), 1860-1 (when it was first published), and 1874 (when it was republished). The thirteenth-century action, as Rossetti came to see, would unfold itself in his own life before he knew Elizabeth Siddal; at the end of his life with her; and in the midst of his devotion to Jane Morris, Rossetti's 'Donna della Finestra.' In this sense, Rossetti's 'angel' is Dante or (perhaps) the whole mythic constellation of Dante's life and works. Some such eventuality Rossetti clearly hoped to realize, though surely not in the dark form that it actually took.

12. 'That lady of all gentle memories' (*EIP*, 295)

This sonnet with alternate beginning lines completes the sequence of traumatized texts that began with 'Stay with me now and listen to my sighs.' It comes in the narrative in Chapter XXXIV as the poem written to celebrate the first anniversary of the death of Beatrice, when Dante set himself to drawing angels. In terms of the action of the autobiography, Chapter XXXIV shows Dante making a turn from his arrested state toward more deliberated action. This meaning, announced in Dante's two different acts of angel-drawing, is refigured in the sonnet's alternative commencements. Note that in the second commencement Dante, as if rethinking the first, says explicitly that Beatrice 'led you to observe' the poet in his first, only half-conscious act of drawing. The acts of drawing and poem-making thus replicate each other as doubled events, the second in each case coming to repeat the first in a more self-conscious way. Because the second sonnet commencement refers back to the first act of drawing, the structural pattern reflects the order of the sonnet's quatrains, ABBA.

Rossetti's 'lighted on my soul' (2) introduces a double meaning not in Dante, but one that seems especially apt for a poem so concerned with the idea of spiritual enlightenment. It is thus one of Rossetti's characteristically 'interpretive' translational moments. The rendering of the sonnet's conclusion is more literal but equally effective in leaving open, as Dante does so carefully, the referent of the 'noble intellect'; for, of course, Dante's own intellect has in a sense been 'gone' since Beatrice left the poet. Dante's version of this double reference is altogether a more happy one, in several senses, than Rossetti's. In Dante the intellect is represented as having ascended to heaven ('oggi fa l'anno che nel ciel salisti'), whereas Rossetti's words inevitably carry a darker overtone.

13. 'Mine eyes beheld the blessed pity spring' (*EIP*, 296-7)

This sonnet focuses the climactic sequence of the *Vita Nuova*, the episode
of the Donna della Finestra (Chapters XXXV-XXXVIII), after which Dante
turns back toward Beatrice with greater devotion than ever. In the narrative's final movement (Chapters XXXIX-XLII), Dante undergoes two
successive visionary experiences: one of Beatrice, the second 'wherein I
saw things which determined me that I would say nothing further of this
most blessed one, until such time as I could discourse more worthily
concerning her' (Chapter XLII). This second (undisclosed) vision has
always been taken to be a forecast of Dante's *Commedia*.

Read in a Rossettian perspective, the Donna della Finestra episode
makes its own uncanny forecast. Its four sonnets – besides this one, the
sonnets 'Love's pallor and the semblance of deep ruth,' 'The very bitter
weeping that ye made,' and 'A gentle thought there is will often start,' all
carry themselves forward into the central texts of Rossetti's *House of Life*.
The connection, as well as its difficult moral and psychic ambivalence,
appears in an explicit way in line 11 of this sonnet. 'Thine eyes' compas-
sionate control' refers to the benignant look of the Donna della Finestra,
but in *The House of Life* that phrase comes to announce 'The Portrait' and
the countenance of that sequence's Beatrice figure, Elizabeth Siddal, not
its Donna della Finestra, Jane Morris.

In the Donna della Finestra episode, Dante represents a final struggle
between his Soul and his Heart. This struggle, for all the trouble it causes
Dante, ultimately functions in a benevolent way in the economy of grace
being celebrated in Dante's work. The benevolence appears in Chapter
XXXIX as a condition of endless martyrdom for the soul whose commitments are ultimately toward divine realities; and the heart's Donna leads
Dante to realize that martyrdom in the fullest possible way.

Rossetti, of course, understands this argument perfectly, as he shows in
his interpretive translation of the last two lines of this sonnet, which draw
the expectable equations between the Donna, Beatrice, and Love: 'Lo! with
this lady dwells the counterpart / Of the same Love who holds me weeping
now.' But the word 'counterpart' – it has no Dantean equivalent – insinu-
ates as well the set of distinctions and differences that Dante will also be
working out through the whole of the Donna episode.

14. 'A gentle thought there is will often start' (*EIP*, 301-2)

Perhaps no text in the entire *Vita Nuova* casts itself so far forward as this superb translation of the sonnet that climaxes Dante's Donna della Finestra episode. Free as it is, the translation captures the radical doubleness of Dante's original poem – indeed, it raises that doubleness to a more explicit level, as Rossetti regularly does in his reclamation of Dante's work. So various key locutions – for example, 'secret self,' ''twixt doubt and doubt,' and 'Love's messenger' – have no literal Dantean equivalents, though all perform equivalent functions. 'Love's messenger' is perhaps most revealing in this regard since it picks up the angel theme that is so important in Dante's work.

An appreciation of the 'strange art' of Rossetti's sonnet (that phrase also has no literal Dantean source) can be usefully sought in various poems and poem sequences in *The House of Life* where the strange art of the secret self is developed to such an extraordinary degree. Observing the nuances and ambiguities of a sonnet like 'Life-in-Love,' for example, not only illuminates this translation of Dante, it demonstrates how deeply Rossetti's reading of Dante's autobiography informs his work. Figural palimpsest is perhaps Rossetti's central poetic (and artistic) device, and in this sonnet we see that he has stolen this idea from Dante or, rather, from his reading of Dante.

Various 'uncanny' effects follow from the deployment of this device. Rossetti's poetry, as everyone knows, is replete with haunted texts, where the present world is regularly impinged upon by forces from the past and spirits of the dead. Not least impressive and affecting, however, are those texts where we glimpse living spirits appearing as premonitions of the past. Rossetti's translation of the *Vita Nuova* is exactly that kind of text – less a translation, in the ordinary sense, than a raising from the dead through a secular reinvention of a key Christian economy, prefiguration. The New Life of Dante's autobiography, in this view of the matter, is that one far-off sublime event to which its whole creation, unbeknownst to itself, moved.

15. 'Woe's me! By dint of all these sighs that come' (*EIP*, 303-4)

This sonnet's principal object is to dramatize that Dante has restored integrity and control to his writing, after his troubled passage through the Donna della Finestra texts. Rossetti underscores Dante's poetic purpose by overtranslating, as it were, the first two lines of the sestet. Besides introducing the wordplay 'musings' (for Dante's 'penseri'), Rossetti works Dante's text in several other important ways. Dante, for example, argues no causal relation between his 'penseri' and his 'sospir,' as Rossetti does, nor is there any Dantean equivalent for Rossetti's 'constant' (10). But of course

Rossetti is quite correct to make his translation insist on both of these points, for they are fundamental to Dante's general argument, even if they are not specifically articulated at this point. The lines give a clear view of how Rossetti will seize any good opportunity to render Dante's thought as faithfully as possible, even if it means departures from immediate literality.

The phrase 'These musings' torques Rossetti's sonnet into a sharply reflexive condition, an effect heightened through the way he multiplies suggestive connections by, in effect, rhyming 'musings' with 'Hearing' and thus building a clear structural parallel between the two final tercets. These formal relationships emphasize the agenting power of Dante's (and Rossetti's) verse and forecast the next chapter in the autobiography with its accompanying sonnet addressed to the pilgrim-folk passing through Florence. For while the sonnet says that Beatrice's 'sweet name' (13) is heard continually in the poet's musings and sighs, we search the text in vain for visible or articulate signs of her. And it is quite the purpose of this sonnet to lead its readers to scrutinize the text vainly for these signs. The name will come, unlooked for, in the next sonnet, generated from the desire expressed and brought to focus in this one.

16. 'Ye pilgrim-folk advancing pensively' (*EIP*, 306)

Dante's prose introduction to his sonnet in Chapter XXXIX explicitly calls for a symbolic reading of the pilgrims introduced into the narrative at this point and addressed in the sonnet. As a result, both the events of Dante's life and his textual passage through his narrative become identified as pilgrimages in what he calls a 'general sense': 'for ... any man may be called a pilgrim who leaveth the place of his birth' (*EIP*, 305), which is exactly what Dante has done in entering upon his New Life, both actual and textual.

Line 12 comes into the sonnet in a dramatic way because it fulfils an unheard melody announced in Dante's previous sonnet, 'Woe's me! By dint of all these sighs that come.' There Dante's 'sospiri' carry an invisible representation of the 'dolce nome' of Beatrice. Rossetti renders this absent presence in auditory terms – as Beatrice's unexpressed sweet name heard only in the 'sad sounds' of 'many grievous words touching her death' (14). In the present sonnet, however, Beatrice appears explicitly as both person and idea, 'la sua Beatrice.'

It is crucial to see that she comes into presence here in words of grace, as Rossetti's splendid free translation of lines 13-14 represents the matter. That literal beatific presence crowns Dante's argument about his double pilgrimage: his literal *Vita Nuova* is a reflexive repetition of his life's experience.

Rossetti translates this complex Dantean textual scene into contemporary terms in the most remarkable way. The move is clearly established in the opening quatrain, whose uncanny effect comes from the suggestion that the pilgrim-folk include Rossetti and his Victorian readers. The illusion of Dante speaking across the centuries is raised through the exemplary mediumship of Rossetti's poetic traversal. Rossetti's readers pass through his verse 'in thought of distant things' (2) – like Dante, like Dante's pilgrims, like Rossetti.

The excellence of this poem is notably marred in its last four words: 'and have no choice.' Rarely do Rossetti's translations display this kind of weakness – words introduced merely, it seems, to complete an English rhyme. The passage does not render, freely or otherwise, anything in the Dante original.

17. 'Beyond the sphere which spreads to widest space' (*EIP*, 308)

The Wordsworth allusion in line 4 ('the untrodden ways') is at once deft and shocking: deft because of the clear parallel between Wordsworth's Lucy figure and Dante's Beatrice; shocking because, as Byron would later say of Haidee and Aurora Raby, their beauties differ as between a flower and gem. Rossetti's implicit argument here forecasts his famous declaration: 'Thy soul I know not from thy body' ('Heart's Hope,' 7).

In a Dantean perspective, the sonnet looks forward to the *Commedia*, as Rossetti's prose note to Chapter XLII indicates: Dante's 'sospiro' (2) conceals his guiding 'peregrino spirito' (8), an understanding hidden within a longing desire (9-10, 14). The forecast *Paradiso* thus becomes here a kind of figure for this climactic moment in Dante's autobiography, where he seems poised in an exquisite vision of the relation of the text and journey he is just finishing and the text and journey he has yet to take. This sonnet incarnates that moment of poised awareness. In the sonnet's Rossettian perspective, that entire Dantean dynamic is recuperated in the 'lady round whom splendours move / In homage': the Ideal lady of every idealizing poet's imagination, Wordsworth's natural one as well as Dante's supernatural one. In Rossetti's later famous (and consciously Dantean) words: 'This is that Lady Beauty, in whose praise / Thy voice and hand shake still' ['Heart's Hope,' 8-9]). Rossetti's final sonnet – not Dante's – is a poetic splendour risen to do homage to that figure.

NOTES

1 Rossetti used the phrase twice: first in a note to his early pastiche poem 'Ave' and again later in his critical essay 'The Stealthy School of Criticism': see the 1911 *Works of Dante Gabriel Rossetti*, 661 and 619.
2 See Doughty and Wahl's *Letters of D.G. Rossetti* (2:389; 19 January 1861).

3

Rossetti's Elegy for Masculine Desire: Seduction and Loss in the *House of Life*

E. Warwick Slinn

Seduction is about surfaces, about colours and sounds, about images that distract the eye and ear, evoking admiration and desire for the absorbing specificity of sensory objects with their enticing beauty of shape and form. Yet if seduction is about sensation, it is also about representation and temporal ambiguity. Allure promises satisfaction, but not quite yet. So seduction plays with possibility, flaunting present sensation in order to draw attention to its signifying function, its mark of a referent, of a fulfilment, or even of more desirable pleasure, somewhere else, whether in space or time. In these terms all art is to some extent about seduction, depending as it does on the sensations and promises of a necessary materiality of form. Dante Gabriel Rossetti's art, however, confronts us more than most with seduction by foregrounding that material presence while at the same time evoking its hints of an alluring otherness. A crucial feature of his work, for instance, is that surfaces and details are also signs and symbols: mouths, lips, and eyes are never themselves. A mouth may be the seal of love's immortality (VIII), lips 'music's visible tone' (XXVII), and eyes an oracle of the soul (XXVII).[1] Woman, therefore, as the supremely present object of Rossetti's poetry and painting, is never herself. Like other sensuous appearances, she promises a pleasure beyond imagination and a signification that transcends all boundaries:

> Sometimes thou seem'st not as thyself alone,
>   But as the meaning of all things that are;
>   A breathless wonder, shadowing forth afar
> Some heavenly solstice hushed and halcyon. (XXVII)

Partly through the potency of these levels of meaning and partly through
the potency of their physical beauty, Rossetti's female figures are the main
means by which he portrays the power of seduction: Lilith, who woos the
serpent with her 'warm mouth's cooing' ('Eden Bower'); Helen, whose
breasts are 'the sun and moon of the heart's desire' (Troy Town'); and the
card dealer, whose 'eyes unravel the coiled night' ('The Card-Dealer'). In
such cases, seduction is a principle of allure, power, and signification; it
exploits, provokes even, a desire for fulfilment and plays daringly around
the uncertainties of future possibility. The eyes of Rossetti's women register the exigencies and temporality of earthly beauty, but they also hint at
transcendent or symbolic knowledge. The game in 'The Card-Dealer' is
the game of life and death. The players see only the card that is played,
beguiled by the 'great eyes' of the dealer's 'rings' and caught in the limits
of the moment, but she on the other hand invariably knows the card that
follows. She knows the future, seducing her players by distracting their
attention with rings and cards – signs that only she fully understands. Thus
seduction 'represents mastery over the symbolic universe,' and, immersed
in signs, it 'supposes a ritual order' (Baudrillard, 8, 21), flaunting the
formalism of aesthetic artifice and worship, as in 'Troy Town,' 'Ave,' and
'The Song of the Bower.'

It seems obvious that Rossetti learnt about seduction from his translations of early Italian poets.[2] Large numbers of these lyrics express the
delight and wonderment of poets whose persona has been seduced, transfigured, by female charms. Invariably their adored women are superior to
all others and celebrated as objects of universal desire: 'Who is she coming,
whom all gaze upon, / Who makes the air all tremulous with light?' (Guido
Cavalcanti, *Works of Rossetti*, 358). The power of these women is represented
as the capacity to bestow spiritual value and eternal truth as well as erotic
joy, and while the poet is the main victim of this power, even God may be
seduced, as He is by the 'perfect gentleness' of Dante Alighieri's Beatrice:
her glory evoked 'wonder in the Eternal Sire, / Until a sweet desire /
Entered Him for that lovely excellence' (*Works*, 337). Women in this poetry
are detached and remote, which allows them to be portrayed as ethereal, in
terms of abstract qualities ('high benison,' 'heavenly beauty'), but their
unrealizable status is part of their allure. The idealized fulfilment they
represent, whether erotic bliss or spiritual ecstasy, remains a tantalizingly
separate possibility, outside the poem. When she is spiritualized, presented as the aesthetic manifestation of a spiritual essence, or absolute
love, the worshipped woman of courtly love (Laura, Beatrice) becomes
interchangeable with the purified woman of myth and religion (Venus,

Diana, Mary). Nonetheless, she evokes the poet's desire and admiration, even if the moral sense of seduction as a leading astray is thereby suppressed, or desire sublimated, rendered aesthetically sublime, transformed into the literal displacement that is ecstasy.

The figure of the woman in these medieval love lyrics does not of course stand alone. She is produced within a generic formula where her role as female object of desire is established in relation to a desiring subject who is thereby gendered male. Her role as female seducer, that is to say, exists within a structure that constitutes masculine desire. A useful illustration of this model of seduction is provided in Fazio degli Uberti's 'Canzone' from Part Two of *Dante and His Circle*. The lady's power to enslave is acknowledged from the outset:

> I look at the crisp golden-threaded hair
>   Whereof, to thrall my heart, Love twists a net:
>   Using at times a string of pearls for bait,
>   And sometimes with a single rose therein. (*Works*, 488)

Her seductive force is supreme among women (no woman 'can have display'd / More power upon all hearts') and the 'loveliness' of her body's features – mouth, neck, and chin – conveys to the mind's eye 'every earthly joy.' She offers delights unknown: if the poet-speaker were wound in her arms, 'a life made new' would be born in his veins. And she represents virtue and reverence: 'All that she loves to do / Tends always to her honour's single scope.' Understandably she invokes impassioned desire: 'I would give anything that I possess, / Only to hear her mouth say frankly, "Yes."' But the subjunctive points to distanced fulfilment, and the poet's desire, as we all know, is characterized by frustration and longing – 'Woe's me! Why am I not, / Even as I wish, alone with her alone?' – at which point the politics and psychology of the structure begin to emerge (*Works*, 488-9).

The power of seduction attributed to the silent woman in such courtly love structures is matched by the power of the poet as speaking subject. Indeed, the force and value represented by the woman is implicitly absorbed by the poet to aggrandize his own status. Apparently seduced, he becomes himself the seducer, appropriating her qualities in order to define and qualify his own. This subtle intermingling of active and passive roles appears at the end of the first stanza in Fazio's 'Canzone,' when the speaker anticipates the delight of unbraiding his beloved's hair and turning her eyes into mirrors. There is an ambiguity in the phrasing of Rossetti's translation – 'make myself two mirrors of her eyes' – that blurs the object-subject relationship between poet and beloved. Who will reflect whom? Will he make himself into two mirrors which then reflect her eyes, himself an object to her subjectivity? Or will he make her eyes into two mirrors for (and thereby of) himself? The number of mirrors (two) suggests the latter, in which case the phrasing exposes the means by which the speaker uses the woman to constitute, to reflect, both literally and figuratively, his own subjectivity.

While the speaker's identity as both male and poet is assured within this structure – as speaking subject, the power of expression and interpretation, the assigning of meaning, rests with him – he is at the same time committed to an image of seduction that disallows fulfilment or completion. The woman's silence ensures his continued expression, his existence as poet, but it is her absence and distance that defines and sustains his desire. As long as desire is not consummated, the poet may speak of longing and frustration and thereby continue to affirm his existence as male subject. This affirmation is achieved through the speaker's indirect objectification of his own presence by writing the poem. By identifying his feelings with the woman as other and thus uttering them in the poem, he implicitly objectifies them for his own scrutiny, persuading himself of their existence. Hence the figure of the woman – which in the poem becomes literally a figure (of speech) – and her role as seductive force are sustained by the poet's formulaic language, a realm of signs. Fazio's 'Canzone' illustrates this point explicitly, since in each stanza the poet turns from the lady's features to his own responses, openly foregrounding how his literal looking, exercising the power of the gaze, is transformed into a figurative and discursive representation: 'I, gazing on that lovely one, / Discourse in this wise with my secret thought.' To contemplate what she means is to confront the construction of his own desire: 'Were it not pleasant now ... To have that neck within thy two arms caught / And kiss it till the mark were left behind?' he asks, addressing himself (*Works*, 488). But foregrounding his representations, both of her attributes and what they evoke in him, is also to confront the limits of representation. He may postulate that 'in her are both / Loveliness and the soul's true excellence,' but he cannot be sure about pity, and thence his anxiety: 'woe's me!' (489).

The masculine quality of a poet in this tradition is thus characterized by his condition of rapture, of being consumed by an idealized image to which he attaches supreme value of feeling but which he cannot possess as an object of desire. What becomes a defining feature of this masculine desire therefore is not only its location of feelings and value in an external source (and consequent evasion of responsibility for those feelings) but also its willingness to settle for a lack of fulfilment – for loss and the sorrow that accompanies loss. For these poets 'life's all suffering' (*Works*, 394), and their identity as male poet is defined by the anguish of loss, whether through the loss of their beloved in death, as in the case of Dante's Beatrice, or simply through absence, as in the case of Cecco Angiolieri's Becchina: 'Sorrow has brought me to so sad a pass / That men look sad to meet me on the road' (*Works*, 394). The only means of assuaging this anguish and suffering, Cecco suggests, would be through possession of the absent woman – 'one moment would pluck out these stings, / If for one moment she were mine to-day.' This effectively emasculated sense of the masculine (compared with the triumph and conquering defined by the man-of-action ethos) depends on submission, on a willingness to submit to the sovereign command of the representative of love and beauty, to be seduced, that is, by the forms and promises of love, by present beauty insofar as it functions as a sign of absent perfection: 'if such loveliness be given / To sight here,' asks Fazio, 'what of that which she doth hide?' (488). What attracts the poet, the male idealist, is the enchantment of female form – less the object itself, than what its form, its representation, the sign of its presence (and absence) portends, signifies, offers. For Dante, what Beatrice offers is faith, gentleness, and 'a passion of exceeding love' (334). But a passion of exceeding love is also the promise of all siren songs and the basis therefore of female power when tied to seduction, to the allure of the sign. Through the centuries men have been beguiled by this formula, seduced by the form, by the structure that gave them definition as male and subjects, as much as by any real woman. Indeed, the woman becomes merely a cipher, a means to a masculine end, since as silent object she is hardly allowed the dignity of reciprocal response as a desiring subject in her own right.

The legacy of Rossetti's Italian translations therefore is a nexus of desire and sorrow, where poetic identity is tied to the present absence of a female other and where loss, if not inherent, is certainly endemic. Immediately we find all the features of Rossetti's poetry that have been repeatedly observed: seductive formalism, aesthetic pleasure, idealized women, spiritualized value, the agony of desire and loss. As William E. Fredeman taught us several decades ago, *The House of Life*, Rossetti's sonnet sequence that most obviously embodies this Italian legacy, is predominantly elegiac in tone, inheriting that mood of loss ('Rossetti's "In Memoriam,"' 318-33). In the early sonnets in the sequence, where Rossetti emphasizes the potential for erotic pleasure found more often in the pre-Dantean lyricists, the element of loss is less apparent. In these sonnets, love is consummated:

'bliss,' in an act of 'Supreme Surrender,' is 'attained' (VII).[3] Indeed, the sequence offers moments of both spiritual affirmation (III) and fleshly celebration (VIa), much to the moral horror of Robert Buchanan in his notorious attack on 'The Fleshly School of Poetry.' As we might expect, the moments of consummation, with their affirmation of a literal female presence, generally act as a guarantor of the poet-speaker's masculine identity. Through the beloved's presence, he is structured as powerful, with the capacity to be transfigured from child to god (V), to experience the emotional satisfaction of post-coital bliss (VIa), and to obtain the knowledge of 'powers primordial' (XXXIV).

But the moments of consummation, of satisfied desire, are not moments of unqualified identity or fulfilment. In one sense they suggest an ideological experiment: what happens to structures of seduction – and thence to desire, masculinity, and spiritual value – when the object is possessed? There is a strong indication, in 'Nuptial Sleep,' for instance, that satisfied desire effectively promotes a loss of identity, in the sense that sexual consummation produces a blurring of boundaries where separate selves disappear (identity presupposing an outline or border, a definition, of self). This point is implicit in the way the poem represents the period of post-coital bliss when the two lovers return to consciousness. After separating physically, but drifting further into the loss of separate consciousness which is sleep, they return to their separate selves: 'Slowly their souls swam up again, through gleams / Of watered light.' When the male figure finally wakes, he 'wondered more: for there she lay' (VIa), and in that wonderment, I suggest, is his realization that it is his beloved's separate presence that now restores his identity as a separate self. In the following sonnet, 'Supreme Surrender' (VII), the speaker's climactic bliss is achieved through the paradox of a submission that leads to sovereignty – but for whom is not clear. The 'queen-heart' of the speaker's mistress lies 'in sovereign overthrow' beside his own heart, but 'sovereign overthrow' is virtually an oxymoron, blending the ruler with the ruled, the conquering power with the downfallen power. Who surrendered to whom is therefore indeterminate, suggesting rather that each surrendered to the other, and the ambiguity again suggests a loss as much as a gain of identity – enacting a secular version of the Christian paradox of self-abnegation perhaps. The speaker in the sequence also learns that possession cannot be complete: 'After the fullness of all rapture,' he says to his beloved in 'Soul-Light,' 'there comes to view / Far in your eyes a yet more hungering thrill' (XXVIII). Thus, a sense of incompletion arises from erotic possession, and lurking within each of these moments is exactly that – a sense that it is a moment.[4] The act of 'Supreme Surrender' is a temporal event, 'The sacred hour for which the years did sigh' (VII), and in 'Severed Selves' the separation of 'Nuptial Sleep' is transformed into a future realization that the moment of erotic satisfaction passes all too quickly: it 'blooms and fades,' leaving behind 'the attenuated dream' (XL).

In celebrating the supposed goal of all seduction, consummation exposes the limits of seduction: the dependency of the masculine on woman and how the requirement that the masculine submit to the beloved as symbol depends on remaining attached to signifiers, to representation, not the thing itself. The success of seduction as a means of defining male desire depends, that is to say, on eluding the contingencies of time. Within actual temporal experience, within the world of referential reality, acting out desire leads indeed to loss, to the dissolution of boundaries between lover and beloved, and to the collapse of the seductive image. Hence in 'Soul-Light,' when the woman is not satisfied, evincing 'a more hungering thrill' and implicitly threatening the male speaker with a sense of his own limits, he restores her to the abstraction of signs, affirming her capacity for infinite seduction (as opposed to infinite coitus) by reaffirming her ability to represent 'the changeful light of infinite love' (XXVIII). If ever patriarchal processes contained woman by treating her as symbol, this is it. Yet it is also the restoration of the structure of seduction – the poet's attempt to retain his role as the subject of male desire. A similar enactment occurs later in the sequence, I suggest, when Rossetti adds 'Soul's Beauty' and 'Body's Beauty' to the poem in the final version of 1881.[5] After sonnets about lost opportunities (LXV) and missed marks (LXVII), these two lyrics reinstate woman as an image of seduction, whether in spiritual or physical terms. Both poems record the seductive snare of these symbolic representations: in one, 'Lady Beauty' names the principle that will ensnare the 'allotted bondman' (LXXVII), while in the other, 'Lilith' names the principle of enchantment that will capture heart and body 'in its hold' (LXXVIII). For seduction to work as a structure that sustains male desire, woman must remain with signs and symbols.

Yet even then dependency on woman – on woman as signifying image – remains, carrying the concomitant threat of her absence. So even before the famous sonnets of consummation – 'The Kiss,' 'Nuptial Sleep,' and 'Supreme Surrender' – the poet-speaker expresses anxiety about the potential loss of his beloved and her image:

> O love, my love! if I no more should see
> Thyself, nor on the earth the shadow of thee,

> Nor image of thine eyes in any spring, –
> How then should sound upon Life's darkening slope
> The ground-whirl of the perished leaves of Hope,
> The wind of Death's imperishable wing? (IV)

This sestet, following an octave that celebrates the ritual worship of the beloved as a principle of abstract Love, demonstrates the precarious status of the speaker's attachment to signs. If not even the 'shadow' or 'image' of his beloved could be seen on earth, hope will perish and death will be imminent. At this early stage in the poem the elegiac portent of the last three lines remains a rhetorical hypothesis, a tone of residual anxiety, but its possibility is not merely residual: it is inherent within the poet's dependence upon the role of woman as signifier, since it is through her mediation that Love is 'made known.' Loss, then, or the possibility of loss, is indeed ubiquitous in the poem, found even in the early sonnets, notwithstanding the celebrated moments of sexually inspired ecstasy.

Given that, as Fredeman suggests, the poem is fundamentally elegiac, perhaps what it elegizes is less the loss of a vaguely conceived life that the title too easily implies than the loss of masculine desire. Jerome McGann and David Riede have already observed the extent to which the poem portrays 'personality dismemberment,' 'loss of identity' (McGann, 'Betrayal,' 351-2), and 'dissolution of the self' (Riede, 137), but I wish to distinguish further between identity, desire, and the masculine. The fragmentation of the poem's structural features, its division into 101 sonnets without any clear continuity of narrative or persona, militates against any drama of a single identity, as Riede acknowledges (141-2). Yet the lyrics still work to establish forms of identity throughout the poem (aesthete, artist, self-analyst, philosopher-poet) and retain a desire that underwrites these roles. What is lost is the sense of masculinity, desire as a yearning for woman, that emerges from the structure of seduction that Rossetti learned from his Italian translations. I also want to emphasize the awareness of temporal process in the poem for it is inseparable from an awareness of desire. And by desire I refer throughout to conscious desire, to the need or longing that is desire for a personalized object and that is produced therefore as an aspect of personalized subjectivity, rather than the unconscious desire, or desiring unconscious, that Deleuze and Guattari depersonalize and nominate in their famous formulation, as the only reality along with the social: '*There is only desire and the social, and nothing else*' (29). To be aware of desire in this conscious sense is to be aware of a lack in the present and of the difference between present lack and future (or past) gratification. Alternatively, a construction of desire in terms of the present plenitude of a woman's meaningfulness may provoke an awareness of the possibility of change, of the future loss of that presence (as discussed in sonnet IV). As Fredeman also pointed out ('Rossetti's "In Memoriam,'" 322), the common denominator in the titles of Rossetti's two parts of the poem is change: 'Youth and Change,' and 'Change and Fate.' If Rossetti begins by representing the experience of bliss attained, he quickly acknowledges the built-in aspect of time and process, as has often been noted (Spector, Conners). Nothing stands: 'There is a change in every hour's recall' (XXIV). Consequently, the persona in these sonnets is rarely without a sense of temporal play or the potential for change, and I would stress the persona's consciousness of time rather than time conceived as some independent or reified 'agent of change' (Conners, 20). A feature, therefore, of an enormous number of sonnets is the way they contain within their own immediate intensity a complex shifting of tenses and temporal awareness.

Any number of sonnets register an awareness about desire and time: about 'vain-longing,' for instance, desire that is 'Life-thwarted,' never fulfilled (LIV); about the abstractions of temporally constituted possibility, 'The hour which might have been yet might not be' (LV); or about lovers whose consciousness absorbs all process, who in every kiss 'feel the first' and 'forbode the last' (LVIII). But 'Beauty's Pageant' (XVII) quite directly focuses on change, celebrating the shifting moods that pass across a woman's face. Registering the transience of woman's beauty and outperforming the 'glory of change' in nature, those moods, at the point of speaking, belong to an immediate past, occurring 'Within this hour.' They induce in the speaker an acute awareness of the implications of temporal process, of the relationship between past, present, and future representations of this 'form and face.' Each 'fine movement,' he postulates, was the 'vesture' and 'disguise' of love – a token of the capacity for beauty and desire to produce a threefold result of 'wonder,' 'joy,' and 'sorrow.' The movements that denote love evoke the 'wonder new-begot' of a 'lily or swan,' the capacity of love to renew itself; they evoke joy in the sight of the lover, although a joy that is now inseparable from the sad 'sighs' of being parted from them; and they invoke sorrow in future eyes, in those who 'read these words and saw her not.' In the brief lines of one sonnet the woman's 'form and face' are transformed from the glory of organic process to the outward sign of love's display to the remembered image that evokes sadness for its loss and, finally, to the absent referent of words yet to be read. The poem registers in miniature those features of seduction in a poem like Fazio's 'Canzone' –

the woman's power of beauty, her provocation of desire, her link with loss, and her entry into poetic formulation. What Rossetti emphasizes, however, is the shifting time relationships and representations – what the woman has been, what she is, and what she will be. Beauty is indeed a 'pageant,' always already a sign, a seductive surface that provokes desire and loss. In effect, the woman herself never exists and perhaps never did.

'Winged Hours' (XXV) also portrays the awareness of mixed moments of time, recording the irony of a celebratory 'hour of meeting' that contains an unheard strain of 'wrong,' the sense that within 'contending joys' there lurks the presence of a future violence, a time when the wings of hours that bring the lovers together will be merely 'bloodied feathers scattered in the brake.' The consciousness of this ironic horror is mitigated by the speaker's contemplative detachment as he attempts to stand outside the process by using the language of figurative description: 'Each hour until we meet is as a bird / That wings from far.' But desire, joy, and loss again intermingle. Other sonnets early in the sequence represent less disruptive mixtures of time. In 'Last Fire' (XXX), for instance, the present is constituted through the past rather than the future. Here the speaker constructs a period of blissful languor that is based on retrieving 'mutual dreams' of 'bygone bliss.' While there is nothing substantial in the moment – only dreams and memories – and it exists as an evening 'glow' amidst other images of transience – sun, fire, summer, winter – it offers the passing plenitude of 'full heart's ease.'

Yet such blissful moments always depend on the presence of the woman, and increasingly there are dire portents of what consciousness would be like without it. The poet would lose all authority, become subservient to some other power, the 'servant' of sorrow or the 'thrall' of death (XXXVI), or merely wander without definition, 'A wayfarer by barren ways and chill' (LIII). In 'Sleepless Dreams' (XXXIX), the speaker confronts the 'lonely night' as 'a thicket hung with masks of mockery / And watered with the wasteful warmth of tears.' And in 'Cloud and Wind' (XLIV) the awareness of future change, wondering whether death will be worse for himself or for his beloved, includes recognition that fulfilment of desire is impossible, 'that Hope sows what Love shall never reap.' Alternatively, when his beloved is absent, memory may supply the seductive lure. In 'Parted Love' (XLVI) he portrays himself as a 'wretch' without his beloved's presence, but 'Memory's art / Parades the Past' and 'passionate portraitures' entice him until desire again 'flood[s]' his heart. Masculine desire momentarily returns, therefore, but it is provoked by signs, by representations, not by the woman herself, and in the sestet the sonnet turns back on its own process, in a self-enclosed moment where the speaker addresses himself: 'thy heart rends thee, and thy body endures.' Thus, as the woman disappears, the speaker can no longer define himself through external relationships, and he turns within, signalling another stage in the seduction complex.

The internalized construction of desire is most obviously dramatized in the 'Willowwood' sonnets (XLIX-LII), where it occurs as a moment of narcissistic reflexiveness. Love is now allegorized as male, and in an act of implicit self-division he and the speaker lean together across a well. The conjunction of pronouns – 'I and he' – that suggests the self-division will later become the explicit dramatization of the divided self in 'He and I' (XCVIII). In Willowwood I, however, the reflected image of love gradually transforms itself into the image of the speaker's beloved: 'as I stooped, her own lips rising there / Bubbled with brimming kisses at my mouth' (XLIX). As the image of seduction rises to meet him from the water, the speaker enacts a self-enclosed process of subject-object relationships. In stooping to the reflected lips and through the agency of the divided self, he responds to that image as to a separate self, the beloved woman, who once again offers the sensory gratification of brimming kisses. Thus, the reflection acts as both a reflection and not a reflection: 'The poet kisses his own image ... and not his own image' (Armstrong, 455). Constructed through love as a male principle of self-projection, the image of seduction nevertheless functions also as a discrete other, thereby constituting the speaker as desiring self. Rossetti internalizes the process that the Italian sonneteers rendered external. In this moment of self-constitution, love can sing, celebrating the reconstitution of the structure of seduction and desire. He sings a song that evokes images from the past, a silent throng of 'mournful forms,' each one a shade of lost days; these images, signs of absent selves, provide the objective recognition that allows the kiss to remain as a construction of identity, wrung from the 'abyss,' from absence and meaninglessness (L). Once the song ends, the kiss 'did ... unclose' (LII), suggesting the close association of the kiss of identity with the discursive practice of song and representation. The image then collapses: 'her face fell back drowned.' Seduction fails; desire remains unfulfilled. All the poet can do is drink from the water where she sank, absorbing literally what he otherwise would appropriate symbolically – 'Her breath and all her tears and all her soul' – and conjure an image of self-enclosed unity, the heads of himself and love encircled by love's 'aureole' (LII). The sonnet immediately following this group, 'Without Her' (LIII), takes the effects of the woman's absence a step further. It transfers the drowning greyness of the beloved's face ('as grey / As its grey eyes') in Willowwood IV to the 'blank grey' of the mirror without her reflection. That blank mirror, 'where the pool is blind of the moon's face,' and the 'tossed empty space' of her dress register not merely absence but also the vacuum without sight and without meaning that is left when the seductive image collapses – the abyss in Willowwood II perhaps, from which the kiss was momentarily conjured. In the void of loss remains only 'desolate night,' the sorrow of 'cold forgetfulness,' and the shapeless life of a 'wayfarer' in often 'doubled darkness.' Without woman's seductive presence, the signs that once gave shape to its potency – her mirror, her dress, her 'pillowed place' (LIII) – point instead to its emptiness.

Hence there emerges an increasing sense that seduction, the tantalizing promise of meaningfulness and plenitude, is, in time, empty, the mere play of signs, without durability. Siren songs become the songs of death (LXXXVII). In the earlier sonnets, the allure of physical beauty is justified by treating it as a symbol of transcendent value. Beauty may fade, but it may nevertheless signify permanence, continuity, that which resides amidst all transience (like Wordsworth's 'dwelling' in 'the light of setting suns'): the 'penetrating sense, / In Spring's birth-hour, of other Springs gone by' (V), or the 'silent penetrative loveliness' of 'all things that are' (XX). But as the awareness of change increases, the presence of permanence recedes. Or, rather, as the literal presence of woman recedes, the dependence upon surfaces and signs, with their shifting uncertainties, becomes more apparent. As that happens, the necessary function of woman in relation to the masculine and the poet's dependency upon his own interpretative subjectivity also become more apparent. The sonnets about 'True Woman' (LVI-LVIII), written and added in 1881, are significant in this respect. They celebrate woman's meaningfulness, but they also acknowledge her separate mystery: 'How strange a thing to be what Man can know / But as a sacred secret' (LVI). While on one level woman is again a function of male appropriation, representing a glory beyond sight, on another level these sonnets expose, wittingly or unwittingly, the means by which that appropriation constructs male subjectivity. In 'Herself' (LVI), for instance, the speaker's sense of wonder implicitly acknowledges woman's existence as sign. To recognize that being 'a sweetness more desired than Spring' makes woman 'strange' is potentially to allow the irony that for the male observer woman is effectively *not* 'Herself.' Her body is not her body: it signifies a 'beauty more acceptable / Than the wild rose-tree's arch that crowns the fell.' This recognition of woman's separate strangeness borders on acknowledging that while her symbolic function depends on male interpretation, 'true' woman is more elusive, a 'sacred secret.' In the following sonnet, 'Her Love' (LVII), male appropriation is at its most vigorous, exposing the way male ideology is attached to the woman's role as signifier. Here, woman functions as a reflection of male ardour: 'Passion in her is / A glass facing his fire, where the bright bliss / Is mirrored.' Woman's role is to discriminate: if a stranger faces the mirror, her fire turns to ice. But through this specular structure she produces the poet's male subjectivity, constituting desire as male (her passion reflects 'his' fire) and himself as sovereign: 'With ... circling arms, she welcomes all command / Of love.' In such poems, male lyricism clearly deploys itself as an act of ideological absorption and self-enclosure.

At the end of Part One, the poet-speaker proposes another source of permanence, the relative durability of poetry itself. While all other fruits of love are subject to change, 'Love's Last Gift' (LIX) is the gift of laurel, that which 'dreads no winter days.' This sonnet reminds us that the whole sequence begins with a proposition about poetry, that the sonnet is '*a moment's monument*' (*Works*, 74), a means of substantiating the insubstantial. Nothing stands – except, that is, the representation provided by the artist who constructs a '*Memorial*,' who formalizes the moment in an aesthetic shape. But as Herbert Tucker observes of this prefatory sonnet, it strands us on its surface from the outset (293), insisting on '*its own arduous fullness*' and its '*impearled*' crest; and as a seductive surface, flaunting the allure of image and sensation, art, particularly poetry, is itself also a sign. In Rossetti's own terms, a sonnet is a transient celebration of what was once present but can never now be known other than through the sign that signifies its lost presence – through its absence, in other words. Rossetti's oxymoron of the '*dead deathless hour*' that is memorialized by sonnets cannot avoid the problem 'that the deathless hours are still, in fact, dead' (Riede, 140; see also Conners, 23). What exists are the words, but since words are also temporal, art, like a woman's beauty, also partakes of the 'pageant' of process and possibility. So if the commitment to seduction is a commitment to signs and symbols, and that is what it is to be a poet, then that is a commitment to loss, to the emptiness of signs that lies behind the promised allure of plenitude. What begins therefore as the expression of conventional lyricism and the construction of male desire through the symbolic representations of idealized women, becomes gradually absorbed by the abstractions of its own method – the language of Dantesque idealism and symbol – so that Love as a personified essence or formalized classical cupid becomes increasingly merely an abstract noun, a signifier without a referent.[6] As readers are thrust back on the formalism of the poetry itself, the seductive repetitions, rhythms, and rhymes of its evocative display, they enter into a realm of signs, where Rossetti's words are 'signs of signs, unattached, free from relation and reference' (Granger, 3), or 'a play of signifiers and signifieds' (McGann, 'Betrayal,' 356) – the symbolic universe that may be mastered by the principle of seduction. But that is a world of aesthetic construction and ritual display, and it is exposed also as a world without permanence or stability (see also Gardner).

Hence in Part Two, poet and reader become increasingly lost in a world of insubstantial allure. 'Autumn Idleness' (LXIX) contemplates the enticing effects of November sunlight, but autumnal glow is an ethereal presence, and when evening fosters the renewal of 'lost hours,' the speaker is left with aimless and uncertain desire: 'Nor know, for longing, that which I should do.' At 'The Hill Summit' (LXX), the 'Transfigured' sun may be recalled as the splendid image of 'a fiery bush with coruscating hair,' but it is also time to 'tread downward' and 'travel the bewildered tracks.' And the glories of sunrise and sunset ('The blushing morn and blushing eve') now signify 'shame' (XCII), the realization that material values (wealth, strength, power) have been given over to the weak and corrupt, and that desire has become a fruitless exchange of mutual and unfulfilled yearning. The structure of seduction is now the 'longed-for woman longing all in vain / For lonely man with love's desire distraught.' This, accordingly, is a world of ambiguous signs. 'The Soul's Sphere' (LXII) is now an internalized realm of uncertain portents and conjecture, where yearning is 'fed' by the ambiguities of what may be a 'prisoned moon' or 'dying sun,' and where the mind's images may herald 'golden futures' or the 'last / Wild pageant of the accumulated past.' In this highly figurative personal 'sphere,' there are no stable figures. There are only the oscillations of conscious alternatives or, rather, the oscillations of alternatives whose differences constitute consciousness. 'Inclusiveness' (LXIII) states how ordinary places, even the room one sits in, may provide images for quite different perceptions, whether in heaven of a 'life well spent' or in hell of 'a memory all in vain.' Consequently, signs may be missed: 'Was *that* the landmark?' (LXVII). 'Who knows' if present 'gloom,' like drops of rain, denotes new struggles – a 'Fresh storm' – or the remains of old ones – 'old rain the covert bears' (LXVIII)? The question about the world's physical process – is it all 'a show' or 'decree / Of some inexorable supremacy'? – is ultimately unanswerable by human means: 'Nay, rather question the Earth's self' (LXXXIX). Among such unstable signifiers, the internalized self dissolves, not unexpectedly, into a fragmented enclosure of regret and recrimination. The speaker in 'Lost Days' (LXXXVI) imagines an afterlife confrontation with the images of his squandered days, each one 'a murdered self,' as if every hour of consciousness remains somewhere to be recuperated and ac-counted for. 'A Superscription' (XCVII) dramatizes a complex interaction between a mirrored image that displays the speaker's sense of failure and a projected observer who objectifies the image: 'Look in my face; my name is Might-have-been; / I am also called No-more, Too-late, Farewell.' The speaker's image is merely a 'shadow intolerable' of earlier forms of life and love, and that reduction occurs through a 'spell,' as if the power of seduc-tion to enthral has abandoned him as a 'frail screen' of 'things unuttered.' The sestet then outlines the terrible, foreboding threat of divided selves that dissolve personal integrity. Should one side relax into complacency and peace, the other, 'with cold commemorative eyes,' will ambush its 'heart.' This deeply unsettling image of self-division and sabotage contin-ues in 'He and I' (XCVIII), the most notorious of Rossetti's representa-tions of the dismembered self: 'Whence came his feet into my field, and why?' But as the drama of subjectivity becomes reduced to the antagonism of two pronouns, their uncertain antecedents blur and merge. The pro-nouns are interchangeable: 'Even in my place he weeps. Even I, not he.' At the same time, this internalized separation supplants the defining exter-nality of woman, affirming the sense of the speaker as a subject who is defined instead against the 'new Self' that wanders around his field.

What emerges from *The House of Life*, therefore, is an increasing expo-sure of the shattering implications of that built-in attachment to loss and lack of fulfilment that was inherent in the courtly love formula. Attaching himself to female beauty as a sign of his masculine identity, the male subject dooms himself to absence and loss. This is no surprise to contem-porary feminine psychoanalysis, but *The House of Life* unfolds the process: shifting personae (between first-person affective expression and third-person detachment), fragmentation (of temporal sequence and thence of causation), and a series of memorialized moments that memorialize little more than their own desperate attempt to seize the moment, whether as the shocked realization that death may imitate love (XLVIII), the trans-forming genius of the poet (LX), the choice of youth (LXXI-LXXIII), or the despairing failure of the 'Might-have-been' (XCVII). Perhaps the poem indicates a covert realization that woman represents less the manifes-tation of spirit than the potential for seduction to be merely an empty sign: these sonnets are 'the great conjurors of emptiness' (Armstrong, 453). Desire itself remains, however, even if only in the attenuated form of hope. The internalized division that engenders desire is frequently conceived (from Hegel to Lacan) as an inherent condition of subjectivity, but without woman, it loses its masculinity. It is merely desire, genderless, vaguely seeking some replacement for what it dimly perceives as lost. In 'Memorial Thresholds' (LXXXI), for instance, the speaker yearns for 'one presence' to fill the liminal zone ('a single simple door') that will be his threshold into eternity; otherwise, his life, his words, and the city of the afterlife will remain a formless maelstrom whirled round by 'mocking winds.' Or in 'Lost on Both Sides' (XCI), the separate hopes of a divided self, like two rivals who reconcile after the death of the woman they both lost, now 'roam together' in 'restless brotherhood,' with the object of their desire, the 'one same Peace' they fought over, no longer attainable ('perished since').

But the poem's last sonnet, 'The One Hope' (CI), provides the last expression of desire for the hope of future replenishment. The speaker imagines that after death he still seeks ('Peers breathless') after the qualities earlier associated with woman ('grace unknown'), and still expects to be enthralled, seduced, wishing that no 'alien spell' be present other than the one he desires, 'the one Hope's one name' – 'Not less nor more, but even that word alone' (CI). There is no referent for hope in this sonnet and no specific image to signify one, for the usual seductive signifier, the woman of ideal form who constructs hope as male desire, is no longer available. All the poet-speaker can posit now to sustain his structure of desire is to predicate it upon the presence of a word, a name, a sign that would sustain hope, the symbol of psychological need. This final desire for a symbol is what remains of seduction, and it acts as the only structure for self that the poet can imagine surviving after death. What he desires therefore is desire itself, to sustain a presence of signs, even if only one specific word ('Hope's one name') that would allow even minimal desire to survive.

Seduction seems a term entirely appropriate to the poem's play with desire and disappointment because it focuses that tantalizing tension between physical presence and absent possibility. Despite the poem's and its author's claims in 'The Stealthy School of Criticism' (*Works*, 617-21) to affirm such absences as a feature of spiritual beauty, the poem seems nevertheless immersed in materiality (including its own) and the representations of mortal consciousness. As Isobel Armstrong suggests, 'meaning hovers or dissolves beyond or beneath the material form, or the physical hovers beyond or beneath the state of loss, always incommensurate, always unrealised' (453). That the poem fails to convince readers of any lasting devotion to spirituality is evident from recent discussion (Granger, Mitchell, McGann, Riede, Armstrong), so perhaps we are better to read the poem as Fredeman proposed, as a form of elegy: as a representation, I suggest, of an 'attenuated dream' (XL), of being a self 'severed' from a lost literary and patriarchal ideal; or, perhaps, as a critique, intentional or not, of the bourgeois attempt in Victorian culture to sustain an idealist aesthetic and an essentialist truth about love. In the nineteenth century, courtly love structures could not provide suitable roles for female poets without considerable modification, as both Elizabeth Barrett Browning in *Sonnets from the Portuguese* and Christina Rossetti in 'Monna Innominata' demonstrate; but *The House of Life* shows that these structures also fail to sustain male identity and idealism. If other poets, notably Matthew Arnold in 'Stanzas from the Grande Chartreuse' and 'The Scholar-Gypsy,' were demonstrating that humanist idealism found it difficult to sustain old modes and transcendent values when it attempted to incorporate the material and historical present, Dante Gabriel Rossetti in *The House of Life* shows the same problem in terms of the seductive body and personalized desire.

NOTES

1 *The House of Life*, reprinted in *The Works of Dante Gabriel Rossetti*, pp.74-108. All quotations are from this edition (hereafter cited as *Works*), and all references to *The House of Life* will be given as sonnet numbers within that sequence. *The House of Life* was published in three main versions (1869, 1870, 1881), and *Works* prints the 1881 text, with 'Nuptial Sleep,' which the author withdrew after 1870, restored as sonnet VIa. For the contents of each version, and for a list of the composition and publication dates of each sonnet, see Fredeman, 'Rossetti's "In Memoriam,"' 336-41. The copy of *Works* I am using, which I am pleased indeed to use for this occasion, was a birthday gift from William E. Fredeman in 1968 when I was privileged to be his student.

2 William Rossetti dates most of these translations between 1845 and 1849. They were first published in 1861 as *The Early Italian Poets* and republished in 1874 as *Dante and His Circle*; the later edition rearranged the poems into two parts, 'Dante and His Circle' and 'Poets Chiefly before Dante,' in order to highlight Dante's importance (*Works*, 282).

3 Courtly love traditions of course vary: 'the courtly lover's passion may or may not be adulterous, and it may or may not be consummated' (Mitchell, 48).

4 See also the discussions of 'Silent Noon' (XIX) by Spector and McSweeney (128-30).

5 These two sonnets were first printed as 'Sibylla Palmifera' and 'Lady Lilith' in *Notes on the Royal Academy Exhibition* (1868); they were reprinted in *Poems* (1870) but not incorporated into *The House of Life* until 1881.

6 For the influence of Dante on *The House of Life*, see Rees, 127-40; for Rossetti's undermining of Platonic dualism, see Armstrong, 452-3.

4

William Michael Rossetti
and the Making of
Christina Rossetti's Reputation

Roger Peattie

I

On 29 December 1894, William Michael Rossetti wrote to Theodore Watts-Dunton: 'You and Swinburne will be sorry (and yet, after such lingering stages of illness, one ought not to be sorry) that my dear good Christina died this morning – most peacefully at the last' (*Selected Letters*, 575). A year later, after sorting and assessing her remaining papers, William published *New Poems by Christina Rossetti*, in the preface to which he declared his love, admiration, and reverence for his sister: 'Her memory is one of my most sacred treasures, and her works and their repute are proportionately dear to me' (xiv). Over the next decade or more, as Christina's reputation steadily strengthened, William played a pivotal role as editor, memorialist, and arbiter. Although it turned out to be a more frustrating and contentious task than he had reason to expect, he pursued it with determination and, ultimately, deep satisfaction.

With little more than a year between them in age, William (b. 1829) and Christina (b. 1830) were during their early years (in the words of Christina's biographer, Jan Marsh) 'small allies against their teasing and often imperious elders,' Maria (b. 1827) and Gabriel (b. 1828). Although, as Marsh correctly emphasizes, 'Christina was also aligned with Maria by gender and ... with Gabriel by a shared spiritedness' (5), the protective bond between the two younger children continued throughout their lives. According to William's calculation, for over twenty years, from about 1854 to 1876, Christina was financially 'substantially dependent' on him (*Family Letters*, 214). He was even willing in 1866, when the equally impecunious Charles

Cayley proposed to Christina, to add Cayley to the 'free inmates,' as he
baldly stated it, of the family house in Albany Street (29). The constant
watchfulness necessitated by Christina's always uncertain health continued to be a drain on William's spirits up to the time of her operation for
cancer in 1892, when he confessed to being 'in much sorrow and oppres-
sion of mind' (*Selected Letters*, 555), and during the long, tortuous illness
leading to her death, when he visited her daily.

Although it would be a mistake to attribute William's love for his sister
solely or mostly to the fierce family loyalty that characterized the Rossettis,
there was a strong element of incomprehension in his relationship with
Christina. In 1881, when Christina joined Gabriel and their mother in
trying to dissuade him from publishing his politically charged *Democratic
Sonnets*, William dismissed her concern as being of little '*practical* importance' because of her 'isolated devoteeism' (*Selected Letters*, 396). He con-
fided to Swinburne in 1904 that because he and Christina had been
'entirely hostile' in matters of religion, they 'left them largely in the
background, as being the only course conducive to our mutual comfort'
(639). With Lucy Madox Brown, whom William married in 1874 and who
like himself was a radical liberal in politics and an agnostic in religion,
Christina was never on easy terms. William struggled valiantly not to let
their coolness towards one another extend to his continuing contacts with
his sister, even when he had to tell her (as he reported to Lucy in 1886) that
should she move from London to Rochester, 'the great stumbling-block' to
her receiving prolonged visits from his children 'would be any tendency of
hers to proselytize the kids' (490).

As for her devotional writing, which occupied Christina increasingly
from the mid-1870s, Marsh nicely remarks that William refused to take any
interest, 'presumably for fear of encouraging it' (462). As Christina ap-
proached death, William, on his daily visits, saw only the most negative
aspects of her faith. On 12 February 1895, while these visits remained fresh
in his mind, he responded to Christina's first biographer, Mackenzie Bell:
'Assuredly my sister did to the last continue believing in the promises of
the Gospel, as interpreted by Theologians; but her sense of its threatenings
was very lively, and at the end more operative on her personal feelings. This
should not have been' (*Selected Letters*, 580). In his later writings on Christina,
ambiguously for an agnostic, William tended to side with the strain of
criticism that promoted her as the embodiment of religious conviction and
'Christian womanhood' (Charles, 62). Indeed, he concluded after her
death that he would be an 'inapt' biographer of his sister: 'Someone who
knew Christina intimately, and is an earnest Christian, would be the right

biographer,' he told Mackenzie Bell on 5 February 1895 (*Selected Letters*, 578). How little taste William had for Christina's religion, and how disinclined he was to try to understand it, is nowhere more apparent than in the decade or more following her death.

At the same time, as his sister's executor and as the last surviving member of the pre-eminent Anglo-Italian literary family of Victorian England, William understood his duty and hastened to fulfil it. Even as he announced Christina's death to Watts-Dunton, in the letter quoted above, he sent a few particulars for the obituary he assumed that Watts-Dunton would write for the *Athenaeum*. Two days later, on 31 December, he recorded in his diary that 'the first paper to notify Christina's death, in a long memoir, is the Daily Chronicle. Sent by request to Pall Mall Budget a photograph of her (1861) for engraving';[1] and on 1 January 1895, he noted with approval: 'Press-notices of Christina numerous, & (as they ought to be) very earnestly laudatory.'

Within three days of the funeral, William began the heavy task of sorting the large accumulation of papers, books, pictures, furniture, and personal objects in Christina's house, 30 Torrington Square, into which she had moved with her mother and aunts in 1876. Of the books, he wrote in his diary on 19 January: 'I keep (I suppose) more than I set aside to be parted with.' Some were given to friends named in Christina's will to receive mementoes; Olivia Garnett, the wife of Richard Garnett, for example, selected 'something like a dozen volumes' into which William wrote inscriptions (MS. Diary, 26 February, 11 March 1895). Somewhere between two and three hundred books, mostly presentation copies to Christina or containing inscriptions by members of the Rossetti and Polidori families, were auctioned at Sotheby's on 1 August 1895, when they brought little more than £25. A few items were purchased for £2 by Thomas J. Wise, including several copies of Maria Rossetti's pamphlet *In Morte di Guendalina Talbot* printed by Gaetano Polidori in 1841. The most poignant dispersal was of numerous remainder copies of books by Gabriele Rossetti and Charles Cayley, whose literary executor Christina had been, most still in sheets, including Cayley's translations of Homer, Petrarch, and Dante's *Paradiso*: 'In my own house I have no space for all these works: so ... I can but undertake to sell them off as waste-paper, however reluctantly. I called-in Olyett, who will on Monday remove the entire stock, & pay for it per weight ... He roughly guesses it at 3 cwt, & its value 15/-' (8 June). The few manuscripts and pictures from Torrington Square that William was willing to sell were enthusiastically acquired by Fairfax Murray and the bookseller and photographer, Frederick Evans; the manuscripts of Christina's first

and last poems, 'To My Mother' and 'Sleeping at Last,' were accepted by
Richard Garnett for the British Museum, and a portrait of the Rossetti's
maternal uncle, John William Polidori, and a joint portrait of Christina and
her mother, by the National Portrait Gallery: 'Find letter from National
Portrait Gallery, accepting the joint portraits of Christina & my mother, &
the one of Dr. Polidori. Few things in my life have given me more heartfelt
gratification than this. To get my dear old mother into the Gallery is no
small thing: & how great would have been the delight of my good Grandfather could he have foreseen that his greatly beloved & lamented John
would be there too' (16 September 1895). A substantial quantity of the
furniture was given to Rossetti's ever-needy nephew, Ford Madox Hueffer,
but one item went to 'one of the oldest & best friends of my good Christina'
(*Selected Letters*, 581), Amelia Heimann, whose husband, Adolf, had taught
the Rossetti children German: 'a table in Japanese style (probably Dutch
work of 18th century) which was I believe my own purchase toward 1865: it
was constantly used by Christina, & more especially for her requirements
during her last illness' (MS. Diary, 8 March 1895). Objects of a more
personal character were reserved for Rossetti's children, his daughter
Helen selecting 'my mother's, afterwards Christina's, old watch, a family-
object in daily use as far back as I can remember' (19 January 1895). A lover
of cats, William gladly welcomed Christina's Muff into his own house.

As he moved from room to room at Torrington Square meticulously
examining their contents, William was most intent on finding family manuscripts and letters. Many of the letters that he expected to find were
present, those to and from Gabriele Rossetti and John Polidori, Gabriel's
coveted letters to his mother, and the small group of incoming letters to
Christina that she had not destroyed. What he was surprised to discover
were numerous unpublished poems by Christina. Christina the poet had
always been something of an enigma to William. 'I cannot remember ever
seeing her in the act of composition,' he wrote in the preface to *New Poems*,
and erroneously concluded that her 'habits of composing were eminently
of the spontaneous kind.' Unlike Gabriel, who often sought and paid
careful attention to William's opinion of his poems, Christina, he believed,
'consulted nobody, and solicited no advice' (xii-xiii).

On 16 March 1895, he began looking 'with some attention through that
old series of MS. books in which Christina used to write down her poems as
soon as brought into shape' (MS. Diary). That they contained unpublished
poems that 'might well be included in some future complete edition' was
obvious from even a cursory inspection, but, being intensely busy finishing
the Memoir of his brother published later that year, it was 31 May before he

realized the extent of the new material: 'In going on with Christina's MS books, I find that the quantity of verse which she wrote, & left unpublished, exceeds what I had supposed. Most of it is much more than moderately good, but rather self-repeating in theme & treatment.' Meanwhile, on 20 May, he had written to Macmillan proposing 'a small volume,' and again on 24 May, in response to their immediate agreement to publish it, promising to complete work on the book with his usual promptitude: 'there does not seem to be any reason against its being published in the coming autumn – & of course I shall be all the better pleased the sooner it *is* published.' True to his word, as he further informed the publishers on 1 June, he proceeded with 'due diligence, so that by 3 June he had identified 203 poems for inclusion, and on 21 June began 'a final ... re-reading of the materials, along with requisite notes.' The typewriting of the material took rather a long while, but by 26 September he could record: 'Finished revising the type-writing ... & began putting the whole copy into final order for print-ing,' and finally, on 3 October: 'To my great satisfaction I handed in to George Macmillan the entire copy ... The course adopted will be this: The Printers in England will print, & send me proofs, & the proofs, as revised by me, will be forwarded to the United States, where American Printers will print other sheets' (MS. Diary).

As proofs began to arrive, William objected to the proposed page size, writing to George Macmillan on 13 October that 'the size adopted – which is much the same as that of Goblin Market [1862] – appears to me to entail a volume of unusual thickness: it must I fancy run up to 600 pages at least.' Macmillan agreed and reverted to the larger format of *Poems: New and Enlarged Edition* (1890), the final collected edition published in Christina's lifetime. The binding of the volume was also identical to *Poems*, which used a modified version of Gabriel Rossetti's cover design for *Goblin Market and Other Poems* (1862). William paid close attention as well to the frontispiece portrait of Christina by Gabriel. 'It is a delicate pencil-drawing of old date (say 1849), & needs to be heedfully handled. You will observe that it gives the profile, & *part* of the head-shape (hair). This will make it desirable ... that in the phototype it should be enclosed within a frame-line,' he advised on 11 August. After seeing a proof of the phototype, he suggested on 19 October that because the drawing had 'overmuch space "to let" in it ... it would strike the eye a good deal more agreeably if one cut off all the lower portion. The limiting framework might be brought a little below the chin – cutting off (I should regard this as advantageous) that rather harsh angle formed by line of throat & dress.' Over the wording of the title-page he was characteristically finicky, writing to the publisher on 16 November: 'The difficulty is to indicate with due brevity the real nature of the volume, so that people may understand it to be something quite new to them, & may buy it accordingly. "New Poems by" &c seems near enough to the mark, without anything else. If one added "Hitherto unpublished or uncollected," that would make the title literally as well as substantially accurate. With this addition the word "New" is not absolutely wanted, but I think it still expedient.' Macmillan was in no hurry to publish the volume, so it was 13 January 1896 before William received an advance copy: 'it is to be regularly published on 17 January,' he noted in his diary. Because he was away from England for several months from the middle of January, we have no record of his immediate response to the many and laudatory reviews the volume received. The only review in which he played any part was Watts-Dunton's in the *Athenaeum*, 15 February 1896. After hearing from Watts-Dunton of his intention to review the book, he advised Frederick Macmillan on 3 December 'to send him the book in sheets from your house, with or without any word or message. The *portrait*, along with the sheets, would be a desirable adjunct' (*Selected Letters*, 594).

II

Christina's death and William's retirement from the Inland Revenue Office both occurred at the end of December 1894, and these events propelled him into nearly two decades of memorializing his family. On the last day of 1895, he reflected in his diary on the pleasure that days filled with biographical and editorial work brought to him: 'Close of a year which (spite of painful memories) has been comparatively cheerful to me, owing to perpetual & congenial occupation.' Although William could be as haunted by 'vanished hours' as his brother had been, 'lost hours' were foreign to him; he was usually guided by the third alternative of the sonnet group, 'The Choice': 'Think thou and act' (*House of Life*: sonnets 36; 69; 73). No task, either then or later, that would advance the fame of Christina or other members of his family ever seemed too much trouble for him or too insignificant. Throughout 1895 scarcely a day passed when his diary or correspondence does not record some involvement in the literary and journalistic response to Christina's death. On 23 January, he commented on the manuscript of Watts-Dutton's 'Reminiscences of Christina Rossetti' (*Nineteenth Century*, February 1895); on 3 February he met with William Sharp to discuss his 'Some Reminiscences of Christina Rossetti' (*Atlantic Monthly*, June 1895); on 20 May he objected to a 'Christina Rossetti Birthday Book' that had been submitted to Macmillan on the grounds that 'the selection does not appear to me to be made on quite the right principle.' Later, he suggested that he or his daughter Olivia could produce a more satisfactory volume.[2] For several months at the start of the year, he oversaw the writing of Ellen Proctor's *A Brief Memoir of Christina G. Rossetti* (1895), advised on a publisher, wrote a preface for the volume, and even allowed Miss Proctor to occupy the first floor of 30 Torrington Square while she wrote her book.

At the same time, not every encounter with a former friend or admirer of his sister was equally relished. As the tepid treatment in *Some Reminiscences* and in the preface to *Poetical Works of Christina Rossetti* (1904) of her first biographer, Mackenzie Bell, suggests, William's abundant patience and forbearance were required to ensure that this self-appointed biographer produced an agreeable life of his sister.[3] How well Bell knew Christina is not clear. Packer and Battiscombe have him visiting her 'regularly' or 'fairly frequent[ly]' during the last six months of her life (Packer, 395; Battiscombe, 199); William records only that he met him 'for the first time, in Christina's house some three or four weeks before her decease: he made several visits of inquiry during her illness' (*Some Reminiscences*, 2:542). A man of enormous egotism and vanity, whose will left a large sum of money to establish a museum in his memory, Bell was determined to publish something on Christina from the moment of her death. As early as 1 January 1895, William acknowledged a quatrain that Bell had addressed to her with the suggestion that 'it ought to be published. The Athenaeum is well effected to me & mine, & I fancy if you were to offer it there (especially if you said how greatly I value the verses), it might be accepted.' An article on Christina, checked by William for errors, followed in March in the *Author*, by which time William had given Bell his lukewarm approval to undertake a biography, writing to him on 12 February: 'It seems to me that your project of a critico-biographic study of my sister is one which might very well be carried out, & that you could do it to the satisfaction of your readers, & of all others concerned.' Over the next three years William kept in close contact with Bell, writing him nearly a hundred letters. Since several reviewers of Bell's book attacked William for overdirecting, if not bullying, a weak and submissive biographer, it is worth inquiring into the precise nature of their relationship during the time that Bell was preparing the biography. Stung into reply by the astringency and personal nature of the reviews in *Literature* (probably by Edmund Gosse) and the *British Weekly* (by Robertson Nicoll) (see *Selected Letters*, 609-10) and irritated by Bell's indecisive denial in a personal letter to the editor of *Literature*, H.D. Traill, William wrote first to Traill and returned to the matter in the preface to *Poetical Works of Christina*

Rossetti. But the most succinct response occurs in a letter to Bell himself dated less than a week after the appearance of the *Literature* review:

> I certainly think (as you decide not to write to *Literature*) that it would be well to state in a Preface to a 2nd edition [4] – in very plain and express terms – the facts (1) that I did not prompt you to write the book, nor volunteer to furnish you with materials; (2) that I did not coerce, or attempt to coerce, you in any way during the writing of the book; (3) that what I did was practically limited to answering explicitly the explicit questions which you asked, and to furnishing at your direct request, on perusal of MS. and proofs, corrections of errors and misapprehensions. I remember saying to you very downrightly, in a personal interview which we had in this house soon after you had undertaken the work, that all I did or wanted to do was to reply to such questions as you found occasion to ask – leaving it to you to use or not use my information as you might prefer, and, if you used it, to put it in your own way. (*Selected Letters*, 606)

Wiiliam's reputation as an essentially truthful man is deserved, and his diary and letters to Bell by and large confirm what he says in this letter. Nevertheless, he seldom encouraged Bell and at times treated him with maddening obtuseness. On only one occasion during their early correspondence (16 March 1895), in response to receiving Bell's outline for the book, did he suggest how particular matters might be handled or organized:

> I have read your Synopsis, &, so far as first general impression goes, it seems to me on the right lines. Of old writers with whom to compare Christina's religious poems, you name only 2, Herbert & Crashaw (the latter not well known to me). I think Henry Vaughan, 'the Silurist,' about the most important & admirable: Donne & Herrick might also be considered if space admits. As to contemporary writers, it might be interesting to say something about my father's book of religious poems, L'Arpa Evangelica: I could easily give you a copy. Am not however aware whether you read Italian ... I think Commonplace etc. might be disposed of in the section 'Books for Children – with some such introductory note as – 'Though the following is not in any strictness written for children, we may here consider it without having recourse to a separate section.

Mostly he confined himself to factual details about Christina's doctors, friends, and books. If Bell failed to ask the right leading questions, William refrained from prompting him, or, if he stumbled on something that William preferred he ignore, he would be by turns unhelpful and sharply dismissive. When, for example, Bell first hinted that he knew about Christina's relationship with James Collinson and Charles Cayley, William remained silent. His diary records on 14 September 1896, 'Mackenzie Bell called again ... I find he had, at an early date of his undertaking, consulted Hunt & Shields, who gave him details about Christina's affairs of the heart. I take it he knows the names, but these were not mentioned between us.' Bell evidently persisted, even seeking advice from his publisher, Hurst and Blackett, whose reply he forwarded to William. William responded curtly on 30 July 1897: 'I return the letter of Messrs Hurst and Blackett. Don't exactly see why they should have interfered at all in such a matter, and they "can't possibly" know whether or not publicity "could not possibly offend anyone ..." My *preference* is that they should not be printed' (*Selected Letters*, 600). William's quasi-prohibition meant that only readers who already knew the facts would have understood Bell's references to Collinson as Christina's 'friend' (quoted twice within two lines from a Christina letter, 305) and to Cayley as her 'dear friend ... whose literary executrix she became ' (again a quotation – actually a truncated quotation – from a letter of Christina's; the full passage follows, showing that she wrote 'so dear a Friend,'106).

Earlier William refused Bell's request to see the manuscript of *New Poems* before it was published, but he later agreed, following a common practice of writers and editors in dealing with rivals, to let him examine a set of proofs on condition that he make no use of them before the publication of the volume. On 21 June 1895, he wrote:

> I hardly know what facilities I shall find for letting you see Christina's forthcoming volume before it is issued to the public. Of course the Publishers – & also myself – want the interest of the book to be centred in the book itself: it would not be to our advantage that before the volume comes out, someone else should have utilized its contents (more or less) in some form of publication. *Perhaps*, when I get a complete set of the proofs into my hands, I may be prepared to show them to you: this might perhaps be 5 or 6 weeks prior to the actual publication. Will think about it when the time comes.

Bell must have been remarkably thick-skinned, for they continued to correspond and occasionally see something of one another long after the publication of the biography, even though William's antipathy led to one of the very few instances of unfeeling rudeness in his large correspondence. In November 1895, Bell pestered him to write inscriptions in copies of the forthcoming *D.G. Rossetti: His Family Letters with a Memoir* and *New Poems*; but William retorted on the 16th: 'Don't see what I could write, by way of autograph inscriptions ... Your ownership of them will have nothing to do with me.' A few months later Bell, perhaps already thinking of a Mackenzie Bell museum, had to be chided yet again. Writing on 20 February 1897, William's rebuke this time was more measured: 'Will you pardon me for saying that I don't like being constantly fidgeted to write an inscription or what not – especially when the copy of the book happens to be one with which I have nothing whatever to do. You may reply that it gives me very little trouble to write the inscription: but then I shall rejoin that it does you very little harm to do without it.' William's later letters to Bell are milder and more friendly in tone, probably because the biography turned out better than he had expected. In the course of reading Bell's manuscript, William noted in his diary on 2 September 1896, 'The book is of course pleasing in general tone, but as yet it seems to present nothing of a salient character in treatment'; and on 3 September, 'As I progress with Bell's book I like it somewhat better.' It also helped that Bell was willing to modify his manuscript 'in accordance with notes' (14 September) William sent him. The notes are untraced, but there is no evidence that they went much beyond rectifying details of fact. On 27 July 1897, William returned the proofs of the book to Bell without, it seems, asking for anything beyond minor corrections.

III

As early as 12 May 1895, while he was preparing the proposal to Macmillan for *New Poems*, William noted in his diary the desirability of bringing out 'a revised form of ... [Christina's] complete works [*Poems* (1890)] ... if possible to include those [poems] published by the S.P.C.K.' Just four years after his brother's death, William had issued a two-volume *Collected Works of D.G. Rossetti* (1886), and he was anxious that Christina receive the same kind of tribute from his hands. Although Macmillan agreed in principle to the new edition, it was not published for another nine years. William affirmed in a letter to Macmillan on 24 May that 'a new & complete edition will continue fully present to my mind,' but he seems not to have begun work on it in earnest until late summer 1897, when he suggested to the publisher that he could 'if you like, begin in a leisurely way to make preparations for such an edition, even if *early* publication is not contemplated. One consideration is that I am not far from 68 years of age, and my lease of life is dwindling, and, when it terminates, no one will remain who knows much about the matter' (*Selected Letters*).

That some work on the edition had already been done is almost certain, for by 7 September he was able to inform Macmillan that he had 'traced out with minuteness (so far as I find it possible to do so)' the dates of the poems and that he would soon begin 'the writing of Notes, Preface, etc.' He began work on the Notes, 'which will no doubt be rather long,' on 28 September. Over the following months, 'in the pressure of other work, I don't for the present attend to this every day,' he noted on 6 January 1898. By 28 July, however, he was able to record substantial progress with the volume: 'Got to the end of another of my rather numerous jobs – or rather to the end of its main framework, for a good deal remains to be done by way of prefacing, indexing, looking up casual outlying items, &c.' The next diary entry on the edition is not until 26 February 1899: 'Since ... 28 July I have done a good deal of work upon [*Poetical Works*] ... indexing, re-reading &c: I now seem to have cleared off those preliminaries to such an extent as allows of my commencing a Preface to the book. I propose to include in it a short biographical notice of Christina: I might succeed in saying a few things to the purpose, more condensed & telling than what is to be found in Mackenzie Bell's book.'[5] By 14 May he had finished the Memoir, which he considered 'a serviceable work,' and contemplated being soon able 'to finish up a few straggling ends of the ... Edition'; and by 12 July: 'At last I have got to the end of [*Poetical Works*] ... [and] began a note to Macmillans.' Although Macmillan agreed on 14 July to take a look at the Preface, Memoir, and Notes, they declined, as William expected they would, to launch the edition while 'the sales of Christina's current editions continue to be decidedly good' (MS. Diary, 20 April 1900).

William seems not to have discussed the matter with Macmillan again until 22 March 1903, when he wrote reminding them of the imminent expiry of the copyright of *Goblin Market and Other Poems* (1862, 2nd ed., 1865): 'If under present circumstances you think of introducing any novelty into the form of her publications, I should like to be apprised of any details.' Macmillan replied immediately that the time was now ripe for William's edition, and that they would bring it out 'as one of ... [their] Globe volumes' (MS. Diary, 23 March). An unexpected difficulty arose when Edmund McClure, the secretary of the SPCK, proposed 'rather hard terms' (MS. Diary, 1 May 1903) for the Society's copyright in Christina's devotional poetry, which they had published in *Verses* (1893) and earlier, scattered throughout her prose volumes. William reported to Macmillan on 2 May that McClure expressed a general view that, if you bring out the Complete Poems with the concurrence of the Society, it would be fair that the profits from sale of the Edition should be divided pro rata between your Firm & the Society. I replied that I do not understand you to contemplate such an arrangement as that, but rather that, by payment of a lump sum (I did not define any *amount*), you would purchase the right of reproducing the Society's poems in your Edition.

McClure eventually agreed to a lump sum payment but remained adamant that he would accept nothing less than £100, which was double what the equally intransigent Macmillan was prepared to offer. William complained to his daughter Helen on 21 June 1903 that 'Macmillans (like Scotsmen as they are & used to be) boggle over paying to the Christian Knowledge Society any sum exceeding £50.' To avoid the '*large* amount of trouble of a rather fidgeting kind' that recasting the volume to exclude the SPCK poems would involve and, more especially, because he believed that 'the public should at last see her poetic work as a whole, in one view,' William (never one himself to enter into a disadvantageous financial arrangement) took the unusual step on 21 June of agreeing that Macmillan should 'pay the S.P.C.K. any sum up to £100, with the understanding that the second £50 (or less) making up this amount should be deducted from royalties payable to me' (*Selected Letters*, 638). On 3 July his diary records: 'Macmillans write that the S.P.C.K. accept the offer of £100 for Christina's *Verses* – I paying the second £50. So the Complete Poems can now go forward, to my no small satisfaction.' On the following day, he requested that the publisher send round a messenger to take delivery of the manuscript, which consisted of 'bundles done up in 4 cloth cases.' When in 1899 Macmillan first mentioned bringing out the *Poetical Works* in an 'edition ... uniform with the Tennyson [Globe edition],' William had objected that he was not 'fond of double columns if avoidable' (17 July). He reiterated the objection again on 14 July 1903 ('a rather serious objection to 2-column printing of poetry is that lines of ordinary length have constantly to be extended into 2 lines of type'), but hesitating to create any further problem in what was already an inordinately prolonged undertaking, he decided to 'urge the point no further.'

IV

William may have regarded *Poetical Works* as his crowning monument to Christina, but it was to be expected that a man of his overwhelming industry and predilection for bookmaking would continue promoting her fame in print.[6] About six months after the appearance of *Poetical Works*, on 12 August 1904, he suggested to Macmillan that 'it would be a good thing to bring out (1) a volume of Christina's *best* poems; & (2) a volume of her narrative or quasi-narrative poems' (MS. Diary). Macmillan replied on 16 August that a combination of the two proposals as a volume in their highly successful 'Golden Treasury Series' would suit them best. William began work on it on the following day, and by 28 August had identified 241 poems that might be included, but he suspected that they would 'fill a space beyond what Macmillans have determined.' Evidently this was the case, since the published volume contains only 187 works. On 29 August, he began arranging the poems, with

> at the beginning Goblin Market & Monna Innominata, & at the end Later Life & the Pageant, & about the middle The Prince's Progress. Then I would have Devotional Poems, Narrative Poems, & compositions divided according to those 'Keystones' of feeling which I defined in an Appendix to the Complete Poems. Finally would come some miscellaneous pieces having no special generic quality.

The only difficulty with the volume again involved the SPCK. William had included four of the Society's poems in the copy he submitted to Macmillan, but the publisher refused to negotiate again with McClure, which William considered 'rather tiresome, as it excludes several fine things, & entails the research for substitutes' (5 September 1904). This time, however, he went along with Macmillan's decision and by 9 September had 'pretty well finished the selection of substitutes.' The preface and other preliminary matter were ready for delivery by 27 September, and the first proof of the poems themselves reached him on 1 October. Emery Walker, 'to whom the firm was for many years indebted for counsel of unrivalled authority' in matters of illustration (Morgan, 124), called on William on 11 October to select a portrait to be engraved as a frontispiece: 'I offered the choice of 4 heads by Gabriel. The profile drawn in 1865, & already reproduced in the Pre-Raphaelite Diaries book, appeared to both of us on the whole the most eligible, & Walker carried it away' (MS. Diary). The volume was published in December and reprinted in the same month and again in the following year, swelling William's royalties on Christina's works for the period from September 1904 to September 1905 to £177.5.10. 'The royalties from Christina are always about double what I get from Gabriel's books,' he noted in his diary on 14 January 1910.

V

Although William had only reluctantly undertaken the Memoir portion of his *Dante Gabriel Rossetti: His Family Letters with a Memoir* (1895), his brother's family letters had been contemplated, and in part completed, within a year of Gabriel's death in 1882 (Peattie, 'Reluctant Biographer,' 54-62). As already noted, as early as February 1895, William had firmly resolved not to write a full-scale biography of Christina, but an edition of her letters from his hands was predictable, though surprisingly delayed. For fifteen or more years, William occupied himself with a vast editorial undertaking which he called 'Rossettiana': 'letters, memoranda, &c., proper to various members of the family,' Polidoris as well as Rossettis (MS. Diary, 11 November 1895). Letters by and to Christina formed part of this project, but since it was never published in the form in which it was conceived and executed and was subsequently broken up for piecemeal publication by William himself and since what remained was disordered by subsequent researchers in the Rossetti archive, it is not now possible to know exactly how many of Christina's letters were included or how fully they were annotated. Of the three volumes of 'Rossettiana' that were published, *Ruskin: Rossetti: Pre-Raphaelitism* (1899), *Pre-Raphaelite Diaries and Letters* (1900), and *Rossetti Papers* (1903), only the latter contains letters of hers (thirteen to Dante Gabriel and one to William).

A proposal for a separate edition of Christina's letters is first mentioned in William's diary on 14 December 1906. Shortly thereafter (2 January 1907), he lunched at the Granville Club with Lacon Watson of Brown, Langham & Co. and recorded that 'Watson wants ... to bring out in the Autumn a volume of Christina's Letters, with such supplementary material as may offer. This I will see about at once.' A fuller account of the project occurs in William's letter of 8 February 1907 to his daughter Olivia:

> I compiled 3 volumes (up to 1894) as sequels to the Rossetti Papers already published. These 3 volumes have not proved attractive to the publishers, & I thought of extracting the letters by or to Gabriel & Christina, & dropping the rest of the material ... The 3 volumes being brought under the notice of Lacon Watson ... he started the suggestion of making a separate book of Christina's letters – this firm being associated with another firm, Masters & Co., which has a large religious connection, to which Christina would appeal. I have now put together Christina's letters, & such letters addressed to her as have been preserved ... & am making steady progress with annotations &c.

It appears from William's diary that Watson was for a time uncertain about what he wanted, suggesting on 21 June that William turn the volume into a 'Life & Letters' on the model of *Dante Gabriel Rossetti: His Family Letters with a Memoir*. 'Shan't do this, having already written what I can say by way of Memoir of Christina. Am a little annoyed about this new move.' By October, Watson was raising difficulties over the length of the volume, to which the seventy-eight-year-old William uncharacteristically raised no objection, or at least not initially:

> MS. Diary, 24 October: I replied to Watson: would freely cut down the bulk of the Christina book, either by omitting or abridging some of the letters, or by omitting part of the appendix-matter, or even the whole of it. From the detail given me by Watson I am myself of opinion that the book in its present form is cumbrously long.
> 28 October: I received the copy for Christina, & began the work of abridging it.
> 31 October: Wrote to Lacon Watson to say what I am doing, & pointed out that the reduction he now wishes for is not what he wanted in April, when he wrote to me that there would be no objection to 2 volumes.
> 14 November: Have now done all the substantial part of the curtailment of Christina, cutting out 200 items, more or less, & abridging some of the items that are retained. This ought to be fully enough.
> 18 November: Have finished with Christina, & wrote to Watson that I can deliver the copy any day now. I dare say that the shortening of it is an advantage in the long run.

It was almost another year before the book was finally published and then not before William agreed, on 14 July 1908, that his 'royalty on the American edition ... shall be reduced, as otherwise it appears that a pending arrangement with Scribners is likely to fall through!' On 15 October, William received 'at last ... an advance-copy, as the actual publication is delayed yet for a week or more.' On the following day, he read the volume through once again, no doubt reflecting as he did so that it was likely to be his final publication on his sister, and clearly he was pleased: it 'appears to me to contain sufficient matter of readable interest to offer a fair chance of a selling-success.'

VI

Nine years after William's death, Edmund Gosse was to say, unkindly and inaccurately, of William's writings on his brother (and by implication, of his writings on his sister) that 'At length, not a shilling more could be drained out of the body of the unhappy man, and public curiosity was definitely sated' (*Sunday Times*, 6 May 1928, 8). By his tireless, not to say obsessive, making of books and articles about his family, William laid himself open to such a charge, but it would be fairer to him to point to the fact that he had worked energetically and faithfully on behalf of his family from that day in 1845 when he left King's College School to enter the Inland Revenue Office as a clerk and became the main support of his impoverished family. It was an act of necessity, which produced two often overlooked results: it allowed Dante Gabriel to pursue his art studies and Christina, her vocation as a poet. William would have regarded it as churlish in the extreme for anyone to object that a modest recompense for his arduous labours in the form of royalties was undeserved.

To pronounce a judgement on William's writings on his sister is a more pleasurable task than it might appear. As her editor and memorialist, he was not much better but certainly no worse than the general run of Victorian biographers and editors of poetical works. Throughout the 1860s and 1870s, as an editor of Whitman (1868), Shelley (1870, 1878), and Blake (1874) and as the writer of the memoirs of Shelley and Blake prefixed to his editions, William apprenticed for his future job as the official "historian" of his brother's and sister's life and works. Bold conjectural emendations, retitling, and regularization of metre (in the case of Shelley and Blake) and truncation, rearrangement, and the invention of titles (in the case of Whitman) were editorial practices that William employed without qualms and, for the most part, without being condemned for doing so by reviewers.[7] When he came to edit Dante Gabriel (less so) and Christina (more so), he employed many of these same editorial procedures. In the *Collected Works of Dante Gabriel Rossetti* (1886), he divided the poems into Principal and Miscellaneous (342 pages) and four other groups: Sonnets on Pictures; Sonnets and Verses for Rossetti's Own Works of Art; Poems in Italian, French, and Latin; and Versicles and Fragments (38 pages), an arrangement very like the one he had used in *Poetical Works of Shelley*. A subject division of Christina's works, therefore, came naturally to him; four divisions in *New Poems* (General Poems, Devotional Poems, Italian Poems, and Juvenilia), and six in *Poetical Works* (Longer Poems and Poems for Children and Minor Verse were the two new divisions, with Devotional Poems and Italian Poems further subdivided). In both collections, William arranged the poems in each section according to date, explaining to Macmillan on 20 May 1895, when he first mentioned the need for a *Poetical*

Works, that 'disregarding the present arrangement of her works, & putting them much more nearly into the true order of *date*' was the correct procedure for a complete edition. For the majority of the poems, he added, he possessed 'very exact indications' of date. Bearing in mind that Christina had brought out her own 'Collected Edition,' William added to his an appendix listing the order of the poems in *Poems: New and Enlarged Edition* (1890), but he neglected, unfortunately, to do same for *Verses.* David Kent has argued that this latter omission discouraged a generation or more of critics from reading the volume 'in the sequential order she designed for it,' though strangely he doesn t fault the critics for their failure to consult a copy of the frequently reprinted volume. William's 'radical dismemberment' of *Verses,* he claims, has had 'disastrous' consequences for our understanding of Christina's achievement as a devotional poet (261). William's provision of dates, on the other hand, remains a major achievement of his edition.

Because of the prominence now accorded to Christina as both poet and woman, William's commentary on her life and work is bound to appear thin and inadequate. Beginning with the Preface and Notes to *New Poems,* he amassed a body of biographical, textual, and bibliographical detail relating to Christina and her work that later biographers, editors, bibliographers, and critics, depending on what they were in search of, have treated as consequential or inconsequential, insightful or misleading, admirably direct or evasive. Perhaps it is the fate of brothers who attempt to influence the course of their more famous siblings' reputations to be dismissed as blundering if not incompetent, untruthful over matters involving family honour, unwilling to engage real issues, and ultimately irrelevant. Reviews of his four major publications on Christina show that from the start of his 'Christina' enterprise, William was rarely spared one or other of these accusations. A late, representative example, a review of the 'Golden Treasury' volume in the *Academy,* a journal for which William had written a distinguished body of literary and art criticism between 1869 and 1878, flippantly dismissed him: 'I should value the *Poems of Christina Rossetti* more had the introduction by William M. Rossetti been omitted' (24 December 1904, 641). As friends and Pre-Raphaelite scholars and enthusiasts from Sydney Cockerell and William Rothenstein to William Fredeman and Angela Thirkell have never tired of pointing out, William was not the fool 'for a brother' that Morris had labelled him. So, although we nod with approval when his blunders, evasions, and misapprehensions about Christina are cited by biographers and critics,[8] it is worth attempting to understand his own attitude towards the staggering forty books and pamphlets and twenty-one notes and articles about his family and the Pre-Raphaelites that flowed from his pen between 1881 and 1911. First, he regarded himself as a privileged observer of a decisive period in Victorian art and poetry. That he knew intimately many of the principal painters and poets of the second half of the century was the only authority he needed to publish accounts of their personalities and achievements. What he revealed about them and how (in the case of his brother and sister) he assembled their work for the public were decisions that he considered he had every right to make on the basis of his understanding of what it mean to be loyal to family and friends, his perception of the historical value of what he knew, and, finally, his own previous experiences as a biographer, editor, and critic. In the case of Christina, if William had not undertaken comprehensive editions of her poems and letters, the task of re-evaluating and championing her in the period from 1968[9] to the present would have started from a less secure foundation.[10]

NOTES

1 *Pall Mall Budget* ceased publication on 27 December 1894. Three manuscript
   collections are the major sources for this paper: the diaries and letters of
   W.M. Rossetti in the Angeli-Dennis Papers, University of British Columbia;
   Rossetti's letters to Macmillan & Co. in the British Library; and his letters to
   Mackenzie Bell at Princeton. Some of the letters and diary entries have
   been printed in *Selected Letters of W.M. Rossetti*, ed. Roger W. Peattie (1990). In
   quoting manuscript sources, Rossetti's frequent abbreviations, except for
   the ampersand, have been expanded.
2 Olivia Rossetti published *The Christina Rossetti Birthday Book* (1896).
3 A. Egerton Smythe gives a workmanlike account of Bell.
4 No second edition with revisions or additions was published, though between
   7 January and 19 November 1898 there were four so-called editions, the
   fourth 'Completing Two Thousand Five Hundred.'
5 William's most unguarded assessment of Bell's biography occurs in a letter to
   his daughter, Olivia, 22 March 1898: 'You are certainly right about Mackenzie Bell's book. It is a work not so much to "damn with faint praise" as to
   "praise with a faint (but not inaudible) *Damn.*" The narrative is a labouring
   but unassorted patchwork, & the criticism is at once obvious & halting.
   However, one must not be exactly discontented with the book. It is written
   in a very admiring & kindly spirit, & states most of the few facts which were
   available for being stated. Were I writing to Bell himself, & not to you, I

could without any uncandour say something in the way of definite praise.'

6 For the publication of *Maude*, with a preface by William Rossetti (1897), about which William was unenthusiastic but not unwilling to earn a small fee, while Macmillan was initially unco-operative, see *Selected Letters*, 599-600.

7 For the major exception, R.H. Shepherd's attack on Gabriel's and William's editing of Blake, see *Selected Letters*, 318.

8 In letters to old friends and to his children, William often spoke less circumspectly about Christina's poetry than he does in his published accounts. Writing to his daughter Olivia in 1898, when she contemplated an article on Christina, he encouraged her with an assessment that one wishes he had been willing to expand on in his own writings: 'I think that you can, with a little pains & thought, write a paper on Christina deserving to rank among the really good things that have been done about her: & all the better inasmuch as you are detached in opinion (though not wholly in sympathy) from her ruling phase of thought. She is truly a very great poet; & one cannot read a dozen lines of her without coming upon something which rings true to all time.'

9 1968 is not altogether an arbitrary date, being the year in which Walter E. Houghton and G. Robert Stange, grudgingly one feels, admitted Rossetti as 'a distinguished minor poet' into the second edition of *Victorian Poetry and Poetics* (600), first published in 1959.

10 A whole paper might be written on another aspect of William as 'keeper of the flame' of Christina's reputation. For a quarter of a century he presided over an enormous assemblage of family books, manuscripts, and works of art at 3 St. Edmund's Terrace, Primrose Hill, London. Christina's books and packets of her poems can be found listed in William's beautifully legible hand among the hundreds of pages of the catalogues of his library and works of art. The numbered list of her books, in the order in which they can be seen on the shelves in early twentieth century photographs of William sitting in the drawing room of St. Edmund's Terrace, makes tantalizing reading: '142. Goblin Market, & Other Poems – 3 copies, 1 having coloured Drawings by Christina up to p. 51'; '143. Verses (privately printed) – 4 copies, 1 with pencil Drawings by Gabriel, 1 with coloured Drawings by Christina'; '145. Singsong – Illustrations by Hughes – 4 copies, 2 containing the extra poems & the Italian translations in MS.' Almost every book, manuscript, work of art, or piece of furniture in the house bore an annotation or label in his hand, explaining its origin and significance. From time to time he sold items to collectors, most of them to T.J. Wise, Sydney Cockerell, and Fairfax Murray, whose collections he felt confident would find their way into national and institutional libraries. Because of the terms of his will, which

divided his collections more or less equally among his four children, and the bombing of St. Edmund's Terrace during WWII, though not before a substantial body of material was safely removed, it has been difficult to appreciate the extent and quality of William's custodianship.

5

'Slight Channels': Arthur Hughes and the Illustration of Children's Books

Carolyn Hares-Stryker

In the *Saturday Review* for 17 December 1904, art critic D.S. MacColl wrote that he remembered as a child 'the first wave of Preraphaelite romance that came with the dark coils of the North Wind's hair and the strangeness of that world of imagery.'[1] MacColl was writing about Arthur Hughes's illustrations for George MacDonald's *At the Back of the North Wind* (1870). Early in the New Year (19 January 1906), Georgiana Burne-Jones would write to Evelyn (nee Pickering) de Morgan asking, 'Have you seen Arthur Hughes' illustrations to a child's book called *Babies' Classics*? It is very lovely and shows him to be no day older than when he did *Sing-Song*, bless him! Ah, my dear, it is not fairy gold that we have been laying up – the reality of those treasures never fails for a minute' (Stirling, 232). Hughes's illustrations of children's books were much admired by his contemporaries. Yet, as Stephen Wildman reveals in his introduction to the recent *Arthur Hughes: His Life and Work*, while Hughes often found great pleasure doing the illustrations, they were a means to an end, a source of income that allowed him to paint canvases that year he sent to the Royal Academy year after year. Some years his paintings were accepted, though often badly placed by the Hanging Committee, but in other years his work was rejected outright or slighted in the press with a persistently damning brand of faint praise: 'exquisite,' 'lovely,' 'charming,' 'poetic,' 'sweet,' 'pretty.' His illustrations, however, were a staple; Hughes did nearly six hundred wood engravings and line drawings, and from the very beginning they were well received, publicly and critically. His illustrations for books by George MacDonald, Thomas Hughes, and Christina Rossetti exemplify the enchanting strangeness of that combination of fairy wings and 'dark coils' that characterizes Pre-Raphaelite romance.

Hughes's work as a children's illustrator can best be understood as beginning in earnest with the first five volumes of *Good Words for the Young*, to which he contributed an extraordinary 231 drawings, each a lyrical blending of religious, fantastical, and literary images.[2] A short-lived but extremely influential and popular sixpenny monthly magazine for children, *Good Words for the Young* was founded by a Scottish evangelical publisher, Alexander Strahan, his aim being to provide wholesome Christian reading material for children. Hughes's involvement with the magazine came from his relationship with George MacDonald, who became its editor in November 1869. Hughes had already worked with MacDonald on *Dealings with the Fairies* (1867), and their working relationship would span several decades. Therefore, although MacDonald's tenure was brief, while he remained the editor, he provided Hughes a considerable amount of work. To be precise, Hughes performed the Herculean task of producing thirty-eight illustrations during 1868-9, ninety during 1869-70, forty-six during 1870-1, and thirty-three during 1871-2. Only after the magazine hit a slump and MacDonald was asked to resign, did Hughes's production taper off. Writing to Louisa MacDonald on 26 February 1871, MacDonald speculated that Strahan attributed the magazine's loss in sales to there being 'too much of what he calls the fairy element' (qtd. in Wildman, 26). Although, as Susan Casteras writes, Hughes created 'familiar and comforting situations and figures that emphasized innocence and simplicity, not conflict, earthly woes or sexuality' (34) for *Good Words for the Young*, Strahan had perhaps grown nervous about the direction in which MacDonald and his chief illustrator appeared to be moving the magazine, seeming to favour pixie dust over clear Christian morals. The publisher did not understand this new embellishment of faith that Hughes and MacDonald had brought to the 'good word.'

Yet the 'fairy element' was basic to the golden age of Victorian children's literature, and in his essay 'Fairy Stories' (1868), Ruskin reveals its spirit, if not its mission. Ruskin believed that if such literature was to be progressive, it ought to eschew harsh moralizing and didactic satire. Instead, it should weave into enchantment a 'religious faith' that would seem a 'shadowy image' underlying the narrative and thus cause children at all times to 'seek faithfully for good.' Offering up a type of secular religion, children's literature, Ruskin believed, spoke to the value of goodness in a world that the Victorians may have felt was in need of such gentle purpose. His belief was shared by others. Charles Dickens was referring to these works when he wrote: 'It would be hard to estimate the amount of gentleness and mercy that has made its way among us through these slight channels ... forbearance, courtesy, consideration for the poor and aged, kind treatment of animals, the love of nature, the abhorrence of tyranny and brute force' ('Frauds on the Fairies,' 97).

Many children's books of the period, however, have since proved to be 'slight channels' indeed. The wish may have been to promote Christian virtues, but grim didacticism and rote sentimentality undermined the effort. Yet, ironically, the very characteristic that hurt Hughes's reputation as an artist of oils and canvases assured his success as an illustrator for children: the sweetness and poetry of his interpretations of character and scene allow readers to believe in the possibility of happy endings, the existence of the sacred in the ordinary, and the power of goodness to ultimately transcend dark visions of poverty, conquest, and loss. A study of Arthur Hughes's illustrations for some of the best known Victorian books for children – George MacDonald's *At the Back of the North Wind* and *The Princess and the Goblin,* Thomas Hughes's *Tom Brown's School Days,* and Christina Rossetti's *Sing-Song* and *Speaking Likenesses* – reveals how important his work is to the popular longevity of these books. Kate Flint may be correct when she writes that 'in his depictions of sexuality, of sentimental melancholy, of apprehensions of undefinable, incomprehensible, and unfriendly powers, Hughes can be seen to interrelate intimately with a variety of contemporary forms of anxiety' (219); but while the artist's interrelation with disturbing subject matter certainly explains our current fascination with crisis, to consider Hughes as primarily a purveyor of angst is to limit the influence he has on our response to, perhaps even our memories of, these books. Obviously, Hughes matched his drawings to the moods of the various books he worked on, whether they called for (in)delicate fantasy or boisterous athleticism, but overall his illustrations ultimately do much to soften the adult ferocity of textual worlds beset by economic, national, and personal insecurities.

I

Today, among Arthur Hughes's best remembered illustrations are those he did for George MacDonald's *At the Back of the North Wind* (1870) and *The Princess and the Goblin* (1871). Their collaboration very much embodied the Pre-Raphaelite split between realism and fantasy or spirituality. In some ways, the partnership between MacDonald and Hughes seems an unlikely one. MacDonald had been an ordained minister of the Congregational church before he resigned over a disagreement on doctrine, while Hughes did not seem to have any great religious calling. However, retreating to the

Romanticism of Keats and Coleridge, writer and artist shared a conviction in the transforming power of the imagination, and like Wordsworth, their night-gowned children do walk 'trailing clouds of glory behind them.' In his essay 'The Imagination: Its Function and Its Culture,' MacDonald wrote that imagination is 'that faculty in man which is likest to the prime operation of the power of God' (*A Dish of Orts*, 2). Although Anita Moss correctly notes that MacDonald was not 'always entirely successful in unifying the Romantic and mystic dimensions of his thought with his unmistakably Victorian emphasis upon work, duty, and obedience' (69), Hughes brought a vital element that literally brought vision to MacDonald's religious allegories. Gillian Avery credits MacDonald with the 'power to make holiness natural and desirable, and to show spiritual progress' (135-6), but it was Hughes who made that world so real that we can forever recall in our minds the beauty of the North Wind's hair, the sweetness of Diamond, the moonlight associated with Irene's grandmother, and the menace of mountain goblins. 'We dare to claim,' MacDonald wrote, 'for the true, childlike, humble imagination, such an inward oneness with the laws of the universe that it possesses in itself an insight into the very nature of things' ('The Imagination,' *A Dish of Orts*, 13). Imagination brought one to the centre of truth, and for the childlike, those who wanted to believe in the existence of divine reality within the everyday, MacDonald could throw shadows of the sacred, but Hughes could make that mysticism visible. Their marriage of truth (allegory) and vision (art) was magical.

At the Back of the North Wind tells the story of Diamond, the son of a gentleman's driver and later London cabman, who is befriended by the North Wind. She takes Diamond on many adventures that sweep him over the streets of London, out across the ocean, and into an Arctic wilderness where he discovers the land that lies at the back of the North Wind. Always cheered on by the memories of the North Wind, Diamond is able to remain sweet and industrious through the bad times when his father loses his position and his family is nearly overcome by grinding poverty and sickness. Just as his family's fortunes begin to turn for the better, Diamond undertakes his final journey with the North Wind, returning forever to 'the land of vision ... and everlasting dream' (115).

The North Wind is not God but Death, which works as an agent of divine mystery, and the child's death and the hard realities that he was exposed to while alive have led critics like Lesley Smith to study the biblical overtones of the book, which seem to fulfil Job's melancholy prophecy: 'Thou liftest me up to the wind; thou causest me to ride upon it, and dissolvest my substance. For I know that thou wilt bring me to death, and to the house appointed for all living' (30:22-3) (161). Such readings are prevalent, and the book narrowly escapes the charge of morbidity. MacDonald's deft handling of the material is partially responsible but Hughes's illustrations also serve to keep the reader focused on the beauty of the unearthly and the abiding warmth of domestic interiors and stables. As early as 1928, Forrest Reid, one of the first scholars to critically assess Pre-Raphaelite book illustration, saw Hughes's drawings as having 'been conceived in a mysterious world, out of space and time ... their beauty at once so strange and so homely, seeming to bring into one world the cat purring on the hearth and the wildest gleams of fantasy' (88). Reid recognized that the twin aspects – the strange and the homely – had to coexist comfortably and serve a mutual purpose. In the case of MacDonald's book, readers had to accept Diamond as credible, his sweetness as believable, if they were also to accept the spirituality of the novel. MacDonald declared that 'the *childlike* is the divine' (*Unspoken Sermons*, 3). The child explains the ways of God to Man. Thus, Reid is correct. Diamond has a 'half angelic sexlessness and strange air of dreamy gravity' (87), but because of Hughes, Diamond is also just a little boy literally caught up in the embrace of something larger than himself.

Hughes could have devoted most of his illustrations to the fantastic – to the North Wind or to Nanny's dream of the lady in the moon or to Mr. Raymond's story of the moonlight princess. Instead, he drew Diamond listening through a chink in his wall, stroking the horses, pretending that chairs can be carriages and blankets caves, resting his head on his mother's lap. He shows us Diamond in the grimy streets of London: finding refuge with Nanny inside a barrel, dressing himself in the cold dawn, being beset by street ruffians, and trying to comfort a wailing baby in the lodgings of its drunken, abusive father. Hughes juxtaposes the quotidian with the spiritual to great effect. MacDonald's narrative tells us that Diamond's visions occur over a span of years. But it is Hughes who provides an exquisite touch. Within the visual element of the novel, when Diamond becomes part of the magic of the North Wind, he always appears as a small, curly-haired child, vulnerable in his nightgown. Because of Hughes's haunting images, one understands more profoundly that while vision fades and the returning normalcy of the everyday reveals the ordinary, even in its hero, the divine brings us back to the state of childlike innocence within us.

This quality of innocence is further foregrounded by Hughes's depiction of the North Wind. While the text often insists upon the maternal quality of the North Wind (to Diamond, her voice is like his mother's), Hughes shows us a peculiarly sexualized being. How easy it is thereafter for

us to succumb to the guilty pleasures of Freudian fantasy. Flint is not alone
when she writes, 'The North Wind's hair suggestively billowing round the
actual contours of her body, her physical plenitude threatening to break
out of the bounds of the picture's frames suggests an overwhelming womanly presence which reaches far beyond the realm of the maternal, offering
an as yet dimly understood sensual world' (207). Maurie McInnis also
contends that Hughes's depictions of the North Wind parallel 'a child's
sudden awakening sexuality' (74). As maternal seductress, the North
Wind would seem dangerous to Diamond.

Certainly MacDonald supplies the textual cues for the North Wind's
pale beauty and her hair that streams out into the darkness: 'her hair began
to gather itself out of the darkness, and fell down all about her again, till
her face looked out of the midst of it like a moon out of a cloud' (12). But
Hughes, particularly in his representation of the North Wind's hair (fig.
5.1), seems to mesh MacDonald's description with the favourite trope of
Pre-Raphaelite art begun by William Holman Hunt in his drawing of 'The
Lady of Shalott' for the Moxon Tennyson. Critics often note that in Pre-
Raphaelite iconography, women's hair became a powerful symbol of feminine power, temptation, and beauty, becoming synonymous with the *femme
fatale* and her twin faces, the virgin and the whore. Such signage of double-
edged sexuality is explored by Liana De Girlami Cheney in 'Locks, Tresses,
and Manes in Pre-Raphaelite Painting.' Cheney argues that while braiding
hair or tamed hair is associated with saints or the Virgin Mary and connotes
chastity, long or unbounded hair is commonly associated with Eve, Venus,
or Mary Magdalene and connotes evil and seduction (159-91).[3] Indeed,
anyone familiar with Pre-Raphaelite art can quickly bring to mind John
Everett Millais's *Bridesmaid*, Dante Rossetti's *Lady Lilith*, or John William
Waterhouse's *La Belle Dame Sans Merci* in addition to Hunt's *Lady of Shalott*
and *Isabella and the Pot of Basil*. All these well-known paintings support the
contention that sensual Pre-Raphaelite women drip danger from their
every follicle. So what should say about the iconography in Hughes's
drawings of the North Wind as she embraces and guides young Diamond?
Should we feel nervous?

Hughes uses billowing, twisting hair to connote the mystery of the North
Wind. He captures her fantastic scale and qualities as she looms above
Diamond or carries him within her woven and knotted tresses (fig. 5.2).
Almost Godiva-like, her hair emphasizes her body, but the North Wind's
hair is more significantly her primary point of contact with Diamond. It
envelops him protectively in its depths. There is a 'fleshliness' about her
back-tilted neck, bare arms, and flying hair; however, she is separated from

her 'fallen sisters,' from being overtly sexual or dangerous, by a significant element overlooked by critics. Hughes often draws the North Wind looking directly into Diamond's eyes. For all of her physicality, she lives in his eyes, in his imagination, and not ours. If she is reflected at all, it is in the adoring, innocent gaze of a child. The artist does not depict the North Wind as seductively looking out of the visual frame and into the admiring gaze of the viewer. Nor does he depict her in another favourite Pre-Raphaelite pose, looking at herself in mirrors or in water: the sterility of self-contained existence. Bram Dijkstra describes the troubling aspect of so many of these paintings that portray the 'extinguished eyes' of women, their 'hypnotic, snakelike quality' (177-8). Griselda Pollock has persuasively argued that such autoerotic fixation indeed invites voyeurism and makes us complicit in the tension created between object and viewer. Too often, however, modern criticism, with its persistent focus on menacing, subversive sexuality, falls short when it focuses our overapt attentions on the negative aspects of the female body. Thus, two recent and otherwise thoughtful studies, Kathy Alexis Psomiades's *Beauty's Body: Femininity and Representation in British Aestheticism* and J.B. Bullen's *The Pre-Raphaelite Body: Fear and Desire in Painting, Poetry, and Criticism*, do not help us to fully understand Hughes's beautiful and complex illustrations for children.

Instead, I suggest Elizabeth Prettejohn's discussion of the spirituality of Pre-Raphaelite symbolism is far more rewarding when studying Hughes's illustrations for MacDonald's *At the Back of the North Wind*. In *Rossetti and His Circle*, Prettejohn recalls the criticism of F.W.H. Myers. His 1883 essay, 'Rossetti and the Religion of Beauty,' interpreted aestheticism in terms of 'sensuous images of transcendent Platonic Ideas, leading the spectator on a spiritual journey from the "fleshly" through beauty to contemplation of the divine' (qtd. in Prettejohn, 74). In Pre-Raphaelite art, Myers saw 'sacred pictures of a new religion.' His contemporary perspective seems far better attuned to the spirit of Hughes's imagery, rising as it does to the high seriousness of MacDonald's purpose. MacDonald wanted his readers to believe in the goodness of Diamond and in the child's ability to transform his environment, and Hughes makes us believe in that Christian possibility. In his drawings, the North Wind becomes the perfect aesthetic symbol – supernaturally beautiful, maternal, powerful – a new and alluring divinity for an age of shaken faith.

MacDonald's next book, *The Princess and the Goblin*, is significantly different. *At the Back of the North Wind* is a mixture of fantasy and dingy reality. MacDonald deliberately concentrated on characters from the working class to show that the actions of individuals, not their social rank, could reveal their innate gentility. Some of that thinking still remains in *The Princess and the Goblin* as we read about the adventures of Princess Irene and Curdie, a miner's son; however, this story is a fairy tale, with kings and princesses, castles and turrets, goblins and caverns, fairy great-great-grand-mothers and magical rooms that materialize above the stairs. The plot concerns the goblins, who plan to break through to the upper-world and capture the princess in order to control her father's kingdom. Against this threat from the rather formidable goblins, dwarfed and misshapen with only one weakness – their tender feet – stand two children and an ancient but eternally beautiful woman who can only be seen by those who believe. With her help and the help of her gifts, a ring and a spool of invisible thread, Irene and Curdie defeat the goblins but not before they each rescue the other, dispelling notions of both class and gender superiority.

Far less ostensibly Christian, the book offers age-old archetypes, and it is not surprising that some modern critics view it as MacDonald's version of the quest myth, 'the ancient myth of the hero's descent into the under-world and his confrontation with the creative and destructive power of his own unconscious' (Sigman, 183). In many ways, the story is mythic with its delicate balance between good (the goddess who lives beyond the world and who often holds herself aloof from it) and evil (the goblins who chip away in the darkness at the foundations of the castle). It seldom belabours the virtues of duty and obedience and self-denial; instead, it delights in descriptions of the grotesque, like the goblin's pets who dimly resemble humans, and the mystical, like the cleansing fire of flaming roses and a bottomless silver bath filled with stars. And yet, of course, it is a parable of the precarious security of our lives, physical and moral, and the dangers of complacency and disbelief. Princess Irene's strength comes from her willingness to believe in the existence of her Grandmother, though the child cannot always find her and though she is ridiculed and bullied by her nurse. Even Curdie, though good at heart, grows angry at her insistence that her Grandmother exists when he sees only an empty attic room and a heap of musty straw: 'You must give him time,' her Grandmother tells her, 'and you must be content not to be believed for a while. It is very hard to bear; but I have had to bear it, and shall have to bear it many a time yet ... Seeing is not believing – it is only seeing' (177-8). The story is about the need for faith in a world pushing aside spirituality in favour of earthly kingdoms. The pragmatic world of politics (Irene's father, who constantly inspects his provinces) and industry (the coal mines) has to be balanced by, indeed saved by, the goodness and courage of innocents.

Zack Zipes contends that the novel is a 'conscious social protest' against its age (111), but unlike *At the Back of the North Wind*, its imagery is not Dickensian; its protest does not centre on class and capitalism. MacDonald seems instead to be taking on another reality of the Victorian age: Darwin. John Pennington argues that MacDonald 'Christianizes Darwinism,' and that while 'many Victorians were depressed by Darwin's theories of the survival of the fittest and accidental evolution, MacDonald found them an apt metaphor for his Christian faith: people evolve or regress according to faith; the strongest do survive, but they are the spiritually strong, not necessarily the strong in body' (Pennington, 135). In *The Princess and the Goblin*, the meek do not passively inherit the earth. Unlikely Christian soldiers, they have to fight for it. In time they will grow and become strong physically, but for now their connection to the spiritual prevents the world from sliding into the degenerative medium of the goblins who were not 'absolutely cruel for cruelty's sake' and who were not 'so far removed from the human as [their] description might imply' (10). Strong in spirit though weak in body, the children stand against the powerful but spiritually deficient goblins.

Arthur Hughes met the challenge of illustrating *The Princess and the Goblin* by emphasizing the slightness of the children. For 'Atop the White Charger,' for example, he draws a tiny Irene sitting with her father on a large, muscular horse. Hughes often contrasts the children's slim forms to that of the stocky goblins or of their weirdly shaped goblin-animals. Or he contrasts the whiteness of Irene and Curdie with the darkness of their surroundings, points of light in the mines or forests. Perhaps also not to frighten young readers and to offer reassurance that Irene and Curdie will triumph, Hughes here downplays the supernatural. Well over half of his illustrations are devoted to scenes of soldiers, Irene's father, or Irene following her thread. When he is forced by the story to reflect the menace of the goblins, as in 'Lottie Only Ran the Faster' (fig. 5.3), Hughes makes them shadowy forms silhouetted by moonlight or emerging from behind rocks and between trees. This, his most sinister drawing, depicts Irene and her nurse being chased by the goblins at dusk and employs a skilful blend of light and dark, of the figures' swirling clothes and the leering, squatting figures that surround them. The nurse's terror is evident, and the composition of straining forms and dense detail is unlike the majority of the other illustrations, which simplify the narrative and offer a pared down interpretation of the scene.[4] But for the most part, Hughes's goblins are not scary. They tramp off to work with pickaxes and lanterns, large heads and small feet in poses that prefigure Disney's familiar seven dwarves. His goblin King and Queen, though vicious in the text, are quite silly, and he shows them having fallen down, waving their podgy fists in the air. He also avoids depicting the magic of Irene's Grandmother, this time intensifying, not muddying, the mystery that surrounds her. Only two illustrations depict her: in one, she is shown at her spinning wheel, and in the other, she stretches out her arms to embrace Irene. The fire-roses, the lamp glowing like the moon, the walls spangled with silver stars, the pigeons, all of these enchanting elements Hughes ignores, leaving them instead to the imagination of the reader. Indeed, his best illustration for the book is that of the little princess at the foot of a staircase peering upwards while 'the moon [was] shining down from some window high up, and making the worm-eaten oak look very strange and delicate and lovely' (89) (fig. 5.4). We know that all of the beauty and comfort of Grandmother's rooms await Irene above. The moonlight connects the gloomy stairs to that other world of enchantment – everything is potential and Irene in her nightgown, looking very much like Diamond, is about to pass between consciousness and vision, between our world and the numinous where body matters far less than spirit.

II

What a difference there is in Arthur Hughes's illustrations for Thomas Hughes's *Tom Brown's School Days*, first published in 1857 but not illustrated by Hughes until its sixth edition of 1869. For some, recalling *Tom Brown's School Days* brings back seemingly endless descriptions of scrimmages, cricket matches, and forays for birds' eggs, and elicits overly detailed descriptions of fagging or blanket tossing – of pervasive and sadistic bullying. It seems such an unlikely book in which to find the illustrations of Arthur Hughes, and yet when his career as an illustrator was well established, Hughes chose to accept the commission to provide forty-three illustrations; he even was able to include fourteen designs by his pupil Sydney Prior Hall. Indeed, illustrating this book 'earned the artist celebrity for the rest of the century' (Wildman, 25). Yet the illustrations in *Tom Brown's School Days* have nothing of the sweetness, magic, or spirituality that typifies the others.

Arthur Hughes may have met Thomas Hughes (no relation) at F.D. Maurice's Working Men's College in Great Ormond Street. Maurice was a Christian Socialist and had founded the college in 1854. Its noble principles were to educate the workman in art, and its classes were taught by diverse personalities: John Ruskin taught drawing; Ford Madox Brown taught painting; Dante Rossetti taught evening classes of figure and watercolour painting; and Alexander Munro taught sculpting. As one of the original founders, Thomas Hughes taught boxing, and because Arthur Hughes eventually followed the other Pre-Raphaelites, he would teach there also, though not until 1877.

Although the claim could not be made of Dante Rossetti, many of those linked to Maurice and to the Working Men's College shared his belief in Christian social reform. Donald Hall writes that for Maurice it had meant 'educating the lower classes with the promise of rendering them "fit" for freedom' (47). In *Politics for the People*, a short-lived weekly Socialist paper, Maurice wrote in July 1848 that 'whatever is true, must at last be mighty. The battle with principalities and powers is fought, for the most part by weak arms; which nevertheless, shall prevail.' It is a heady blend of religious metaphor and political call to arms. A response to the insecurities and turmoil of the time, *Politics for the People* ran during a year of profound social crisis, the angry petition of the Chartists to Parliament and, upon its rejection, a massive demonstration on 10 April 1848. For Maurice, however, and for others deeply sympathetic to the workers, the goal was not radical social change but a kinder and gentler reunification of hierarchy, a new Brotherhood of Spirit, though not of class; and Christian Socialists believed it could be accomplished by the calming, civilizing effects of education, strengthening the mind, body and soul.

A decade later, T.C. Sanders coined a term that grew out of Christian Socialism: *Muscular Christianity*. Writing in the *Saturday Review* about Charles Kingsley's *Two Years Ago* (1857), Sanders combines the attributes of physical strength and religious certainty and connects them to freedom and to the land: '[Kingsley's task] is that of spreading the knowledge and fostering the love of a muscular Christianity. His ideal is a man who fears God and can walk a thousand miles in a thousand hours – who, in the language which Mr. Kingsley has made popular, breathes God's free air on God's rich earth, and at the same time can hit a woodcock, doctor a horse, and twist a poker around his fingers' (qtd. in Hall, 7). When Thomas Hughes's book was reviewed in 1858, its hero, Tom, was credited with the same muscular traits, as one who, as Hall eloquently describes him, was 'intended to display the excellence of a simple massive understanding united with the almost unconscious instinct to do good, and adorned, generally speaking, with every sort of *athletic* accomplishment' (Hall, 8). Correctly speaking, therefore, it is not Christian Socialism, with its suggestion of class turmoil, that best characterizes *Tom Brown's School Days*, but Muscular Christianity, with its concentration on the metaphor of the male body to signify a spiritual egalitarianism attained through education and through the healthy physicality of little boys taking their knocks on the rugby fields of their public boarding school and so learning what it was to be good Englishmen.

Within such a frame, one can better understand why among all the illustrations of playing football, climbing trees, running, fighting, and various other depictions of a male world of boundless energy, Hughes's illustration of little Tom and his friend, East, defeating the contemptible arch-bully, Flashman, was used on the front cover. The drawing foreshadows a triumph of good over evil that will occur some 192 pages later: the weak, united, standing up to the brutality of despotic power. Moreover, the frontispiece connects with Hughes's first true illustration for page 1, entitled 'St. George.' This drawing depicts members of the Brown family (fig. 5.5), to whom 'the British nation will be properly sensible of how much its greatness it owes,' 'dogged, homespun,' the salt of the British earth, a 'fighting family.' In the background, a maternal figure holds aloft a sweet faced child still in night-cap and gown; in the middle ground, a young boy holds a wooden sword and shield and sports a paper hat; and in the foreground, a dragon is coiled. Upon closer inspection, the bottom of the drawing reveals four legs, two of which clearly belong to the young boy and two of which belong to a hitherto unnoticed squatting figure whose face is obscured by, or is in, the dragon's mouth. With his left arm, he strains to push at the jaws, and with his right, he tries to prevent the monster's tail from tightening its circle about him. The future defenders of England against Evil are very young and their posturing precarious. Yet no such ambiguity exists in one of the book's last illustrations, 'The Conquering Knight.' The battle won, the knight kneels in supplication, his sword and helmet now placed on the ground before him, while a towering banner above him unfurls to reveal a crown of thorns. Flint rightfully commends Hughes for 'the strength of his young male figure groups' (211-12) and points to an illustration such as 'Tom's First Exploit at Football' (fig. 5.6); however, such praise of Hughes's rendition of the human form misses a subtler, more important, aspect of such drawings. Depictions of masculinity, or its lack, serve a greater purpose than merely to convey 'old boy' nostalgia and memories of school games. In the composition of the figures – Tom's small, limp body in the centre, supported by and surrounded by a dense circle of muscular older boys – Hughes's image evokes a Renaissance deposition, the viewers' comfort being that a resurrection will soon occur, as in Roger Van der Weyden's *Deposition* (1435). A finer attention to the book reveals what Thomas Hughes captured so well: the interlace between muscular Christianity and nationalism.

While Part I of *Tom Brown's School Days* is dedicated to Tom's gradual removal from his family and to his introduction to sports and schools, to their rules and hierarchies, Part II is dedicated to conversion, to the tempering and gentling of institutions and individuals. The fire produces a finer metal. In fact, in the preface to the sixth edition (1882), Thomas Hughes defends his book's attention to the scenes of bullying, one of which features the brutal burning of little Tom's legs. His rationale is curiously offered by means of a letter sent to him by a Mr G. De Bansen who writes, 'my conviction is that [bullying] must be fought, like all school evils ... [but] by getting the fellows to respect themselves and one another, rather than by sitting by them with a thick stick' (xii). Bullying can only be eradicated if boys themselves respect each other, and they can only do so if they are allowed to be boys without interference. Physical trials, therefore, are necessary proving grounds; only afterwards can a peaceful unity exist. Thomas Hughes had a mission when writing about school days. 'My whole object in writing,' he states in that preface, 'was to get the chance of preaching!' (xii). The parable of the sermon, a boy's boarding school, stands for the needful reinvigoration, re-education, of England itself. Clearly he believed that England was dangerously enfeebled. In the past, his narrator reminds us, young men had no other amusements but bracing walks and riding; they knew 'all the country folk, and their ways and songs and stories by heart' (7). 'We,' the narrator continues, and one can almost hear the thumping of the fist, 'were Berkshire, or Gloucestershire, or Yorkshire boys' (7). Now, rings the accusation, 'You're young cosmopolites, belonging to all counties and no counties' (16). The past of the 'We' had been fitter, more egalitarian, and more patriotic; the present of the 'you' is a sorry shadow. For pages before the action truly begins, Thomas Hughes writes passionately about the land, Ashdown, and White Horse Hill, but what he is actually writing about is not the west country of Victorian England but the Wessex of England's romanticized Anglo-Saxon heritage. Himself an 'Angular Saxon,' he scorns, as well as fears, the self-indulgence of the rootless cosmopolitan 'gadding over half Europe every holiday' (16). Addressing his audience as 'young England!' (6), he paints a picture of the debilitating, isolating ennui of the present-day Englishmen, racing not on horses but on railways, living for holidays and not for the camaraderie of their school chums, dropping copies of Tennyson on the tops of Swiss mountains, pattering French, eating sauerkraut, and lying on their backs 'in the paternal garden ... and half bored to death' (6). In 'Young England: Muscular Christianity and the Politics of the Body in "Tom Brown's Schooldays,"' Dennis Allen argues that Thomas Hughes redefines Disraeli's term 'Young England' to 'suggest that the national idea is also incarnated in the bodies of the boys, who stand as a living embodiment of the nation. Thus, as signifiers of the same signified ('England'), the land and the bodies of the boys themselves are interchangeable' (119). Tom Brown, then, is a reminder of, and call from, the nobler, more masculine England of the past. Like Tom, Young England too needs to stand on its own feet.

Yet as Part I of the book shows again and again, undirected, purposeless strength does not shape young men but leads to physical tyranny (the cruelty and influence of Flashman) and to arrogance (Tom's and East's descent into sneakiness and their snubbing of the dorm's rules), and Arthur Hughes' illustrations capture this misdirection. 'Roasting a Fag' depicts the gang assault on little Tom, and the last illustration for Part I, 'Tom discovered by Velveteen,' is the ignoble depiction of Tom hiding in a tree above Velveteen the Gamekeeper.

Part II introduces Tom's moral education. In danger of being expelled from school, Tom is tamed by a charge: to take care of the sickly new boy, Arthur. Here at last we see the blending of the muscular and the Christian, 'high animal spirits' and spirituality. Dennis Allen writes that 'this task is designed to imbue Tom with moral principles, to make him Christian as well as muscular, both through the responsibility of his role and through his association with the high-minded and sensitive Arthur. By the same token, the relationship is supposed to make Arthur more sturdy, to supplement his spiritual strength with physical vigour' (116). The narrator tells us that 'constant intercourse with Arthur' does much for Tom, 'a great strapping boy'; Arthur, 'still frail and delicate,' has nonetheless 'learned to swim, and run, and play cricket' (301). The true test occurs when Arthur becomes sick and nearly dies. Will his association with Tom have given him the strength to fight death, and will Tom's association with the preacher's son have taught him compassion and brotherhood? In the sick-room scene, Thomas Hughes stresses the significant differences between their bodies. Arthur lies on a sofa, his white face and fair hair illuminated by the rays of the setting sun and the blue veins on his thin hands clearly visible. Transparent, golden, and spirit-like, he reminds Tom of 'a German picture of an angel.' Ashamed and angry 'at his own red and brown face, and the bounding sense of health and power which filled every fibre of his body,' Tom kneels next to Arthur and gently puts his arm around him. At that moment, Tom realizes that 'his little chum had twined himself round his heartstrings,' and symbiotically Arthur draws on 'this very strength and power so different from his own' (305). Arthur does survive and Tom, in his thankfulness, repents and gives up cribbing. Arthur Hughes chose to illustrate this encoded scene and was faithful to its iconography.

Moreover, Arthur Hughes produced a number of final illustrations that accentuate this vital combining of body and spirit for the greater good. 'The Conversation during the Match' shows Arthur sitting on the grass looking up at Tom, while Tom sits on a bench next to a clergyman, their sixth-form master. The drawing emphasizes that this little group represents the mature unity of mind, body, and spirit. As if to further stress this message, Hughes shows us that while they are still students, Arthur and Tom have left off childhood games and now merely hold their cricket bats loosely in their hands. Two illustrations later, 'Chairing Tom in the Quadrangle' depicts joyful brotherhood on the eve of their leaving school and the literal ascension of Tom as he is carried on the shoulders of his friends, all sturdy Young Englanders now. Finally, the last illustration, 'Visit to the Tomb of Dr. Arnold' evinces Tom's obeisance to his old nemesis and master, to the stern but requisite authority that had forged him.

So well does Arthur Hughes meet and match the mission of Thomas Hughes's *Tom Brown's School Days* that just as they had done for MacDonald's fantasies, Hughes's illustrations complement the narrative. They are not merely 'static figure subjects,' as Wildman characterized them (26); instead, they powerfully engage with Thomas Hughes's sometimes dark, always evangelical sermon of nationalism.

III

Such illuminating engagement with the text occurred also when Hughes worked with Christina Rossetti. As with George MacDonald, Arthur Hughes seems to have had a close relationship with Rossetti. Hughes and Rossetti were friends, though the beginning was not auspicious. She confessed in a letter to Pauline Trevelyan, 'I fancy when one has gone a certain depth [with him], one will fail to find a deeper still, intellectually of course' (1859, qtd. in Trevelyan, 140). But on Hughes's part, there was no ambivalence at all. After her death in 1895, he wrote to Alice Boyd that 'the most beautiful soul of these latter days is at rest, and we shall not see the like again, and truly we may be very grateful for the privilege we have had' (qtd. in Fredeman, 'Pre-Raphaelite Gazette, 58). Discovering that he had been bequeathed a pair of her candlesticks, he confesses, 'these wonderful things are now owned by unworthy me! only, I think in one way I may be worthy to hold them, for I don't think anyone could have felt a much greater respect and love for her mind than I have' (ibid., 59-60). Hughes reveals his genuine affection, and upon her death, he also reflects on the only two works that he illustrated for her: *Sing-Song* in 1872 and *Speaking Likenesses* in 1874. 'I like to think,' he wrote, 'I did the "Sing Song" and regret dreadfully that I did not make better drawings to the *Speaking Likenesses*' (To Agnes Hale-White, 11 January 1895, MS: Tate, qtd. in Wildman, 27).

From a modern perspective, Hughes's self-appraisal reflects the keen division between *Sing-Song*, a nursery-rhyme book, and *Speaking Likenesses*, a disquieting tour de force. Hughes's drawings for *Sing-Song* have an enduring quality and appeal. Sidney Colvin of *The Academy* noted that 'the volume written by Miss Rossetti and illustrated by Mr. Hughes is one of the most exquisite of its class ever seen, in which the poet and the artist have continually had parallel felicities of inspiration' (qtd. in Bornand, 170), and twentieth-century book historians continued to echo the praise, noting that its 'great simplicity in both words and the accompanying pictures' sets *Sing-Song* apart as 'a new standard in children's books' (Whalley and Chester, 84). But the ambivalence felt by Hughes concerning *Speaking Likenesses* is still shared. In their anthology of *Fairy Tales and Fantasies by Victorian Women Writers*, Nina Auerbach and U.C. Knoepflmacher describe *Speaking Likenesses* as 'the most brilliant, and certainly ... the most unsettling, work in this collection,' almost gleefully announcing that it is 'unapologetically unhappy,' a 'perverse release from the cheerfulness demanded of good women' (317). On the other hand, Stephen Wildman describes it as 'a disappointing sequel,' 'odd,' 'weird' (27). And perhaps there is such dissension between the merits of these two books precisely because of Hughes's illustrations. In *Sing-Song*, Hughes's art alleviates the book's pervasive morbidity. In *Speaking Likenesses*, he often made vivid all too truthfully its disturbing lexicon of anxiety, distortion, and helplessness.

During the autumn of 1869, Rossetti wrote the 120 poems that would make up *Sing-Song*, its title suggested by her mother and immediately adopted. Her brother, Dante Rossetti, in mixed praise, described them to Algernon Swinburne as 'admirable things, alternating between the merest babyism and a sort of Blakish wisdom and tenderness' (*Letters*, 2:797). More negative was John Ruskin's reaction. He had been given a draft of the book some time before its publication. 'I sat up till late last night reading [Christina's] poems,' he wrote ruefully, 'They are full of beauty and power. But no publisher – I am deeply grieved to know this – would take them, so full are they of quaintnesses and offences' (W.M. Rossetti, *Ruskin*, 258-9). Ruskin would be proved wrong; at the time of its publication in 1872 *Sing-Song* was well received – in all probability, in great part as a result of Arthur Hughes's work.

It had not been certain, however, that Hughes was going to be the illustrator at all. There seems to have been some confusion at first about whether Rossetti wanted to illustrate the rhymes herself. She had prepared some sketches to accompany them. However, her intent appears to have been to allow her friend Alice Boyd to provide the illustrations. But both the original publisher, F.S. Ellis, and her brother disapproved of the samples they saw. Indeed, Ellis chose to withdraw from the project. Into the void stepped Ford Madox Brown, who suggested that he, Dante, and perhaps some others might each lend three or four designs in a collaboration reminiscent of *The Music Master*. This project, too, however, never materialized. Instead, the brothers Dalziel, leading Victorian wood-engravers who had by now stepped in to prepare the book for publication by George Routledge, recommended F.A. Fraser, a rather uninspired illustrator. This time it was William Michael Rossetti who objected, recommending not to his sister but to the engravers that Arthur Hughes be given the job. With the Dalziels' full agreement, Hughes was invited to join the project and to be its only illustrator (McInnis, 73). Hughes accepted, and critics have long assumed that he took full artistic control. The assumption arose because of the Dalziel brothers' recollection that 'the manuscript of this book was somewhat a curiosity in its own way. On each page, above the verse, was a slight pencil sketch, drawn by Miss Rossetti, suggesting the subject to illustrate, but of these, Mr. Hughes made very little use, and only in two instances actually followed the sketch' (*Brothers Dalziel*, 91-2). However, Lorraine Janzen Kooistra's study of the history of Rossetti's publication negotiations with the Dalziel Brothers' engraving firm argues convincingly that the evidence shows that Hughes used 'the poet's sketches as the basis for his designs, not only for page layout, but also for specific pictorial interpretations' (Kooistra, 'Jael,' 58-9). Kooistra shows that, with Hughes, the poet 'achieved the dialogic interaction of image and text so essential to her purpose' (58), and when *Sing-Song* was finally published, the Rossettis were more than pleased. With no lingering qualms, Dante Rossetti wrote to a friend, 'Christina's book is divinely lovely both in itself and in Arthur Hughes' illustrations which are quite unequaled in sweetness' (Bornand, 116); William Michael Rossetti wrote in his diary that 'the poems are about Christina's finest things, and Hughes the first of living book-illustrators' (Doughty and Wahl, 2:808). As for Christina Rossetti, so pleased was she with the final results that she insisted that the artist's name be set in a larger type on the title page, declaring that his designs alone 'deserve to sell the volume' (qtd. in Weintraub, *Four Rossettis*, 117).

Their 'cooperative dynamic interchange' (Kooistra, 'Jael,' 62) meant that the very appearance of the book set it apart: clean and uncluttered, each page was devoted to a single, often very brief, poem and an accompanying illustration that took its cue from a single element from within that poem. Yet Dante Rossetti was correct. *Sing-Song* does oscillate between two audiences, that of the nursery and that of the drawing room, between children and adults. For the very young, there is the sing-song quality of the poems and visual imagery can be "read" of loving mothers, protective angels, rabbits and chickens, flowers and impish fairies. For adults, however, the poems' imagery unmistakably dwells on maternal desire, fragile happiness, and aching loss. Perhaps that is why *Sing-Song* has begun to attract critical attention more recently. Jan Marsh describes it as 'emotionally autobiographical,' Rossetti's attempt to reach and mother the child within (379). Lila Hanft believes that the poems 'suggest maternal ambivalence ... and offer resistance, expressed in infanticidal wishes and confusion about how to read the baby, to the conflation of feminine identity and maternal identity' (216). Sharon Smulders interprets Rossetti's dedication – 'RHYMES DEDICATED WITHOUT PERMISSION TO THE BABY WHO SUGGESTED THEM' – as pointing to the book's dependence upon 'an ideological cipher that not only yields before feminine power in the nursery but reproduces feminine powerlessness outside the nursery' (103).

Much of the criticism focuses on the darker aspects of *Sing-Song*. In scrutinizing the poems, critics seem most aware of the sadness and sometimes the menace of Rossetti's nurseries and landscapes. Again, more recent studies, such as Lorraine Janzen Kooistra's 'The Dialogue of Image and Text in Christina Rossetti's *Sing-Song*,' draw our attention to the affirmation of the book brought about by the collaboration between illustrator and poet: 'Through the happy partnership of Christina Rossetti and Arthur Hughes, *Sing-Song* became more than an illustrated book for children: it became a work of composite art whose simple surfaces resonate with profound social and spiritual meanings.' As Jan Marsh points out, even the overall sequence of poems mimics a child's day. They begin with cradles and cradling, roosters at sunrise, collecting the post, eating, exploring outside, and then gradually 'build up to a final series on sun, moon and stars, which naturally leads to bedtime' (381) with its 'cool white curtains about my bed,' mother singing lullabies, and being tucked in:

> Lie a-bed,
> Sleepy head,
> Shut up eyes, bo-peep;
> Till daybreak

> Never wake: –
> Baby, sleep.

Hughes's lovely images give that world materiality.

Visually, the child's world consists of the familiar and comforting: cradles, beds, high chairs, firesides, daffodils, rainbows, dovecots, butterflies, blackboards, toys, sundials, shops, orchards, chicken coops, gardens, snails, and the companionship of other children. The pages are filled with children of every age: tiny babies, chubby toddlers, little boys and girls, young men and women. They sleep, eat, sew, swing, play, serve, cry, and most often stay close to their mothers. Second only to the children are the depictions of animals. While a few are bizarre and even intimidating (the huge baby owl that surprises the little girl from behind, in 'I dreamt I catch a little owl'; the hissing cat with its cat-o-nines tail, in 'A city plum is not a plum'; the parrot who holds a ripped doll's head in its beak and stands on the doll's sawdust-spilling torso, in 'I have a Poll parrot'), others are humorous (a ministerial mole, in 'Hurt no living thing'; a dainty lizard beneath its parasol, in 'When fishes set umbrellas up'; an incongruous pig who trots along while a horse is beset by the wind, in 'Who has seen the wind?'; and a mincing pig, resplendent with wig, top hat, cane, and pince-nez, in 'If a pig wore a wig'). Of the more than one hundred illustrations, only four disturb the comfortingly domestic mood: an exotic peacock, the aforementioned profoundly maladjusted pet parrot, the crows for 'If a mouse could fly' (an illustration, interestingly enough, that Rossetti particularly liked), and an unavoidably dead thrush for 'Dead in the cold, a song-singing thrush.' For the most part, the pages team with friendly animals: lambs, cats and dogs, frogs, voles, donkeys, and one very endearing rabbit. Birds also figure largely, and again most have soothing domestic associations: geese, ducklings, chickens, roosters, linnets, robins, and skylarks.[5]

In this sweetly ordered world, the supranatural also plays a role. Balancing five explicitly morbid scenes (a dead mother, a mother kneeling over an empty cradle, a dead thrush, children at a cemetery, and a baby being handed to a woman over a little grave) is an equal number of drawings of angels. With Raphael wings and long gowns, they guard an infant's cradle, bend over a ring of children, walk protectingly behind others, and pluck the stars. And as if a foil to their prettiness, Hughes sprinkles in the absurd: five goblins for 'A toadstool comes up in a night' – two bare-bottomed, one sticking out his tongue, one rubbing his eyes, and one tipping his acorn cap at us; a circle of madly somersaulting pixies for 'In the meadow – what in the meadow?'; and a caricature husband and wife for 'Wee wee husband' who seem a piquant version of 'Peter, Peter Pumpkin Eater.'[6]

Between text and art, a delicate balance: despite verses alluding to death and loss, Hughes's art soothes and consoles. While, on the surface, it may not appear so, there is a structure at play. Specifically, a number of facing pages complement each other: within these verso/recto pairs, the first page introduces a sorrowful or painful element and the second offers closure and sometimes contains iconography denoting Christian affirmation. Pages 18 and 19 are obviously connected. On the left page, to capture the bitterness of the wind 'wandering, whistling to and fro,' Hughes provides a frozen snowscape with a motionless wind-mill and barn. On the right, he again draws a snowy scene, but in this one a mother trudges through the snow, her child in her arms. The two designs form a unit of sensibility. 'Whereas,' Maurice McInnis says, 'the border of the facing image is ragged, this one is contained within an ovoid, encircling shape whose form emphasizes the action of the mother protecting and shielding her child from both bad weather and peril' (71). The technique is repeated on other pages. On page 4, the poem 'Our little baby fell asleep,/ And may not wake again' is accompanied by a drawing of an angel floating above an empty cradle and holding a baby; on page 5, there is a seemingly unrelated poem about a rooster. Yet Hughes's illustration of its crowing and the rising dawn is resonant with the traditional symbols of resurrection. Page 8 features a poem about a child feeding robin red-breast, reinforced by the drawing of the child sprinkling bread crumbs on a snowy window-sill; page 9 turns to warm interiors and shows a little girl, perhaps rewarded for kindness, eating by the fire, her 'clothes ... soft and warm.' The dead thrush illustrating the poem on page 10 is companioned on the next page by the verse 'I dug and dug amongst the snow' and an illustration of a little girl digging with a spade. Hughes, however, relieves the bleak scene with snow-drops emerging from the snow and a tiny bird, unmentioned by the verse, that looks on. The illustration for 'Why did baby die' on page 24 shows two children at a gravesite; on the facing page, for the verse 'If all were rain and never sun, / No bow could span the hill,' a small child and its grandmother can be seen returning home: the bottom half of the picture is lightly sketched and predominantly white, while the top half, though still dark with the remnants of a thunderstorm, reveals as well a great rainbow, God's covenant of cessation from suffering.

More generally, one senses an overarching structure of visual point and counterpoint. Critics correctly note *Sing-Song*'s disquieting beginning. The first verse, 'Angels at the foot, / And Angels at the head,' evokes the childhood prayer 'Gentle Jesus, Meek and Mild' which ends with the haunting request 'If I should die before I wake,/ I pray to God my soul to take.' Hughes's attendant image of gathered angels leaning almost expectantly over a baby's cradle confirms our unease. Taken as a first page, the effect is morbid. However, turning to Hughes's final illustration, to the verse 'Lie a-bed,' we perhaps unconsciously register that it is the very same cradle, with its heart-shaped cut-out at the foot, but that this time it is watched over by a mother, who now lovingly arranges her baby's blanket before saying good-night. The first claustrophobic illustration fed our anxieties, while the last is a serene shadow.[7] If one doesn't understand the Vinaver-like interweave that Hughes creates with his careful illustrations, then it does become tempting to treat a poem as a divisible unit instead of as one part of an indivisible book. 'Read' purely as text, for example, even *Sing-Song*'s second verse, 'Love me, – I love you,/ Love me, my baby,' raises tension. Lila Hanft, arguing that *Sing-Song* abounds in symbols of maternal ambivalence, writes that the seeming demand to 'love me [*because*] I love you' suggests 'the fear that one side might love without reciprocity: in order for the mother to be confirmed in her role as mother, an exchange must take place that completes the circle' (217). Yet by focusing on the single poem, something vital goes unnoticed: the willing reciprocity that occurs with Hughes's illustration of 'My baby has a mottled face.' There he lovingly draws a toddler leaning into its mother and kissing her, the circle of the child's fallen dress echoing the larger circle of the composition and emphasizing the intimacy of their embrace (fig. 5.7).

Because Hughes's illustrations take up half, and sometimes more, of each page, we can simply delight in the world of security that they portray – seeing can be believing, after all. In favour of the illustrations, one can gloss over the didactic verses, such as lessons about numbers or telling the time ('1 and 1 are 2 – / That's for me and you' or 'How many seconds in a minute? / Sixty, and no more in it'), and the more adult, metaphysical pieces ('What are heavier? sea-sand and sorrow:/ What are brief? to-day and to-morrow'). One can gloss over quite a bit.

The outcome of the partnership with Hughes on their second book project was a boon to critics raised on feminist and psychoanalytic theory. The appreciation of *Speaking Likenesses* is still admittedly limited. Its three linked stories taken as a whole contain more than latent subversiveness, they are manifestly subversive and seem not really suitable for children at all. Indeed, it is hard to imagine a more unlikely sequel to *Sing-Song*. Rossetti offered it to the publisher Alexander Macmillan early in February 1874, describing it as 'a little prose story, such as might I think do for a child's Xmas volume ... Properly speaking, it consists of 3 short stories in a common framework – but the whole is not long' (qtd. in Marsh, 418). She described it to her brother, Dante Gabriel, as 'merely a Christmas trifle, would-be in the Alice style with an eye to the market' (W.M. Rossetti, *Rossetti Papers*, 44). Seemingly, therefore, she believed she could capitalize on the recent popularity of Lewis Carroll's *Alice's Adventures in Wonderland* (1865), and yet she originally titled her manuscript *Nowhere*, only changing it upon the advice of her brother. Even the final title, *Speaking Likenesses*, seems hardly a tribute to sweet, always well-behaved Alice; indeed, Rossetti chose it because, as she explained, 'My small heroines perpetually encounter 'speaking (literally speaking) likenesses' or embodiments or caricatures of themselves or their faults' (Marsh, 425). When it was published, the *Athenaeum* suggested that the 'fanciful little stories would have been more original if Alice had never been to Wonderland' (Marsh, 425), and the *Academy* noted with bemusement that her Christmas offering gave only 'the uncomfortable feeling that a great deal more is meant than appears on the surface, and that every part of it ought to mean something, if only we knew what it was' (ibid.). Nevertheless, the sales of the book must have been gratifying. More than a thousand copies were sold, although the author herself had seemed uncertain of its success. 'I only hope the public appetite will not be satisfied with 6 or 60, but crave on for 600 or 6000 at least!' she wrote to Macmillan. A month after the book's release, she wrote again, confessing 'truth to tell, I had feared the reviews might this time have done me a very real injury with the buying public' (ibid.). Perhaps the sales were so healthy because the public expected something along the lines of *Sing-Song* and were confirmed in their expectations because Arthur Hughes was again the illustrator.

Rossetti had asked for Hughes early in the negotiations with Macmillan. 'I am glad to accept your offer for *Nowhere*,' she wrote on 20 April 1874. 'About illustrations: nothing would please me more than Mr. Arthur Hughes ... should do them.... This would give me pleasure' (Packer, 100). Less than a month later, she wrote to her brother William: 'To my great satisfaction yesterday heard from Mac[millan] that Arthur Hughes engages not only to do my illustrations but to do them by mid-June' (qtd. in Cowan, 82). Once he accepted, Hughes also seems to have been influenced by *Alice*, and hence, as Kate Flint has noted, there is a similarity between some of his illustrations in *Speaking Likenesses* and Tenniel's illustrations for the *Alice* books (215-16). However, it is important to recognize that in the 1870s Hughes was beginning to branch out in his painting toward a more natural-ist style, and he was in the happy position of being recognized as largely responsible for the glowing accolades *Sing-Song* had received. In this decade, therefore, he seemed 'perfectly content to follow his own predilections' (Wildman, 28). He had achieved an artistic confidence and independence. Perhaps that is why, though he himself had originated the formula of sweet, reassuring designs for *Sing-Song* only a few years before, for the second book, Hughes seems emboldened and his illustrations very modern in their representation of Rossetti's antifantasies.

Speaking Likenesses keeps the reader constantly off balance. The three stories have no common character and begin with the voice of the narrator who ostensibly will lead us through this maze of narratives. Yet the narrator's voice, frequently interrupted, is none too comforting. Aunt first gathers the little girls around her to listen to stories while they sew, but she is not a warm, maternal figure: 'Put away your pout and pull out your needle, my dear; for pouts make a sad beginning to my story. And yet not an inappropriate beginning ... Silence! Attention! All eyes on occupations' (325).

Speaking Likenesses begins with the tale of Flora, who wakes up on her birthday to 'a sense of sunshine' and her mother's kiss. The sunny mood quickly fades when the narrator intrudes and informs her little listeners that 'I tell you, from the sad knowledge of my older experience, that to every one of you a day will most likely come when sunshine, hope, presents and pleasure will be worth nothing to you in comparison with the unattainable gift of your mother's kiss' (326). Things become even worse when Flora's birthday party turns into a disaster of cruel children and spoiled food. Flora retreats in misery to a yew alley where she finds herself before a strange door, an entrance to her own Wonderland. The charm of animated furniture and countless mirrors, however, is soon replaced by horrible children drinking tea who will not offer her a chair or a cup (a Mad Hatter's Tea Party to which she is not invited) and a girl who tells Flora, 'It's my birthday, and everything is mine' (333). The party games begin: Hunt the Pincushion, the goal of which is to select the weakest player (Flora) and chase her around the room while sticking pins into her, and Self Help, the goal being pretty much the same but now 'every natural advantage, as a quill or fishhook, might be utilized to the utmost' (338). The violence and sexuality of these games are plain enough, played as they are by boys who 'bristled with prickly quills' and 'raised and depressed them at pleasure' and girls who 'exuded a sticky fluid [that] came off on the fingers' (335). Flora's 'party' reaches its crescendo when she finds herself bricked up, alone, with a now Carroll-like red faced Queen, her speaking likeness of impotence and fury, amidst a hailstorm as the children throw bricks at the glass houses that now encase each of them. When Flora magically finds herself back in her familiar garden, we are not surprised that she has 'a conscious look in her little face that made it very sweet and winning' (342). She has learned to be good, and in this story to be very good is to be happy.

For Flora's story, Hughes's first illustration, very much in the vein of Tenniel, is integral to the arrangement of the entire page,[8] and it does much to take the sting out of the narrator's waspish promise of 'the unattainable gift of your mother's gift.' Instead of having a separate space dedicated to the illustration alone, Hughes draws a rooster standing on top of a number of full-justified lines that serve as the landing at the bottom of a flight of stairs at the left hand side of the page. Then he lightly sketches the stairs to Flora's room mounting steeply upwards, and tops off the page with the scene of Flora lying in her bed and being awakened by her mother who lovingly leans over her. To add even more movement to the illustration, he places a little dog stretching up on its hind legs and a cat that walks along the foot of the bed. The other illustrations are more traditional in their format. However, from the bare-breasted Medusa that Hughes imaginatively uses as the embodiment of the party's Apple of Discord to the curtsying chair, his illustrations linger on the bizarre and he dedicates a full page to the horrible game of Hunt the Pincushion.

The second, much shorter, story concerns Edith who 'thought herself by no means such a very little girl, and at any rate as wise as her elder brother, sister, and nurse' (343) and tries, unsuccessfully, to light a fire for a picnic by herself. Unable to boil a kettle (literally unable to boil water), and though surrounded by a number of animal helpers who at any moment promise to transform into good fairies or helpful princes (there is even a frog!), Edith is sent back home by her nurse who arrives with a whole box of matches. The (non)events put her squarely in her place. She is not capable and grown up; she is not even a fairy tale princess. Hughes offers only two illustrations for this relatively tame story. For both, however, he surrounds Edith with the animals, who stare at her, expectantly.

The final story describes the 'rewards' of Maggie. The orphaned granddaughter to the owner of the village 'fancy shop,' Maggie is sent out late on a bitterly cold Christmas Eve to bring candles to a doctor's family for their Christmas tree. In the woods, she is confronted by her own desires for self-gratification: children who invite her to play the familiar, angry games of the first story; a gluttonous wide-mouthed boy who demands food (a nasty step-brother to Tweedledum and Tweedledee) (Marsh, 419); and a dozen people who toast themselves around a warm fire, 'all yawning in nightcaps or dropping asleep' (358). Passing those tests and remaining dutiful,

Maggie reaches the house – where she receives no reward but only a firm 'Thank you' as the door swings shut. Before she returns safely to her grandmother's house, where she will be hugged and given tea and toast before bedtime, Edith sees a beautiful but foreboding vision worthy of the Book of Revelation: 'the sky before her flashed with glittering gold, and flushed from horizon to zenith with a rosy glow ... each hill ... smouldered ready to burst into a volcano. Every oak-tree seemed turned to coral, and the road itself to a pavement of dusky carnelian' (359). However, always more drawn to characters and their narratives than to landscapes, Hughes illustrates each of Maggie's temptations. In a full Little Red Riding Hood costume, Hughes's Maggie is a sharply defined figure set against a background of swirling wraiths, one of which pulls at her hand as if to draw her into their world. If the wolf of the folk tale had wanted to eat the heroine, Hughes's ghostly children just want to play with her – to death. The trope of bottomless hunger occurs again in the repellent illustration of the big-mouthed boy and his fat tabby cat who clutches a kitten in its mouth.

After Maggie's story, *Speaking Likenesses* stops, and its narrative frame is broken. The narrator never returns, not to explain the moral nor to release the little girls from their sewing. *Speaking Likenesses* simply concludes with the bits and pieces of each tale's problematic ending. Readers are left to wonder whether Rossetti's story teaches the necessity of control and self-reliance, whether she uses it to criticize Victorian sexual politics, or whether it reveals a domestic tyranny endured by girls that will in time shape them also into self-hating narrators of their own stories. Jan Marsh offers other possibilities: that the story can be understood as autobiographical, cathartic in its final defiance of phallic figures, or as allegorical, the '"progress" of a young princess – the victory of duty over self-indulgence, another version of the moral tale' (418-31). A very different reading is offered by Sharon Smulders, who suggests that we should understand that as the children and their Aunt sew, their efforts contribute to her 'charity basket' and 'create a seamless link between domestic and social service,' valorizing the maternal and feminine creativity (122). And Ruth Parkin-Gounelas asks us to consider the story's threatening spaces and transgressive impulses as simply falling within the 'burgeoning of women's fantasy writing in the genres of Christmas tales and children's fiction [that provided] women with a fictional outlet previously provided by the Gothic romance' (148).

I would argue, however, that while all of these questions and readings have validity, they are limited if they do not also take into account the influence of Hughes's illustrations. As in the case of the other authors whose work he softened, gently redirecting us to the possibilities of happy

endings, in the case of *Speaking Likenesses* Hughes seems again to attempt to alleviate our disquiet at the story's ending. The story itself cruelly plays with our anticipations: we want Flora to be happy when she returns home, but instead she is browbeaten and contrite; we want Edith to be triumphant, but instead she is humiliated; and we want Maggie to be granted a deserved apotheosis, but instead she merely retreats to bed. The story's textual disruptions are sharp, and so many readers gratefully hold on to the final comforting image. Hughes reassures us, and his illustration for the last page shows us Maggie tipping out a basket now filled with true Christmas presents: the peaceful dove, the loyal puppy, and the playful kitten (fig. 5.8). Hughes obscures Dame Margaret's face with a large, dark bonnet that suggests that she had been preparing to go out in search of her grandchild. But worries fade. Still in her Little Red Riding Hood cloak, Maggie has ultimately arrived safely at grandma's house. As the story closes, we remember the picture of the kitten who contently rubs itself against maternal skirts and the child who gazes sweetly up at a woman who bends at the waist so as to draw closer to the little girl at her feet.

NOTES

1 Unsigned review, *Saturday Review*, 17 December 1904, supplement, vi. (The reviewer is identified as D.S. MacColl in a letter by Hughes to F.G. Stephens, 21 December 1904, Bodleian MS Don. e. 83, fo. 147.)

2 The range and diversity of Hughes's illustration work, however, should not be underestimated. He had begun to work with George MacDonald as early as 1862 (*Dealings with the Fairies*, published in 1867) and did illustrations for books such as William Allingham's *The Music Master* (1854), Tennyson's *Enoch Arden* (1866), William Bell Scott's *Autobiographical Notes* (1891), William Holman Hunt's *Pre-Raphaelitism and the Pre-Raphaelite Brotherhood* (1904), and Greville MacDonald's *Jack and Jill* (1913). For sources that detail Hughes's prolific career as an illustrator, refer to Forrest Reid (1928) or to the marvellous *Arthur Hughes: His Life and Work*, by Leonard Roberts (1997).

3 Other discussions of the negative symbolism of women's hair in Pre-Raphaelite art include Virginia M. Allen's '"One Strangling Golden Hair": Dante Gabriel Rossetti's "Lady Lilith,"' *Art Bulletin* (June 1984): 285-94; Elizabeth G. Gitter's 'The Power of Women's Hair in the Victorian Imagination,' *PMLA* (1985): 936-54; and Samuel J. Wagstaff, Jr.'s 'Some Notes on Holman Hunt and The Lady of Shalott,' *Wadsworth Athenaeum Bulletin*, 5th series, no. 11 (1982): 1-21.

4 This illustration almost anticipates the swirling movement of Laurence
   Housman's illustrations to Rossetti's *Goblin Market* (Macmillan, 1893), particularly that of the heroine being pawed at by the frenzied goblinmen.

5 It has to be said, though, that Hughes's choice to draw crows for 'If a mouse
   could fly' carries with it all of their archetypal menace and that his stiff
   thrush for 'Dead in the cold, a song-singing thrush' is quite convincingly
   dead. In the latter case, the verse offers no option.

6 In 'The Dialogue of Image and Text in Christina Rossetti's *Sing-Song*,'
   Kooistra offers another visual association – Punch and Judy dolls – and,
   additionally, her comparison of Rossetti's sketch and Hughes's illustration
   reveals that the wee husband's large hat did seem to find its inspiration from
   Rossetti's similarly shaped and ridiculously oversized one.

7 Interestingly, Hughes uses this identifiable cradle once more, again offering a
   subtle punctuation of visual reassurance. On page 15, to illustrate 'A baby's
   cradle with no baby in it, / A baby's grave where autumn leaves drop sere,'
   Hughes draws a woman dressed in black, kneeling over a starkly white and
   empty cradle. As described above, though, in the final illustration on page
   130, the cradle reappears, except this time it contains a clearly visible, sleeping baby. The cradles and the women are mirror images of one another: one
   dark and the other light.

8 *Speaking Likenesses* was not the only work for which Hughes blended text and
   illustration together. Hughes also creatively interwove text and image for
   George MacDonald's *Phantasies* (1905) and Hall Caine's poem 'Graih My
   Chree: A Manx Ballad' (1895).

ILLUSTRATIONS

Fig. 5.1. Arthur Hughes, 'I Am Afraid of Falling Down There.' *At the Back of the
North Wind* by George MacDonald. London: Strahan, 1870.

Fig. 5.2. Arthur Hughes, 'Fear Invaded His Heart.' *At the Back of the North Wind*.
London: Strahan, 1870.

Fig. 5.3. Arthur Hughes. 'Lottie Only Ran the Faster.' *The Princess and the Goblin*
by George MacDonald. London: Strahan, 1871.

Fig. 5.4. Arthur Hughes, 'The Light in the Stairwell.' *The Princess and the Goblin*.
London: Strahan, 1871.

Fig. 5.5. Arthur Hughes, 'St George.' *Tom Brown's School Days* by Thomas
Hughes. 6th edition. London: Macmillan, 1869.

Fig. 5.6. Arthur Hughes, 'Tom's First Exploit at Football.' *Tom Brown's School
Days*. 6th edition. London: Macmillan, 1869.

Fig. 5.7. Arthur Hughes, 'My Baby Has a Mottled Fist.' *Sing-Song* by Christina Rossetti. London: Routledge, 1872.

Fig. 5.8. Arthur Hughes, 'Maggie Drinks Tea and Eats Buttered Toast with Grannie.' *Speaking Likenesses* by Christina Rossetti. London: Macmillan, 1874.

Fig. 5.1 Arthur Hughes, 'I Am Afraid of Falling Down There.'
At the Back of the North Wind by George MacDonald. London: Strahan, 1870.

Fig. 5.2 Arthur Hughes, 'Fear Invaded His Heart.'
At the Back of the North Wind.

Fig. 5.3 Arthur Hughes, 'Lottie Only Ran the Faster.'
The Princess and the Goblin by George MacDonald. London: Strahan, 1871.

Fig. 5.4 Arthur Hughes, 'The Light in the Stairwell.'
The Princess and the Goblin.

Fig. 5.5 Arthur Hughes, 'St George.' *Tom Brown's School Days* by Thomas Hughes. 6th edition. London: Macmillan, 1869.

Fig. 5.6 Arthur Hughes, 'Tom's First Exploit at Football.'
Tom Brown's School Days.

Fig. 5.7 Arthur Hughes, 'My Baby Has a Mottled Fist.' *Sing-Song* by Christina Rossetti. London: Routledge, 1872.

Fig. 5.8 Arthur Hughes, 'Maggie Drinks Tea and Eats Buttered Toast with Grannie.' *Speaking Likenesses* by Christina Rossetti. London: Macmillan, 1874.

Fig. 6.1 William Morris, *The Woodpecker*.
Tapestry, wool, and silk on cotton warp. Morris & Co., 1885.
Courtesy of the William Morris Gallery, Walthamstow.

Fig. 6.2 William Morris, *Lea*.
Hand-block printed cotton. Morris & Co., 1885.

Fig. 6.3 William Morris, *Strawberry Thief.*
Hand-block printed cotton. Morris & Co., 1883.

Fig. 6.4 William Morris, *Trellis*.
Hand-block printed wallpaper. Morris & Co., 1864.

Fig. 6.5 William Morris, *Honeysuckle.*
Hand-block printed cotton. Morris & Co., 1876.

Book ij.   Chapter j.

OF A DAMOSEL WHICH CAME GIRT WITH
A SWORD FOR TO FIND A MAN OF SUCH
VIRTUE TO DRAW IT OUT OF THE SCABBARD.

FTER the death of Uther Pen-
dragon reigned Arthur his son,
the which had great war in his
days for to get all England into
his hand. For there were many
kings within the realm of England, and in Wales, Scotland,
and Cornwall. So it befell on
a time when King Arthur was
at London, there came a knight
and told the king tidings how
that the King Rience of North
Wales had reared a great
number of people, and were
entered into the land, and burnt and slew the king's true
liege people. If this be true, said Arthur, it were great
shame unto mine estate but that he were mightily withstood.
It is truth, said the knight, for I saw the host myself. Well,
said the king, let make a cry, that all the lords, knights, and

Fig. 6.6 Aubrey Beardsley, *Le Morte Darthur* by Sir Thomas Malory.
London: J.M. Dent, 1893–4, 27.

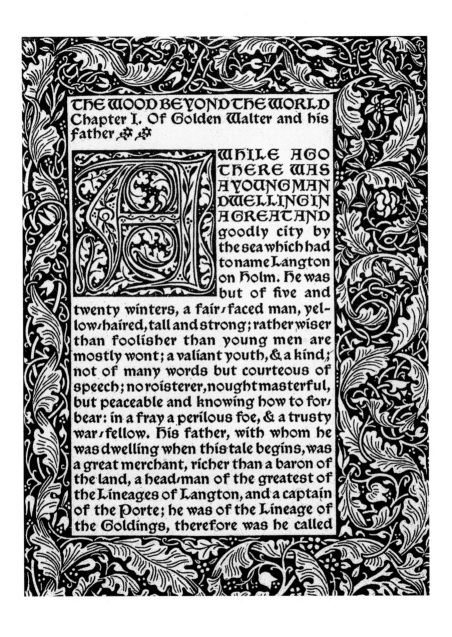

THE WOOD BEYOND THE WORLD
Chapter I. Of Golden Walter and his
father ❀ ❀

A WHILE AGO THERE WAS A YOUNG MAN DWELLING IN A GREAT AND goodly city by the sea which had to name Langton on Holm. He was but of five and twenty winters, a fair-faced man, yellow-haired, tall and strong; rather wiser than foolisher than young men are mostly wont; a valiant youth, & a kind; not of many words but courteous of speech; no roisterer, nought masterful, but peaceable and knowing how to forbear: in a fray a perilous foe, & a trusty war-fellow. His father, with whom he was dwelling when this tale begins, was a great merchant, richer than a baron of the land, a head-man of the greatest of the Lineages of Langton, and a captain of the Porte; he was of the Lineage of the Goldings, therefore was he called

Fig. 6.7 William Morris, *The Wood Beyond the World.*
Hammersmith: Kelmscott Press, 1994, 1.

Fig. 7.1 J.A.M. Whistler, *The Little White Girl: Symphony in White.* 1864,
oil on canvas; Tate Gallery, London. Photograph with inscription on frame
courtesy of Mark Samuels Lasner.

Fig. 7.2 *The Little White Girl.*
Detail of bar, hand, signature, and reflected painting.

Fig. 7.3 *The Little White Girl.*
Detail of fan.

Fig. 7.4 J.A.M. Whistler, *Nocturne in Blue and Silver: Cremorne Lights*. 1872, oil on canvas, 50.2 × 74.3 cm; Tate Gallery, London.

Fig. 7.5 J.A.M. Whistler, *Harmony in Grey and Green: Miss Cicely Alexander.*
1872–4, oil on canvas, 190.2 x 97.8 cm.; Tate Gallery, London.

Fig. 8.1 Arthur Boyd Houghton, 'Schehera-zade [*sic*] Relating the Stories to the Sultan.' Frontispiece for *The Arabian Nights' Entertainments.* London: Warne, [1865].

Fig. 8.2 Arthur Boyd Houghton 'Prince Firouz Schah Beseeching
the Protection of the Princess of Bengal.' *Dalziels' Illustrated Arabian Nights'*
Entertainments ed. H.W. Dulcken. London: Ward, Lock, and Tyler, [1865], 729.

Fig. 8.3 Arthur Boyd Houghton 'The Journey of Prince Firouz Schah and the Princess of Bengal.' *Dalziels' Illustrated Arabian Nights' Entertainments*, 737.

Fig. 8.4 Arthur Boyd Houghton 'The Princess of Bengal.' *Dalziels' Illustrated Arabian Nights' Entertainments,* 745.

Fig. 8.5 Arthur Boyd Houghton 'The African Magician Embracing Aladdin.'
Dalziels' Illustrated Arabian Nights' Entertainments, 577.

THE MAGICIAN COMMANDING ALADDIN TO GIVE UP THE LAMP.

while he was contesting the matter with him some person might come and make that public which he wished to be kept quite secret, that he completely defeated his own object.

"When the magician found all his hopes and expectations for ever blasted, there remained but one thing that he could do, and that was to return to Africa; and, indeed, he set out on his journey the very same day. He was careful to travel the by-paths, in

Fig. 8.6 Arthur Boyd Houghton 'The Magician Commanding Aladdin to Give up the Lamp.' *Dalziels' Illustrated Arabian Nights' Entertainments*, 585.

THE BRIDEGROOM SHUT UP IN THE LUMBER-ROOM.

princess privately gave him; and this officer then introduced him into the apartment of
the princess his wife, and conducted him to the chamber where the nuptial couch was
prepared. The vizier's son retired to bed first; and in a short time the sultana, accompanied by her own women and those of her daughter, brought the bride into the room.
The sultana assisted in undressing her; and, wishing her a good night, she retired with
all the women, the last of whom shut the door of the chamber.

Fig. 8.7 Arthur Boyd Houghton 'The Bridegroom Shut up in the
Lumber-room.' *Dalziels' Illustrated Arabian Nights' Entertainments*, 605.

disperse the crowd, but the people increased so fast in number that the guards thoug
better to dissemble, well satisfied if they could conduct Aladdin safe to the pala
out his being rescued. In order to prevent an attempt of this kind, they took gre
e to occupy the whole space, sometimes extending, and at others compressing the
ves, as the streets happened to be more or less wide. In this manner they arrived

THE SULTAN'S SURPRISE AT THE DISAPPEARANCE OF ALADDIN'S PALACE.

open square before the palace, where they all formed into one line, and faced ab
keep off the armed multitude, while the officer and guard who led Aladdin entered
ce, and the porters shut the gates, to prevent any one from following.
"Aladdin was brought before the sultan, who waited for him, with the grand vi:
his side, in a balcony; and as soon as the prisoner appeared, the sultan ang
manded the executioner, who was already present by his orders, to strike off his he

Fig. 8.8 Arthur Boyd Houghton 'The Sultan's Surprise at the Disappearance
of Aladdin's Palace.' *Dalziels' Illustrated Arabian Nights' Entertainments*, 633.

Fig. 9.1 Aubrey Beardsley, 'Aubrey Beardsley's Bookplate' (retitled
'Mr. Pollitt's Bookplate'). *The Later Work of Aubrey Beardsley.*
London: John Lane, 1901, 155.

Fig. 9.2 Aubrey Beardsley, 'How Sir Launcelot was known by
Dame Elaine.' *Le Morte D'Arthur* by Thomas Malory. Vol. 2.
London: J.M. Dent, 1894, facing 670.

Fig. 9.3 Aubrey Beardsley, 'How Sir Tristram Drank of the Love Drink.'
Le Morte D'Arthur. Vol. 1. London: J.M. Dent, 1893, facing 334.

Fig. 9.4 Aubrey Beardsley, 'The Woman in the Moon.'
Frontispiece for *Salome* by Oscar Wilde. London: John Lane, 1912.

Fig. 9.5 Aubrey Beardsley, 'The Toilette of Salome.'
Salome. Facing 50.

Fig. 9.6 Aubrey Beardsley, title-page design for *The Savoy*,
No. 1 (January 1896).

Fig. 9.7 Aubrey Beardsley, 'The Lady at Dressing Table.'
The Later Work of Aubrey Beardsley, 163.

Fig. 9.8 Aubrey Beardsley, 'D'Albert in search of his Ideals.'
The Later Work of Aubrey Beardsley. 162.

6

'Reading Aright' the Political Texts of Morris's Textiles and Wallpapers

David Latham

For William Morris, to 'read aright' is to recognize the social production of a text. Seamus Heaney's poem 'The Bookcase' provides a good example of what Morris meant by presenting a subtle distinction between Heaney's way of 'seeing things' and Morris's more radical ideology. Not books, but the bookcase itself is what Heaney reads in a very Morrisean manner, recognizing as equally important furniture and literature. When Heaney speaks of 'each vellum-pale board,' he is referring not to vellum-bound books but to the 'ashwood or oakwood' shelves on which the books stand. When he speaks of 'the lines' and 'a measuredness,' he is referring again to the boards on which the volumes of verse stand shelved. Vertical rows of dust-jackets are described in terms of his memories melded with the domestic chores of the kitchen:

> Whoever remembers the rough blue paper bags
> Loose sugar was once sold in might remember
> The jacket of (was it Oliver & Boyd's?)
> Collected Hugh MacDiarmid. And the skimmed milk
>
> Bluey-white of the Chatto Selected
> Elizabeth Bishop. (Heaney, 5-10)

Heaney's bookcase is less a collection of books that catalogues an education than a recollection of home, an objective correlative for the need to look homeward amidst the flood of chaos.

Morris looks the other way. Ever-forward looking, Morris saw furniture and literature as interchangeable parts of his political agenda. First, the book is not only a means for transporting its reader to other realms; it should also be for its viewer and handler an aesthetic object, itself a well-designed work of art: 'Well, I lay it down, first, that a book quite unornamented can look actually and positively beautiful, and not merely un-ugly, if it be, so to say, architecturally good' (*WM:AWS*, I:311). Secondly, we should be able to enjoy the book as an integral half of the furniture of our daily lives: 'If I were asked what is at once the most important production of Art and the thing most to be longed for, I should answer, A beautiful House; and if I were further asked to name the production next in importance and the thing longed for, I should answer, A beautiful Book. To enjoy good houses and good books in self-respect and decent comfort, seems to me the pleasurable end towards which all societies of human beings ought now to struggle' (*Ideal Book*, 1).

To help establish this new social order, Morris foregrounds in all of his work the integral relationship between art and politics. My own understanding of his revolutionary vision arose from a most memorable moment at the British Library when I was researching Morris's manuscripts. I was primarily interested in Morris's poetry at the time, and I did not fully understand his development as an artist, a development that appeared to leap through a succession of stages from theology, architecture, and painting to poetry and decorative arts and then to a whirlwind decade of political action, before finally winding down with printing and with prose romances. E.P. Thompson's monumental study of Morris's conversion from romantic to revolutionary, with its climactic chapter on Morris's crossing the river of fire to become a committed socialist, was an essential text, but somehow with everyone quoting Morris's growling confession about 'ministering to the swinish luxury of the rich' (qtd. in MacCarthy, 412), I was still uncertain about the relation between decorative arts and political action.

As I was reading through the manuscript of a socialist lecture entitled 'Commercial War' – only half mindful of the argument while noting the watermarks, paper size, and penmanship changes, I came to this blunt sentence: 'All workmen are exploited.' In writing the word 'exploited,' Morris crossed through the 't' with a line that continued over to the right margin where it then dipped and swirled into an elaborate pattern of acanthus leaves.[1] This was the first time I recognized Morris's remarkable consistency. He remained committed to all of his many and varied interests throughout virtually all of his life.

The consistency of his vision concerning the decorative arts and political action transcends the apparent paradoxes repeated so often: repeated not as inevitably embedded aporia but as superficial responses to much more complex matters. How, for example, can the most revolutionary artist be dismissed as an escapist, not just by those who take at face value the ironic persona idly singing of an empty day but by anyone who reads Morris's definition of art as the expression of our 'pleasure in labour'? ('Art of the People,' *CW*, XXII:42). The apparent paradox I wish to investigate in this essay concerns the relationship between work and rest. Its resolution will clarify the relation between the decorative arts and political revolution and show how Morris's interests in paradise, the walled garden, and wallpaper are integrated.

Comparisons of Morris's lectures and designs reveal the consistency of his theory and practice. Such comparisons encourage us to consider his decorative designs as texts to read. To do so takes us away from the conventional manner of previous studies, which focus on his textiles and wallpapers in terms of their technical production – the vegetable dyes and the pearwood blocks – or in terms of the chronology of patterns: the naturalistic with vertically hinged repeats (1862-75), the formalist with horizontal repeats (1876-82), the diagonal rivers (1883-90), and the floriated swirls combined with rigid grids (1890s). But to read Morris's decorative designs as texts, we have to learn how to read textiles of line and colour without the written text of type and how to read paper not from the pages of books but from the decoration of walls.

John Ruskin learned to 'read rightly' such things as stones, and Morris followed his example to become an instinctive reader of all aspects of culture. 'Read rightly' and 'read aright' are phrases both theorists use. Ruskin asked the readers of *The Stones of Venice* to distinguish the signs of slavery from the signs of creativity: 'Alas! if read rightly, these perfectnesses [the 'accurate mouldings and perfect polishings' of an English room] are signs of slavery in our England.' The crudely carved stones of the Gothic cathedral, in contrast, 'are signs of the life and liberty of every workman who struck the stone; a freedom of thought, and rank in scale of being, such as no laws, no charters, no charities can secure; but which it must be the first aim of all Europe at this day to regain for her children' (*Works*, X:192).

In poems written long before his political lectures, Morris similarly addressed his readers. In the 'Apology' to *The Earthly Paradise*, Morris compares the poet to a wizard who entertains a northern king by diverting him from the drear December winds to the wondrous window views of spring, summer, and the autumn harvest. The 'Apology' concludes as an *apologia* for poetry:

So with this Earthly Paradise it is,
  If ye will read aright, and pardon me,
  Who strive to build a shadowy isle of bliss
  Midmost the beating of the steely sea. (36-9)

To 'read aright' is to recognize the difference between reality and art,
between the limitations of the brazen world and the imagination of the
golden world. Recognizing the dream words of the creative act of fantasy as
an alternative to the drear winds of the idle day of reality may inspire us 'to
regain' the theoretical conditions Ruskin envisioned for nurturing 'life
and liberty' and 'freedom of thought' in future generations.

Before we learn to 'read aright' the decorative designs of textiles and
wallpapers, we need to understand Morris's radical version of Ruskin's
prescription for the renewal of art. As Northrop Frye observed, 'Morris
started out, not with the Marxist question "Who are the workers?" but with
the more deeply revolutionary question, "What is work?"' ('Varieties of
Literary Utopias,' 129). Morris answers with a number of theoretical discussions of the relation between work and rest.

After mocking the hypocrisy of the idle class who promote 'the sacred
cause of labour' in 'Useful Work vs Useless Toil,' Morris acknowledges that
nature must 'give us some compensation for this compulsion to labour,
since certainly in other matters she takes care to make the acts necessary to
the continuance of life in the individual and the race not only endurable,
but even pleasurable. You may be sure that she does so, that it is in the
nature of man, when he is not diseased, to take pleasure in his work'
(XXIII:98). In ' The Art of the People' he elaborates, using inspirational
poetry as his example:

> A most kind gift this is of nature, since all men, nay it seems all things too,
> must labour; so that not only does the dog take pleasure in hunting, and
> the horse in running, and the bird in flying, but so natural does the idea
> seem to us, that we imagine to ourselves that the earth and the elements
> rejoice in doing their appointed work; and the poets have told us of the
> spring meadows smiling, of the exultation of the fire, of the countless
> laughter of the sea. Nor until these latter days has man ever rejected this
> universal gift, but always, when he has not been too much bound by dis-
> ease or beaten down by trouble, has striven to make his work at least
> happy. (XXII:42)

History dwells on the diseased, remembering kings and warriors because they destroyed. On the other hand, art remembers the people because they created (XXII:32). As Morris explains: 'Not everyday ... was slaughter and tumult, but every day the hammer chinked on the anvil, and the chisel played about the oak beam, and never without some beauty and invention being born of it, and consequently some human happiness' (XXII:42). Art thus is not made by 'daintily' cultivated, privileged artists, 'guarded from the common troubles of common men' (XXII:40; 41). It is quite the opposite: created by 'common fellows ... in the common course of their daily labour' (XXII:40).

If art is to be revived, it must gather strength in simple places. Yet, surprisingly, these 'simple places' are not the places of work but rather the refuges from work where the farmer, the weaver, the scholar, the painter retreat from their labour:

> The refuge from wind and weather to which the good man comes home from field or hillside; the well-tidied space into which the craftsman draws from the litter of loom, and smithy, and bench; the scholar's island in the sea of books; the artist's clearing in the canvas-grove: it is from these places that Art must come. ('Making the Best of It,' XXII:113-14)

Art is reborn in the place of rest from the struggle of work. This elevation of the state of peace, of leisure as the prerequisite of art, may seem curious when we consider how persistently Morris deconstructs over several pages a single sentence from a speech that disturbed him, a sentence presented by the orator as a self-evident axiom that ignores the pleasure of work: 'No man would work unless he hoped by working to earn leisure.' Morris subverts this axiom with what he in turn regarded as an equally obvious axiom: 'No work which cannot be done without pleasure in the doing is worth doing' ('Prospects of Architecture,' XXII:141). He considers his own case:

> It was clear to me that I worked not in the least in the world for the sake of earning leisure by it, but ... because I love the work itself ... If I were forbidden my ordinary daily work ... I knew that I should die of despair and weariness.' (XXII:142)

When he next turns his thoughts to his friends, he finds 'that the one thing they enjoyed was their work, and that their only idea of happy leisure was other work' (XXII:142). When he then turns from his artist friends to people in public positions like Gladstone, he 'could see no signs of their working merely to earn leisure: they all worked for the work and deeds' sake' (XXII:143). Morris makes it clear that the work must be human, serious, and pleasurable, not machine-like, trivial, or grievous (XXII:139). 'For the word art to be rightly understood, people need hope and pleasure in their daily work. These conditions are the foundation of art and of general happiness in all life' (XXII:139). Useful work and art are virtually synonymous. Why, then, does Morris locate the revival of art in the refuge from the litter of the loom, on the island from the sea of books, in the clearing from the canvas grove? In 'Making the Best of It,' he describes these refuges as the requisites for art to 'ever again be enthroned in that other kind of building, which I think ... whether you call it Church or Hall of Reason, or what not, will always be needed; the [communal] building in which people meet to forget their own transient personal and family troubles in aspirations for their fellows and the days to come' (XXII:114). The key here is the need to establish a link between the personal and the social, between the craftsman and the aspirations of others; the worker needs a refuge for 'time to read and think and connect his own life with the life of the great world' (XXII:116). Modern civilization has divorced us from this traditional kinship meaning of the arts, which, Morris contends, 'is surely the expression of reverence for nature, and the crown of nature, the life of man upon the earth' ('Prospects of Architecture,' XXII:125). Morris later defines art as the stories we tell of our relation with nature and with human nature, with the trees and winds and beasts, and with our ancestors and our neighbours, whose deaths give our lives meaning and whose sorrows cathartically give our lives joys:

> Freed from the bondage of foolish habit and dulling luxury [we] might at last have eyes wherewith to see: and should have to babble to one another many things of our joy in the life around us: the faces of people in the streets bearing the tokens of mirth and sorrow and hope and all the tale of their lives: the scraps of nature the busiest of us would come across; birds and beasts and the little worlds they live in; and even in the very town the sky above us and the drift of the clouds across it; the wind's hand on the slim trees, and its voice amid their branches, and all the ever-recurring deeds of nature; nor would the road or the river winding past our homes fail to tell us stories of the countryside, and men's doings in field and fell. And whiles we should fall to muse on the times when all the ways of nature were mere wonders to men, yet so well beloved of them that they called them by men's names and gave them deeds of men to do; and many a time there would come before us memories of the deeds of past times, and of

the aspirations of those mighty peoples whose deaths have made our lives, and their sorrows our joys. (XXII:151-2)

Here again in 'The Prospects of Architecture,' he explains that artistic vision cannot be experienced without the 'leisure from toil, and truce from anxiety' that provide us with 'time to brood over the *longing* for beauty' we are all born with (XXII:134). In this same lecture Morris also explains the river of fire metaphor: 'Between us and that which is to be, if art is not to perish utterly, there is something alive and devouring; something as it were a river of fire that will put all that tries to swim across to a hard proof indeed, and scare from the plunge every soul that is not made fearless by desire of truth and insight of the happy days to come beyond' (XXII:131). He identifies that fire as 'the hurry of life bred by the gradual perfection of competitive commerce' (XXII:132). In his lecture on 'The Beauty of Life,' he foregrounds 'our work, our thought, and our rest' (XXII:77) as a sort of trinity of co-dependents that stand against the 'hurrying blindness of civilization' (XXII:53).

As the proponent of 'thoughtlessness, of hurry and blindness' (XXII:65), 'modern civilization is on the road to trample out all the beauty of life' (XXII:54). The recurrent military metaphors in Morris's lectures present modern civilization making a siege on art. The hurrying blind toil of commerce has overrun and devoured all but the last remnant of art, now held at bay in its citadel ('Prospects of Architecture,' XXII:147). Art's resistance is expressed with organic metaphors, fragile yet natural and thus persistent: 'How can we spread the decencies of life, so that at the least we may have a field where it will be possible for art to grow?' ('Beauty of Life,' XXII:67) The hope for its revival and fruition is founded on the yearning for art and beauty that is deep-rooted in our souls ('Prospects of Architecture,' XXII:151). However, confronted with the evidence that the root of the tree of art we are cultivating is not well, Morris has come to the realization that what art needs is not an evolutionary re-*routing* in a new direction but a revolutionary upheaval and ultimate re-*rooting* in newly prepared ground. Morris thus yearns for the cleansing flood of a new barbarism to bring an end to civilization: 'The arts have got to die, what is left of them, before they can be born again' (*Letters*, 2:217; 21 August 1883).

The campaign begins with language. Such words as 'cultivation' and 'originality' must be wrenched from their present debasement. For Morris, cultivation has nothing to do with an elevated status to be showcased in the drawing rooms of the 'swinish ... rich'; cultivation has to do with the re-rooting of art from a privileged domain into a daily practice. And he understood that originality depends on a return to origins. His innovative experiments in the decorative arts retrieve the acanthus leaf from ancient Greek motifs and revive traditional printing techniques with indigo dyes and pearwood blocks.

As Morris outlines in his lecture on 'The Decorative Arts' and in his 'Address on the English Pre-Raphaelite School,' neoclassical rules had infected art with an inorganic academicism that promoted an hierarchical division between the greater and lesser arts, the elevation of a few traditional crafts to the status of fine art and the demotion of the rest to the lower status of practical handicrafts. Raymond Williams reminds us that the word 'art' from the thirteenth through the seventeenth centuries designated a wide variety of skills: mathematics, medicine, even angling. But in the eighteenth century, it began to assume a more 'specialized application to a group of skills not hitherto formally represented: painting, drawing, engraving, and sculpture.' The Royal Academy was founded, and in a short time it excluded engraving from its ranks and endorsed the hierarchical distinction between artist and artisan, 'the latter being specialized to "skilled manual worker" without "intellectual" or "imaginative" or "creative" purposes' (41).

Henry Cole's summation of the hegemonic results – a hundred years later – shows how soon within three generations the corrupt practice legitimized the theory: 'We have no principles, no unity; the architect, the upholsterer, the paper stainer, the weaver, the calico-printer, and the potter, run each their independent course; each struggles fruitlessly; each produces in art novelty without beauty or beauty without intelligence.' Cole's complaint was one of resignation. The 1861 formation of the Morris firm was an aggressive counterattack. In Walter Crane's words, Morris's ultimate aim was to eliminate the 'artificial distinction between art and labour' (*Claims of Decorative Art*, 57). The 1861 prospectus of the Morris firm addresses this loss of unity from the division of labour: 'Fine Art Workmen in Painting, Carving, Furniture, and the Metals [ready to] undertake any species of decoration, mural or otherwise, from pictures ... down to the consideration of the smallest work susceptible of art and beauty.' Here, Morris gives a long list ending with 'ornamental work in other such materials, besides every article necessary for domestic use.'

For Morris the romance of life depends upon the harmonious relationship between art and the beauty of the earth. The arts must be unified in an architectural nature that is ultimately an environmental nature: 'It is this union of the arts, mutually helpful and harmoniously subordinated to one another, which I have learned to think of as Architecture ... [including] the whole external surroundings of the life of man ... and the moulding and altering to human needs of the very face of the earth itself' (110). Morris thus acknowledges the moral responsibility of the artist in determining the harmonious relationship between civilization and the earth.

How do we re-establish the harmony between ourselves and the beauty of the earth? The statistics from the 1996 World Habitat conference in Istanbul revealed that thirty years ago one-third of the world's population lived in cities and that a mere thirty years from now two-thirds of the world will do so. This complete reversal of the rural country, urban city ratio suggests that we are hurrying so fast in the opposite direction of the village communities envisioned in *News from Nowhere* that an eventual backlash will indeed switch us in Morris's direction toward a harmonious relationship with what is left of the beauty of the earth. As *News from Nowhere* shows, the point is not so much whether or not such a utopia could ever become a reality; rather, what horrifies Morris is that we no longer even wish for it to happen. Too many of us prefer to dream of some technological computer paradise, of new shopping malls, of more cable television choices, of holding the winning lottery number. As Herbert Marcuse noted, 'capitalism's real power is to make unthinkable the alternatives' (141). Morris explains how the capitalist system has 'reduced the workman to such a skinny and pitiful existence, that he scarcely knows how to frame a desire for any life much better.' Art provides the anwer: 'It is the province of art to set the true ideal of a full and reasonable life before him, a life to which the perception and creation of beauty, the enjoyment of real pleasure that is, shall be felt to be as necessary to man as his daily bread' ('How I Became a Socialist,' 382-3).

Morris's prescription for changing the hurrying course of civilization is to awaken us from our blindness by restoring our vision. Responding to the 'extraordinary acuity' of a descriptive passage from 'The Story of the Unknown Church,' Jerome McGann identifies Morris's practice in fiction and poetry as an 'aesthetic of observation' ('A Thing to Mind,' 59): 'It is as if in reading descriptions of such common familiar things, one were being led to a recovery of the powers of vision, to see again for the first time' (59). McGann recognizes that Morris's Pre-Raphaelite attentiveness to detail, which translates the familiar into the strange, 'comes as a kind of benevolent reproach. It tells us that though we live in the world, we commonly do not see the smallest part of its material particularity, which for Morris is its wondrousness' (59).

Perhaps even more integral to the recovery of vision are the decorative arts since they are central to that balance between work and rest and thus not escapist but integral to social revolution. As Morris explains in 'Some

Hints on Pattern-Designing,' because the extremes of tragedy or beauty can harden us if we are subjected to them all the time, we need 'lesser art' to relax us (258-9). Oscar Wilde's confession that 'my wallpaper and I are fighting a duel to the death; one or the other of us has got to go' (qtd. in Ellmann, 556) is thus layered in irony. Morris contends that we need 'to clothe our daily and domestic walls with ornament that reminds us of the outward face of the earth, of the innocent love of animals, or of man passing his days between work and rest as he does.' The ornament 'must be suggestive rather than imitative ... because scientific representation ... would again involve us in the problems of hard fact and the troubles of life, and so once more destroy our rest for us' ('Pattern-Designing,' 259).

For Morris, the ornamental patterns of wallpaper and chintz are meant to lead the mind outdoors. How far beyond the door is suggested by Morris's metaphors. The haunting lyric for November in *The Earthly Paradise* examines the poet's vision struggling against a formless veil: 'Art thou so weary that the world there seems, / Beyond these four walls, hung with pain and dreams?' The walls should be hung not with formless veils but with ornament: 'Any decoration is futile and degrading when it does not remind you of something beyond itself' ('Pattern-Designing,' 260). The walls should be hung with ornament that leads us outside, yet once beyond the doors of our homes, we should find ourselves in a garden which, in turn, should be walled: 'A garden ... should be well fenced from the outside world' ('Making the Best of It,' XXII:91). Morris's metaphors locate the proper bounds within the walled garden (the word 'paradise' originating from the Persian word for 'walled garden'). Literally this walled garden is part of his prescriptions for 'making the best of it,' wherein he explains how each of us can strive to improve the conditions for art by cultivating a garden outside our house and creating ornament inside our house. But the walled garden is more than a paradisal refuge from the hurrying blindness of modern civilization. It provides the conditions for the 'delight in skill [that] lies at the root of all art' ('Pattern-Designing,' 263).

Our walls should be clothed in an ornamental pattern comprised of 'beauty, imagination, and order' ('Pattern-Designing,' 261). The pattern will be suggestive rather than imitative when we apply the principles of order and beauty to nature. This technique of conventionalizing nature 'builds a wall against vagueness and opens a door therein for imagination to come in by' (262). Morris suspends his own ornamental patterns in an organic balance between nature and abstraction, between depth and flatness, between melodic swirl and firm grid. The design appears organic when based on the abstractions of geometry because these same ordered principles are inherent in nature, from snowflakes to starfish, from peacocks to pine trees.

The material itself provides walls for the artist's imagination to work within:

> Every material ... imposes certain limitations within which the craftsman must work. Here again, is a wall of wonder against vagueness, and a door for the imagination ... These limitations are not hindrances to beauty but are enticements and helps to its attainment ... The artist says I want to make such and such a pretty thing out of these intractable materials, straightway his invention will be quickened and he will set to work with a will; for, indeed, delight in skill lies at the root of all art. (262-3)

In comparing the theory of Morris's lectures to the practice of his art, it is clear that his subversion of the greater arts and support for the lesser ones is demonstrated by his own 'regression' from oil painting to decorative designing. But how may we see his individual patterns as demonstrating his re-rooting of art? By 'gardening with golden thread' Morris demonstrates how we can re-root art in the common soil of our daily lives and thereby raise our grinding toil to the joy of useful work, as work, play, and art become synonymous[2] ('Pattern-Designing,' 276).

To 'read aright' Morris's decorative designs is to recognize their intertwining stems and blossoms as an integral part of a socialist agenda. His *Woodpecker* tapestry (1885) (fig. 6.1) provides a transitional example that combines the written text with the woven textile. The tapestry may be the elitist medium, 'the noblest of weaving arts,' as Morris identified it ('Textiles,' 23); however, the lush richness of the *Woodpecker* tapestry is subverted by the ribbon of poetry woven within the honeysuckle border above and beneath the bird. The uncoiled scroll spells out the song of the woodpecker amidst the curled acanthus, as Morris politicizes Ovid's myth of Circe spitefully turning the king into a scavenging bird for refusing her love:

> I once a King and chief
> Now am the tree-bark's thief,
> Ever 'twixt trunk and leaf
> Chasing the prey. (IX:192)

The king's appearance as a lowly thief in pursuit of its prey is not a physical transformation but rather a revelation of the king's true nature. Morris thus updates Ovid by replacing Circe's sorcery with insightful psychology. When Morris reprinted the four lines of 'The Woodpecker' as a poem on its own in his *Poems by the Way* (1891), he placed it among the 'Verses for Pictures' that mark the political shift in the collection from love to art, a shift from personal fulfilment to public commitment. The subtext that emerges is not the urgency of personal renewal through love but the resolve for social renewal through revolution.

What tales does the weave of his textiles tell us when they have no written text? Bernard Shaw observed that Walter Crane's lectures were always well attended even though Crane was not a lively speaker. But whenever Crane picked up chalk and turned to the wall to illustrate a point, the whole audience would perk up and lean forward. Morris, however, though occasionally illustrating his lectures on pattern design or typeface with drawings or slides usually limited his illustrations to a verbal explanation of his theoretical positions.

Morris is specific in one way and elusively allusive in another way. He is very specific in discussing the use of planes in relations to the use of line and colour. There are two ways of clearly contrasting or delineating the pattern forms, he tells us: by creating the effect of different planes overlapping for depth or by using contrast in colour. The use of different colours is limited to a flat design, and the multi-plane effect is limited to a few shades of colour. If there are several colours and several different depth effects, the result is an inarticulate mess. The *Lea* chintz (1885) (fig. 6.2), with its flow of continually turning acanthus leaves, is an example of a few shades of colour used with a complexity of planes, while the *Strawberry Thief* chintz (1883) (fig. 6.3) has many contrasting colours existing on a few simple planes.

Morris remains poetically suggestive in his demonstration of the effect of planes as walls for visionary means. In paper and chintz, he presents a foliage of leaves and blossoms, of stems and vines, of birds and trellises: a surface thicket of two or three planes that form a veil over a flat monochrome plane beneath. The papers more often present dark-coloured growth over a light-coloured background, while the chintzes are more often a lighter foreground on a dark background. The effect is of a garden thicket with the sky beyond or a thicket wall with an open field beyond. The *Trellis* wallpaper (1864) (fig. 6.4) is typical in presenting the birds in the foreground, the climbing rose weaving before and behind the trellis in the middle, and the butterflies hovering within the wooden-framed squares to accentuate the mystery of the blank plane behind the trellis. The *Jasmine* wallpaper (1872) is marginally more complex with its planes of jasmine and hawthorn: the circling vines and veined leaves and starred blossoms of jasmine are entwined over and under the meandering climb of the branches of stemmed leaves and blossoms of hawthorn. The blank plane beyond is thus more obscured. The *Honeysuckle* chintz (1876) (fig. 6.5), with its dense boughs of evergreen forming a wall of layered needles that prevent a view into the background, is an exception. Normally, 'mere air and space' are essential. As Morris prescribes in 'Making the Best of It,' for the 'spacing out of the wall for decoration ... it is best to put nothing that attracts the eye above a level of about eight feet from the floor – to let everything above that be mere air and space, as it were' (XXII:96-7).

The repeats of the pattern should be somewhat masked so that while we are enticed to pursue its outline, the masking lulls our curiosity to trace it out. The *Strawberry Thief* chintz is a brilliant example (fig. 6.3). With the raised and lowered tails of the birds, the turnover hinge appears to shift elusively from one pair of birds to another, drawing the eye from the vertical relationships between the different coloured singing birds and thieving birds to the horizontal relationships between the same-coloured face-to-face birds and back-to-back birds. The foregrounding of the pair of plucked strawberries, whose stems pass toward us through the birds' beaks, serves to integrate the birds within the weave of the two planes of berries and flowers. The variety of plants range from small strawberry blossoms to large artichokes. The five planes, from the closest to the distant – the plucked berry (1), the birds (2), the entwined flowers (3, 4), set against the flat indigo background (5) – create an illusion of depth. Yet, with each berry, bird, blossom, stem, and all but two turned leaves presented as flat arrangements of colour, the *Strawberry Thief* pattern retains a relatively flat surface of intricate colours.

Such masterful patterns are designed to produce a satisfying mystery. What diverts our attention to the repeat may be the charm of a particular surface detail, or it may be the freedom of light or the mystery of the dark beyond the fenced foreground. The successful pattern may invite us to dwell on the busy surface, or it may lure us to delve beyond the surface to the blank space beyond, to an unfettered imagination, to see again, inspiring us to envision our own dreams. Lulling rest and pensive vision: the *Strawberry Thief* exemplifies that delicate balance between fulfilment and anticipation. While its pattern depicts a paradisal abundance of foliage, fruit, and song, its title invites a satirical wink at the capitalist notion of property and the biblical notion of humanity's dominion over the natural world.

Wallpaper and the walled garden thus merge with the paradisal vision.

As a metaphorical construct through which Morris envisions a revolutionary social order, decorative art is a political concern with its aesthetic
principles of 1) order, 2) beauty, and 3) imagination leading us away from
the 'thrall of muddle, dishonesty, and disunion' toward establishing the
desired social conditions of 1) order, 2) goodwill, and 3) union ('Pattern-
Designing,' 283). Decorative art is thus not only the essential foundation
upon which all art must stand but also is among the fundamental needs of
humanity.

A comparison of a page from a Kelmscott Press book designed by Morris
with a page from the Dent *Morte d'Arthur* (fig. 6.6) designed by Aubrey
Beardsley reveals how different a similar design can turn out when the
aesthetic principles of order, beauty, and imagination are divorced from
the social principles of order, goodwill, and union. Beardsley may have
taken as his example any number of Morris's Kelmscott Press books. A page
from *The Wood Beyond the World* (fig. 6.7) is typical. Beardsley follows Morris's
example by framing the text with a decorative border and then repeating
that border as an inner frame whose foliage is intertwined with the opening initial. Morris's curved stems with leaves and blossoms are circular like
halos. Beardsley's thick stems with thorns and satyrs are coiled like ser-
pents. Morris's initial is rounded; Beardsley's initial extends downward
like a sabre through the thorns. His androgenous satyrs scowl and crouch
and crawl. Morris's design is one of organic growth, suggesting the walled
garden of paradise. Beardsley's design is a demonic artifice, aggressive and
menacing. His overemphasis on ornament at the expense of naturalistic
detail makes his art appear overly sophisticated. It thus exemplifies the
'disunion' of the intrusively artificial. Beardsley's parodic design bears no
trace of Morris's faith in a paradise regained through the integration of
aesthetic and social principles.

When J.W. Mackail identified Morris's wall-hangings (his 'printed cotton goods, the celebrated "Morris chintzes,"' 2:56) as a style that did not
catch on – 'People dressed themselves in his wall-hangings, covered books
with them, did this or that with them according to their fancy; but hang
walls with them they would not' do – the conservative and commercial-
minded Mackail revealed the shortsightedness of his literal reading of
Morris's art by overlooking the profound importance Morris would have
attributed to Mackail's own reference to people doing 'this or that with
[wallhangings] according to their fancy' (2:57). Morris aimed to transform
our concept of art from ' a phantom of bygone times' to 'a living thing with
hope in it' ('Pattern-Designing,' 283). The wall-hanging was not intended
to set a fashion; rather, it was part of Morris's effort to transport us to the

walled garden of paradise by inspiring us to commit our lives to art. This is the revolutionary ideal he devoted his life to. Lecturing at the loom in order to demonstrate what 'we each and all of us who have the cause at heart may do to further the cause' (283), Morris sought to inspire us to envision the means to construct the walled garden wherein we may all live creative lives.

NOTES

1 Similarly, in his lecture on 'Communism,' such notations as 'old age pensions' and 'luxury or necessity' are wrapped in ornamental floral designs. The versos of the last two folios of 'Socialism' are filled with floral designs. On folio 6 of 'Communism, i.e. Property,' the margins and the ends of the paragraphs are decorated with foliage. These lectures were written between 1885 and 1892. All four lectures are in the British Library, Add.MSS. 45333. Eugene LeMire lists the dates for the composition and delivery of each lecture in *The Unpublished Lectures of William Morris*, 302, 310, 318, 319.
2 See also 'How I Became a Socialist' for similar gardening metaphors: Art cannot 'grow when it has no longer any root ... Its roots must have a soil of a thriving and unanxious life.' 'Amidst all this filth of civilization the seeds of a great change, what we others call Social-Revolution, were beginning to germinate' (382-3).

ILLUSTRATIONS

Fig. 6.1 William Morris, *The Woodpecker*. Tapestry, wool and silk on cotton warp. Morris & Co., 1885. Courtesy of the William Morris Gallery, Walthamstow.
Fig. 6.2 William Morris, *Lea*. Hand-block printed cotton. Morris & Co., 1885.
Fig. 6.3 William Morris, *Strawberry Thief*. Hand-block printed cotton. Morris & Co., 1883.
Fig. 6.4 William Morris, *Trellis*. Hand-block printed wallpaper. Morris & Co., 1864.
Fig. 6.5 William Morris, *Honeysuckle*. Hand-block printed cotton. Morris & Co., 1876.
Fig. 6.6 Aubrey Beardsley, *Morte d'Arthur* by Sir Thomas Malory. London: J.M. Dent, 1893-4, 27.
Fig. 6.7 William Morris, *The Wood Beyond the World*. Hammersmith: Kelmscott Press, 1894,1.

7

Whistler/Swinburne: 'Before the Mirror'

J. Hillis Miller

William E. Fredeman was a man of the manuscript and printed book epoch if there ever was one. He also knew, however, that a printed book, like a manuscript, was not disembodied words that might be printed without loss in any type size and font on any sort of paper. A book or a manuscript is a material object, and the form of its materiality is part of its meaning. Moreover, as William E. Fredeman also knew, books have also always been in one way or another multimedia productions, most obviously in the case of illustrated books. Fredeman's magnificent collection of Pre-Raphaelite materials, like his published writings, took that particular group of artists, poets, bookmakers, and artisans, the Pre-Raphaelites, as a paradigmatic example of the need to go back to originals in order to study the literature of the printed book epoch adequately. This small paper attempts to reflect on the changes in such study being brought about by new communications technologies. They are radically altering the way we examine the sort of material that Fredeman collected in his own library as the indispensable means of access to the cultural meanings embodied in Pre-Raphaelite productions.

The transformations now being wrought by new communications technologies in shaping humanistic research and teaching are hard to define and understand, partly because we are in the midst of them. The digital revolution, however, is clearly as radical and as irreversible as the move from a manuscript to a print culture. Email, faxes, computerized library catalogues, composition on the computer rather than in longhand or on the typewriter, the increasing use of computers and networks in instruction, the availability of more and more material online, the move from linear print media to multimedia hypertext, the online publishing of articles and monographs that is altering the way research results are disseminated – all these are irrevocably transforming the way teachers and students of literature (and of other humanistic disciplines) do their work.

In striking passages written by one of the protagonists of *La carte postale* (*The Post Card*), Jacques Derrida says the following:

> An entire epoch of so-called literature, if not all of it, cannot survive a certain technological regime of telecommunications (in this respect the political regime is secondary). Neither can philosophy, or psychoanalysis. Or love letters. ('Envois,' 212; *Post Card*, 197)

> Refound here the American student with whom we had coffee last Saturday, the one who was looking for a thesis subject (comparative literature). I suggested to her something on the telephone in the literature of the 20th century (and beyond), starting with, for example, the telephone lady in Proust or the figure of the American operator, and then asking the question of the effects of the most advanced telematics (la télématique la plus avancée) on whatever would still remain of literature. I spoke to her about microprocessors and computer terminals, she seemed somewhat disgusted (avait l'air un peu dégoutée). She told me that she still loved literature (me too, I answered her, mais si, mais si). Curious to know what she understood by this. ('Envois,' 219; *Post Card*, 204)

What Derrida or, rather, his protagonist in *La carte postale* says in the citation is truly frightening, at least to a lover of literature like me or the protagonist's hapless interlocutor, the American graduate student in comparative literature who was looking for a dissertation topic. What the protagonist says arouses in me the passions of anxiety, doubt, fear, disgust, and perhaps a little secret desire to see what it would be like to live beyond the end of literature, love letters, philosophy, and psychoanalysis, all prime examples of 'humanistic discourse.' To live beyond their end would be like living beyond the end of the world.

Derrida's words perhaps also generate in most readers the passions of disbelief and even scorn. What a ridiculous idea! We passionately and instinctively resist the statement that Derrida makes in such a casual and offhand way, as though it goes without saying. How could a change in something so superficial, mechanical, or contingent as the dominant means of preservation and dissemination of information, the change, to be precise, from a manuscript and print culture to a digital culture, actually bring to an end things that seem so universal in any civilized society as literature, philosophy, psychoanalysis, and love letters? Surely these will survive any change in the regime of telecommunications? Surely I can write love letters by email! Surely I can compose and transmit literature or philosophy or even a love letter on a computer connected to the Internet just as well as I can with handwriting or a typewriter or through a printed book? How is psychoanalysis, based as it is on face-to-face interlocution (it's called 'the talking cure'), tied to the regime of print and to be brought to an end by a shift to digital culture?

Derrida's curt and even insolent words arouse in me a passion of disgust like that in the graduate student to whom he gave such strange advice. This advice, by the way, was taken by Avital Ronell, in her own way and no doubt not as a response to any direct communication from Derrida. Both Proust on the telephone and Derrida's *The Post Card* figure in Ronell's admirable *The Telephone Book*, itself in its format an anticipation of the new regime of telecommunications. Laurence Rickels has also already written brilliantly on the telephone in modern literature, psychoanalysis, and culture generally, as has Friedrich Kittler.[1]

Nevertheless, that is what Derrida is claiming: the change in 'regime of telecommunications' does not simply transform but absolutely bring to an end literature, philosophy, psychoanalysis, and even love letters. It does so by a kind of death-dealing performative fiat: 'Let there be no more love letters!' How in the world could this be? Insofar as Derrida's words, either those he (or one protagonist of *The Post Card*) said to the graduate student or the words you or I read now in that book, generate the passions of fear, anxiety, disgust, incredulity, and secret desire, those words are a 'felicitous' performative utterance. They do what they say and help bring about the end of literature, love letters, etc., just as saying 'je t'aime (I love you),' as Derrida argued in a seminar, not only creates love in the speaker but may also generate belief and reciprocal love in the one to whom the words are spoken.

In spite of all his love for literature, Derrida's writings, for example *Glas*, or *La carte postale* itself, have certainly contributed to the end of literature as we have known it in a particular historical epoch and culture, say the last two and a half centuries in Europe and America. The concept of literature in the West has been inextricably tied to Cartesian notions of selfhood, to the regime of print, to Western-style democracies and notions of the nation-state, and to the right to free speech within such democracies. 'Literature' in that sense began fairly recently, in the late seventeenth or early eighteenth century, and in one place, Western Europe. It could come to an end, and that would not be the end of civilization. In fact, if Derrida is right, and I believe he is, the new regime of telecommunications is bringing literature to an end by transforming all those factors that were its preconditions or its concomitants.

One of Derrida's main points in *The Post Card* is that it is a feature of the new regime of telecommunications to break down the inside/outside dichotomies that presided over the old print culture. The new regime is ironically allegorized in *The Post Card* in somewhat obsolete forms, that is, not only in the many telephone conversations the protagonist (or protagonists) have with their beloved or beloveds but also in an old-fashioned remnant of the rapidly disappearing culture of handwriting, print, and the postal system: the postcard. The postcard stands as a proleptic anticipation of the publicity and openness of the new communications regimes. A postcard is open for anyone to read, just as email today is by no means sealed or private. If an example of either happens to fall under my eye, as Derrida makes explicit for post cards and letters not only in *La carte postale* but also in the admirable essay called 'Télépathie,' I can make myself or am magically made into its recipient. The postcard message or the email letter that happens to fall under my eye, is meant for me, or I take it as meant for me, no matter who it is addressed to. This certainly happens when I read the passage from *The Post Card* I have cited. The bad or even disgusting news the speaker conveyed to the graduate student, news of the end of literature, philosophy, psychoanalysis, and love letters, is also conveyed to me. I become the recipient of this bad news. The passions that what the protagonist said generated in the graduate student are also generated in me.

Perhaps the most disturbing thing Derrida says in the passage is that in the power the new regime of telecommunications has to bring an end to literature, psychoanalysis, philosophy, and love letters, 'the political regime is secondary.' More exactly, Derrida says, 'in this respect the political regime is secondary.' 'In this respect' means, I take it, that he does not deny, nor would I, the importance of political regimes but that the power of the new regime of telecommunications is not limited or controlled, except in a 'secondary' way, by the political regime of this or that nation.

The second industrial revolution, as everyone knows, is the shift in the West, beginning in the mid-nineteenth century and accelerating ever since, from an economy centred on the production and distribution of commodities to an economy increasingly dominated by the creation, storage, retrieval, and distribution of information. Even money is now primarily information, exchanged and distributed all over the world at the speed of

light by telecommunications networks that also transmit literature in digitized form. Several of Henry James's novels, for example, are now available
on the Internet, along with innumerable other literary works, works belonging to the now rapidly fading historical epoch dominated by the
printing press.

Photography, the telegraph, the typewriter, the telephone, the gramo-
phone, cinematography, radio, tape recorders, television, and now CDs,
VCRs, DVDs, cell phones, computers, communication satellites, and the
World Wide Web – we all know what these devices are and how their power
and effects have accelerated over the last century and a half. The possession and consequent effect of these devices, as Masao Miyoshi and others
have frequently reminded us, is unevenly distributed among various countries and peoples of the world. Only about 50 per cent of U. S. households
presently have personal computers, and, of course, the percentage is
immensely smaller in many other countries. Nevertheless, in one way or
another and to one degree and another, almost everyone's life has already
been decisively changed by these technological gadgets. The changes will
accelerate as more and more people come, for example, to have access to
the Internet, and they will include a transformation of politics, nationhood
or citizenship, culture, and the individual's sense of selfhood, identity, and
belonging, not to speak of literature, psychoanalysis, philosophy, and love
letters.

The decline or weakening of the nation-state's autonomy, the development of new electronic communities, communities in cyberspace, and the
possible generation of a new human sensibility leading to a mutation of
perceptual experience making new cyberspace persons, persons deprived
of literature, psychoanalysis, philosophy, and love letters – these are three
effects of the new telecommunications regime.

What is perhaps most scandalous about the radical effects of new telecommunications is the way none of the inventors, so far as I know, intended or foresaw any of the effects their inventions have had. The inventors
of the telephone or of the magnetic tape recorder were doing no more
than exploiting technological possibilities, playing creatively with wires,
electrical currents, vibrating diaphragms, plastic tapes, and so forth. They
had no intention, so far as I know, of putting an end to literature, love
letters, philosophy, or the nation-state. It is the incommensurability between cause and effect plus the accidental aspect of the huge effect – no
less than a radical disruption, interruption, break, or reorientation in
human history – that is so scandalous.

My claim is that this new digitized existence will change literature and literary study in manifold and as yet unforeseen ways. I would go so far as to say that it will transform, is already transforming, the concept of literature or of literarity, killing literature and giving it a new existence as the survivor of itself. Students of literature will and should remain as the guardians and surviving witnesses of previous historical epochs, just as classicists bear witness to what was the nature and function of Greek tragedy within a vanished classical culture. Literature as we know it, as Derrida has argued, is inextricably associated with democracy, that is, with freedom of speech, the freedom to say or to write anything and everything (never completely obtained, of course). Even the concept of free speech is being changed by the electronic revolution. 'Literature' is also, I further claim, concomitant with industrialization prior to the electronic revolution, with the age, now coming to an end, of the printed book, and with Cartesian and post-Cartesian conceptions of selfhood, along with their associated notions of representation and of 'reality.' All these factors are intertwined and mutually self-sustaining. Literature as a distinctive way to use language arises not from any special way of speaking or writing but from the possibility of taking any piece of language whatsoever as fictional or, on the other hand, as possibly truth-telling, as referential in the ordinary sense. This 'taking' happens according to complex historically determined conventions, codes, and protocols. That neat opposition between fiction and truth-telling is a feature of print culture. In the digitized world of the Internet, the distinction breaks down or is transformed, just as it has already been transformed by television. In television, advertising cannot always be distinguished from news, and wars like the one in Somalia or the Gulf War are presented as media spectacles, not all that different from war movies.

The computer-adept person, I am arguing, will read literature of the past differently and think of its relation to other cultural artifacts differently. I shall exemplify this with an example from Swinburne.

Swinburne's 1866 poem 'Before the Mirror,' is subtitled '(Verses Written under a Picture)' and then designated as 'Inscribed to J.A. Whistler.' The picture is Whistler's *The Little White Girl.* The poem and painting together make a double work of art, each illustrating or interpreting the other. About this interaction and about Swinburne's admirable insight into what is going on in Whistler's painting, there is much to say. Mark Samuels Lasner has been kind enough to send me a reproduction of a photograph of the painting in its original frame with a manuscript copy of the poem attached to the left and right sides of the wide frame border. The photograph is inscribed 'To Swinburne' 'from JA McNeill Whistler' (fig. 7.1). Mr. Lasner has also provided me with a reproduction of the original autograph manuscript of 'Before the Mirror,' used as copy-text for the poem in *Poems and Ballads* (1866). At some point the painting was exhibited with Swinburne's poem attached to make a double work of art. My stress now, however, is on the way the easy accessibility of both literary texts and graphic images on the World Wide Web invites and facilitates certain forms of literary study. I was able to download Swinburne's 'Before the Mirror' from my computer terminal on Deer Isle, Maine, in a few minutes from the Chadwyck-Healey database available through my university. A few more minutes' search also produced a Whistler Web site with about forty Whistler paintings in JPEG format, including *The Little White Girl*, which I downloaded in a few seconds. I was then easily able to manipulate this digital image in various ways, for example, by printing it on my Epson 800 colour printer, or by blowing up details. Here are five details I found useful in interpreting the painting: details of the fan, hand, bar, and signature, and reflected painting (figs. 7.2 and 7.3).

Such manipulations make it possible to see that the picture on the fan is a seascape or riverscape, as is the Whistler painting reflected in the mirror from the wall behind the viewer or painter. The most similar Whistler painting to the one reflected in *The Little White Girl* is *Nocturne in Blue and Silver* (fig. 7.4). Whistler has painted one of his characteristic black bars down the middle of the mirror in *The Little White Girl*. Another such painting is *Harmony in Grey and Green* (fig. 7.5). Whistler has also superimposed his signature, oddly just his last name with a period or dot after it, on the upper right hand corner of the painting, as if to call attention to the way his proper name is also a common noun, meaning someone or something that whistles, though I am at a loss to incorporate that into the reading of either painting or poem. That failure to find significance is significant. Apart from the black bar, the signature is the only thing painted on the canvas that is not reflected or able to be reflected by the mirror. Both bar and signature are outside the loop of representational mirroring and doubling, neither inside nor outside, neither before nor behind the mirror. In one sense, they are non-significant, but in another sense, they belong to a different register of significance. The black line, you may argue, might be seen as part of the mirror, a division between one piece of glass and another. Nevertheless, I answer, Whistler need not have painted it even if it was actually there. It is an intrusive bar, not centred over the middle of the mantel and cutting through the reflected Whistler painting in the background. It is like the black smudge of mortality across the surface of social life in Densher's imagination of it in an eloquent passage in Henry James's *The Wings of the Dove*. 'It was a conspiracy of silence, as the

cliché went, to which no one had made an exception, the great smudge of
mortality across the picture, the shadow of pain and horror, finding in no
quarter a surface of spirit or of speech that consented to reflect it' (2:299).
The black bar exceeds its representational function. It looks like the raw
material from which the signature is painted, as though the same brushfull
of paint were used for both or as if the straight line of the bar had been
curved and broken to make letters that still ostentatiously contain their
non-signifying material base, since they are rather crudely drawn.

Whistler's painting, like Swinburne's poem, and like the poem in its
relation to the painting, is a provocative and enigmatic series of doublings.
These vertiginous doublings and redoublings are neither of opposites nor
of mirrored identities but of differential complementarities. Perhaps the
most striking instance is the difference between the girl's expression and
that of her ghostly sister in the mirror. The girl looks calmly, meditatively, at
the wedding ring on her left hand. The girl in the mirror, however, has a
look of ineffable heavy-lidded sadness and suffering, whether of pain
received or pain imposed it is not quite possible to tell. The girl is doubled
and redoubled again by the riverscape paintings on the fan and reflected
from the wall behind the viewer and by the two oriental pots on the mantel,
one red, one a cool white and blue. The girl's hidden body, chastely
covered from sight by the white dress, is doubled by her left hand, which
looks so provocatively like female legs. Two of these finger-legs are chastely
together, while two others (one the same finger) are spread lubriciously
apart. This doubleness is picked up by the poem in the (presumably) male
speaker's questions about the girl's sexual innocence or knowledge. Is she
chaste or is she 'fallen'? Her hand is said by the girl herself to be 'a fallen
rose' that 'Lies snow-white on white snows, and takes no care' (35). The
question of her degree and kind of sexual knowledge cannot, the poem
says, be answered, not even, against common sense, by the girl herself.
Speaking of her sister ghost, her mirrored image, the girl says: 'She knows
not loves that kissed her / She knows not where' (29-30), and then the girl
says of herself: 'I cannot see what pleasures / Or what pains were' (36-7).
The girl in the painting is doubled by the roses. As the poem says, 'White
rose in red rose-garden / Is not so white' (1-2). These lines pick up a motif
frequent in Swinburne's poetry that sets red rose against white rose and
compares people, especially women or lovers, to flowers, gardens, or to the
landscape generally (in his early play *Rosamund* or in 'The Forsaken Garden' or in *Atalanta in Calydon*). The structure of doublings within doublings
in a receding series is present again in the painting in the wooden frames
within frames of the mantelpiece enclosing the black hole of the fireplace

proper, of which nothing can be said because nothing can be seen. The fireplace is an emblem of the non-knowledge so insistently asserted in echo in Swinburne's poem. The doublings in the painting are redoubled by the way the poem brackets the middle part spoken by the girl with first and last sections spoken by the poet. 'Before the Mirror' brilliantly manipulates the analogy between the girl and the seascape that the painting proposes. Presenting a painted replica of a painting raises the unanswerable question of the priority of original and mirrored copy that the poem repeats. At the exact middle of the poem, the girl asks her mirrored image:

> Art thou the ghost, my sister,
>   White sister there,
> Am I the ghost, who knows? (31-3)

Though of course someone reading Swinburne's poem could study Whistler's painting in a book of Whistler reproductions or by going to see the original painting in the Tate Gallery, the Internet makes it possible to compare them far from any good library and far from the original painting. The way in which the poem and the painting can exist side by side on the computer screen or in a single file encourages thinking of the poem and the painting as a single unit made of manifold doublings, mirrorings, and enigmatic echoings. The ease of manipulating so easily both poem and painting encourages new kinds of multimedia study. It tends to break down the divisions between picture and text that are strongly institutionalized in university departmental divisions. Moreover, these new technologies to some degree free me or any other scholar-critic from the need to own or to have access to the sort of comprehensive collection of original materials William E. Fredeman collected. This essay was prepared using all the appropriate resources of the new technologies. Nevertheless, as a person of the printed book epoch myself, though one strongly attracted by the new technologies and fairly adept at using them, as in the composition of this essay, I would relish the experience of seeing the original of Whistler's *Little White Girl* face to face, thereby interrupting her self-contemplation, or the experience of holding one of those old books in William Fredeman's collection in my hands. Like many scholars today, I remain somewhat uneasily poised between two epochs, the printed book epoch and the epoch of the Internet.

NOTE

1 See Avital Ronell, *The Telephone Book* (Lincoln: U of Nebraska P, 1989);
Laurence Rickels, 'Kafka and Freud on the Telephone,' *Modern Austrian
Literature: Journal of the International Arthur Schnitzler Association*, 22: 3/4 (1989):
211-25, and *Aberrations of Mourning* (Detroit: Wayne State UP, 1988), esp.
chapters 7 and 8; Friedrich Kittler, *Essays: Literature, Media, Information Systems*,
ed. John Johnston (Amsterdam: G+B Arts International, 1997), esp. 31-49.

ILLUSTRATIONS

Fig. 7.1 J.A.M. Whistler, *The Little White Girl: Symphony in White*. 1864, oil on
canvas; Tate Gallery, London. Photograph with inscription on frame by Mark
Samuels Lasner.
Fig. 7.2 *The Little White Girl*. Detail of bar, hand, signature, and reflected paint-
ing.
Fig. 7.3 *The Little White Girl*. Detail of fan.
Fig. 7.4 J.A.M. Whistler, *Nocturne in Blue and Silver: Cremorne Lights*. 1872, oil on
canvas, 50.2 x 74.3 cm; Tate Gallery, London.
Fig. 7.5 J.A.M. Whistler, *Harmony in Grey and Green: Miss Cicely Alexander*. 1872-4,
oil on canvas, 190.2 x 97.8 cm; Tate Gallery, London.

8

Scheherazade's 'Special Artist': Illustrations by Arthur Boyd Houghton for *The Thousand and One Nights*

Allan Life

A work of art, as the title of this volume reminds us, is haunted. It is haunted by associations conjured by its admirers, and, like Keats's Grecian Urn, a legend may haunt its very shape. Deciphering that legend, we may apprehend the spectre of a vanished mind. In the study of such Pre-Raphaelites as Dante Gabriel Rossetti, such a retrieval is especially difficult. Rossetti's imagination was possessed by a time in which he did not live and by a country he would never see. To interpret the legends that haunt his work, scholars must venture beyond biography and their own academic territories. Like so many manifestations of Romanticism, Pre-Raphaelite art demands an interdisciplinary and transcultural perspective.

Throughout his career, William E. Fredeman encouraged such a perspective, both through his own breadth of erudition and through his acknowledgement of the multivalent achievement of the Pre-Raphaelites. That acknowledgement included his promotion of artists and writers affiliated with the movement and his advocacy of new approaches to their work. In the spirit of Dick Fredeman's legacy, I am devoting this paper to the Victorian artist Arthur Boyd Houghton (1836-75).

Though his personal contacts with the Pre-Raphaelites were sporadic (see Life, 387-400), Houghton began his career by emulating the style of Ford Madox Brown. Like Rossetti, he was inspired in his mature work by a culture unfamiliar to him at first hand but intimately experienced in his domestic circle. In Rossetti's art, the ruling locale is Italy. In Houghton's, it is India.

Houghton is now best remembered as an illustrator, and his reputation has been upheld by other graphic artists of distinction. Laurence Housman

devoted a handsome volume (1896) to Houghton's illustrations, while
Edmund J. Sullivan chronicled his career in a two-part article (1923). Paul
Hogarth documented Houghton's art in a series of publications, culminat-
ing in a biography (1981). The subtitle of Edmund J. Sullivan's article, 'An
Artists' Artist,' was anticipated by no less a judge than Vincent Van Gogh,
who rejoiced in volumes of the London *Graphic* containing Houghton's
impressions of America, which he had visited as the paper's 'Special
Artist.' 'He has something mysterious like Goya,' Van Gogh wrote, 'with a
wonderful soberness which reminds me of Meryon' (qtd. in Hogarth,
Artists, 50).

However, while Houghton the draftsman and Houghton the pictorial
journalist have been appreciated, Houghton the interpreter of literature
has been neglected. Only Laurence Housman (1896) and Terry Reece
Hackford (1982) have intimated the complexity of his literary responses
and his success in continuing the interpretive sophistication of Pre-
Raphaelite book illustration. In this paper, this aspect of Houghton's
achievement will be exemplified by his illustrations for *The Thousand and
One Nights.*

When he began to illustrate this book, Houghton had already published
several designs in *Good Words, London Society*, and other periodicals. Most of
these early illustrations resemble the series of cityscapes in oil that he
began to exhibit in 1859 (see Hogarth, *A.B.H.*, 16-18). In many of them,
groups of figures are disposed across a picture plane where the geometrical centre lacks a dominant motif. Compounding this unsettled focus is
the juxtaposition of frontally disposed figures with others in profile. The
result is a series of secondary centres defined more in terms of colour and
formal structures than of 'narrative interest.' For that very reason, 'lines of
sight' – evoked by the emphatic gaze of people depicted – take on a
tangible significance for the viewer.

Though analogous effects can be identified in the work of Madox Brown
and other Pre-Raphaelites, Houghton's exploration of them endures
throughout the stylistic transitions of his career, and he employs them with
notable success to reinforce the interpretive dimension of his illustrations.
The fact that Houghton was blind in his right eye from childhood may have
reinforced his sensitivity to secondary centres and to lines of sight and
hence to their recurrence in Pre-Raphaelite art.

The turning point in Houghton's career came in 1863, when the Dalziel
Brothers, whose firm engraved most of his early designs, invited him to
contribute to their *Illustrated Arabian Nights' Entertainments.* Serialized in
weekly penny numbers by Ward, Lock, and Tyler from 17 December 1863

and in monthly parts from January 1864, the entire work, in one- and two-volume formats, was available for the Christmas trade in December 1865.[1] Though well publicized, this project lost money for the Dalziels and their partners (Dalziel, 226). Part of the reason must have been the text, a leaden, bowdlerized translation of *Les Mille et Une Nuits* of Antoine Galland, 'revised and emendated throughout' by H.W. Dulcken. As for the 'upwards of two hundred illustrations by eminent artists' promised on the title page, these were the work of eight draftsman, ranging in style from John Everett Millais to John Tenniel. Ninety of the illustrations were contributed by Thomas Dalziel, a brother of the engravers and as inconsistent a technician as the period can claim.

For some purchasers, this unwieldy edition was redeemed by the contributions of Houghton, and his ninety-three designs for the *Arabian Nights* (counting an engraving on the title page) have been cited ever since as his masterpiece as a book illustrator. 'It seems,' William Michael Rossetti recorded in 1866, Houghton 'was in India in his childhood, being the son of an Indian officer, and has some knowledge of oriental matters, which influenced his *Arabian Nights* designs' (W. M. Rossetti, *Rossetti Papers*, 196). Though his personal experience of the 'Orient' ended in infancy (Hogarth, *A.B.H.*, 11), Houghton was born in the hill station of Kotagiri in the Nilgiri Mountains in South India in 1836. His father was a captain in the East India Company's Marine, and Houghton had an older brother and friends who were officers in the Indian army. His illustrations were prepared amid 'fine collections of articles of virtu, curios, costumes, and every sort of thing invaluable for the illustrator's purposes' (Dalziel, 226). A modern critic praises the 'circumstantial detail and wide scholarship' of these designs (Caracciolo, 34).

However, Houghton's 'circumstantial detail' seems niggardly beside that of naturalistic artists who actually worked in the Middle East and South Asia; in this respect a contemporary like William Carpenter, who painted in India in the 1850s, is obviously superior (see Archer and Lightbown, 138-9). And Houghton's 'scholarship' should not be confused with the antiquarianism of such High Victorian machinery as Edward John Poynter's *Israel in Egypt*. Given the historical period of the *Nights*, his 'invaluable' wardrobe and props were anachronistic. Typically, he costumes a prince of medieval Persia (fig. 8.2) for an early Victorian durbar, complete with a *pagadi* hat more appropriate for a subordinate (cf. Doshi, 172). In comparison, the Persian nobility in John Tenniel's designs for *Lalla Rookh* (1861) are plausibly attired. At times, Houghton disdains fidelity: warriors in some designs (e.g. 747, 801)[2] are equipped with matchlock rifles; a princess of

Bengal (fig. 8.4) and Scheherazade herself (frontis.) sport hoopless crino-
lines. If Houghton's designs reflect 'scholarship,' his erudition is alien to
Victorian Orientalism.

What is certain is Houghton's growing affinity for 'Oriental' themes
during his work on Dalziels' *Nights*. For him, the 'East' meant South Asia,
and even the Biblical subjects he illustrated for the *Sunday Magazine* (1866-
70) are transported to the India of his imagination. As he was to demonstrate as a 'Special Artist' in America, a little exposure goes a long way in
Houghton's art, and if his designs for the *Nights* are deficient in factual
detail, they do contain surprising insights into South Asian culture. Ultimately, such insights have less to do with 'articles of virtu' than with
temperamental affinity and a profound understanding of British Romanticism. In Western art and folklore, Houghton encountered symbolic por-
trayals of the psyche analogous to those in South Asian iconography and
myth.

In illustrating *The Thousand and One Nights*, Houghton had every incen-
tive to draw on his conceptions of India. Dulcken commences his edition
with an excerpt from the Austrian Orientalist Joseph von Hammer-Purgstall,
who argues that 'the collection ... may be traced back to an Indian or
Persian source' (viii). This scholar's 'evidence' reflects the Orientalism of
his time, when admired works were freely associated with 'the "good"
Orient,' defined by Edward Said as 'a classical period somewhere in a long-
gone India' (99). Yet Muhsin Mahdi, the leading modern authority on the
Nights, relates the frame of the work to 'adverse circumstances in the
history of the ancient Indo-Persian royal house of the Sassanids ... The
stories ... are narrated by a wise heathen girl to a heathen king in a heathen
land in heathen times' (127). Even now, Houghton's 'Indo-Persian' slant
on the work can be justified.

In the remainder of this essay, I will discuss examples of Houghton's
designs for *The Thousand and One Nights*. My focus is on the interpretive
sophistication of his designs, which I will relate not only to the texts he
illustrated but also to current scholarship on the Arabic *Nights*. Underlying
Houghton's interpretations is a personal conception of mutual realization
through love, which the artist conceives in terms reminiscent of a wide
range of narrative and figurative traditions.

The Frame of the *Nights*

As a sort of apologia for his recycling of Antoine Galland, Dulcken prefaces
the Dalziels' edition with a quotation from Edward Lane, whose edition of

the *Nights* had appeared in 1838–41. For the first time, Lane provided English readers with a direct translation from Arabic of most of the work. Adding to the credentials of this edition were copious notes appended to each of the tales and scores of wood engravings after William Harvey, with 'accurate' depictions of Arab dress, furnishings, and architecture.

Despite the obvious claims of Lane's edition, however, some readers preferred the English versions taken from Galland, whose twelve-volume *Nuits* had been completed in 1717. After all, Galland had introduced into the West such favourites as 'Ali Baba and the Forty Thieves' and 'Aladdin, or the Wonderful Lamp' – favourites omitted by Lane since they have nothing to do with authentic manuscripts of the *Nights*. And Lane's magisterial footnotes, his one-to-one equations between Islamic Egypt and the world of the *Nights*, struck some critics as intrusive. They were also uneasy with Lane's subordination of Scheherazade, who is the pervasive narrator of the tales in the Arabic manuscripts. As these original texts confirm, the young sultana is the mistress of the cliffhanger – she is, to paraphrase the Victorian essayist James Mew, the mother of serialized fiction! (Ali, 84). Yet this fact can only be sustained by due acknowledgement of the frame of the work.

The frame begins with the tribulations and consequent derangement of Schahriar, sultan of the Persian Empire. Having executed his sultana for indulging in orgies during his absence, Schahriar resolves to marry a virgin every day and have her executed by his grand vizier the next morning. In three years, the city is depopulated of eligible victims, except for Scheherazade, the elder daughter of the vizier. This young lady is an *adiba*, a 'woman learned in the arts of literature and society' (Malti-Douglas, 21), and to save her people, she insists on being married to the sultan. Her name, *Shahrazad*, means 'of noble race,' while her sister's name, *Dinarzad*, denotes 'of noble religion' (Mahdi, 131). With Schahriar's permission, Dinarzade sleeps in the nuptial chamber, and an hour before daybreak she requests from Scheherazade 'one of the delightful stories of which you have read so many' (10).

Though Galland has been censured for attributing 'perfect beauty' to Scheherazade as well as erudition (see Sallis, 101–3), he retains more of her presence in the work and more of her ingenuity in keeping her sultan in suspense than the 'scholarly' Lane. In Dulcken, this process is facilitated by enclosing Scheherazade's entire narrative in quotation marks, while the preliminary wood engravings highlight 'introductory' events. Houghton's frontispiece shows the conclusion of the frame, where 'The sultan pardons Scheherazade' as she kneels before him. In the original drawing, Houghton may have conjured what one scholar terms 'the dream space' that, from the first night in the sultan's bedroom, 'is established ... in the relationship of the three participants' (Sallis, 94). In the published engraving, the shimmer of cascading bedcurtains has dulled into thickets of brittle hatchings, and though the love between the royal couple is suggested in their expressions and gestures, these suggest an equally coarse translation of Houghton's original.

Far more satisfactory, both as a rendering of this artist's style and as an interpretation of the frame of the *Nights*, is Houghton's frontispiece for an adaptation of Galland published by Warne in 1865, the same year Dulken's serialization was concluded. Houghton's success in portraying the dramatic context of the work is especially welcome in this bowdlerization, whose editor resolves 'so to purify the text that the most innocently-minded maiden may read [it] aloud to her brothers and sisters without scruple or compunction' (Townsend, v). In this purified version, Scheherazade exits on page 13, only to reappear 616 pages later to witness the sultan's change of heart.

At least when our maiden turned to the frontispiece of the Warne edition, she would encounter a big sister's role in the creation of the *Nights* (fig. 8.1). In this small (5 ¼ x 3 ½ in.) wood engraving, Houghton presents a Scheherazade who reconciles Victorian expectations with a sophisticated interpretation of the character. And though this design was not published in the Dulcken edition, it parallels not only the frontispiece to that volume but also Houghton's illustrations for the rest of the work.

Here and elsewhere, Houghton interprets his text in formal terms, and his illustrations must be related to his working methods. Though by 1867 Houghton spoke of drawing 'his wood-cut designs straight off on the block, taking as a rule only some two to three hours per design' (W.M. Rossetti, *Rosesetti Papers*, 242), a number of pencil studies exist for his *Arabian Nights* illustrations in which the general disposition of motifs is established (Hogarth, *A.B.H. Check-list*, 31). Even in these cases, however, many details were added when the preliminary compositions were transferred to the blocks of boxwood provided by the Dalziels. The polished upper surface of each block was lightly coated with Chinese white, and the drawing was executed in pencil and in ink, normally applied with a fine brush. Pen and ink, which is simulated in the finished engravings, was employed sparingly on the block by experienced illustrators like Houghton, who could assume that their hatchings in pencil would darken – and stiffen – when they were engraved and printed. Each separate line in these wood engravings has been cut in relief by the engraver, and comparing Houghton's surviving designs on wood with their engraved 'translations,' it is clear that the Dalziels rendered clusters of hatchings and crosshatchings better than lines in isolation. Inevitably, the process of engraving and printing – especially from electrotypes – diminished recession, and subtle facial expressions can be reduced to caricature.

In figure 8.1, Houghton employs more tone than usual; the parallel hatchings of the background display a standard method of rendering an India ink wash, though the artist must have introduced directional lines to guide the engraver. The sultan's figure is a black silhouette, highlighted with curves and flecks of the burin. The same technique is employed on Dinarzade's skirt, though the shadow on her bosom and face is more linear. As for Scheherazade, her figure and her portion of the bed consist largely of the white of the paper. She is spotlighted to a degree that is more than theatrical, since Victorian gaslight was incapable of this degree of satura-tion. Nor can this light be natural since by definition her recitations must end at daybreak. Is the lady herself its source? This possibility is both appropriate and ironic, since a male ruler (including a sultan) is sup-posed to be the sun to his consort's moon (see Galland, 1:13n).

Houghton's chiaroscuro emphasizes the sinuous curve of his heroine's bare arms. Such an absence of jewellery on elbows and wrists may seem anachronistic, though Houghton appears to remember what a reader of this 'purified' edition would hardly suspect: each hour of recitation is preceded by a night of sex, and by showing a relatively unencumbered sultana, Houghton acknowledges the fact. He also evokes a flow of energy that passes from her torso to her upturned palms and fingers fanned in a subtle curve. This gesture is related to the main divisions of his composi-tion: the vertical axis passes through Scheherazade's right palm and touches her left fingers, while the horizontal axis, which passes through her waist, coincides with the lower contour of her right hand.

Scheherazade's gesture can be variously interpreted. To a Victorian, the 'exotic' atmosphere would recall the sleights of hand of conjurers, with their introductory disclaimers (*Nothing up my sleeves, Sultan!*). Palmistry might also come to mind, and here the heroine's candour is stressed; she displays her hands to the sultan, while he conceals his own. This gesture also connotes supplication, and if the artist had banded her wrists with bracelets, he would have emphasized the 'manacled' condition of the heroine, who is less the sultan's bride than his prisoner at the outset. This Scheherazade, however, is more free than the constrained dark figure before her; accustomed to the sustained, emphatic gestures of Victorian actresses, Houghton's contemporaries could have animated her elastic pose. And Houghton would certainly have heard from his family about the *abhinaya* ('gesture language') of South Asian dance forms, frequently witnessed by military officers in India like his father and his elder brother. Especially when a dancer was seated and interpreting a text that she herself might sing, the emphasis was less on miming every word than on mirroring in repeated motions of arms and hands the prevailing sentiment of a passage.

These kinesthetic responses to Scheherazade's gesture are encouraged by the figure of Dinarzade, hovering like a shadow between the sultan and his bride. The shading on her dress emphasizes an arc defined by her sister's fingers and sweeping up to her own hands. Unlike her sister's, Dinarzade's wrists are tightly banded, and her arms are folded before her. She reminds the viewer of the dark side of the luminous heroine's predicament as well as the arts of concealment and 'enchantment' she must employ. Yet she also signals that it is Dinarzade, 'of noble religion,' who initiates each hour of storytelling. In Mahdi's words, Dinarzade serves as 'an instrument ... of secret wisdom' (131).

In Houghton's frontispiece, a literal instrument is present, leaning conspicuously in the foreground. It represents an Arabic lute or '*ūd* (literally, 'wood'), and Houghton integrates this motif into the structure of his design. The elongated pegboard (minus tuning pegs) parallels the angle of Scheherazade's upper arms and counters the downward diagonal of the fan that hangs from the ceiling. With its curved white highlights, the lower portion of the lute resembles Dinarzade's skirt, while the angles of its upper sections suggest those of her torso. The form of the sultan too is echoed in the rendering and disposition of the lute.

Analogies between such instruments and the human body are traditional. According to legend, the '*ūd* was contrived by a bereaved father to approximate the skeleton of his dead son (Shiloah, 36-7). In today's classical lute, the back (displayed by Houghton in this picture) is its 'body'; the vault of the body is composed of separate 'ribs'; the soundboard is the 'belly'; the slender fingerboard is the 'neck'; and the oblique pegbox is the 'head' (Harwood, 3-4).

In Renaissance art, playing a lute can symbolize romantic concord; the most famous example is 'Giorgione's' *Le Concert Champêtre*, which inspired one of Dante Gabriel Rossetti's sonnets on art, first published in the *Germ* (May 1850: 181). In Daniel Fischlin's interpretation, 'the interwoven expressions of the two males and one of the women are focussed on the lute as emblematic of the theatre of shared privacy that is this visual and allegorical concert' (Fischlin, 58).

The lute beside Scheherazade sits unplayed, but she is speaking, and the fall and rise of her voice are evoked by the wavelike line inscribed on the base of the bed. The low point of this curve marks the point of separation between her and the sultan, and (like analogous descents and pauses in the violin solo of Rimsky-Korsakov's *Scheherazade*), it suggests the breaks in her narration. Associations between the voice that rises from her diaphragm and the sound of the lute are reinforced by the posture of her hands, which could simulate holding the body of this instrument. Holding, but not playing; the strings must be plucked by other hands, and those must be the hands of the sultan, defensively hidden from view. Meanwhile, with her voice and gestures, she must play on him: and here is where the similar rendering of lute and sultan passes from formal resemblance to figurative analogy.

This analogy anticipates Bruno Bettelheim's response to the frame. To Bettelheim, Scheherazade's tale-telling is therapeutic, effecting psychic integration. Bettelheim especially parallels Houghton's imagery when he interprets sultan and sultana as a single fractured psyche, with Scheherazade personifying the ego; Schahriar, the id. Focussing more on Scheherazade as a character in her own right, he observes that

> only a person whose ego has learned to draw on the positive energies of the id for its constructive purposes can then set that ego to control and civilize the murderous propensities of the id. Only when Scheherazade's love for the king further inspires her storytelling – that is, when superego (the wish to deliver 'the daughters of the Muslims from slaughter') and id (her love for the king, whom she now also wishes to deliver from his hatred and depression) both endow the ego – has she become a fully integrated person. [She] ... is able to deliver the world from evil as she gains happiness for herself and for the dark other, who believed that none was available to him. As she declares her love for the king, he declares his for her ... Murderous hatred has been changed into enduring love. (89)

In his frontispiece, Houghton has not only anticipated the healing of the 'dark other' but also something of the inner reconciliation described by Bettelheim. He suggests it above all by the disposition and rendering of Dinarzade. Scheherazade's young sister hovers like her darker self, manifesting the anxieties that any woman must experience in the arms of a serial killer. Yet this dark self is the 'instrument' that initiates the process of narration, which is kaleidoscopic in its range. Such narration can only be essayed with the full-throated candour evoked by Houghton, by the kind of

psyche revered by Dryden when he spoke of Shakespeare's 'comprehensive soul.' In addition, we should remember that the psychotherapy described by Bettelheim would have been associated in South and Southeast
Asia with exorcism, whereby the 'therapist' becomes possessed by powers
that have invaded the patient. By acknowledging her own misgivings,
Scheherazade is able to minister her husband's.

The ritualistic connotations of Scheherazade's pose are clarified by the
artist's description of a Shaker ceremony he witnessed in Massachusetts a
few years later (1869). Houghton records how in the dance called the Gift
of Love, 'the meeting forms into lines for dancing, the women on one side,
the men on the other. They are holding their hands up [at chest level] with
the palms upward, as if waiting to catch the grace and blessing of the Deity'
(Hogarth, *A.B.H.*, 77).

For Houghton, the Shaker ceremony manifests the *expectation* of grace.
By making Dinarzade so conspicuous in the design and by linking her with
a musical symbol of *communitas* that sits unplayed, Houghton mirrors a
growth that continues within Scheherazade and within the sultan. Characteristically, the artist achieves this effect partly through a line of sight that
crosses the vertical axis of the composition; here, the line between the eyes
of the sultan and Scheherazade corresponds to the lower contour of
Dinarzade's right hand. There is also a secondary line of sight – from
Dinarzade's eyes to her sister's brow – and Houghton emphasizes this
invisible trajectory with the shading on the wall behind them. The result is
an acute angle thrusting rightward: an angle emphasized by the recession
of the bedframe and the diagonal of the ceiling fan. The movement of the
composition is strongly to the right, to Scheherazade's side of the picture,
as if the dark sultan is being drawn steadily towards the light through the
collaboration of all three characters in the picture. This rightward movement is so pronounced that it creates a distinctly nautical impression: with
the slanted hatchings of the background and the swirls of shadow on the
wall, the bed seems to ride the wave inscribed on its base, with the ceiling
fan for a sail and the lute for a rudder. This analogy anticipates the stories
in the collection associated with the sea, including the tale in which
Princess Giauharè comes from beneath the ocean. In Houghton's design
(413), Giauharè reclines beside an identical lute whose form matches
those of ships and the princess herself. This analogy also recalls the finest
poetic tribute to Galland's *Nights*, a rhapsodic lyric by Tennyson:

> When the breeze of a joyful dawn blew free
> In the silken sail of infancy,

The tide of time flowed back with me,
The forward-flowing tide of time.
('Recollections of the Arabian Nights,' 1-4)

In the process of enlightenment effected by these two sisters – or, figuratively, by the reconciliation of psychic forces within the same woman – Schahriar must move back as well as forward: back to the period before his disillusionment with his first wife and, in consequence, with all women. For if the bed is conceived as a boat, and if the lute is conceived as its rudder, that boat is sailing stern first! – back into the morning of life, beheld with eyes scorched dim in the glare of noon.

The Enchanted Horse

In some of his illustrations, Houghton echoes the frame of the *Nights*. Such echoes resonate through his illustrations for 'The Story of the Enchanted Horse.' Dulcken provides a reasonably faithful translation of Galland, who obtained this story (along with such favourites as 'Aladdin' and 'Ali Baba') from Hanna Diab, 'a Maronite Christian Arab from Aleppo' (Irwin, 16-17). At the opening, an Indian presents a mechanical flying horse to the king of Persia. Angered by the Indian's effrontery in requesting the hand of the king's daughter, the crown prince of Persia, Firouz Schah, mounts the horse and impetuously sails off on it before he learns how to make it descend. After he discovers the lever 'peg' to accomplish this, he lands at night on the terraced roof of a palace, which Galland sets in Bengal. Creeping into a bedchamber, he discovers a beautiful princess asleep on a bed elevated on a sofa, with her women sleeping around her. In his Gallic elaboration of Hanna Diab's narrative, Galland urges that 'instantly [the prince] felt the flame of love in his heart.' '"Ciel! ... Ne dois-je pas m'attendre à un esclavage certain, dès qu'elle aura ouvert les yeux"' or, in Dulcken's clanking rendition, '"Oh heavens! ... Must I not expect inevitable thraldom when those eyes are unclosed, which must add a yet greater lustre and brilliancy to that assemblage of charms? Yet I must be content to submit, since I cannot quit the spot, and necessity compels me to await the decree of my destiny!"' (728; Galland, 2:471).

The attraction is mutual; on waking, the princess of Bengal grants Firouz Schah her protection, and prevails on him to remain in her palace two months. She and the prince hunt together, and they converse at such length and with such vacuity that Galland seems to be penning a manual for his patroness, the 'Marquise d'O,' on the art of speaking while sleeping. Finally, they agree to elope on the flying horse. Off they sail to Persia where complications (naturally) ensue, with the princess carried off on the horse by its Indian inventor. She is rescued by the sultan of 'Cashmere,' who decapitates the Indian and proposes to the princess. But she remains loyal to her prince and feigns madness to prevent the sultan from marrying her. The prince arrives in Cashmere disguised as a healer of lunacy, and amid his ritual 'cures' for the princess, they mount the horse and escape to Persia.

In the meantime, where is the 'sultan' of Bengal? His existence is acknowledged when the princess debuts and exits, but in the two months of his daughter's dalliance with a stranger he is never introduced. However, though the unchaperoned courtship of the young lovers strains credulity, the result is a private ritual analogous to the nights of Scheherazade and her sultan, though in this story the verbalizing is mutual. Echoes of their encounters abound in later literature, from Porphyro kneeling by Madeline's bed in Keats's 'The Eve of St. Agnes' to the erotic interview between Guendolen and Sebald in William Morris's 'Rapunzel.'

In his first illustration for the story (725), Houghton records the distress of the king of Persia at the disappearance of the horse – with the crown prince on its back. The original design, which the Dalziels preserved on the woodblock (Hogarth, *A.B.H. Check-list*, 34; Housman, pl. 3), displays a command of pictorial dynamics and characterization unrivalled in the British art of this period. Regrettably, the published version, engraved from a photograph of the design transferred to another block, is a graphic equivalent of the text's Dulckenized French. Especially deplorable is the extinction of the king's expression, a blend of aggression and panic directed downward (via a diagonal with an upward thrust) at the Indian magician, who coils like a viper at the foot of the dais. Behind the king, the eyes of courtiers are turned to the sky, in a medley of lines of sight that act as foils to his own fixed gaze. The king's dismay, and perhaps his vulnerability, is shown in the loss of his left sandal, which sits empty beside his foot; his threat of retribution ('your head shall be the forfeit, if, in three months, the prince my son does not return in safety' [727]) is mirrored in a scimitar, whose blade he is drawing from its scabbard.

The next illustration (fig. 8.2) is captioned, 'Prince Firouz Schah beseeching the protection of the princess of Bengal,' which suggests that the prince has traded places with the Indian in the previous design. Other than having their hands clasped before them, however, there is little resemblance between the two figures, and whereas the scene in the Persian court portrayed divergent lines of sight, all eyes here are fixed on the prince. With the eyes of the princess opened, the 'thraldom' Firouz Schah anticipated has possessed him, and his 'destiny' is decreed. Houghton's challenge is to substantiate the mutual gaze of prince and princess, while evoking the elective affinities between them.

In manipulating the lines of force within an oblong rectangle, Houghton employs devices he had perfected in his early canvases of London life. The vertical axis is practically vacant, though it meets the contours of the prince's hands and his shadow on the bed. The horizontal axis coincides with the top of the mattress and the lower edge of the table on the right, but its point of intersection with the vertical axis lacks a centring motif. Its absence reinforces the prominence of secondary centres, which are defined by 'playing black against white,' in Laurence Housman's epitome of Houghton's 'common method' in his designs. And the upper right of this illustration, which consists almost entirely of the page where it is printed, shows Houghton's appreciation for what Housman terms 'the value of "whites"':

> his tone scheme ... [is] at once full of colour and colourless. As black and white it is admirable, bold, effective, and sweeping; yet all that it suggests is curiously bound down to monochrome. It ... seems only to say 'white is white, and black is black, and midway lies grey.' (19-20)

In this design, the sombre knot of the prince's hands constitutes a secondary focal point, and so do the black eyes and hair of the princess and two of her women, who are peering through the silk curtains. Beneath the descending triangular folds of the silks on the left and a cluster of anklets, the bare foot of the standing woman forms another centre, reinforcing the tendency to weight an oblong rectangle on the left (see Arnheim, 47). The angle of this foot, placed above the edge of the dais and the artist's signature, corresponds to the diagonal axis ascending through the geometrical centre of the design and into the darkly shaded cheek of the prince. This upward diagonal is weakened, however, by the vertical group of women massed behind the prince and by the absence of motifs in the upper right. In contrast, the downward diagonal axis coincides with the eyelid of the standing woman on the left, the lower jawline of the princess, and the angle of the princes's left shank. Parallel to this diagonal axis is the line of sight from the eye of the woman who stands above the princess to the eye of the prince. In comparison, the line of sight between the eyes of prince and princess is less emphatically slanted, and though the eddying silks between the couple define a movement from her to him, the prince's dark shadow ascending the bed is one of several devices that oppose the usual narrative direction and encourage a movement to the left. The contour of his back is an upward counter to the downward diagonal axis, and his right foot parallels that of the woman who stands on the left. The form of his billowing white sleeves is inverted into the mattress overlapping the arm of the sofa. And a descending, leftward movement is reinforced by the opening cut into the wooden frame of the sofa, which echoes the silhouette of the head and shoulders of the princess.

The most conspicuous parallel, however, is between the profiles of the future lovers. Like Dante Gabriel Rossetti, Houghton manifests 'elective affinity' with a family likeness. There is in addition a clear resemblance between the princess and the two women who eye the prince through the curtains. Like the shadowy servants converging in the background, these denizens of the *zenana* multiply the princess's line of sight and manifest the ambivalent emotions of a woman finding a handsome intruder in her bedroom. In South Asia, a stare exchanged between a woman and a man was more than provocative, especially when accompanied by the woman's naked shoulder. Yet the princess cocoons her silks and her hair round her torso, and the woman above her exposes only a single eye as she rears on tiptoe. The woman standing on the left grips the dais in suspended retreat and pulls the silk against her breasts. Beneath those veils, however, the same woman has turned at the waist to contemplate the prince, and her pose evokes the titillation of an erotic dance. Houghton is playing on Western fantasies of *purdah*, of women secluded in a Turkish bath of famished lust, but he does so without violating the courtly tone of his text, where love at first sight is couched in the language of 'hospitality, humanity, and politeness,' to quote the princess (729). Even the prince's bare feet show a respect for 'Indian' etiquette as well as the dramatic necessity of making as little commotion as possible. But they also remind us that this bedroom for him is sacred ground, where the flame of love, as Galland says, has risen in his heart. Transfixed by the eyes of his hostess, his dark figure bends with monumental solidity, weighted by the downward thrust of the triangular folds of his leggings and the Celtic knot of his waist cloth.

To provide further weight to the lower right of his composition and to reinforce the downward vectors that connect the two lovers, Houghton sets beside a table leg an Arabic lute identical to that in figure 8.1. Had he emphasized the upward thrust of its head or pegboard, this instrument would be associated with the prince, whose back ascends at the same angle. But the head of the lute is largely covered by the edge of the table, directing attention to the body or back of the instrument and the soundboard or belly with its strings bisecting the soundhole or 'rose.' Given the strong diagonal connecting the lute with the princess, the soundboard suggests a photographic negative of her torso, with her face analogous to the black oval of the 'rose' and her hair corresponding to the grey that surrounds it. In a 'positive' analogy, the dark hatchings on the back of the lute suggest her hair, with the soundboard approximating her face and torso. Though these parallels are merely implicit in this design, they become important in a later illustration.

The hatchings on the body of the lute also echo the shadow of the prince, sliding up the sofa and mattress towards the princess. The verticality of his shadow is echoed in a vase on the table. The slender vase and the neck of the swelling lute seem near enough in shape to merge, except for the intervention of the table. Here again are analogous shapes that Houghton will explore as the tale proceeds.

As in figure 8.1, there is an aqueous quality to this interior. The Bengali ladies and their visitor dwell in light that is fluid, yet tangible enough to be etched like glass. By this late point in the series, Houghton has mastered an expressive freedom in delineation that helps to explain the enthusiasm of other graphic artists for his work. Designs like this one convey the physical process involved in their creation, and for kindred spirits such an evocation is substantive, encouraging an emulation of this creative action. If Houghton 'became his admirers,' he endured in their nerves as much as in their memories.

In this case, the hatchings on the curtains evoke a shifting fabric, fragile as silkworms' gauze yet formidable as water – or fire. The princess and her two companions seem to emerge from a descending river: was Houghton acquainted with the myth of the river Gaṅgā's descent from heaven and how the river goddess was wed to Śiva in the very act of flowing through his hair? He would certainly have known of the water nymphs of Greek mythology and their sisters of Hindu myth, the apsarasas. Especially current in Victorian Britain were the mythical heroines classified by Barbara Fass Leavy (1994) as swan maidens: denizens of the waters (like Giauharè in Galland's *Nights* and de La Motte Fouqué's *Undine*) who marry mortals and suffer as a result. The basis of their suffering is epitomized in Wendy Doniger's interpretation of Hans Christian Andersen's 'The Little Mermaid': her immortality depends on her lack of feet, but without feet 'she cannot dance (surely a euphemism for the sexual act) ... Through the fatal link between sexuality and death, when the mermaid gets feet, she can dance, and love, and bleed (menstruate?), and suffer – and finally die' (*Splitting the Difference*, 184). The pairing of the princess, shrouded in a vaporous cloud, with the standing woman on the left with her exposed bare feet recalls the transformation scenes in such tales. Houghton presents the initiation into love of his princess in somewhat ominous terms, reminiscent of the 'shadow self' of Scheherazade in his frontispiece for the *Nights*.

Such mythological parallels reinforce the trepidation of Galland's prince, who must sacrifice his freedom in the flame of his own heart. The hatchings between his eyes and those of the princess wave much like flames, and this blend of fire and water testifies to the elemental – and unquenchable – nature of their passion. In Hindu mythology, there is a fire beneath the sea that issues from the mouth of a subterranean mare: a notion with its parallels in Victorian Scotland, where country folk believed in the kelpie or water horse (see Keightley, 360, 385). The fire under the waves is directly associated by Kālidāsa, the Sanskrit poet, with the passion of Śiva for Pārvatī, his dark bride of the mountain:

> and his thirst for the pleasures of loving
>   never became any less in him
> as the fire that burns below the ocean
>   is never satisfied by the rolling waters.   (Heifetz, 131)

Given such precedents, it is notable how 'equine' Houghton has made the *zenana* and the princess herself. While Galland's description of this room conjures rococo elegance, Houghton presents an interior of bedouin – or 'early Maratha' – simplicity. The prodigious hair of the princess curls round her like a mane, and her mattress rests on a tasseled rug like the caparison of the horse on which, in Galland's narrative, she rides off to hunt.

In Houghton's next illustration, 'Prince Firouz Schah Declares His Love for the Princess of Bengal' (733), the princess sits cross-legged on a couch in a swan-like attitude, while the bare right foot protruding from her skirt is distinctly hoof-like. Above her head perches a cockatoo, who bends towards her ear. In addition to their reputation as voyeurs and gossips (see the story in Dulcken, 24-6), such domesticated parrots are liminal creatures – birds who seldom fly, but use their feet like hands; birds that talk, but are not human. This cockatoo seems to exhort the princess to board a wingless horse for a 'liminal' elopement from the security of Bengal. Meanwhile, Firouz Schah is reassuring the princess, with a gesture that anticipates placing a ring on her left hand. In a Hindu marriage, the analogy for a wedding ring (besides the wedding *tali* round the neck) is a pair of rings banding the second toes; on the big toe of her right foot, Houghton's princess already wears a ring.

This minor detail becomes significant in the next illustration (fig. 8.3), where the couple is in full flight. Riding the mechanical horse sidesaddle, the princess grips her right sandal with her bare left sole, as its sandal is suspended in the air below her. This sandal floats before a pinnacle of rock, crossed by crescents of cloud reminiscent of the silks in fig. 8.2. Like the princess herself in this illustration, the sandal is dark. But its mouth is bordered with pearls. In addition to suggesting the gravitational force defied by the ponderous horse, in its disposition and rendering this sandal has multiple connotations.

When it is related to mythical archetypes, this motif demonstrates Houghton's capacity for embroidering Galland's narrative. The idea of a beautiful woman's shoe descending to some unknown place recalls the story in Strabo's *Geography* of the Egyptian courtesan Rhodopis, whose sandal was stolen by an eagle. It proved a fortunate theft for Rhodopis, for the eagle dropped the sandal into the lap of Pharaoh, who mounted a search for its owner. When she was discovered, Pharaoh married her (Strabo, 8:93, 95). Folklorists have identified similar narratives in many cultures and periods (see Dundes); 'Cinderella' is the most enduring Western version. Contemplating the ubiquity of such stories, Wendy Doniger enquires, 'Why do [they] regard a woman's foot as the key to her identity? Why do some variants regard a ring … as the equivalent of the shoe in other variants? What do a ring and a shoe mean, together, for the cultural formulation of a woman's sexual identity?' (*Implied Spider*, 94).

In his psychoanalytic reading of 'Cinderella,' Bruno Bettelheim confronts these questions. Like Doniger (*Implied Spider*, 140-1), he argues that 'the shoe must be a slipper that does not stretch, or it would fit some other girl, such as the stepsisters.' Also like Doniger, he praises Charles Perrault for his 'subtlety … in … saying the shoe was made of glass, a material that does not stretch, is extremely brittle and easily broken.' Focusing on versions of the tale in Perrault and the Brothers Grimm, he continues:

> A tiny receptacle into which some part of the body can slip and fit tightly can be seen as a symbol of the vagina. Something that is brittle and must not be stretched because it would break reminds us of the hymen; and something that is easily lost at the end of the ball when one's lover tries to keep his hold on his beloved seems an appropriate image for virginity … Cinderella's running away from this situation could be seen as her effort to protect her virginity. (264-5)

Bettelheim finds these identifications confirmed when Cinderella passes the 'shoe test.' Cinderella accepts the prince 'because he … lovingly

accepts her vagina in the form of the slipper, and approves of her desire for a penis, symbolized by her tiny foot fitting within the slipper-vagina ... as she slips her foot into the slipper she asserts that she, too, will be active in their sexual relationship.'

Doubtless to lessen the anxiety (or worse) aroused by this interpretation, Bettelheim marshals 'support' from the ring ceremony at a wedding, where 'the ring, a symbol for the vagina, is given by the groom to his bride; she offers him in return her outstretched finger' and thereby acknowledges that, 'from now on, her husband to some degree will have possession of her vagina, and she of his penis.' Noting that in the Brothers Grimm 'Cinderella' the slipper is gold instead of glass, Bettelheim finds a direct equivalent to the wedding ritual (271-2).

Houghton's design corresponds to portions of Bettelheim's reading. On a narrative level, it often does so in reverse: the princess of Bengal does not require a prince to achieve royal status, and she has lost her slipper, not while her 'lover tries to keep his hold' on her but while she is holding onto him. The grip of her naked foot on her remaining sandal can suggest exhilaration, and it is likely she has kicked off – not lost – a shoe that appears too narrow for her. Interpreting 'Indo-Persian' narratives in a Victorian culture where 'well bred' women bared their feet only in front of intimates, Houghton shows another royal lady, the princess Badoura, ascending out of her left sandal as she embraces her other half, Prince Camaralzaman (328). In Victorian terms, the baring of the hoof-like (or, following Bettelheim, 'phallus-like') foot of the 'crinolined' princess in the preceding courtship scene is a sign of erotic commitment, and the ring on her big toe encourages this reading.

Bettelheim comes nearest to Houghton's design when he equates the loss of the glass slipper with a threat to Cinderella's virginity. The sandal of Houghton's princess is not glass, but its opening bordered with pearls strengthens its connection with virginity and its resemblance to the vulva. In a vertical division of the psyche that is fundamental to Hindu iconography and is paralleled in many other cultures, the left side of the 'subtle body' is the 'feminine' side, and in placing the left sandal of the princess against a narrow pinnacle, Houghton symbolizes the surrender of her virginity, at least on a psychic level.

Combined with the slipper, the pinnacle of rock is phallic, and (thinking of Bettleheim's interpretation of the ring ceremony), the descending bands of cloud on this rock can suggest the stages of sliding a ring onto a bride's finger. However, such identifications undercut the formal parallels established by Houghton in the design, and these parallels encourage a figurative reading not only of the pinnacle and slipper but also of the horse and its riders. The parallel angles of the slipper and the decorated 'horse collar' reinforce the resemblance between the pearl-studded mouth of the slipper and the collar, and both shapes are echoed by the studded reins. The disposition of the slipper against the right slope of the pinnacle corresponds to that of the collar against the bodies of the riders as well as their mount. In this context, the pinnacle becomes an elongated and 'growing' analogy for the combined forms of the two lovers, with the shade on its left side corresponding to the dark hatchings on the princess. The intersecting streamers of cloud that frame the pinnacle echo the arms of the lovers as well as the backward swirl of the lady's veil, which suggests her escape from *purdah*. The ramp of cloud beneath her descending slipper parallels the windswept skirts of the young couple, and all three misty arcs suggest the speed of their flight despite the apparent immobility of their vehicle.

Such a union, Houghton suggests, has become possible through the sacrifice by the princess of the kind of luminous isolation she enjoyed in figure 8.2, where she seems to inhabit the middle world that stretches beneath her. Her reward, it seems, is ascent to a higher plane of realization, though the darkening of her form is notable, and, if anything, she is even more 'equine,' with hair resembling the tail of the magic horse. Though it parallels the clasping of her hands on the prince's chest, the clenching of her left foot over the right suggests more than infatuation; the loss of a shoe may connote distress and regression, as we find in the first illustration for the tale, in which the king of Persia has shed his left sandal amid the uproar following the disappearance of the prince. Once the horse lands, Houghton's princess must either limp about with one shoe or go barefoot; both alternatives enforce an earthbound status and vulnerability unfamiliar to her. Here is where Doniger's comment on 'The Little Mermaid' is especially pertinent.

The fact remains that this illustration is one of Houghton's most jubilant, and the expressions of the lovers reinforce this impression. So, in a more oblique fashion, does the mount they share. Less the 'skilfully carved' facsimile described in Dulcken (723) than a levitated hobby horse, it matches certain features of the princess's bed in figure 8.2: note especially the fringed caparison. And there is another object in figure 8.2 that this wonder horse resembles, though we must set the design on its left side to perceive the fact. Viewed this way, the horse's abdomen resembles the body of a lute; its back highlighted by the sweeping skirts, the soundboard; its neck, the equivalent part of the lute; and its head – turned by the artist to conceal the eyes and mouth – the 'head' or pegbox of that instrument. Turning the design right way up again, the lovers themselves take on something of the same configuration. And this analogy is pursued in Houghton's next design (fig. 8.4), captioned simply, 'The Princess of Bengal.'

In this scene, the princess is not in her native kingdom but in 'Cashmere,' and she is feigning madness to elude marriage to its sultan. Her performance is heightened by her loathing for a ruler who tried to marry her after a day's acquaintance, a 'violent and tyrannical' action that she repels with 'extravagant' speech and gestures so menacing that she 'seemed ready to tear him to pieces.' The physicians he summons get a similar reception; she greets them with 'violent marks of aversion, endeavouring to tear their faces if they came near her.' They content themselves with prescribing 'potions, which she made no objection to swallow, as she well knew that it was in her own power to continue her feigned madness as long as she pleased' (742, 744).

When the prince appears disguised as a physician, the princess reveals the heartache that motivates her performance. At the beginning of this scene, the prince has viewed her apartment through a lattice that opens on a balcony and spied 'his beloved princess, seated in a negligent posture, and singing, with tears in her eyes, a song in which she deplored her unhappy destiny, which, perhaps, would deprive her for ever of the sight of him she so tenderly loved' (744). In Lane, there is a translation from Arabic of such a song, though it is sung by 'a handsome slave-girl' in Persia, not by the princess:

> Think not that absence hath made me forget: for if I forget you, what shall I remember?
> Time passeth; but never shall our love for you end: in our love for you we will die and be raised. (2: 530)

Houghton shows the princess in a virtual mirror image of her pose in the earlier engraving of the prince declaring his love. In this engraving the prince, with his white *pagadi* hat, has been replaced (again, in a mirrored substitution) with a fountain. Even the cockatoo from the courtship scene is remembered, with a ragged feather in the princess's back hair. In the 'courtship' scene, the princess wore a sleeveless bodice with fur trim at the collar and bust; here, her arms are sheathed in sleeves and she wears a jerkin apparently composed of fur.

Comparison with figure 8.3 reveals additional transformations. The fringed caparison of the flying horse is echoed in the tasselled ceiling fan, which is magnified in the carpet on the floor, with a billow that matches the central rib of the fan. Both the fan and the carpet recall the blanket of the princess's sofa bed in figure 8.2. The tuft adorning the head of the horse is parallelled by the feather in the hair of the princess.

These motifs are rigidly structured around the central vertical and horizontal axes. The tilted head of the princess is bisected by the vertical axis, and a line drawn at the halfway point between the horizontal axis and the design's upper border meets the top of the fountain, the crest of the lady's hair, and the top of the cushion on the right. The tectonics of the design are echoed in the niche or cupboard in the upper right, which corresponds to the 'lattice' through which the prince is able to see the princess. Instead of the prince's face, Houghton frames a vase in this enclosure. Though this object recalls the 'potions' inflicted on the prin-cess, its disposition suggests a symbolic meaning.

Since this vase is a more bulbous equivalent of the vessel sitting on the table at the right of figure 8.2, and since the vase in this earlier design can be associated with at least a portion of the prince's vertical shadow, this object in the niche could be interpreted as a symbol for the absent male. However, the swelling lower portion is distinctly womb-like, and the vase is a more symmetrical version of the pinnacle of rock in figure 8.3, which was analogous to *both* the lovers. In figure 8.2, furthermore, the slender vase is juxtaposed with the Arabic lute which in this engraving is balanced on the folded legs of the princess. Given the association between the horse in fig. 8.3 and the shape of the lute, her devotion to this instrument matches her obsession. While riding on the horse, the princess gripped her right foot with her left; here, she presses her concealed left foot against the body of the lute, which in figure 8.2 was linked with herself at the first 'sight of him she so tenderly loved.'

Interpretation of both the vase and the lute is related to that of the fountain on the left. Here, the aqueous veils of figure 8.2 and the vapours of figure 8.3 have been compressed into a shape as clearly bounded as a lamp shade. The fountain rises from a circular base, and inscribed on the flank of this base is an Arabesque motif that inverts the upward thrust of the vase in the niche. In the courtship scene, the princess gives her left hand to the prince. In this mirror image of that pose, her right fingers drift in the spray from the fountain, while her left fingers hover above the fingerboard of the lute. The gesture of her right hand reinforces the connection between the crest of water and the prince, and this, in turn, associates the prince with the upper portions of the lute. As for the Arabesque motif on the base of the fountain, it strongly suggests the female generative organs (Sanskrit, *yoni*) and their representation in Hindu iconography. Fountain, lute, and vase connote a horizontal division between masculine (upper) and feminine (lower), a division at variance with the symbolic androgyny in figure 8.3, in which the split within the pinnacle of rock and the union it symbolized was presented vertically. Neither 'division' nor 'split,' however, accords with the ideal fusion that Houghton is suggesting: the stem of the vase rises gradually from the base; the strings bond the head and neck of the lute to the belly, and bring forth its latent sound.[3] And the water in the fountain is apparently recycled: like the love celebrated by the slave girl in Lane, its circuit will not end; it dies back to its place of origin only to rise again. This place of origin is the circular tank, rendered oval through recession and thereby linked with the oval belly of the lute. The place where the fountain rises corresponds to the 'rose' of the lute, which Houghton lowers to the vertical centre of the belly. The sound of the water – its intermittent plash against the fingers of the princess – evokes the harmony of love within the unplayed lute.

Swirled around her legs, the skirts of the princess are also oval, and their billowing folds recall the 'swan maiden' analogy of figure 8.2 and the swan-like posture of the courtship scene. Here, the lower half of her figure is clearly associated with the base of the fountain, and hence with the belly of the lute and the 'womb' of the vase. The upper half of her body is parallel with the fountain, and the tilt of her head approximates the oblique angle of the head of the lute. Brooding on the concord she achieved with the prince aboard the enchanted horse, the princess has become an emblem of her yearning for that concord. Unlike the emblems that surround her, however, she cannot achieve that ideal harmony without the prince; there is a stark division in her form between upper and lower body, between the hair and fur above and the liquid satin below. In mythopoeic terms, the princess has become an anomaly: a sort of inverted centaur with the lower extremities of a swan maiden and an equine torso. These 'mare'-like qualities, furthermore, parallel the madness that she feigns: tearing objectionable males to pieces is typical of the mare women of Hindu mythology. Wendy Doniger has chronicled the attributes of these females (who include the 'dark goddesses' of the Hindu pantheon). They present the antithesis of the nurturing 'cow': they are phallic and murderous and behave much as the princess behaves to her tormentors (see O'Flaherty, 149-280). In this design, the jutting head of the lute, with the tuning pegs flattened to an inlaid pattern, is distinctly reminiscent of a blade – or a fang; and the fingers of the princess are curled like ivory claws above the strings.

Perhaps to emphasize the resemblance, Houghton places a ring, not on the customary finger but on the 'middle' and longest one.

The princess, it might be argued, is only feigning a mare while she nurtures the organic union with the prince embodied in the objects around her. But to resist the 'violent and tyrannical' imposition of the sultan she must resort to the 'equine' qualities that were apparent from her first appearance in figure 8.2. Similarly, Scheherazade, resisting the greater violence and tyranny of her own sultan, must draw on her darker self to defeat the darkness within him. In the process, she transforms the sultan into someone she can unite with while uniting the forces within herself.

Aladdin and His Lamp

In such designs, Houghton follows the Pre-Raphaelites in investing circumstantial detail with figurative meaning; in Erwin Panofsky's phrase, he creates 'disguised symbolism' (1:135, 141). Not surprisingly, this power is conspicuous in Houghton's illustrations for 'The History of Aladdin, or the Wonderful Lamp.' Coming quite late in the series, these twenty designs show the artist in full command of a stylistic repertoire he had evolved in his illustrations for earlier tales, and he succeeds both in interpreting the story itself and in relating it to the frame of the *Nights*. Though a selection of these designs can only suggest this achievement, it reinforces points already made about Houghton's depictions of the frame and of 'The Enchanted Horse.'

Unlike most tales in the *Nights*, the story of Aladdin is still proverbial, despite (or because of?) the fact that it is largely the invention of Antoine Galland. Recollection of this 'History' is encouraged by Houghton in his first illustration (fig. 8.5), which anticipates high points of the entire narrative. To the right of the central axis, the African magician is greeting Aladdin as the son of his long-lost (Chinese!) brother. In the text, the magician 'threw his arms round Aladdin's neck, and embraced and kissed him repeatedly' (576). Houghton shows the boy almost smothered by an Arab of stupendous height. Adding to the magician's stature is a tree snaking up behind him: its tentacles and billowing 'pollen' ascend to a ramshackle edifice populated by regal mandarins. Beneath the Islamic gate sways a lady under a parasol, while a destitute Chinese man slouches on a crate beside her. Before her some street boys are huddling.

The ascending tree evokes the powers within the magic lamp, an association reinforced by the Chinese lanterns to the right of its trunk. It also anticipates Aladdin's climb from a street boy to the son-in-law of a 'sultan.'

As for the perilous balcony on which the courtiers balance above the gateway, it portends Aladdin's fall from grace when the magician exchanges a 'new lamp for old' and transports Aladdin's palace to Africa – along with his princess. Deprived of his wife and the magic to regain her, Aladdin wanders in despair, like the dejected fellow on the crate. Yet the princess of China, like her sister in Bengal, holds the fort till Aladdin arrives to save her. She repels the advances of the magician, and after Aladdin appears, she is instrumental in poisoning her captor and regaining possession of the lamp. In the process, she comes down to earth – often a qualified victory, as Wendy Doniger reminds us, but preferable to the insubstantial and confining world in which she has been raised. Here, Houghton suggests the evolution of the princess by placing his stately lady on the ground. The street boys both correspond to Aladdin's activity at the inception of the plot and anticipate the acquisition of worldly knowledge – and cunning – he requires to use magic wisely. Soon enough he surpasses the magician himself, whose eyes are black with fraud and avarice. The mongrel at lower left, leaping in jubilation at this 'reunion,' parodies the moral stature of Aladdin's 'uncle.'

As in the 'Enchanted Horse' designs, Houghton associates this scene with fairy tales. The most obvious echo is of 'Jack and the Beanstalk,' which Bettelheim relates to a boy's confrontation with his oedipal complex (with 'father' personified by the ogre) and his discovery of the resources and advantages of manhood (187-93). In Houghton's illustration, the father is a towering surrogate complete with vaporous horns, and the origin of the beanstalk is suggested by the sprout in the right foreground. In some respects, the fairy tale and this 'History' are opposites: Jack receives the magic beans from a benefactor, while Aladdin wins his magic through the bungling of an enemy. But the tales end on a similar note, with Jack cutting down the beanstalk and Aladdin relying on the love of his wife and his people instead of magic. Houghton anticipates this conclusion in the lower right, where shards of a lamp are strewn in the dust.

Given its evocation of an 'Oriental' street, the design recalls two staples of South Asian magic, at least according to Oriental Annuals and the memoirs of sahibs. The first is the 'Mango Tree Trick,' where a street magician conjures a thriving plant from a sprout. As Lee Siegel notes, this trick was associated with the Parijata, 'a magical, wish-granting tree' (165). The second is the 'Indian Rope Trick,' which begins with a rope ascending into the air. Accounts of the trick vary, but they feature an ascent up the rope either by a young assistant or by the magician himself. Atop the rope, the climber becomes invisible and simulated dismemberment follows, with pieces of the victim falling to earth. This grisly spectacle is followed by the 'resurrection' of the performer (see Siegel, 189, 197-221). This 'Rope Trick' corresponds to aspects of the 'Beanstalk' tale as well as simulations of death and rebirth found in many *rites de passage*.

Aspects of such *rites* are conspicuous in the next illustration, 'The magician commanding Aladdin to give up the lamp' (fig. 8.6). Equipped with a magic ring provided by his 'uncle,' Aladdin retrieves the lamp from a subterranean cavern. When the magician demands that Aladdin hand him the lamp without leaving the mouth of the cave, the boy refuses. The enraged magician throws 'a little perfume' on the fire beside him, and 'he had hardly pronounced two magic words when the stone which served to shut up the entrance to the cavern returned of its own accord to its place' (584).

Though Houghton's magician makes an unlikely shaman, this illustration does present analogies for the liminal phase of initiation into manhood. Aladdin himself occupies the ambiguous, 'invisible' status attributed by Victor Turner to the liminal 'passenger,' who is at once dead and unborn. He is also, during this phase of initiation rites, untouchable by the initiated, from whom he must be secluded: note that the magician cannot follow Aladdin into the cavern, portrayed by Houghton as both sepulchral and womb-like. It seems the magician cannot touch Aladdin either – not in this liminal phase of the boy's experience – and Houghton embodies the magician's frustration with a frenzied ogre bellowing from the fire. This thrashing monster corresponds to the grotesque and shifting nature of such transformative rituals. It also recalls their ludic aspects, since the magician, for all his occult knowledge, is a hotheaded fool. After years spent locating the magic lamp and an arduous journey to China in search of it, he relinquishes its powers in a moment of bad temper. For Aladdin, however, the result is the kind of liminality defined by Turner: 'a realm of pure possibility whence novel configurations of ideas and relations may arise.' In a realm that is 'essentially unstructured (which is at once destructured and prestructured),' neophytes are brought 'into close connection with deity or with superhuman power, with ... the unbounded, the infinite, the limitless' (Turner, 94-9). The raging ogre anticipates the fertile genies of the magic ring and, once Aladdin reenters society, of the lamp itself.

Houghton visualizes the 'destructured' nature of Aladdin's initiation. The angled contours of the rocks and the jagged, painterly hatchings of the foreground convey an ongoing act of creation. Amid these erupting vectors and the billowing curves of smoke, the only stable shapes are those

of the magician and Aladdin, and despite the magician's downward gesture, they are separated by opposing lines of force, including the sluggish
drift of the magician's head cloth. That trailing head cloth and the
impercipient stare of the magician's shadow self in the fire help to cancel
any line of sight between the figures. If the magician can see anything, it is
the lamp, thrust into Aladdin's bosom and pressed with his left hand. And
Houghton's rendering of this lamp suggests a reason for its potency.

By emphasizing the circular opening at the top of the lamp and its
highlighted rim, Houghton fuses two magic objects. Imprisoned in the
cavern, Aladdin is delivered when he rubs the magic ring on his finger.
This action produces a genie, who also comes to his aid when the magician
steals the lamp and transports Aladdin's palace to Africa. Adapting
Bettelheim's interpretation of the ring ceremony, a ring on a finger connotes an interpenetration between male and female forces; rubbing the
ring (female) while it is on the finger (male) is analogous to playing the
strings of the lute that bond the female belly with the masculine neck and
head. Similarly, rubbing the magic lamp merges circular 'womb' with
phallic spout: a magic equivalent of inserting a wick into the oil in the belly
of a lamp and lighting that wick with a flame whose generation is also
symbolic of sexual intercourse, with 'male' and 'female' sticks or metals in
creative friction.

Consistent with this interpretation, the magician can only retrieve the
lamp with the help of a youth like Aladdin, whose social identity is the
proverbial tabula rasa. The magician is seeking to control a power whose
origin he has relinquished within himself; in nineteenth-century Romantic terms, his motive for seeking the lamp is exclusively 'masculine.' He
aspires to become 'the most powerful monarch of the universe' (584), and,
as his callous betrayal of Aladdin confirms, he lacks the 'feminine' gift of
imagination, with the empathy it confers. In Aladdin's experience, he
resembles the ogre in 'Jack and the Beanstalk'; both boys have mothers but
no fathers, and they confront their oedipal anxieties with a vengeance
courtesy of these surrogates. Galland's tale makes this association explicit,
with the slobbering paternalism of the magician transformed into chastise-
ment and homicide.

If the magician lacks the 'feminine,' Aladdin's mother fears the 'masculine' and its encroachments. When she inadvertently rubs the magic lamp
and the genie appears, she faints. In a ludic complement to figure 8.6,
Houghton shows her hiding her eyes with her apron from the lamp, while
Aladdin manipulates it with confidence (589). Aladdin's acceptance of
the genie suggests his acceptance of the creative fusion between mascu-

line and feminine inherent within the lamp. This acceptance prepares
him for love at first sight of a single woman, the princess of China. In a
simulation of 'Islamic' antecedents, Galland insists that until this moment
Aladdin has never seen a woman without her veil, save for his own mother;
his notion 'that all women resembled his mother' is dispelled on behold-
ing the princess on her way to the bath. Like the prince of Persia in the
enchanted horse story, Aladdin is 'entranced'; the image of the princess
'had penetrated to the very bottom of his heart' (594). Until this event,
Aladdin has not exploited the magic of either the ring or the lamp; now he
must conjure spectacular riches to win the hand of the princess from her
father. First, he must sabotage the marriage between the princess and the
son of the grand vizier, which he achieves by having the couple's nuptial
bed transported to his own chamber. The genie of the lamp accomplishes
this feat on two successive nights, leaving the bridegroom standing paralyzed
in a privy, a symbol of enforced regression that Dulcken transforms into
'the lumber-room' (606; cf. Galland, 2:284).

Houghton's illustration of the bridegroom's predicament (fig. 8.7) is
one of his most meticulous designs, and the Dalziels' translation of its tonal
shifts is spectacular. Nevertheless, this engraving does not appear in collections of the artist's work, perhaps because the design, viewed in isolation,
might be taken for a sinophobic peep at an opium den. The next illustration (609) could arouse additional unease; the 'sultan' of China is a
swaggering mandarin complete with pigtail, while his daughter is as Aryan
as the artist's Scheherazade.

Considered in relation to Galland's text, however, Houghton's juxtaposition of exaggerated national types is not only defensible but appropriate.
The entire 'Orient' of Galland's *Nights* is uniform in language and, where
the characters 'approved' by the narrator are concerned, in race as well. A
notable example comes in the 'History of Prince Camaralzaman,' where a
prince hailing from 'Khaledan' ('twenty days' sail from the coast of Persia'
[300]) can be impersonated with Shakespearean ease by a princess of
China. People other than the norm in appearance and behaviour are
inwardly corrupt. In Houghton's interpretation of the Aladdin story, the
sultan of China and his surrogate, the vizier's son, are as 'other' as the
African magician.

If figure 8.6 shows a liminal phase in a passage to manhood, figure 8.7
suggests the paralysis of this transition. An event intended to assert the
masculine dominance of the bridegroom (and, through him, of the sultan) is portrayed as a symbol of regression, division, and impotence –
regression, in his dread of two black mice who are drawing near. As he

recoils from them, he places his right foot over his left, in a reversal of the princess of Bengal's posture as she rides the enchanted horse. While the princess in that image embraces her prince, this brideless bridegroom embraces himself. In the process, he magnifies the silhouette of the mice. A similar emulation can be found in plate 4 of Houghton's *Home Thoughts and Home Scenes* (1865), where a little girl shrinks from a crab she has met at low tide. *You become what you fear.* Division – internal no less than external – is symbolized in the separation of the phallic vase in the lower left from the womblike jug above it and of the circular bowl beside the bridegroom's feet, with its ringlike periphery, from its conical lid. Impotence is evoked by the 'feminine' moonlight caressing his ironically phallic upper body and by the empty containers surrounding him, including the box and basket on the right, which echo the angles of his skirt and torso.

Above all, the ruptured box connotes the escape of the princess from a marriage imposed by the sultan. As for the perforated basket, it strongly resembles the titular prop in the 'Indian Basket Trick.' The conjuror's assistant would be fastened inside this style of wicker basket and emerge unscathed after the basket had been lanced repeatedly with swords.[4] The balance of peril and salvation in this performance is parallelled in Houghton's next illustration, where the princess, returned to the sultan's palace after her second night with Aladdin, is threatened by her father with a saber. 'Irritated' by her refusal to explain the odd behaviour of herself and the vizier's son after their nuptials, the sultan delivers an ultimatum: 'tell me what you thus conceal, or I will instantly strike off your head' (608).

Throughout the tale, this sultan is a caricature of the disillusionment and vindictiveness of Scheherazade's husband. With his pendulum swings from blubbering solicitude to lethal tyranny, the sultan of China is not without his 'feminine' side, but a 'masculine' infatuation with power and wealth subordinates it. His affection for Aladdin is based on the magnificent palace the genies construct; when the palace disappears, he orders Aladdin arrested and decapitated. Aladdin is saved by the people of Peking, who stage a revolt to rescue him. At the end of the story, Galland's Scheherazade declaims a lengthy 'moral,' but she leaves it to her own sultan to perceive that he too might confront an uprising if he persists in executing his wives – herself included.

For deliverance from her father's 'love,' the princess relies on Aladdin and his magic – and his self-restraint. For on both the nights that he replaces her bridegroom, Aladdin places 'a drawn sabre between the princess and himself, as a sign that he deserved to be punished if he offended her in any way' (606). Aladdin has learned, as the sultan has not, to control the impulses personified by the African magician.

In the long run, the disappearance of Aladdin's palace confronts the sultan of China with truths about his realm, his priorities, and his own heart. Galland begins the process with a passage of considerable realism, even in Dulcken. The morning after the palace has vanished, the sultan

> did not fail to go as usual to his cabinet and look out, that he might have the pleasure of contemplating and admiring Aladdin's palace. He cast his eyes in the direction where he was accustomed to see it, but saw only the open space that had been there before the palace was built. He thought he must be deceived. He rubbed his eyes, but still he could see nothing more than at first, though the air was so serene, the sky so clear, and the sun so near rising, that every object appeared distinct and plain ... His astonishment was so great that he remained for some time rooted to the spot, with his eyes turned to the place where the palace had stood.

Long past sunrise the sultan waited, 'to see if he were not under the influence of some delusion. He at length retired, looking once more behind him as he left the cabinet' (631).

In the entire passage, which is twice the length of this extract, there is not a word of the sultan's daughter and son-and-law; his only concern is for a palace interposed between himself and the sun. So congenial is this interposition, to the court no less than to its monarch, that the grand vizier and his attendants fail to notice that Aladdin's palace has vanished! 'Even the porters,' Galland adds, 'when they opened the gates, did not perceive its disappearance' (632). As for that aspiring 'monarch of the universe,' the African magician, he admires the gaudy pile enough to transport it to his own domain. Genies of the lamp, it seems, are sound judges of their patrons' minds.

Might Galland, approaching the end of his career as a glorified civil servant, have intended any allusion to France's 'Sun King' with this episode? At any rate, Houghton has mirrored the essence of the text even as he deviates from it. In his illustration (fig. 8.8), the sun is blazing into the 'cabinet,' and its light strikes the sultan with the force of an explosion. In Arabic aesthetics, this sultan experiences *'ajab*, defined in one scholastic text as 'the change of the *nafs* [spirit or soul] through something the cause of which is unknown and goes out of the ordinary' (Mottahedeh, 30). Arguably, versions of such 'astonishment' sustain the interest of the *Nights* both for Sultan Schahriar and for assorted auditors within Scheherazade's narrative, though their 'souls' are affected at best by gradations. Here, however, there is an overwhelming of the faculties that seems to unite the entire psyche and threatens to disrupt the balance of the design itself. To reinforce the point, Houghton has smuggled the mongrel from figure 8.5 into the sultan's chamber; the 'masculine' right foot has stomped on the tail of the dog, and the animal rears in a reflex of the sultan's stagger. A ruler of Plato's cave could not appear more bewildered if his wall of shadows fell into the light.

The sultan of course is still among the shadows; his 'off with his head' reception of Aladdin confirms that. And his own shadow, fanning backward across the wall, bears a distinct resemblance to the silhouette of the African magician in a subsequent illustration (641). There, the magician rears back in a death fit after drinking the poison administered by Aladdin's princess, and the analogy shows the debasement of the sultan's 'spirit or soul.' Yet it also offers hope for the sultan, who must conquer the forces in himself that the magician embodies. The very composition of figure 8.8 offers reassurance; despite its threat to topple rightward, it remains anchored to its axes, thanks in part to the cropping of the upper corners and the disposition of stabilizing motifs. These motifs include the shadow of a pair of swallows mating in the air; they are birds of earth and changing skies, and their shadows are cast by the light that sets to men as quickly as it rises. Yet in that light they mate, and in that mating is their magic and the magic of lovers who live through Houghton's art. Underlying the symbols of 'feminine' and 'masculine' in his work, of union and division, is faith in the reality of love between a woman and a man and the power of that love to validate the world. In Galland's *Nights* he found a mirror of that faith, and in Houghton, Galland found his perfect illustrator. So, I believe, did Scheherazade herself.

NOTES

1 Publisher's Circular, 8 December 1863, 'illustrations 50-51'; 8 December 1865, 'illustrations 72.' A copy of the work with the original monthly wrappers (January 1864 to September 1865) is in the British Library.
2 Unless otherwise cited, page references to the *Nights* refer to the one-volume Dulcken edition [1865]. However, the transliteration of proper names in the *Nights* follows Antoine Galland, whose consistency in such matters is violated by Dulcken.
3 In terms of Hindu iconography and ritual, this reading recalls the interpenetration between *śiva* and *śakti* in various tantric systems. In an adaptation of

these concepts, Heinrich Zimmer sees the primary object of Saiva worship, the *Śivaliṅga*, as the union of 'the symbol of male creative energy ... with the primary symbol of female creative energy, the yoni, the latter forming the base of the image with the former rising from its centre' (127). This interpretation has been discounted by such scholars as Gritli v. Mitterwallner, who calls it 'a highly abstract and wishful idea of Tantric inspiration' (27). But it has been paralleled in recent studies of South Indian ritual; Richard H. Davis speaks of the *liṅga* as 'a smooth, cylindrical shaft set in a pedestal (*pīṭha*) identified with Sakti' (62). Even if the *Śivaliṅga* is conceived as exclusively 'male,' its presence in the 'womb-room' (*garbhagṛha*) of the temple lends some support to Zimmer's intuition.

4 For an account of this trick, with illustrations, see Branson, 65-75. I am grateful to Mr. Michael Claxton for sharing with me this and other rare publications relating to 'Indian conjuring.'

ILLUSTRATIONS

Fig. 8.1. Arthur Boyd Houghton, 'Schehera-zade [*sic*] Relating the Stories to the Sultan.' Frontispiece for *The Arabian Nights' Entertainments*. London: Warne, [1865].

Fig. 8.2. Arthur Boyd Houghton, 'Prince Firouz Schah Beseeching the Protection of the Princess of Bengal.' *Dalziels' Illustrated Arabian Nights' Entertainments*. Ed. H.W. Dulcken. London: Ward, Lock, and Tyler, [1865], 729.

Fig. 8.3. Arthur Boyd Houghton, 'The Journey of Prince Firouz Schah and the Princess of Bengal.' *Dalziels' Illustrated Arabian Nights' Entertainments*, 737.

Fig. 8.4. Arthur Boyd Houghton, 'The Princess of Bengal.' *Dalziels' Illustrated Arabian Nights' Entertainments*. 745.

Fig. 8.5. Arthur Boyd Houghton, 'The African Magician Embracing Aladdin.' *Dalziels' Illustrated Arabian Nights' Entertainments*, 577.

Fig. 8.6. Arthur Boyd Houghton, 'The Magician Commanding Aladdin to Give up the Lamp.' *Dalziels' Illustrated Arabian Nights' Entertainments*, 585.

Fig. 8.7. Arthur Boyd Houghton, 'The Bridegroom Shut up in the Lumber-room.' *Dalziels' Illustrated Arabian Nights' Entertainments*, 605.

Fig. 8.8. Arthur Boyd Houghton, 'The Sultan's Surprise at the Disappearance of Aladdin's Palace.' *Dalziels' Illustrated Arabian Nights' Entertainments*, 633.

9

Sartorial Obsessions:
Beardsley and Masquerade

Lorraine Janzen Kooistra

In the 1960s, during the major exhibit of Beardsley's drawings at the Victoria and Albert Museum that inspired a renewed interest in the artist and his work,[1] the following headline appeared in the *New York Times*: 'Beardsley Prints Seized in London. Shop Wares Called Lewd – Museum Showing Originals' (11 August 1966, I:25). The story drew attention to the ironic situation in which reproductions of art on open display at a public institution whose very name – The Victoria and Albert – confered dignity and respectability had been seized by Scotland Yard at a bookseller's shop only two blocks from the museum (Salerno, no. 128; in Langenfeld, 298). The irony illuminates the arbitrary categorization of art as 'high' or 'low.' High art is work sanctioned by the elite structure of museum culture, which protects its subject matter from censorship by philistines, prudes, and policemen. Low or popular art, on the other hand, is defined not only by its theoretical accessibility to all purchasers through the capitalist market system but also by its subject matter, which, outside the academy, is open to the charge of 'lewdness.' In other words, within the context of the exhibit, Beardsley's drawings may have been erotic, but they were not pornographic. Outside the museum, on sale to every Tom, Dick, or Mary who walked into the shop with sufficient funds, the prints became obscene – they became pornography.

Beardsley himself referred to his work in similar terms in his famous last letter to Leonard Smithers, the publisher of pornography who was also the artist's friend and patron:

Jesus is our Lord and Judge

Dear Friend,

   I implore you to destroy all copies of Lysistrata and bad drawings. Show
this to Pollitt and conjure him to do same. By all that is holy all obscene
drawings.

                                                    AUBREY BEARDSLEY

   In my death agony. (*Letters*, 439; 7 March 1898)

This letter may mark a sincere deathbed remorse, but it may also enact
Beardsley's last mask – that of the penitent preparing for death under the
watchful eye of his mother (Easton, 115, 261n58; Reade, *Re-Mounted*, 37).
Just as his art has oscillated between claims that it is high art and charges
that it is pornography for the last one hundred years, so too has Beardsley's
life eluded the defining strategies of the most determined biographers.
None of them has been able to categorize Beardsley's sexual practices any
more definitively than critics have been able to categorize the erotic content of his work.[2] Beardsley's last plea also activates a moving posthumous
irony, for Smithers kept the 'bad drawings' and even sold facsimiles of the
letter itself as a special enducement to collectors of the *Lysistrata* prints
(*Letters*, 394). From first to last, from production to reception, Beardsley's
art moves between the public and the private, the erotic and the pornographic, the man and the mask – and always with an ironic playfulness that
blurs boundaries and disrupts categories.

   I want to examine this disruption of binaries in Beardsley's life and work
by looking specifically at the theatricality of his art. Beardsley is undoubtedly interested in sexual subjects, but the erotic content has tended to
distract critics from the performative aspects of an art obsessed with dress,
undress, and the liminal states between. With his theatrical costuming, his
delight in disguised and masked figures, his fascination with the details of
feminine attire and toilettes, and his ubiquitous cross-dressing themes,
Beardsley shows the sartorial obsessions that dominate his oeuvre from his
earliest to his latest works. I will argue that the function of masquerade in
Beardsley's art is to call into question the basic notion on which we ground
all our binary oppositions: the male/female division. Both performative
and transgressive, masquerade operates by the carnivalesque construction
of alterity through costume, disrupting fixed notions of personal identity
by permitting the subject to inhabit opposing positions simultaneously.
The function of masquerade in Beardsley's art is to challenge the hierarchical distinctions of the late-Victorian patriarchal society. By presenting
clothing that overpowers the human body, as in his 'Black Cape' design for

Salome, and nude figures of ambiguous gender, as in the book plate he designed for his transvestite friend Herbert Pollitt, Beardsley challenges the viewer to move beyond the limitations of sex and gender categories to a liminal third space. This liminal positioning is aligned with the contemporary conception of the 'third sex,' which for *fin-de-siècle* sexologists was inextricably connected to the whole notion of 'dressing up.' If Beardsley was, as his *Letters* suggest, an occasional cross-dresser himself, his personal interest had a political edge to it, for his art is engaged in disrupting the Victorian dogma of essential sexual difference by demonstrating the ways in which our basic notions of identity are constructed, artificial concepts – masquerades.

I: The Man: Beardsley Mystique and Masquerade

In a cartoon published in *To-Day* in September 1894 with the caption 'An Illustration of the Gospel of To-Day by Baudry Weirdsley,' Beardsley appears as a cross-dresser in the costume of Yvette Guilbert, the popular French café singer. The caricature is an intriguing one, for it not only, as Bridget Elliott points out, 'placed Beardsley and his illustrations in the realm of popular entertainment' ('Beardsley as Performer,' vi, viii); it also positioned him as an artist who could be recognizably represented as a man dressed as a woman. The cartoon seems to be a visual version of the familiar charge that Beardsley's art is 'effeminate' or 'sexless' (Haldane MacFall, qtd. in Weintraub, *Beardsley*, 131): surely the most direct attack against a man's sexuality is to represent him in feminine attire. But – as so often in Beardsley criticism – it is not entirely clear if the caricature is responding to perceived tendencies in Beardsley's work or his public persona or both; Beardsley was, after all, given to theatrical self-display. And it was only a year earlier that Beardsley apparently did appear in a dress at a public venue. In a letter to John Lane postmarked 12 September 1893, Beardsley wrote: 'I am going to Jimmie's on Thursday night dressed up as a tart and mean to have a regular spree' (*Letters*, 53). 'Jimmie's' was St James's Restaurant in Piccadilly, a site where prostitutes, homosexuals, and other 'tarts' could make their pick-ups (Easton, 148).

As always with Beardsley, it is difficult to know whether this statement is a verbal mask assumed to shock his publisher or whether the event described really did take place: there are no corroborating reports from witnesses, and there is no mention in his *Letters* of similar public escapades. We do know, however, that Beardsley played female parts in the private theatricals he put on with his sister Mabel (Easton, 154), and Brian Reade speculates that Aubrey and Mabel enjoyed exchanging clothes (*Re-Mounted*, 28; *Aubrey Beardsley*, 20). Indeed, Malcolm Easton suggests that on that mysterious night in September 1893, both Beardsleys went to St James's Restaurant cross-dressed. Easton draws our attention to W. Graham Robertson's oil sketch of Mabel in male attire inscribed 'To Philip Beardsley' and suggests that Mabel here appears in costume as her brother, indicating a lifelong pattern of sibling identification through sartorial exchange. Easton's speculative answer to the 'Beardsley riddle' is that Aubrey and his sister were transsexuals and that the secret of Beardsley's life and art lies in his wish to be a woman (243).

The 'wish to be woman' is not, of course, an exotic deviance limited to such 'rare birds' (Easton, 243) as transsexuals. It can be understood in a wider cultural context involving aesthetic, sexual, and political positioning. As Richard Dellamora argues in *Masculine Desire: The Sexual Politics of Victorian Aestheticism*, 'the rhetorical wish to be woman' (130) expressed itself in a variety of art forms at the *fin de siècle*, enabled principally by Walter Pater's espousal of an androgynous ideal in *The Renaissance*. Moreover – if we move from the rhetorical to the actual for a moment – sociological, psychological, and historical studies of transgender behaviour indicate that cross-dressers not only wish to be but also identify themselves as women – that is, women in terms of their gender rather than their biological sex. Among the recent studies of this wish to be woman – including Richard F. Docter's psychoanalytic theory of cross-gender behaviour, Harry Brierly's psychological case studies, John T. Talamini's sociological survey, and Peter Ackroyd and Marjorie Garber's cultural analyses – Ackroyd makes important distinctions that are relevant for contextualizing Beardsley's work. In distinguishing transsexualism, drag, and transvestism, he points out that the desire of transsexuals 'is to assume the genitals and the body of the opposite sex,' while the misogynistic function of drag is to mock and parody women. The goal of transvestites, on the other hand, is 'to create at least the illusion of femininity – "to pass" as a woman, either publicly or privately.' Ackroyd concludes 'it is possible to dress, behave and even think like a woman – as many transvestites do both in public and in private – without in fact being trans-sexual' (13, 14). While I might contest Ackroyd's assumption that a woman thinks in a gender-specific way accessible to masculine mimics, his point that transvestites identify themselves as women and express that identification through performance and costume seems particularly applicable to Beardsley's sartorial obsessions.

Like the story of Beardsley's escapade at 'Jimmie's,' the caricature of him cross-dressed as a French café singer is part of the Beardsley riddle –

part of the mystique of the man and his many masquerades. As Linda Zatlin remarks, no published account of the artist's sexual practices is satisfactory; they must remain a matter of speculation. His very theatricality, his adoption of different masks in different situations, make definitive statements about his sexuality impossible ('Drawing Conclusions,' 114, 130-1). Yet there are many suggestions in Beardsley's life and art that indicate he was fascinated by clothing and its ability to confound preconceived notions of sex and gender difference by altering the persona and mystifying the physique. Contextualizing Beardsley's critique in terms of the *fin-de-siècle* culture out of which it was produced and in which it was received, I will focus first on the aspects of his biography that seem to support this theory and then move on to examine the political implications of the transgendered tropes in his designs.

Beardsley was supported, in his last years, by three intriguing *fin-de-siècle* figures: Leonard Smithers, Herbert Pollitt, and André Raffalovich. His letters to Smithers are, by and large, the most detached and professional, relating almost exclusively to business dealings, commissions, payments, and the like. His usual salutation is 'My dear Smithers' or (on occasion) 'My dear Leonardo.' By contrast, Beardsley's letters to the other two are much warmer, frequently addressing Pollitt as 'My dearest Friend' and Raffalovich as 'My dearest Brother.' Since the money necessary to support Beardsley in his final illness depended on the continued goodwill of all three men, we do not, perhaps, need to look far to find his motivation for maintaining good relations with them. The basis for each friendship was, however, markedly different.

Smithers was Beardsley's publisher in the *Savoy* venture and the *Rape of the Lock* edition as well as the distributor of his drawings to collectors. Raffalovich, on the other hand, who disliked and distrusted Smithers, was connected to Beardsley through their shared interest in the Roman Catholic Church, which Beardsley joined with his friend's encouragement in March 1897 (*Letters*, 237). Raffalovich was homosexual, whereas Smithers's interest in sexual matters, though diffuse professionally, seems to have been heterosexual personally. Between these two men is the mysterious figure of Herbert Charles Jerome Pollitt (1871-1942), a man only one year older than Beardsley and an undergraduate at Cambridge when he met the artist sometime in late 1894 or early 1895 (Hobbs, 520-1). In some ways, Pollitt may be likened to Smithers by his interest in erotic art and to Raffalovich by his homosexual orientation. But he also introduces a new element into the erotic and sexual mix of the Beardsley mystique: cross-dressing and theatre.

Besides being a collector of erotica and a practising homosexual, Pollitt
was also, when Beardsley first met him, a female impersonator particularly
applauded for his rendition of the '"Serpentine," a scarf dance executed
in the style of the American dancer Loie Fuller.' His stage name for his
performances at Cambridge's Footlights Dramatic Club, Diane de Rougy,
invoked the Folies-Bergère dancer Liane de Pougy (Hobbs, 520) with the
same campy panache as the *To-Day* caricature's association of Beardsley
with the French café singer Yvette Guilbert. Although there is no evidence
that Beardsley ever saw Pollitt perform, the curiously sexless drawing of
'The Stomach Dance' in *Salome* may owe something to his friend's version
of the veil dance on the Cambridge stage. Beardsley certainly used transvestite tropes in his illustrations for Wilde's play to highlight its underlying
homoerotic themes (Kooistra, *Artist as Critic*, 140-1). Significantly, Pollitt
introduced himself to Wilde by sending photographs of himself in a variety
of costumes, including one in which he wore only a transparent robe
(Wilde, *Letters*, 777). The teasing play with dress and undress, the body and
the costume, homo- and heterosexual identities, and the categories of
male and female that characterize what little is known of Herbert Pollitt's
life and theatrical activities has many affiliations with Beardsley's own
interests, as no doubt the artist was well aware.

The precise nature of Beardsley's relationship with the man he addressed as 'My best good Friend' and for whom he signed himself 'Yours
entirely, pen and pencil' (*Letters*, 286) may never be known, but it seems
likely that the two shared an interest not only in erotica and theatre but also
in transvestitism. The evidence of Beardsley's bookplate design (fig. 9.1)
suggests an implicitly acknowledged identity, perhaps even a psychic trans-
ference, between the two men. Beardsley's design was first intended for his
own use and given to Smithers as a catalogue cover. Later, the artist changed
its title from 'Bookplate of the Artist' to 'Mr. Pollitt's Bookplate,' adding the
appropriate lettering on the print in Pollitt's copy of *A Book of Fifty Drawings
by Aubrey Beardsley*. In the spring of 1897, Hentschel made up the block from
the amended print and the book plate became officially Pollitt's (Hobbs,
524). This reassignment may have been merely a matter of expediency –
Beardsley had already received the money for Pollitt's bookplate, but he
had failed to produce it despite many promises (Hobbs, 524-5). At the
same time, the transfer of ownership also suggests a hidden affinity between Beardsley and Pollitt – a shared secret, perhaps, about the pleasures
associated with role reversals, mistaken identities, and confusions between
origins and destinations, signs and signatures.

The bookplate features the prominent backview of a statuesque woman wearing nothing but an elaborate hat reaching out to a platter of books held by a bald and paunchy male grotesque. The design highlights the strength and power of women, involving both designer and owner, perhaps, in the 'wish to be woman' that characterizes the transvestite. There may be a hint of the same interest in Beardsley's relationships with Raffalovich and Smithers. In some letters, Beardsley addresses Raffalovich as 'Mentor' and signs himself 'Télémaque,' two characters taken from Fénelon's *Télémaque*, in which 'Mentor, though in appearance a wise old man, was in reality the goddess Minerva disguised!' (Easton, 60). Even Beardsley's occasional reference to Smithers as 'Leonardo' may involve a veiled allusion to the pleasures of transvestitic transformation. As Dellamora shows so persuasively in *Masculine Desire*, the name of Leonardo da Vinci had become, ever since Walter Pater's famous description of his paintings in *The Renaissance*, a specialized code in decadent circles for an androgynous aesthetic based on 'the transforming power of "becoming-woman"' (146). My purpose here is not to establish Beardsley as a transvestite (the fragmentary evidence makes any conclusion speculative) but rather to point out his documented interest in cross-dressing and to examine the effects of this fascination with masquerade in his art. Ultimately, the sartorial tropes in his designs are far more interesting for their critique of conventional sex and gender roles than they are for whatever insights they may give us into the artist's personal sexual practices.

II: The Art: Sartorial Obsessions and Transgendered Subjects

In a paper entitled 'Womanliness as a Masquerade,' first published in the *International Journal of Psychoanalysis* in 1929, Joan Rivière, a Freudian analyst, moved the debate about female sexuality into a new phase by arguing that womanliness is nothing more than 'a mask' that produces the effect of femininity. Since she argues that 'genuine womanliness and the "masquerade" ... are the same thing' (38), Rivière opens the door to an understanding of gender as a performative effect only coincidentally related to an 'originary' sex and hence – theoretically, at least – a masquerade available to both male and female performers. Later, Simone de Beauvoir reinforced the conception of femininity as a social construction with her famous statement, 'One is not born, but rather becomes, a woman' (267). Her maxim highlights the self-conscious, performative aspect of gender that has intrigued post-structuralist theorists and made cross-dressing a crux of cultural studies. With his concept of the 'mask' behind which 'femininity takes refuge,' Jacques Lacan identifies masquerade as the means by which

feminine subjectivity establishes itself (84-5). This element of performance in producing femininity is highlighted by cross-dressing practices
that unsettle the whole concept of 'sex' as a natural, pre-existing given –
what Foucault ironically terms the 'anchorage point that supports the
manifestations of sexuality' (152) – precisely because transvestites operate
by assuming a mask of a femininity, *which is in itself always already a mask.* In
effect, cross-dressing enacts a playful deconstruction of the concept of
unified and originary subjects. Taking female impersonation as her starting point in *Gender Trouble: Feminism and the Subversion of Identity,* Judith
Butler asks 'is drag the imitation of gender, or does it dramatize the
signifying gestures through which gender itself is established?' (x). Butler
goes on to argue that 'questions of primary identity' are not the issues
feminist critics ought most to engage in but, rather, the 'political possibilities' that follow from 'a radical critique of the categories of identity' (xi).

It is precisely such a radical critique of the basic categories of identity –
male and female – that Beardsley launches with his sartorial tropes and
motifs of masquerade. His transgendered subjects, confronting, confound-
ing, and transgressing Victorian concepts of essential identity and polarized sexual difference are shocking not so much for their eroticized
content as for their political implications. That his audience was, on some
level, aware of the cultural ramifications of his art is evident in such articles
as 'How to Court the "Advanced Woman"' in the *Idler* magazine of 1895.
The magazine prefaced its series on 'The Development of the "Emanci-
pated"' – glossed in the article itself as a '"Man-Woman"' (194) – with a
Beardsley illustration of a woman contemplating an elaborate hat on a
stand. Contemporary reviews of his work also focused on the affinities
between Beardsley's designs and the sexual deviance and corruption of
the masculinized New Woman (Elliott, 'New and Not So "New Women,"'
33-4; Zatlin, *Aubrey Beardsley,* 81). Indeed, after the public uproar caused by
Beardsley's illustrations for *Salome* and *The Yellow Book,* one newspaper
called 'for "a short act of parliament to make this sort of thing illegal"'
(A.J.A. Symons, 99). Clearly, Beardsley's audience was profoundly aware of
the political implications of his art.

While Beardsley's style underwent many changes in the course of his
brief career, his fascination with clothing and his interest in transgendered
subjects continued throughout, from the *Morte d'Arthur* (1893-4) to *Mlle de
Maupin* (1897-8).[3] His interest in the theatrics of masquerade is evident in
his many toilette scenes, which comprise a fifth of his drawings (Eaton,
117), while his ubiquitous hermaphroditic and androgynous figures highlight his ongoing challenge to fixed notions of a stable sexual identity.

Although a comprehensive study is beyond the scope of this essay, a representative sampling of Beardsley's sartorial tropes and gender-bending themes suggests that – despite the fact that he worked almost exclusively in black and white – his art was engaged in challenging, not reinforcing, the rigid binary oppositions implicit in the black/white dichotomy and basic to the late-Victorian conception of polarized sexual difference.

In the *Morte d'Arthur* designs that launched his career as an illustrator, Beardsley's critique of the chivalric world of Malory's romance undermines the sexual hierarchy on which that society depends (Kooistra, 'Beardsley's Reading,' 55-77). The critique is a double-edged sword, for it cuts against both the Arthurian world of the text and contemporary Victorian society, which idealized that world and reclaimed its chivalric values for itself. As Debra N. Mancoff's study of the nineteenth century's production and reception of Malory suggests, 'in reviving the Arthurian legend Victorian artists and writers, and their eager audience ... forged a mirror of the present, projecting their own ideals and ambitions, dreams and fears, onto legendary characters and events' (*Return of King Arthur*, 8). Since many of these idealizations were produced and circulated in the 'high art' of literary and visual imagery, Beardsley was fighting in the front lines of the battlefield when he accepted the challenge of illustrating the legendary Round Table. Sir Edward Burne-Jones, for instance – who became a knight himself while Beardsley was working on the *Morte* and whose Pre-Raphaelite presence haunts Beardsley's early designs for the book – pursued the chivalric theme almost obsessively in his paintings. As George P. Landow comments, 'taken together, these works comprise a sexual myth that had great appeal for the artist and his contemporaries' – that is, the myth of 'the dominant male's rescue of the helpless maiden' (40).

Far from reinforcing this chivalric myth, Beardsley's art undermines the presupposition of essential sexual difference with its representations of dominant women and weak men, its playing with the motif of disguise, and its many hermaphroditic and androgynous figures. In 'How Sir Launcelot Was Known by Dame Elaine' (fig. 9.2), for example, Beardsley focuses on a theme he returns to again and again in the *Morte* – that of the ineffectual or inactive knight. More than a quarter of his full-page illustrations show knights asleep, entranced, or ill, and many of the initial vignettes further develop the motif.[4] In the full-page illustrations, the knights' ineptitude is highlighted by their lack of a complete set of armour: none of them has a helmet or upper body mail or even a sword. Moreover, both their languid bodies and their delicate faces give them an androgynous look. In the illustration of Elaine and Launcelot, this androgyny is reinforced, as so often in Beardsley's work, by the mirroring effect of the proximate faces of the man and the woman. At the same time, the strength of women is enhanced by the details of the composition, which suggest that Elaine, rather than Launcelot, is in control of the situation, actively engaged in a rescue aided by the bevy of female 'squires.' By focusing on such moments, Beardsley directly attacks the chivalric myth that artists like Burne-Jones perpetuated in the Victorian popular imagination. Christopher Snodgrass has shown how Beardsley's campy distortions of Pre-Raphaelite conventions (the romanticized middle ages, the 'feminine ideal,' the 'aura of high art' itself) subvert the representation of 'a hierarchical, unified and univocally ordered world' ('Decadent Parodies,' 193; *Aubrey Beardsley*, ch. 6). Indeed, as Mancoff comments in her study of *The Arthurian Revival in Victorian Art*, despite the fact that J.M. Dent commissioned the artist precisely for his 'ability to emulate Burne-Jones,' Beardsley inverted the 'iconographical formulations of the Arthurian Revival' as established by the Pre-Raphaelites and challenged 'three generations of heroic imagery with his androgynous phantoms' (260, 264).

The androgyny motif is repeated, but with different effect, in the illustration for 'How Sir Tristram Drank the Love Drink' (fig. 9.3), which anticipates the double image in the celebrated design of John the Baptist and Salome, produced for *Salome* but not used. In both illustrations, the locked gazes of the mirroring subjects suggest equality, not hierarchical distinctions. In these images of male/female mirroring, Beardsley elaborates a costuming that cloaks the form of the body, so that – especially in the design for Tristram and Isoud – the human figure becomes nothing more than a geometric shape, a pattern outlined by draperies, and, hence, apparently protean. The body's shape-changing potential, underscored by the dramatic use of clothing as both concealer and revealer, is also explored in the *Salome* illustration, where Salome's breasts and navel are more decorative aspects of the costume than female body parts.

After his first illustration commision for the *Morte* Beardsley began to incorporate specifically transvestitic themes in his art. In his famous frontispiece design for *Salome*, for instance, Beardsley's playful presentation of dress and undress proposes that gender is a cultural sign subject to interpretation (fig. 9.4). The discrepancy between the gender-specific caption ('The Woman in the Moon') and the lunar face of Oscar Wilde[5] underscores Beardsley's technique: he wants the eye to be tricked while the mind is left oscillating between two incompatible categories. The principal figures of Beardsley's frontispiece also work to disrupt our confident reading of that most basic category of human identity, sex. The androgynous dress of the figure on the far right has made the usually simple matter of naming the frontispiece characters a contested critical issue. While the exposed genitalia of the male figure leave no question as to his sex, his personal identity is dependent on his relation to the androgynous clothed figure. If this figure is taken to be Salome herself, then the naked man is Jokanaan (Dellamora, 'Traversing the Feminine,' 256; Marcus, 9). If, on the other hand, the clothed figure is taken to be the effeminate Narraboth, then the naked man is the Page who suffers unrequited love for him, and the frontispiece highlights the homoerotic themes of the play rather than its ostensible subject (Fletcher, 77; Heyd, 101; Showalter, 155; Snodgrass, 'Decadent Mythmaking,' 74; Wilson, 11). Beardsley's frontispiece, which refuses the anchor of either caption or text, draws our attention to the degree to which all our readings, even of so 'obvious' a matter as sexual identity, are artificial and constructed rather than natural or transparent. Clothes, like words, become rhetorical devices that can be manipulated to produce the effects of gender while casting into doubt the possibility of a fixed and stable originary identity. As Snodgrass comments, 'in Beardsley's world garments, like identities and allegiances, oscillate from one owner to another, a part of both, but ultimately belonging to neither' ('Decadent Mythmaking,' 77).

In *Salome*, as in his designs for *The Rape of the Lock* and his illustrations for *The Yellow Book* and *The Savoy*, Beardsley's many toilette scenes draw attention to the performative nature of gender by focusing on the site where the effect of femininity is artificially produced. Two of the sixteen full-page illustrations Beardsley designed for *Salome* feature toilette scenes,[6] while others – notably 'The Peacock Skirt' and 'The Black Cape' – emphasize clothing's ability to mask the 'natural' form of the body. In his two designs for 'The Toilette of Salome,' one of which was produced as a substitute for the original drawing suppressed by John Lane, Beardsley reinforces the theatrical conventions of the play he is illustrating by focusing reader attention on the dressing room where the actress prepares for her role (fig. 9.5). The implication is that womanliness is, like the calculated effects of the actress, a masquerade self-consciously contrived with the assistance of powder and paint, coiffure and costume. The theme of masquerade is highlighted in both drawings by the masked Pierrot who attends Salome at her dressing table. Moreover, in each case, the lines of Salome's dress confound our expectations of anatomy by masking the presence of the human figure within the robe. Indeed, in the first version, Salome's draperies double as the lines establishing the foreground of the composition so that the figure who appears to be sitting is, in reality, groundless. By teasing the eye with the oscillations of figure/ground relations, Beardsley draws attention not only to the artifice of his composition's constructive principles but also to the arbitrariness of all conventional relations that rely on an originating 'ground' for a fixed meaning – including the conception of the sexual body as the 'ground' for the effects of gender.

In his later work, Beardsley increasingly draws on cross-dressing and masquerade as subjects for – rather than simply stylistic features of – his art. His titlepage design for the first two issues of *The Savoy*, for example, focuses on the rituals of eighteenth-century masquerade, with its masks, elaborate headgear, and fancy dress (fig. 9.6). As other illustrations in his 'eighteenth-century phase' suggest, one of of the reasons for Beardsley's interest in that period is precisely its delight in sartorial transformation – its recognition that one could become the 'other' through masquerade. As Terry Castle writes in *Masquerade and Civilization: The Carnivalesque in Eighteenth-Century English Culture and Fiction*:

> The masked assemblies of the eighteenth century were in the deepest sense a kind of collective meditation on self and other, and an exploration of their mysterious dialectic.... One became the other in an act of ecstatic impersonation. The true self remained elusive and inaccessible – illegible – within its fantastical encasements.... The pleasure of masquerade attended on the experience of doubleness, the alienation of inner from outer, a fantasy of two bodies simultaneously and thrillingly present, self and other together, the two-in-one. (4-5)

By the Victorian period, however, with the public masquerade rooms closed, the sartorial code rigidly established for genders and classes, and the carnivalesque relegated to children's pantomime, the outlets for the subversive pleasures of masquerade were limited to the public stage of the theatre, the private practices of the home, and such fringe venues as St James's Restaurant, Piccadilly. Whether or not Beardsley took personal pleasure in becoming the 'other' through cross-dressing, his artwork attests to an ongoing interest in sartorial exchange and the subversive potential of transvestitic transformation. His adaptation of an eighteenth-century decorative style toward the end of 1895 (Wilson, 23) signals a fascination with that period's engagement with masquerade and its socially disruptive potential. Hence the array of Pierrots and Harlequins, masked figures, Scaramouches, Don Juans, and Sgnanarelles in his later works. As Castle remarks, the erotics of costumed concealment paradoxically permit the revelation of enacted truths about the artificial nature of social hierarchies (346). In his art, Beardsley employs an ironic and erotic tropology of costume that produces a graphic version of Oscar Wilde's famous aphorism in 'The Decay of Lying': 'Truth is entirely and absolutely a matter of style' (981).

The 'truth' Beardsley returns to again and again with his sartorial tropes is that the categories of 'man' and 'woman' are conventional and constructed, arbitrary and artificial – purely a matter of *style*. His interest in gender as a stylistic effect reconstructed with each new performance is evident in all his imagery of androgynous and hermaphroditic figures, toilette scenes, and masquerades, but it really comes out of the closet in illustrations that take cross-dressing itself as their subject. I have argued elsewhere that in *Venus and Tannhäuser*, Beardsley is less interested in exploring sexual encounters than in luxuriating in transvestite fantasy and that both images and text take cross-dressing as their principal theme (*Artist as Critic*, 226-35). Beardsley's focus on cross-dressing as the subject for his unfinished novel produces a fantastic exploration of sexual border-crossing and the freedom from proscribed social roles that such ambiguity licenses. Featuring the procuress Priapusa in 'The Toilette of Helen' as a cross-dressing Oscar Wilde, a portrait of Tannhäuser as an effeminate eighteenth-century chevalier troubled about 'the labored niceness of his dress' (25), and a design of Saint Rose embraced by the Virgin, which suggests the saints are stand-ins for the cross-dressing Spiridion who entertains his hosts at dinner by singing as a virgin in drag, Beardsley's illustrations indicate that his real interest is not so much sexuality as artificiality. His cross-dressing theme investigates the ways in which sex and gender are constructed by the cultural clothing that teaches us to identify man and woman, 'masculine' and 'feminine.'

This theme is explored in other drawings that pursue transvestitic tropes, such as the *Savoy* drawing of 'Mrs. Pinchwife' rigged out in the pantaloons, coat, and wig of a dandified gentleman and looking like she is enjoying herself very much in her assumed role (*Best Works*, 101). Among Beardsley's most interesting work on this theme is the series of six drawings he produced for *Mlle de Maupin*, Théophile Gautier's famous novel about gender confusion and sexual transformation that became a cult favourite among aesthetes of the *fin de siècle*. 'The Lady at the Dressing-Table' (fig. 9.7) reveals Beardsley's ongoing fascination with the production of feminine effect. The composition depicts a voluptuous woman having her hair dressed by an obese attendant while a chained parrot on the stand beside the table draws attention, by its own decorative plumage and talent for mimicry, to the performative nature of the masquerade in progress. 'D'Albert in Search of His Ideals' (fig. 9.8), on the other hand, focuses on a male figure not unlike the Chevalier Tannhäuser with his feminine hips, hour-glass figure, and nice attention to dress but also akin to Mlle de Maupin herself as she appears in drag in Beardsley's frontispiece. Since Albert is entangled in confusion about his own sexuality, in love with a man whom he hopes, but is not sure, is a woman, the composition of the figure satirically highlights the liberating possibilities that such confusions license. If Albert is in love with a man, then he must be 'womanly' himself – hence the full hips. If, on the other hand, Albert is in love with a woman, then his instinctive masculine desires have penetrated Mlle de Maupin's disguise, and he is a virile male after all – hence the hooded eyes, sensual mouth, and elaborate attire of the libertine. The ambiguity of the design implies that Albert is, like Mlle de Maupin herself, both of these. 'I belong to a third sex of its own which has not yet been given a name,' declares Mlle de Maupin; 'My imaginary ideal would have to be of each sex in turn' (qtd. in Ackroyd, 144). In search of his own ideals, Beardsley's Albert seems also to be imagining a world in which he could occupy a liminal third space that permits the play of enacted identities, allowing him to be 'each sex in turn' and both at once.

III: *Fin de Siècle* and Cultural Critique

All of Beardsley's art engages in border-crossing, his images teasing out and playing with the differences in such opposing categories as 'high' and 'popular art,' 'pornographic' and 'erotic' representation, hetero- and homosexualities, and male and female identities. Taken as a whole, Beardsley's transvestitic tropes launch an attack on the binary oppositions on which Victorian society based its hierarchical power relations. As Peter Ackroyd argues in *Dressing Up*, transvestism – in both its literary and cultural manifestations – flourished in the late-nineteenth century precisely as a countercultural critique of mainstream society:

> Victorian materialism represented the triumph of bourgeois morality in which 'love' itself was used as a form of male oppression. The two sexes were torn apart in the process, and that great divide was reflected in the dress of the period: women had never looked more graceful and more useless, and men shrank into tight, utilitarian clothing. In this context the male transvestite would seem offensive on every level. His cross-dressing is entirely useless and essentially visual, an expression of pleasure rather than

of principle and of sexual play rather than of moral duty. He flouts economic sense and sexual custom. (60)

Beardsley's visual play with sexual identities and cultural conventions was certainly as offensive as cross-dressing to many in his contemporary audience and for similar reasons. His transgendered figures should be read in the context of the critique on the nature of difference launched by both decadent men and avant-garde New Women as outlined by critics such as Linda Dowling (434-53) and Elaine Showalter (chapter 9). As the best-known and most notorious decadent artist of the *fin de siècle*, Beardsley was associated, especially through his illustrations for *Salome* and his drawings for *The Yellow Book*, with Oscar Wilde and the homosexual subculture, and he paid for this association with the loss of his income after Wilde's arrest and conviction. Under pressure from a group of conservative writers, Lane fired Beardsley as art editor of *The Yellow Book* because Wilde had been carrying a yellow-backed French novel, mistakenly thought to be a copy of the avant-garde magazine, at the time of his arrest (Weintraub, *Beardsley*, 126-9). Beardsley's association with 'decadent' homosexual culture was compounded by an equally strong connection to the defiant New Woman. His illustrations of female figures linked him in the public mind with the women who were challenging patriarchal conventions by demanding increased personal and political power and autonomy.[7] His connection with feminist aspirations was reinforced through his association with John Lane. As Lane himself acknowledged in an interview printed in *The Sketch* in 1895, 'I publish for Sappho' – a reference not just to the feminist writers the Bodley Head promoted (and their implied sexual orientation) but also to the advanced views they, and their readers, represented. The *Sketch* article concludes with a poem entitled 'The Bower of Sappho,' which not only spoofs the New Woman writer who now 'sings in Vigo Street,' but also specifically connects her feminist art with Beardsley's:

> They sing, the modern Muses Nine,
>   On hand-made paper, gorgeous print,
> With Aubrey Beardsley's weird design
>   Of satyrs, leering-eyed and squint;
> Nor pipe they for a vulgar set –
> Their price, you know, is always net.
> The hearts of women throb and beat
> For Mr. Lane in Vigo Street.

What though the fire of Greece has gone?
    The seed of Sappho multiplies;
And London has its Helicon,
    On which man turns his longing eyes.
A heavenly throng, they chant their aims
To Mr. Lane, the Squire of Dames;
And sentiment is not effete,
For Sappho sings in Vigo Street. ('Publisher of Minor Poets,' 6)

While the popular imagination figured the New Woman as culpably masculine and the decadent artist as both effeminate and 'effete,' Beardsley's art challenged the received notion that masculine and feminine identities were poles apart. His critique of Victorian sexual conventions through transvestitic tropes complements the studies of such contemporary sexologists as Havelock Ellis and Edward Carpenter, who were fascinated by sex/gender/sexuality distinctions. Basing his argument on the pioneering work of K.H. Ulrichs, the first sexologist to describe the male homosexual as a man with a 'feminine soul enclosed in a male body' (117), Carpenter used the trope of the 'Intermediate Sex' to break down traditional binary oppositions by proposing a more fluid understanding of sex and gender difference. Arguing that 'the sexes do not or should not normally form two groups hopelessly isolated in habit and feeling from each other,' Carpenter maintained that 'sex' should not be understood as two mutually exclusive categories but rather as a continuum between opposite poles (114-15). The *fin-de-siècle* conception of the 'Intermediate' or 'Third' Sex was based on an understanding of homosexuality as an interior identity whereby a male homosexual might express his interior 'womanliness' and a female homosexual, her interior 'manliness' by such outward signs as wearing the clothing of the other sex. For this reason, the notion of the 'Third Sex' was intimately linked, as we have seen in Gautier's *Mlle de Maupin*, with transvestitic transformation (Ackroyd, 144).

With its playful disruption of binary oppositions and hierarchies, Beardsley's art is based precisely on such a fluid understanding of sex and gender difference. His effeminate men and masculine women, his images of toilette scenes and attention to costume, effectively stage a critique of an oppositional understanding of self and other by suggesting the ways in which all identities are constructed masquerades based on recognizable cultural idioms and social conventions. His critique has a particularly *fin-de-siècle* edge, for the 1890s were a decade of increasing sexual anxiety. This anxiety was expressed not only in attacks on the patriarchy by women, decadent artists, homosexuals, and intellectual radicals (Showalter, 11) but also in a reactionary effort to consolidate existing systems of power by entrenching traditional roles and distinctions. Taking up transvestitic tropes as a means of undermining their subjects' masculinity, the cartoons of the popular press set out to spoof and mock such obvious targets as Beardsley and Wilde for their perceived threats to social norms. Wilde was associated with both women's clothing and female emancipation through his editorship of *Woman's World* (1887-9), a magazine that focused on female fashion and dress but whose keynote was 'the right of women to equality of treatment with man' in such articles as 'Women Wearers of Men's Clothes' and 'The Fallacy of the Superiority of Man' (Schmidgall, 70-1). A contemporary caricature by Alfred Bryan depicts Wilde dressed as a cigarette-smoking New Woman (Ellmann, plate 48), while a *Punch* cartoon of 1894 presents Beardsley in exaggeratedly feminine attire as 'The Servant of the New Woman' (Zatlin, *Aubrey Beardsley*, 81; see plate 41).

The *fin-de-siècle* anxiety that expressed itself in a powerful concern that male and female difference be clearly distinguished by dress comes out clearly in a *Punch* spoof of 1891 entitled 'The Sterner Sex!' The drawing shows a pair of very modern young ladies about to play tennis, one of whom is wearing her brother's hat and coat. Asked whether she likes the outfit, her friend replies: 'Well – it makes you look like a young man, you know, and that's so effeminate!' (147). The satire attacks the transgressions of both dress and sex, for the connection between cross-dressing and homo-sexuality is not principally attached to the cross-dressing woman in the sketch but rather to the absent male, who has apparently abdicated his proper authority over her and whose own sexuality is thus called into question. As happens so often with the cross-dressing trope, 'the unex-pected or supplementary presence of a transvestite figure in a text ... indicates a *category crisis elsewhere*' (Garber, 17), in this case in the Victorian ethos, which was becoming increasingly destabilized by the transgressive behaviour of effeminate young men and masculine New Women. It is part of Beardsley's brilliance that he used his incisive black-and-white lines to underscore the category crisis of his world by producing figures that inhabit neither one end of a spectrum nor the other but both at once – a liminal third space that encompasses both male and female but moves beyond them to a transgendered subjectivity. With his performative mas-querade of nude and costumed figures of ambiguous gender, Beardsley directly attacks the Victorian notion of essential sexual difference by draw-ing attention not only to the constructed, artificial nature of hierarchical distinctions but also to the dangerous politics such polarities put into play.[8]

NOTES

1 The exhibit, which was held at the Victoria and Albert Museum in the summer of 1966, was organized by Brian Reade and, as Simon Wilson observes, 'marked the appearance of a level of interest unprecedented since Beardsley's own day' (in Langenfeld, xv). The exhibit was also taken to New York and Tokyo (see Lasner, Nos. 196, 196a, 196b, 196c).

2 Linda Gertner Zatlin argues that Beardsley's sexual nature was probably unformed but that his work, which is erotic rather than pornographic, demonstrates a strong affinity with, and support of, women (*Aubrey Beardsley*). Brian Reade suggests that Beardsley may have had an incestuous relationship with his sister, Mabel, with whom he liked to exchange clothes (*Aubrey Beardsley*, 20). Malcolm Easton concludes that Beardsley was a transsexual (243ff).

3 Beardsley began work on *Mlle de Maupin* in February 1897, planning to illustrate the novel in monthly parts; he abandoned work on the text in the fall of 1897 (*Letters*, 250, 354-5, 381-2, 384-5, 393). Smithers published *Six Drawings Illustrating Théophile Gautier's Romance Mademoiselle de Maupin* in 1898 (Lasner, 121).

4 Six of the twenty full- and double-page illustrations for the *Morte* focus on this theme. See 'How King Arthur Saw the Questing Beast and Thereof had Great Marvel'; 'How Four Queens Found Launcelot Sleeping'; 'How La Beale Isoud Nursed Sir Tristram'; 'How King Mark Found Sir Tristram Sleeping'; 'How King Mark and Sir Dinadan Heard Sir Palomides Making Great Sorrow and Mourning for La Beale Isoud'; and 'How Sir Launcelot Was Known by Dame Elaine.'

5 The caption, however, was provided by John Lane; Beardsley's original, ironic, title for the picture was 'The Man in the Moon' (MacFall, 52).

6 Only thirteen of the sixteen illustrations Beardsley designed for *Salome* were printed in John Lane's 1894 edition; 'John and Salome,' 'Salome on the Settle,' and the first version of 'The Toilette of Salome' were excluded.

7 Zatlin has given the most sustained argument for Beardsley's support of female emancipation and his critique of conventional gender roles and sexual attitudes in *Aubrey Beardsley and Victorian Sexual Politics*. See also Bridget Elliott's 'New and Not so "New Women" on the London Stage' for a detailed exploration of the ways in which Beardsley's images of actresses were aligned in the public mind with feminist demands for increased autonomy.

8 I am grateful to the Social Sciences and Humanities Research Council of Canada and Nipissing University for supporting the research for this essay and to Dr. Donald Mason for his interest and encouragement as well as for his generously shared knowledge of the *fin-de-siècle*.

ILLUSTRATIONS

Fig. 9.1. Aubrey Beardsley, 'Aubrey Beardsley's Bookplate' (retitled 'Mr. Pollitt's Bookplate'). *The Later Work of Aubrey Beardsley.* London: John Lane, 1901, 155.

Fig. 9.2. Aubrey Beardsley, 'How Sir Launcelot Was Known by Dame Elaine.' *Morte d'Arthur* by Thomas Malory. Vol. 2. London: J.M. Dent, 1894, facing 670.

Fig. 9.3. Aubrey Beardsley, 'How Sir Tristram Drank of the Love Drink.' *Morte d'Arthur.* Vol. 1. London: J.M. Dent, 1893, facing 334.

Fig. 9.4. Aubrey Beardsley, 'The Woman in the Moon.' Frontispiece for *Salome* by Oscar Wilde. London: John Lane, 1912.

Fig. 9.5. Aubrey Beardsley, 'The Toilette of Salome.' *Salome.* London: John Lane, 1912, facing 50.

Fig. 9.6. Aubrey Beardsley, titlepage design for *The Savoy*, No. 1 (January 1896).

Fig. 9.7. Aubrey Beardsley, 'The Lady at the Dressing Table.' *The Later Work of Aubrey Beardsley.* London: John Lane, 1901, 163.

Fig. 9.8. Aubrey Beardsley, 'D'Albert in Search of His Ideals.' *The Later Work of Aubrey Beardsley.* London: John Lane, 1901, 162.

10

W.E.F: Question Marks, Exclamation Points, and Asterisks

Ira B. Nadel

Midway in a 1972 review of a reprint of *The Germ*, Dick Fredeman called attention to the question mark. Distinguishing between Elliot Stock's line-for-line type facsimile of the Pre-Raphaelite magazine and the original edition, Dick noted the accuracy of the 1901 reprint. Celebrating the photofacsimiles of wrappers and frontispiece etchings and the completely reset line-for-line reprint in a font closely approximating the original 1850 printing, Dick nevertheless undertook a collation of the two versions to show that textual variants *did* exist. Paper stock differed, as did heavy type embossing, with minor variations in the type face, which 'appears to be fractionally smaller' (Rev. of *The Germ*, 88). But what really underscored the difference between the original and the facsimile was the question mark.

In the 1850 printing, the question mark exists in both roman and italic type. In the Stock reprint, italic question marks are employed exclusively until page 112; roman and italic appear together intermittently after that following the type of the original. In Number Four of *The Germ* reprint, there is a single instance of the italic question mark that follows the 1850 text. Exclamation points and the asterisk also differ in the reprint, which surely undermined its authenticity. Such attention to detail was not unusual as anyone Dick reviewed can attest. Such microscopic analysis not only characterized Dick's method but also excited him as a reviewer and editor. Indeed, the more minute the detail, the greater the concentration of scholarly energy and investigation. In reviewing the 1971 reprint based on the Stock facsimile, for example, he carefully notes that the occasional punctuation mark has been whited out 'as has Signature K on page 145' (92). The 1971 text, he concedes, is legible, but the 'book is essentially unusable in that it cannot be referred to bibliographically except by the most awkward circumlocution' because of its pagination: *The Germ* itself is not continuous with its editorial matter, and the dual numeration creates chaos (92). The editor did not reproduce the original *Germ* but the inaccurate Stock facsimile.

With the attention of a medieval scribe and the enthusiasm of a graduate student, Dick would pore over texts. No detail was too minute to escape his attention, from spacing and leading to the alignment of rules, indented sections, and individual letters. Compositor departures from the line-for-line resetting were an anathema, as were differences in the position on the page of signature and page numbers. Dick, whose eyes appeared magnified behind his thick glasses, read microscopically and frequently proved his points with detailed appendices that listed textual variants or sources overlooked, neglected, or disregarded by the hapless editor of the text at hand. Often, he would turn the occasion of the review into a survey of all the bibliographical scholarship relating to the text or the author. And with confidence, evidence, detail, and lengthy footnotes, Dick, like some latter-day scholastic, would sweep the scholarly stables of error, laxness, or sloth. No element was too small, no error too minor to escape his censure. He was quick to point out, for example, that *The Germ* appeared not in a black slipcase, as the unfortunate editor Robert Hosman states in his 1971 reprint, but in either a black envelope case or in a blue-gray box with a white spine. How did Dick know? He owned the original, as well as all the various reissues.

Dick's bibliographical and textual standards were uncompromising, and his reviews constantly reflected them. He took reviewing seriously and published essays that often ran fifteen pages or more. His scrupulosity drove him to query, question, and quantify the errors in the work before him. His reviews also opened new areas of scholarly pursuit for himself as well as for others. None provides a better example than his 1968 review of Volumes III and IV of the *Letters of Dante Gabriel Rossetti*, edited by Oswald Doughty and John Robert Wahl.

Dick could hardly contain his outrage at their inept, careless, and desultory approach to gathering material. The adjectives are his, summarized in the cautious but cutting term he uses for the entire edition: 'deficient' ('Rossetti's Letters,' 104). The four volumes, he quickly shows, are anything but comprehensive; his criticisms begin with the editors' failure to note which letters had previously appeared and reach a near fever pitch when he cites the at least 1,600 letters the editors *excluded* from their edition. He then carefully reviews the nature of the excluded material, indicating how their absence invalidates the edition.

With precision (and a certain relish), Dick dismantled the edition, not only in terms of its lacunae but also in terms of its apparatus, reliability, and purpose. From eight manuscript sources alone, he points out 1,000 missing letters. To drive home the point, or to provide the *coup de grâce*, he then lists, at the conclusion of his review, thirteen letters to eleven recipients, all from common sources, that do not appear in the Doughty-Wahl edition. The number of letters to many recipients is unconvincing, especially to such figures as Elizabeth Siddal (1),William Morris (1), Burne-Jones (2), and Ruskin (1), the last especially bizarre since there are seventy letters from Ruskin to Rossetti in the Cook and Wedderburn edition of Ruskin's works. Material in the Angeli Papers at the University of British Columbia and available to the editors includes 104 correspondents who are not represented in Doughty-Wahl. The edition 'lamentably falls short' of being the definitive edition of Rossetti's letters, but it would become, as many soon learned, the spur to Dick's long-term project to produce a comprehensive, multi-volume edition of the poet/painter's correspondence (107).[1]

The co-editors of a 1982 edition of Tennyson's *In Memoriam* suffered a similar fate. In his review of this Clarendon edition, Dick again proved his mettle, criticizing the effort to combine the twin functions of a critical and a variorum edition. He praises the editors' lengthy catalogue of accidentals and their collations of variants from the Trinity College, Cambridge, manuscripts, which were unavailable to Christopher Ricks when he published his 1969 Longman's Annotated Poets edition of Tennyson's poetry. He also praises the editors, Susan Shatto and Marion Shaw, for their selection of the 1884B edition as copy-text.

Contentious matters soon emerge, however, from the editors' decision to use arabic rather than roman numerals for the sections, deviating from the copy-text and marking a concession to pragmatic rather than textual considerations. Dick makes clear that since the title of the poem is in Latin, the formality of roman numerals is more appropriate to the subject and tone of the elegiac form. He then begins with the numerous production errors, the most grievous being the transposition of the opening pages of the text of the poem owing to the presence of an erratum slip that itself contains an error (the reversed pages are not '36 and its facing leaf' but 36 and the verso of its facing page, the facsimile of the title page of the first edition of the poem, which should occupy the verso of the fly-title [Rev. of *In Memoriam*, 308]). Serious and detailed textual criticisms follow, related, most importantly, to Dick's belief in their importance for interpretation:

'these [matters] affect the way a reader approaches the poem critically' (309). Objecting to the editors' substitution of 'Introductory Stanzas' for 'Prologue' to the poem, Dick uses physical evidence and the textual history of the work to question their decision.

Examining the non-textual sections of the edition, he points out further errors and complains that there seems to have been no evidence of copyediting by either the co-editors or the Press. Repetition of various points becomes an outright annoyance since the editors do not relegate information to one section or another. Every fact, description, or anecdote, especially if it relates to the manuscripts, is repeated at least once and sometimes three or four times, often in identical language. To insure his readers understand the point, Dick devotes an entire page to documenting only one set of repetitions. He then moves on to a larger problem, introduced with characteristic reason, tinged with poison: 'there are so many technical faults to find with the Shatto-Shaw edition that one hardly know where to start ... or stop' (310).

But Dick was not always negative. When an edition met his stringent standards, he could be generous, as he was in his 1990 review of editions of Tennyson's work by Christopher Ricks and Cecil Lang. The occasion was the publication of the second edition of Ricks's poems of Tennyson and two volumes of Lang's Tennyson *Letters*. Beginning with the new access to the Trinity College manuscripts, the new edition of the poems substantially improves upon the old one, which Dick had earlier praised. Accepting the continuation of an editorial policy outlined in the original 1969 version, he concedes that 'microscopic scrutiny' of Ricks's approach is not necessary ('Tennyson,' 2). In a note, he praises Ricks's attention to detail: 'no error is too minuscule to evade detection and correction,' adding 'see the inserted caret in the notes to *The Princess* (between ii and iii, last line 2: 219), inadvertently omitted in 1969' (26). Such scrupulosity earned approval.

After citing further corrections and the addition of new biographical and publication information, Dick explains that the main feature of the second edition is the 'textual intercalations in the notes and appendices of unpublished drafts, rejected readings, fragments, and new poems' made possible via the now available manuscript notebooks at Trinity College. More than 250 pages of new and revised material in the second edition made a three-volume edition necessary. The care, research, and 'unpretentious erudition' (3) of Ricks gains high praise from Dick who in a rare display of scholarly hyperbole, declares that this second edition 'approaches definitiveness' (4). But, of course, Dick could not resist collating the first and second editions, beginning again with numeracy, challenging the claim made by Ricks that there are 'about a dozen poems, about a thousand lines of verse and countless variants' added to the second edition (5). Dick leaps on the 'about' and clarifies its reference through another microscopic, textual *tour de force.*

Despite this detail, Dick complains that his remarks are only an 'abbreviated survey' that cannot, despite its 36-page length, do justice to the 'magnitude of Ricks's revisions' (12). But caveats must be offered, although 'the few editorial peccadilloes spotted in fine-combing the edition are herein relegated to footnotes' (13). A note nearly three pages long then documents the errors, although Dick cites only a single typo in the text itself 'and that in Appendix A' where the first line of 'The Ring' (III: 577) reads 'Litte' for 'Little' (29). He does add, however, that while the 'notes are unusually generous, there are lacunae' (30). A long paragraph follows.

In praising the extensive revisions to every element of the edition, from the prelims to the index, Dick delights in its thoroughness and accuracy, declaring the work 'reliable and readable' because it 'reproduces in an admirably economical format almost all the substantives and significant variants without imposing on the reader the clutter of minutiae that too easily obscures rather than illuminates the text' (10). Dick was similarly pleased with the first two volumes of the Tennyson letters edited by Cecil Y. Lang and Edgar F. Shannon, predicting that when the final third volume appeared, the entire edition would become one of the indispensable research tools for Tennyson scholarship. Because the number of surviving letters to Tennyson are small by comparison to those of Dickens, Browning, or Carlyle, the editors have had to provide other documents 'to flesh out the running life-narrative' (17). Doing so results in multiple perspectives that constitute a new genre, 'somewhere between biography and an edition of letters' (17). The selection of documents that complement the correspondence add immeasurably to the value of the edition. Acknowledging minor typos and occasional inconsistencies in the two volumes, he agrees with the editors' decision not to attempt diplomatic texts of the letters but objects to the exclusion of details relating to the publication history of the letters.

Dick bestows particular praise upon the lively annotations, praising in particular their humour as in this note for Daniel Barron Brightwell, unauthorized compiler of the first Tennyson concordance: '[He] remains as obscure as Tennyson could have wished him' (21). James Furnivall is described as an 'enthusiastic and intemperate scholar, sculler, editor, antiquary, teacher ... and polemicist (all his life) ... His virtues, though numerous and conspicuous, did not include moderation or modesty, self-restraint or self-doubt' (20). But erudition is never absent in the notes that Dick admires. The occasional lapses in the editing occur mostly in the cross-references and are of little importance given the general level and accuracy of the annotations. The only factual error spotted in the entire edition is the publication date of Rossetti's 'My Sister's Sleep,' which first appeared in 1848, not in 1850 as the editors state.

Dick's reviews were not limited to bibliographical and textual matters, as his 1993 essay entitled 'Silent Margins' demonstrates. Indeed, in this work, he takes up the cudgels against feminist criticism and slays the beast in his most aggressive style. Taking objection to the phrase 'clitoral hermeneutics' found in an early work by Naomi Schor entitled *Breaking the Chain*, he abbreviates it to 'Clit Crit' ('Silent Margins,' 157). He then demolishes a feminist reading of the Pre-Raphaelites in Lynne Pearce's 1991 study *Woman/Image/ Text: Readings in Pre-Raphaelite Art and Literature*. Questioning the value of a 'fully armed militant feminist' approach to Pre-Raphaelite painters who created constant images of sex-starved women, Dick challenges the personal war on the Pre-Raphaelites undertaken by Pearce (158). Dismissing the disclaimer that the 'I' in the text is not personal, Dick notes that the point of view throughout is 'predominately perpendicular' and that the pronoun appears no fewer than 150 times in the text with more than 200 other first-person pronouns. The introduction and conclusion alone use 'I' 72 times, and only 27 pages of the text are free of first-person intrusions. (Dick's love of numbers is nowhere more apparent than in such citations.) But in her assault on the 'tyranny of the patriarchal context,' Pearce misfires, relying on 'practical cliticism disguised as a serious gallery-guide to a decade of Pre-Raphaelite literary pictures' (159). Her style and approach are awkward and often 'incoherent, pleonastic, convoluted, repetitive, and breezily careless' (160). Unrelenting, Dick notes that the errors and inconsistencies in fact, idiom, diction, and mechanics are so rampant that he cannot believe the author is a university instructor in English. Solecisms and jargon vie with subject verb disagreement and dangling modifiers. And if such strictures are 'phallocentric and therefore irrelevant [or] old fashioned,' there is more, Dick gleefully writing that 'repetitions are almost as prolific as the virgulitis that punctuates virtually every page in the book.' There is also the unscholarly habit of quoting primary material from secondary sources (160-1). Surprisingly, Dick believes that constructive feminist criticism has a point, although 'Clit Crit' does not. Nothing more than 'the crotch' is the 'neural command center in the Clit Crit-feminist war on patriarchal literature and art' he declares (161). Regrettably, Dick concludes, the excesses of Clit Crit produce 'trivial, biased and perverse assertions that reveal more about the author than either about the pictures or poems discussed' (165).

Dick's love of accuracy carried over to his own editorial work, proof of his commitment to textual exactness and the privileged role of the editor, which he believed superseded that of the critic. *The P.R.B. Journal,* published in 1975, was an early sign of this devotion. The volume, William Michael Rossetti's diary of the Pre-Raphaelite Brotherhood, is the sole contemporary authority, other than correspondence, for the history of the PRB. William Michael was the Secretary of the movement and Dick, for the first time, offers the whole of the surviving manuscript along with important ancillary materials. The edition, with its ten plates, seven appendices, and four-part critical apparatus, which includes his 'Editorial Introduction,' provides the most thorough and comprehensive edition of this crucial document, the single most important record of the movement, to appear so far. Work on this much-praised volume was made easier when Dick acquired the manuscript as part of the Angeli Papers housed in the Special Collections Division of the University of British Columbia Library.

The four volumes of the *Dictionary of Literary Biography* – two each on the Victorian novelists and poets – plus two special issues of *Victorian Poetry* he edited further display Dick's editorial acumen and insight. And it was a credit to Dick's reputation that he always attracted the top contributors in the field. For the *DLB* project (1983-5), a distinguished set of scholars participated, including John F. Stasny, then editor of *Victorian Poetry,* George Ford, Anne Humphreys, Jacob Korg, Robert Kiely, Juliet McMaster, Norman Page, Barry V. Qualls, G.B. Tennyson, Joseph Wiesenfarth, and Tom Winnifrith. Dick himself contributed entries on Oliver Madox Brown and William Bell Scott. For the special *Victorian Poetry* issue on Queen Victoria (1987), Richard Altick, Jerome McGann, Christopher Ricks, John D. Rosenberg, Richard L. Stein, and G. Robert Stange were among the contributors. However, he never let friendship interfere with his scrupulosity: one contributor to the *DLB,* exasperated by frequent requests to change (i.e., improve) his essay, demanded its withdrawal. Dick refused, arguing that since he had already re-written so much of it, he had part ownership. The original author chose to withdraw his name and the essay appeared with the *sobriquet* 'anon.'

The 39-volume *Victorian Muse* project for Garland (1985-6) also demonstrated Dick's editorial talents, especially in organization. Originating out of a mutual need for ready access to obscure or un-reprinted primary documents of the Victorian period, from criticism to parody, which only Dick seemed to know, the two of us, with the help of John F. Stasny, prepared a daunting collection of material that ranged from the satiric *Poems inspired by certain pictures at the Art Treasures Exhibition, Manchester* by Tennyson Longfellow Smith of Cripplegate, in the same volume as *The Laughter of the Muses, A Satire or The Reigning Poetry of 1869*, to R.H. Horne's *A New Spirit of the Age*. *The Fleshly School of Poetry* by Robert Buchanan appeared in the same volume as Swinburne's *Under the Microscope*, while the parodic *Anti-Maud* was printed with *Every Man His Own Poet*. Walter Hamilton's *The Aesthetic Movement in England*, plus a three-volume reprint of the bio-critical introductions to *The Victorian Poets* by A.H. Miles, a ten-volume anthology published between 1891 and 1897, expanded the series. Especially useful was Dick's volume, *Victorian Prefaces and Introductions*, a facsimile set of key documents such as Palgrave's 'Preface' to *The Golden Treasury* and D.G. Rossetti's introduction to *The Early Italian Poets*. William Michael Rossetti and Arnold also appear in the volume, which contains four important introductory notices to Victorian editions of the works of three major Romantic poets: Keats, Blake, and Shelley. Dick's introduction to the volume is a masterful synthesis of Victorian aesthetics and criticism.

As co-editor of the *Journal of Pre-Raphaelite and Aesthetic Studies* from 1987-1990, Dick at last found a vehicle to promote the direction and research of Pre-Raphaelite studies. Using the journal as a means to publish the best criticism and latest developments in the field, he made it a publication befitting its subject, introducing colour plates, longer articles, and a new format.

Dick and I inherited the journal, which was originally titled *The Pre-Raphaelite Review*, from Frances Golffing, who began the publication in 1977. In 1980, it was retitled *The Journal of Pre-Raphaelite Studies* in an effort to strike a balance between the art-historical and the literary studies. In the summer of 1987, Dick and I took over the operation and retitled the journal once more in an attempt to expand further its coverage and range as the pre-eminent journal in the area of Pre-Raphaelite studies. Dick's prominence made this effort easy, and submissions soon arrived, even though our first editorial had made it clear that all submissions would now be refereed. An illustrated title page replaced the colour cover illustrations, in response to the tendency of libraries to discard covers in bound volumes of journals. Volume 1 under the new editors contained contributions by Adeline R.Tintner, George Landow, David Latham, and Dick himself. A cumulative index of the preceding ten years appeared as the final article. In an effort to be current, the journal devoted part of the spring 1988 issue to papers from the special MLA session on the Pre-Raphaelites held at the 1987 Modern Language Association Convention in San Francisco.

Little did the authors know the intensity with which their work would be scrutinized by the editors *before* it went out to referees. Once an essay arrived, I would glance over it to judge its possible suitability for the journal and check if we had or had not recently published on the same subject. We would then determine the accuracy of the facts in the essay. Were primary sources employed? Were facsimiles? Dick would begin to work it over, which meant that he would examine almost every reference, 90 per cent of the time relying on his own resources and books in his library. Shoddy scholarship or sloppy writing would disqualify a work immediately, and it was the rare piece that passed his eye uncorrected. If the submitted essay was deemed legitimate, it would go out to two readers for an assessment. Invariably, items would be returned to the author with numerous queries and questions.

Once enough suitable material was received and corrected for an issue, we would begin to deal with our designer, Ron McAmmond. Dick's determination to have every issue look as handsome as its content, including colour plates and black and white illustrations, also meant working carefully with an expert printer who cost us more but provided us with superior work. The arrival of a new issue was cause for celebration and admiration, and colleagues were often invited to Dick's library to praise the work. One of his last efforts with the journal was the handsome *A Rossetti Cabinet: A Portfolio of Drawings by Dante Gabriel Rossetti,* by now a collector's item, documenting the largest collection of the artist's work remaining in private hands. Appearing in 1991, this special and final issue of *JPRAS* from Vancouver displayed Dick's assiduousness, detail, and fine aesthetic sense, both in his selections for the 113 plates and in the layout and design of the volume. Through our editorship, Dick believed that the study of the Pre-Raphaelites was enhanced and that the journal provided a specific outlet for new scholarship. Only a lack of funding, essential to maintain the production standards and publication of illustrations, curbed the appearance of the journal from Vancouver. It went on to other hands, ironically at a time when Pre-Raphaelite studies were flourishing in the form of exhibits, conferences, monographs, and new societies.

Dick's major editorial enterprise was the multi-volume edition of the *Correspondence of Dante Gabriel Rossetti,* the first two volumes of which were in page proofs at the time of his death. This project consumed Dick, who prepared a detailed fifteen-page prospectus of the edition in 8-point type. Of course, it was something more: a condensed summary of Rossetti's life and work, an account of his critical reception, and an evaluation of the dire state of his letters. It also contained vintage Fredeman language: 'biographical quidnuncery always attaches to Bohemian artists and writers,' he complains, although 'Rossetti's case was exacerbated by the sheer number of melodramatic episodes punctuating his life' ('Correspondence,' 2). After confronting the Rossetti legend, Dick outlines his rationale for a new edition, skewering the Doughty-Wahl effort once more, highlighting not only its unreliability but also its lack of an index and extensive lacunae. The editors, he repeats, printed something less than half of the surviving correspondence.

Dick would take up the challenge in his energetic, focused, take-no-prisoners way that combined scholarly objectivity with zeal. He planned to account for 'every *known* letter written by Rossetti,' which already totalled 5,700 letters to some 300 recipients, not the paltry 150 recipients cited by Doughty-Wahl ('Correspondence,' 5). Nearly 2,000 unpublished letters would be included, and his edition would restore the full text of many letters so far only available in fragmentary form, as well as some 100 drawings included in the letters. Some 300 letters, however, would be calendared rather than printed in full letter format: most are undated invitations or responses to invitations. Such material would appear in a projected *Companion* volume, the tenth, of the edition.

Three sets of letters published at intervals to correspond with three principal chronological periods of Rossetti's life formed the basic plan of the edition. The first was 'The Early Years,' in two volumes ranging from 1835 to 1862, when Elizabeth Siddal died. The last two sets were to be in three volumes each. Naturally, each set would be comprehensive, containing a census of the included letters plus two indices, one of recipients and repositories, one of names, places, and literary and artistic works referred to in the letters. Index references would be to letter number rather than page. Each year would be preceded by a cover sheet indicating major literary and artistic works, a summary of the contents of the letters, and a chronology. Indices to the sets would contain brief biographical identifications, although full annotations would be reserved for the *Companion* volume designed to serve as a reference guide to the entire edition and intended to eliminate multi-volume cross-references. In his outline of research, editorial approach, and plan, Dick was preparing to execute a full assault on Rossetti archives worldwide. He did, mounting a campaign that often had a team of researchers checking sources, clarifying references, and aiding in annotations. This was a monumental project to which Dick devoted years, and his inability to complete it was perhaps the only serious scholarly disappointment he faced.

Where did all this work take place? In Dick's library, and one of the frightening strengths of Dick as a reviewer was that his library – that wonderful two-storey addition to the rear of his home, itself a repository of outstanding Victorian furniture, painting, and collectibles – contained *all* the major Pre-Raphaelite texts and most of the other Victorian works needed to survey, investigate, and challenge the books he reviewed. Over the years, his Victorian reference materials equalled, if not exceeded, the reference section of most major research libraries.

As a collector, Dick was both omnivorous and omnipresent. Beginning in the mid-1950s, he began to amass one of the largest private collections of Pre-Raphaelite books, including drawings and paintings, in North America. It was no surprise, then, that Andrew Lloyd Webber, himself a collector of Pre-Raphaelite art, came to call, as did most of the major Victorianists of Dick's generation. Scholars like Lionel Stevenson, George Ford, John D. Rosenberg, Christopher Ricks, and Jerome McGann often appeared in Dick's living room, a space replete with authentic Victorian furniture, with a Kelmscott Chaucer page lying framed on an inlaid table, overlooked by several Rossetti drawings around the fireplace.

Dick loved to show off his collection, displaying his rare items on a long library table of medieval design piled high with journals, first editions, offprints, manuscripts, and Victoriana. Close to one of his favourite reading chairs was a bronze statuette of Victoria seated with a dog by Sir Joseph Boehm and dated 'Osborne 1869.' A second copy, he would grandly announce, was in the Queen's collection. Perpendicular to the library table on the other side of the long room was his desk, which was a mountain of paper, disrupted only by his ashtrays; to his right, his computer purred, insulated by a floor-to-ceiling corner bookcase of reference books. An additional wooden bookcase on wheels that contained the most essential materials fenced in the enclosed space that contained Dick's surprisingly unbaronial desk chair.

The library table, evoking the Arts and Crafts tradition of Morris, withstood the weight of reprints, review copies, pamphlets, books, articles to assess, bookseller's catalogues, unopened packages, odd bits of Victoriana, and mail. The glass-covered bookshelves that filled the long room contained not only numerous first editions but also later issues of major and minor Victorian poets with obligatory sets like the Cook and Wedderburn

Ruskin or the loathed Doughty-Wahl collection of Rossetti's letters. An open Webster's *International Dictionary* stood at the ready on a lectern. The second storey of the library, reached by a narrow wrought-iron circular staircase, contained duplicates, twentieth-century literature, and texts deemed unworthy to be situated in the privileged confines of the first floor. Above, a lonely graduate student might be found, checking references or collating. Below, in the basement, in the early stages of his massive edition of the Rossetti letters, a team of assistants worked in a large room surrounded by identical red binders and containing a pool table covered with plywood and a drop cloth that served as additional counter space. The displacement of his collection of *Playboy* magazines and his beloved Marilyn Monroe archive from this workroom was the only bibliographical sacrifice he made, although his plan to provide the first complete index to *Playboy*, undertaken with a colleague, also had to be sidelined.

Dick's particular passion was printing, and the works of Thomas Bird Mosher received special prominence, their own bookcase standing in the dining room.[2] To the side and on a wall was his collection of Victorian spoons; on special occasions, an embroidered Victorian tablecloth celebrating Victoria's Jubilee appeared, acquired during a lecture trip to Australia.[3] A large cast of the Boehm Victoria, nearly two feet high and protected under a glass dome, presided over the room. Receipt of a new item for the collection was cause for celebration, and colleagues were often summoned to the library at 1649 Allison Road to admire his latest purchase and sit in one of three low and uncomfortable Victorian armchairs while Dick narrated the provenance or bibliographical history of the item, which then disappeared onto his shelves. The publication of colour photos of his artefact collection as the Appendix to the special issue on Victoria he edited for *Victorian Poetry* especially pleased him, while readers were astonished as they realized the wealth of Victoriana he had accumulated ('England Our Home,' 223-41).

Acquiring Queen Victoria commemoratives was a passion for Dick. His collection encompassed mugs, plates, plaques, busts, statuettes, tea towels, pipes, bookmarks, match holders, needle and cigarette cases, thimbles, watches, tea caddies, mirrors, flags, aprons, handkerchiefs, inkstands, dishcloths, photographs, and prints. This is by no means an exhaustive list, and it overlooks the commemorative jewellery, coins and stamps, paintings, flags, magazines, menus, and invitations he owned that related to the Queen. Victorian sheet music, woodcuts, and even a Pre-Raphaelite stained glass window were also part of the collection.

One could not take a step in his home without bumping – literally – into an item of Victoriana. The Queen's image appeared painted on alabaster or in a caricature from *Vanity Fair*, while a montage of medals, pins, brooches, and coins commemorating occasions from her wedding to Prince Albert to her two Jubilees resided prominently on a sideboard in the dining room. And the collection constantly grew, the result of his many successful forays to antique shops and flea markets throughout England and the Pacific Northwest. No item was too small or, it seemed, too large for his collection, including a velvet needle case with a Baxter miniature of the young Queen or a Royal Worcester perfume bottle with a stylized head of Queen Victoria in relief on the front. The arrival of a new catalogue from a British bookseller was also cause to cheer or to jeer; it often contained glaring errors or highly priced items that Dick had already purchased cheaply. But the text always required immediate verbal or written annotation.

Dick was a scholar who thrilled in the details others neglected. But he was also an iconoclast, who recognized that academia had changed during his career, a point he elaborated with some disdain in one of his many sardonic verse epistles he penned for various occasions. His retirement after thirty-five years of teaching at UBC prompted one of these rhymed extravaganzas, which also celebrated the very thing that he loved:

> Ensconced in my double-deck book room secure,
> I annotate letters *de jour après jour,*
> All the world is a text, and as every text fetters,
> I'm locked to my prosser, editing letters.

This was Dick – in his scholarly glory.[4]

NOTES

1 The review in *Victorian Studies* was actually a synthesis of a longer, two-part review that first appeared in *The Malahat Review* (January 1967, April 1968).

2 One of Dick's last pleasures shortly before his death was to receive a copy of Philip R. Bishop's *Thomas Bird Mosher: Pirate Prince of Publishers* (1998), a bibliographical and critical survey of Mosher's work containing Dick's introductory essay.

3 Dick lectured worldwide, preparing by altering his sartorial splendour to suit the country. For a visit to Communist Poland in 1977, he acquired a bright red leisure suit accented with new white patent shoes; for lectures in the States, he purchased a metallic blue suit. Three-piece suits, however, were

preferred around the UBC English Department, occasionally worn with saddle shoes and always with a gold chain on which hung a large gold nugget.

4 The author would like to thank Herbert J. Rosengarten, a long-time friend and colleague of Dick Fredeman, for his assistance with this essay.

11

The Great Pre-Raphaelite Paper Chase: A Retrospective

William E. Fredeman

More than three decades have passed since I invented the field of Pre-Raphaelite studies, and I thought it might be appropriate in this keynote address to the Armstrong Browning Library conference on 'The Pre-Raphaelites and Their Circle' to retrace for you some of the highlights of those years by way of a retrospective anecdotal account of my personal involvement with the Pre-Raphaelites: where I came from, where I am, and how I got here.[1]

As a bibliographer, editor, and reluctant book collector, I have maintained a systematic watching brief both on the new directions and developments in Pre-Raphaelite criticism and scholarship that have won for the field a gradual, if sometimes grudging, academic respectability and on the multifarious other activities, such as conferences, societies, serial publications, auction sales, exhibitions, booksellers' catalogues, and ephemera that reflect and promote the increasingly widespread popularity of the movement. The growth industry that I last surveyed in 'Pre-Raphaelitism Revisited: Dr. Frankenstein Reprograms the Monster' at the *JPRAS* seminar at the MLA in 1987 has since that date been steadily bullish: Pre-Raphaelite stock, as a recent *New Yorker* cartoon showing a TV news anchor reporting a 15 per cent increase indicates, has never been higher, an assessment confirmed by the attendance at this conference.

Malcolm Warner, now keeper of Prints & Drawings at the San Diego Art Gallery, who has been engaged on a catalogue raisonée of Millais for almost as long as I have been working on the new edition of Rossetti's letters, said to me when we first met in Chicago a few years ago, 'It's like meeting Moses!' Modesty precludes my accepting his analogy, for, while on occasion, largely owing to a series of 'Mack-the-knife' reviews for which I have become undeservedly famous, I may have served as the 'Sorcerer's Apprentice,' the Moses of the Movement was not I, but William Michael Rossetti, without whose contribution to Pre-Raphaelite scholarship none of us would be here this evening. I should like to dedicate this lecture to him. In another venue, I might propose a Bacchanalian toast to his memory; but on this occasion – here, at Baylor, where tamer libations prevail – I am constrained by Dionysus' incredulous response to his wife, Ariadne, in Garrison Keelor's story, 'The Mid-Life Crisis of Dionysus,' in *The Book of Guys,* after she berates him for drinking too much: 'Look,' he says, 'I'm the God of wine, okay? I'm not the God of iced tea.'

I

For most of my academic life, I have been involved in a great Pre-Raphaelite paper chase. The first decade was spent tracking down the primary and secondary materials necessary to document the Brotherhood and the Movement, a chase that culminated in the publication in 1965 of *Pre-Raphaelitism: A Bibliocritical Study.* That work followed on my 1956 doctoral dissertation on the Pre-Raphaelites at the University of Oklahoma, only the second written on the subject, which, since my committee did not regard Pre-Raphaelitism as a *bona fide* area of research, I was allowed to pursue only because Cecil Lang, the greatest paper-chaser of all Victorian scholars, had pioneered the field in his Harvard dissertation six years earlier.

I had no intention during those years of devoting my entire career to what Rossetti called the 'visionary vanities of half-a-dozen boys' (qtd in Caine, *Recollections* 219) until the chase led, in 1963, to two events that altered dramatically the course of my research pursuits. The first was what I like to think of as my 'mini-Malahide,' the discovery of the Pre-Raphaelite manuscripts at Penkill Castle that focus mainly, but not exclusively, on William Bell Scott and Alice Boyd. The second was my introduction in the same year to Helen Rossetti Angeli, the doyen of the Rossetti family, who, a few years later, generously arranged for the transfer of the remaining Rossetti Family archive, now known as the Angeli-Dennis Papers, to the University of British Columbia, where I spent my entire academic career. Coincidentally, about the same time, Dr. Frank Taylor invited me to contribute to the John Rylands Library *Bulletin,* a journal whose format and generous length allowance proved fortuitously ideal for presenting the major caches of manuscripts discovered at Penkill: the letters of Arthur Hughes to Alice Boyd (1967); the documents relating to Rossetti's breakdown and attempted suicide in 1872 (1971); and a selection of the extensive correspondence between William Bell Scott and Alice Boyd (1976).

If Serendipity, my tenth muse, played a crucial role, as she assuredly did, in shaping these two scholarly adventures, I am convinced that a third, the invitation to review the Clarendon edition of Rossetti's letters (1965-7) was orchestrated by some malicious cosmic jester, bent on revenge. The concatenation of events that led me recklessly in 1973 to agree to re-edit Rossetti's letters is too lengthy to rehearse. Twenty years on, on the eve of publishing the first two volumes, covering the formative years from 1835-62, Rossetti has become my personal nemesis, and I am seriously considering resubtitling the work, originally planned as the 'Centenary Edition,' for publication in 1982, as the 'Albatross Edition' of Rossetti's correspondence. Still, if the paradigm credited to the first prime minister of India has any validity – that 'the cards a man is dealt represent determinism, how he plays them free will' – I hope to convince you by the end of this narrative that it was not so much hubris as naiveté that led me to embark alone on the edition and that notwithstanding the evidence of inordinate delay in bringing the first set of letters to fruition, my career has not been wholly a scholarly *mis*adventure.

I am often asked how I became interested in the Pre-Raphaelites in the first instance. Like most Ph.D. students, after finishing my comps, I was casting about for an unploughed field that would meet the dissertation demand of originality when I hit on the Pre-Raphaelites, then, essentially, except for the Rossettis, virgin territory. With all the bravado of a stereotypical tyro, I embarked on a doctoral dissertation pretentiously entitled: 'The Pre-Raphaelites and Their Critics: A Tentative Approach toward the Aesthetics of Pre-Raphaelitism.' Forty years later, notwithstanding my own research, the entry into the field of dozens of excellent scholars, and the publication of literally hundreds of general and specialized articles and books, I'm not certain that either my own or 'our' collective approach to the aesthetics of the movement is any less tentative or, for that matter, that we are any closer to articulating a precise definition of Pre-Raphaelitism that accommodates comfortably and accurately the forty or so writer and artists who share the label. General and specialized studies of the individual Pre-Raphaelites and of their visual and verbal texts are plentiful, but there is still no single book that provides a critical overview of the entire movement; indeed, there is not even an adequate historical narrative to replace William Gaunt's highly readable and anecdotal *Pre-Raphaelite Tragedy* (1942).

I did not consciously plan in 1956, when I completed my degree, after having taught for five years in a high school in Oklahoma City, that my graduate courtship with Pre-Raphaelitism would eventually become a marriage any more than I planned, in accepting a position in a Canadian university, that I would become a permanent expatriate. The decision to go to Canada proved to be as important as my choice of field, for not only were Canadian universities, like their American counterparts, poised on the cusp of the enormous expansion that would transform academe over the next two decades, the Canadian Government had enacted, just the year before, legislation creating the Canada Council to fund academic and artistic pursuits. In 1958, eight leave fellowships were introduced across the country, and because I was fortunate enough to win one of these, in part perhaps owing to the novelty of my field, the university granted me paid leave in 1959-60, and I set sail, literally, for England, where the first phase of the great paper chase began in earnest.

II

Determined not to waste my dissertation and to publish a work on the Pre-Raphaelites that could not be ignored, I conceived the idea of a bibliocritical study of Pre-Raphaelitism that would serve as a guide or map to open up the subject to students and scholars interested in either the individual poets and painters or in the movement as a whole. It is difficult to realize from today's perspective how discredited the Pre-Raphaelites actually were in 1959. After a brief flurry of interest generated by the half-dozen token centenary exhibitions of 1948 and the publication of Oswald Doughty's and Helen Rossetti Angeli's biographies of Rossetti in the next year, they had once again fallen into disfavour, if not disrepute. Their pictures brought next to nothing at auction – Burne-Jones's four large panels of *The Seasons*, for example, that were on offer a few years ago for £400,000 and would certainly realize substantially more today, actually went through the rooms in 1960 for £38. One of the few dealers who carried Pre-Raphaelite works was Abbott & Holder in Kew, where framed drawings such as those for the Moxon *Tennyson* could be bought for as little as £5. One of my great regrets is that I didn't have the courage to mortgage my $6,200 salary to purchase one of the large Rossettis that Leger Brothers had in stock in 1959, when W.D. Paden acquired *La Pia* for the University of Kansas for £550; two years earlier, the National Gallery of Canada acquired from the same gallery *The Salutation of Beatrice* for £500. One of the partners in the firm offered me *The Roman Widow*, also priced at £550 for £100. Would I had heeded his advice: 'Fredeman,' he said, 'I know you think you can't afford it, but you really should own a Rossetti; they can't go anywhere but up.' No one then could have predicted how far up: in 1964, L.S. Lowry secured for £5,250 the *Proserpine* for which John Paul Getty Jr., who occupied Rossetti's house in Cheyne Walk, paid the then record price of £1.5 million in 1987. The under-bidder on Getty's *Proserpine,* Andrew Lloyd Webber, later purchased his first Rossetti oil, *A Vision of Fiammetta,* for £3.5 million!

If quality art works by the Pre-Raphaelites were in 1959 ridiculously inexpensive by today's standard, albeit still beyond my reach, books – which were almost literally 'going for a song,' and which were, after all, my primary concern in compiling the *Bibliocritical Study* – were not. When I said earlier that I was a 'reluctant book collector,' I meant that I have never collected books as an investment. I do not collect press books, such as Kelmscotts, of which I have only the three Rossettis and the cheapest volume produced at the press, Morris's *Gothic Architecture*; nor do I collect presentation or association copies, unless they come my way by accident, fine bindings, or first editions *per se.* I am, however, both by instinct and background, a collector; but my motivation in forming the largest collection of printed material on the Pre-Raphaelites in private hands has always been purely pragmatic: to form my own working library of books, ephemera, xeroxes, and offprints to free me from having to depend on university and public libraries. Because Oklahoma's library had only a handful of the books I needed for my dissertation and interlibrary loan was then in its infancy, I began ordering books on the Pre-Raphaelites from English dealers as a graduate student, at a time when it was possible to get from someone like George Sexton of Brighton eight or ten books for under £3, including postage. When the UBC library proved equally deficient, I set about system-atically to assemble a Pre-Raphaelite collection and made my first foray on the New York City bookstores at the end of my first year of teaching in the summer of 1957, funded by my first modest research grant: an unprincely sum of $500 (tax free) that was nevertheless sufficient to cover a month's travel expenses, and the purchase of nearly two hundred books. One I passed up because it was too expensive was George Price Boyce's copy of *The Germ,* bound in full green levant by Reviere, offered in a binding sale at Inman's for $37.50. Happily, a mature student who accompanied me on that research trip presented it to me as a gift, and it remains still, after nearly forty years, one of the cornerstones of my Pre-Raphaelite collection.

Lest you think the grant was awarded to send me on bookman's holiday, I hasten to add that the main purpose of the trip was to consult the Pre-Raphaelite resources in the major research centres: the Berg Collection in the New York Public Library, the Pierpont Morgan, and the Frick Art

Reference Library in New York; Harvard, Yale, and the Wilmington Society of the Fine Arts (now the Delaware Art Centre), which houses the only discrete collection of Pre-Raphaelite art in North America. On a similar grant in the following year, I worked at the Huntington Library in San Marino and finally met my mentor, Cecil Lang, then teaching at the Claremont Graduate School and proofing the first two volumes of his monumental edition of Swinburne's letters.

I was, thus, reasonably prepared when I reached England to begin serious research on the *Bibliocritical Study*. My base, naturally, was, the British Museum, whose amenities then for foreign scholars were far more civilized than they are today. Not only was I given a permanent named desk in the North Library, across from Geoffrey and Kathleen Tillotson, on which I could keep fifty books, I also had an assigned parking place in the foreyard of the Museum for my new Mercedes! (Canadian academics on leave abroad at that time, because they escaped income taxes at home and in England, enjoyed an affluence unknown to succeeding generations.) While the Museum's printed and manuscript resources were indispensable, the Printed Catalogue proved of limited value in compiling a subject bibliography, and I spent nearly half my time in bookstores, where for a few shillings I could buy, not just consult, the books I needed, and where also I discovered hundreds of items, especially catalogues and other ephemera, that I should otherwise have missed. The standard price of ordinary books in England, which is now between £5 and £10, then ranged from 1s.6d to 3s.6d. I well remember standing in the basement of Shaw's Bookshop in Manchester for half an hour seriously debating whether to spend 50 shillings for Simeon Solomon's *A Vision of Love Revealed in Sleep* (1871); save for two $10 books, which I splurged on during my first trip to New York, I had never spent that much on a book. Luckily, I succumbed, for I have never again seen Solomon's book for sale in a shop, though it occasionally turns up in booksellers' catalogues or at auction, where it can fetch as much as eighty times the price I paid, to judge from the last copy offered (in 1989) by Ian Hodgkins, the only specialist Pre-Raphaelite book dealer in Britain.

When I arrived in England, there were only a handful of people seriously interested in the Pre-Raphaelites, among them a group that I used to refer to as the three Johns and three Marys: John Woodward, John Bryson, and John Gere, and the three Pre-Raphaeladies: Lady Mander, Virginia Surtees, and Mary Bennett. When it became known that a brash young American was stalking the Pre-Raphaelites, a kind of jungle telegraph was launched to keep tabs on me, as I discovered when I met in turn each member of the group. Lady Mander, who, under her pen name, Rosalie Glynn Grylls, published a flighty biography of Rossetti in 1964, later did the perfunctory notice of my *Bibliocritical Study* in the *TLS*, and Virginia Surtees, who compiled the invaluable catalogue raisonée of Rossetti, remained always civil but coolly suspicious. John Bryson, of Balliol, the editor of the reciprocal correspondence of Rossetti and Jane Morris, eventually warmed, and I obtained from him two of the black orchids in my Pre-Raphaelite library: a pair of tract volumes containing all the major articles on Rossetti published in the nineteenth century and Oliver Madox Brown's novel *Gabriel Denver*. John Gere, who curated the 1948 Birmingham exhibition and went on to become Keeper of Prints and Drawings in the British Museum, was always willing to share his wide knowledge of the Pre-Raphaelites with me; and Mary Bennett, the formidable art scholar who curated the three major retrospective exhibitions of Ford Madox Brown, Holman Hunt, and Millais in the 1960s, was equally generous on the many occasions that I visited the Walker Gallery. But it was John Woodward, the Keeper of Art at the Birmingham gallery, whose tragic end precluded his fulfilling his role as successor to Ellis Waterhouse, who really opened the doors of the Pre-Raphaelite world in England by preparing my way with the key personnel in the major repositories of Pre-Raphaelite art – the Ashmolean, the Victoria & Albert Museum, and the provincial art galleries in Manchester, Liverpool, and Port Sunlight, in each of which I spent one to two weeks examining the collections and archives and scouting the local bookshops. It was from the Birmingham Gallery duplicates that I secured most of my early exhibition catalogues of the Pre-Raphaelites in exchange for cataloguing their extensive collection.

Books, of course, accounted for only perhaps half the items in the bibliocritical study, and much of my time was spent examining the periodical and newspaper resources at the British Museum (and Colindale). The problem was accessing the complete runs of the two to three hundred journals I had determined I needed to consult. To expedite this enterprise, I enquired of the two neophyte Keepers of the North Library – Dennis Rhodes, the now retired distinguished Italian incunabulist, and Ian Willison, also now retired, who went on to become the Keeper of English Language Books in the British Library – whether I might be allowed to work in the stacks. The answer was a definite 'No! Impossible! No one is allowed to work in the stacks!' My response, to put it bluntly, was 'revengeful grievance.' Accordingly, I prepared call slips for the complete runs of all the journals and presented them together, in a huge stack, at the bulb in the Reading Room. Angus Wilson, then the Keeper, angrily demanded to know what I thought I was about, but I remained recalcitrant: I persisted in reporting that I needed to examine all the material requested. In short order, I was summoned by Rhodes and Willison, who informed me that they had reconsidered their decision and that I would be allowed to work in the stacks, which I did – for three long and painful months, hovering over a library cart, going meticulously through the contents of the journals and making notes on the articles – *sans* chair, *sans* table, and with precious little light! The stacks, I discovered, at the expense of permanent foot and back damage, were not designed for readers. But I made two of my closest British friends in Dennis Rhodes, who later coached me in Italian, and Ian Willison, whose apartment I share whenever I am in London, having told him years ago that he would simply have to put me up because I couldn't afford to pay hotel charges and buy books too!

III

What I did *not* accomplish in 1959-60 was meeting Mrs Angeli, then living in Rome, in the Via Marghutta, just above the Piazza d'España. In the letters we exchanged before I left Canada, she had been most friendly and generous with advice and information. But when I went to Rome and tried to contact her – sending letters, telegrams, and flowers – there was no response. I was fearful that she had become offended by an enquiry I had sent her pertaining to a letter I discovered at Texas that appeared on the surface to implicate her father in the nefarious machinations of T.J. Wise, subsequently published in the *Book Collector*. But my fears proved unfounded: what I did not know was that she was nursing her older sister, Olivia Agresti, who died in 1960, and would have seen no one. When I returned, disappointed, to England, Serendipity once again intervened. During a fortnight spent in Oxford, working at the Bodleian and Ashmolean, I was splurging at the Randolph Hotel (then £3.10 shillings a night). One evening after supper I went into the lounge for coffee, where I struck up a conversation with a handsome, young Anglo-Italian a couple of seats away, who, after we introduced ourselves, asked where I was from and what I was working on. When I told him I was working on the Pre-Raphaelites, he informed me that William Michael Rossetti was his great-grandfather. He then asked me whether I would like to meet his mother, Mrs. Dennis, Mrs. Angeli's daughter. That casual encounter with Edward Dennis, precipitated a life-long friendship that terminated only when Imogen Dennis died on 29 December 1993. Coincidentally, both William Michael and Helen Angeli died in their 90th year; Imogen Dennis was just six days short of her 90th birthday. Genes, it appears, always *will* out!

Mrs Angeli returned to England after the death of her sister, and I first met her in the summer of 1963, when she was 84. It was, reciprocally, love at first sight, and I spent much of that summer with her and Mrs Dennis in Woodstock. She took a great interest in my research and read meticulously through the advance proofs of the bibliocritical study, admonishing me in a marginal annotation to a comment of mine that 'Ford Madox Brown was a minor painter': 'My grandfather was not a minor anything!,' she fumed. Because her days and nights were not always distinguishable, we used to sit after dinner, smoking my cigarettes, until two or three in the morning as she regaled me with family lore and tradition and reminisced about her own past. She had never known 'Uncle Gabriel,' but she had distinct memories of 'Aunt Christina' and, of course, of her father. She was warm, engaging, intelligent, and extraordinarily witty; and she retained in old age redolent reminders of the great beauty she had been in her youth; but she was no docile little old lady. She would often bring me up short when I stepped out of line, as she did one early morning when, having seen her to bed in the little house she had in the back garden, I was reading to her from *The Times* as she dozed. Suddenly, an enormous spider crawled across the table beside her bed, and I rolled the paper up and killed it. She came to like a shot, berated me for my insensitivity, and dismissed me summarily. I remained in her bad books for several days.

In a very real sense, Mrs Angeli was my first (and only) patron, and her generosity to me was unbounded. The only Rossetti oil I have is the fragmentary head for *Desdemona's Death Song* that she gave me – the last oil Rossetti worked on before his departure for Birchington. When the family home at 3 St. Edmund's Terrace was damaged by bombs during the war, Mrs Angeli and Imogen went up to London from Barnstable, hired fourteen taxis, rescued her invalid sister, Mary, and took away as much as they could of the contents of the house. From the four unfinished Rossetti oils in the basement, including my *Desdemona*, she removed the heads with a butcher knife. That night there was a direct hit on the house and whatever remained was destroyed. She also said she wanted me to have all the duplicate books in her library, many of which were association copies, stipulating only that she would choose the one I was to have. Many of the greatest treasures in my collection are doubly precious because they were gifts from her: the Gaetano Polidori private printings of *Sir Hugh the Heron* and Christina's *Verses*, and the even rarer 'To my Mother'; sample letters from the family papers; several volumes of William Michael's 'Miscellanies'; and his clipping book on Dante Gabriel, which a few years ago I commissioned

the distinguished Canadian binder Courtland Benson to bind in a full
levant binding decorated with Rossetti's family crest and the monogram he
had designed as the letterhead for his stationery. Annotated by William
Michael as having been purchased at the sale of Jefferson Hogg's daughter,
Prudentia Lonsdale, at Sotheby's 6 Nov 1897, it was signed by HRA in 1919,
and, finally, inscribed to me: 'To Dick Fredeman / Pre-Raphaelite
Pantologist / Woodstock 1963.' That summer I acquired a Jubilee photo
album for my Queen Victoria collection, which houses a music box that is
activated when the front cover is opened. Mrs Angeli was so enchanted with
it that she insisted (to my great delight) in filling it with original family
photographs – of all the Rossettis and Madox Browns; of Ruskin, Morris,
and Swinburne; of William Bell and Letitia Scott and Alice Boyd; and of
Whitman and others.

When I departed for Penkill Castle, the retreat of Alice Boyd and
William Bell Scott, near Girvan in Ayrshire, Scotland, that same summer, I
could not have imagined either that the thirty-six hours I had allocated for
the visit would prove to be the most exciting of my life or that what I would
find there would so significantly alter the shape of my future research.
Collating two Sotheby sales of Scott and Penkill materials a decade apart
(1952, 1962) against a typescript inventory of the Castle made early in this
century, I went to Penkill with a fairly clear expectation of what I might find
in the way of books, portfolios, pictures, and drawings. Arriving from Glasgow at lunchtime on the Saturday, I was graciously received by May Courtney
Boyd, a half-cousin by marriage of Alice Boyd and the then Laird of Penkill,
who gave me free access to the castle's treasures. To my surprise, little of
what I thought to be there was in evidence, and by supper time on Saturday,
I had exhausted the collection and written my description.

On Sunday morning, I packed my bag and brought it downstairs, thinking to while away the day walking about the grounds and searching out the
glen where Rossetti composed 'The Stream's Secret.' Coming out of my
room on the third floor of the castle, I noticed a ladder running diagonally
up the wall to a landing with a crawl space and small door. When I asked
Miss Boyd about it, she said it led to a room called the 'Ark,' where Scott and
Alice used to paint, but assured me there was nothing up there except
some old trunks and painting props; she also told me that no one had been
up there since Alice's death in 1897, except for the electrician who wired
the castle a few years earlier. She readily acceded to my request to see it and
after some searching produced a key. I changed into some old clothes and
went up. As soon as I opened the door of the Ark, which was a long garret
studio with a full-length skylight, I saw lying on top of the trunks, which

lined one side of the room, all the portfolios for which I had been looking and a number of framed paintings and engravings, including Sandys's *A Nightmare*, which because Miss Boyd disliked it heartily, she gave me as a memento of my visit. I then started going through the trunks, most of which contained rotting clothes, memorabilia, and correspondence between Alice Boyd and her niece. I then came to a trunk that was locked. Fortunately, there was a screwdriver nearby, and, using my experience as an ex-military policeman, I jemmied the lock. Inside, on top of a pile of clothes, was a large, tin manuscript box, also locked. On opening it, I discovered several packets of manuscript letters – from Morris, Christina Rossetti, Swinburne; a packet of seventy-two letters, wrapped in a paper cover marked 'To be destroyed,' dealing with Rossetti's breakdown in the summer of 1872; a box of seventy-two letters from the painter Arthur Hughes to Scott and Alice Boyd; and, tied up in pink ribbons, the complete correspondence from Scott to Alice, from 1859, when they met, to 1885, when they removed from London to Penkill. My emotions ran the gamut from elation to frustration because I had arranged to leave Girvan at 6:00 p.m. to return to London, where I had appointments the following day. Before I left, Miss Boyd agreed not to let anyone into the Ark before I could return in a fortnight's time; she also kindly allowed me to take away some of the letters to examine at my leisure and to give UBC first option to purchase the material. The pickings were slimmer on my return visit to the Ark, but I did discover some letters from Scott to Alice and the complete run of her day-diaries, which proved invaluable for documentation, since she recorded every letter she sent and received and kept a minute record of the periods when she and Scott were together and apart. Together with the reciprocal correspondence, the diaries provided irrefutable evidence to disprove the ridiculous speculations that Scott was Christina Rossetti's innominate lover, a thesis that undermined Lona Packer's otherwise incisive biography of the poet.

The later history of the exploitation of May Boyd and the plunder of Penkill by a succession of unethical professionals and tradesmen, including Wally the Milkman, and the acquisition of Penkill by the American millionaire Elton Ekstrand, who sought to restore it to its former glory, is too lengthy to recount here. When the sale of the castle and its contents was advertised in 1992, the Penkill Trust was established in an attempt to interest either a private charity or the National Heritage Memorial Fund to purchase the Castle for the nation at a reputed price of £1,000,000. The Christie sale of the contents of Penkill was held on 5 December 1992. Stripped of its Pre-Raphaelite associations, the castle has now apparently

been sold to another American for an undisclosed sum: *Sic transit* for a
residence that, like Kelmscott Manor, Red House, and Cheyne Walk,
reportedly still shelter the restless ghosts of the Pre-Raphaelite saga.

Several letters from Scott to Alice Boyd in the Penkill Papers offered the
first concrete evidence of a physical relationship between Rossetti and
Jane Morris, a discovery subsequently confirmed in the pillow talk recorded in her letters to her later paramour, Wilfrid Scawen Blunt, and in
his even blunter diary. Because Mrs Angeli requested that I refrain from
publishing them until after her death when I showed them to her, they did
not appear in print until my *Prelude to the Last Decade* was published in 1971,
where, with the other letters intended for destruction, they were put into
the context of Buchanan's attack and Rossetti's breakdown and attempted
suicide. Between 1963 and her death in 1969, I saw Mrs Angeli in most
years; in 1965-6, when I was in England on my first Guggenheim, she
expressed the desire that the Rossetti archive, which she kept beneath her
bed, should be where I was, and the papers accordingly came to UBC in
1966. Surprisingly, most of Rossetti's letters published in Doughty/Wahl
with Angeli provenances were missing, and it was not until I was in England
on my second Guggenheim in 1970-1 and recuperating from cataract
surgery, when I undertook a thorough search of the house after Mrs
Dennis asked me to sort through all her mother's papers, that Allan Life
and I unearthed a trunk containing about 650 letters, bringing the total in
the collection to 820. Mrs Angeli's correspondence and papers, with the
exception of a few notebooks, are now in my personal collection, a gift from
Mrs Dennis, who later gave me permission to photograph the miscellaneous, unpublished drawings of Rossetti, reproduced in *A Rossetti Cabinet*
(1989), which comprised the last issue of *JPRAS* under my editorship.
Though I did not see Mrs Angeli in the summer before her death, my
relationship with her ended on a poignant note, for among her papers I
found wedged in the back of a drawer in her desk a tiny sketch she had
made for her gravestone, a simple design capped by a little owl that now
marks her resting place in the churchyard at Woodstock.

IV

The manuscript collections at UBC, comprising the Angeli-Dennis and
Penkill Papers, as well as a smaller group of letters from the collection of
Rossetti's Newcastle patron, James Leathart, which I secured in 1968 from
his grandson, Dr Gilbert Leathart, established Vancouver as a 'must see' on
the scholarly Baedecker trail. Lacking, however, was a comparably impor-

tant collection of printed books to complement the manuscripts, a lacuna soon to be remedied, thanks once again to Serendipity. I first met the legendary Bournemouth bookseller Norman Colbeck in 1966 at the Lytton Strachey Sale, where I purchased Strachey's copy of *Modern Love*. Afterwards, Norman accompanied me to Bertram Rota's, where I acquired for £65 one of the scarcest Pre-Raphaelite items, Evelyn Waugh's first book, *The P.R.B.* (1926), privately printed at Leicester in 50 copies, replete with misprints, as Waugh wrote me in a letter in 1960. For several years it remained my most expensive book, but its acquisition was the turning point in my career as a collector. Reasoning that I either had to buy the Waugh without quibble or cease pretending to build a Pre-Raphaelite library, I agreed to take it without even asking Anthony Rota the price.

On Norman's invitation, Matt Bruccoli and I travelled together to Bournemouth during an early spring snowstorm the following April. His bookpremises at Ophir Road were located in a disused dance hall at the end of his garden, which was connected to his house by a long corridor. His private collection, consisting of some 13,000 volumes of Victorian and Edwardian poetry and *belles lettres*, a high percentage of them presentation or association copies, plus a large number of manuscripts and letters, he kept in his house, which he shared with his 90-year-old mother. When I enquired what he intended to do with the collection when he retired from bookselling, since the Inland Revenue would certainly regard it as part of his business and tax it away, he said he wanted to give it to an institution that would allow him to do what he had never had time to do: to work with his books. With no authority, I immediately said, 'We'll do that for you,' whereupon he informed me that Gordon Ray, the President of the Guggenheim Foundation and one of his best customers, thought they should go to the British Museum. I protested, on the grounds that, first, it would be carrying coals to Newcastle since the Museum would certainly have 80 per cent or more of the books; second, that the BM would not house Norman's books together as a collection; third, that there was no way the Museum would find a position for Norman; and, finally, that the condition of his books was too good for the Museum, whose books, because there was then no conservation department, were falling apart. Since overtures had already been made, Norman was eventually summoned to London by the Director, not for lunch or a drink (Norman didn't drink), not even for a cup of tea, but to see whether the books of an ordinary tradesman were worthy enough for the Museum to deign to accept them as a gift. In due course, a keeper came to Bournmouth to view the books, but the British class system had already lost the collection.

Meanwhile, back at the ranch, I had initiated negotiations with UBC's President and Librarian, and we held a conference call with Norman, inviting him to come out to Vancouver at our expense, to which he readily agreed, much to the chagrin of Julian Roberts (now at Bodley) who wanted to return to Bournmouth to check Norman's holdings against xeroxes from the *General Catalogue* on the very day Norman was flying to Montreal. When I met Norman, he had never had a transatlantic telephone call, never had a vaccination, never had a passport; he had also never been out of England except to visit Yeats's grave at Sligo, never been in an aeroplane, and never been married. Before his arrival, the Librarian and I had worked out a formula that would enable Norman to give away his major asset: British Columbia, being a book-poor province, the three BC universities would buy his stock in trade as a bookseller and pay to have the collection and the stock shipped to Vancouver. The stock would be distributed among the three universities, UBC would get the collection, and we would employ Norman for five years to curate his own collection, for which a special room would be created, and prepare a catalogue that the UBC Press would publish. Three days into his visit, Norman agreed to these arrangements, and in June 1967, just prior to his 65th birthday, the bookseller and his collection took up permanent residence in Vancouver. Conflating the next twenty years into a single sentence: Norman lived with me for the first year; married a retired colleague (now 95) in the English department in the second, inheriting an instant extended family; made annual pilgrimages either to England or to his wife's shared resort in Spain; saw the publication of *A Bookman's Catalogue* and received an honourary doctorate from UBC in the penultimate year of his life; and died in 1989, aged 86. A bookseller by default, Norman Colbeck was one of the most knowledgeable bookmen I have ever known; he was also one of my dearest friends. Though we were totally dissimilar as personalities, my aggressiveness seemed to complement his natural shyness and reserve, and he used to say that his life was divided into two unequal halves: pre- and post-Fredeman. I only learned in his last year that I was the only person to whom he had ever shown his collection, so perhaps we were, indeed, fated to meet. Had I consulted Norman in 1959-60, when I began serious research on the *Bibliocritical Study*, my work would have been greatly facilitated, but the Colbeck Collection would almost certainly never have come to UBC: the timing would simply not have been right for either of us.

V

The greatest paper chase of all, of course, has been the editing of Rossetti's letters. The new edition was originally commissioned by the Clarendon Press in 1973, with whom I had already contracted *The PRB Journal*, published in 1975, following on my reviews of the Doughty/Wahl edition, published in four volumes (*sans* index) by Clarendon in 1965-7, in which I exposed the major lacunae of the edition, pointed to a few of the editors' shortcomings, and suggested that Clarendon might like to consider publishing an 'Aladdin' edition, offering new lamps for old. Dan Davin, then Englit editor at Clarendon, originally proposed that I should either do a supplementary volume or two, picking up the missing letters, or, alternatively, an intercalated revision that would salvage as much of the Doughty/Wahl typeset letter-texts and notes as possible. It soon became obvious, however, that simple surgery was out of the question; the edition was too unreliable to risk even using it as a primary source for a new edition.

My edition of *The Correspondence of Dante Gabriel Rossetti* will consolidate within a single chronology all the published and unpublished correspondence in three sets of letter volumes to appear in two, three, and four volumes respectively, each terminating in a crisis year, or turning point, in Rossetti's life: 1862, with the death of Elizabeth Siddal and his removal to Cheyne Walk, his last permanent residence; 1872, with his breakdown and attempted suicide, the prelude to the last decade; and 1882, the year of his death. Each set will contain a biographical and analytic index. A final 'Companion' volume containing much of the apparatus and a synoptic index will round out the edition. The first set, 'The Formative Years: From Charlotte Street to Cheyne Walk,' will be published early in 1996.[2] Subsequent sets will follow at two- to three-year intervals.

By contrast with the Doughty/Wahl edition (hereafter D/W), the new edition will print over 5,700 letters to some 330 recipients from 125 manuscript repositories, public and private, and 50 printed sources, doubling in every category the number in D/W, which contained 2,615 letters to 150 recipients, gathered from 23 private and 17 public repositories and three dozen printed sources. The edition will contain approximately 2,000 letters never before published, many from correspondents unrepresented in D/W. It will also restore the complete texts of letters heretofore available only in fragmentary form and reproduce the 100 or more drawings in the letters that were not reproduced in D/W, only a few of which appear in Virginia Surtees's *Catalogue Raisonné*. It will also incorporate a limited number of letters to Rossetti. Some 300 undated and undatable trivial

invitations and responses to invitations to major recipients, such as Frederic
Shields, will be relegated to a calendar in the 'Companion,' where every
known letter written by Rossetti, including unlocated letters in booksellers' catalogues and those mentioned in the letters themselves, which have
not turned up, will be accounted for. Located letters probably amount to no
more than two-thirds of Rossetti's epistolary corpus.

Three major caches of correspondence, amounting to nearly three hundred letters, have not surfaced. Of these, the eighty to ninety to Ruskin,
which almost certainly no longer survive, are the most vital, for while their
content can be deduced from Ruskin's side of the correspondence, one
can only imagine the stylistic and tonal frustration and intemperance of
Rossetti's responses to Ruskin's repeated and tyrannical attempts to im-
pose his vision of life and art on his protegé. The missing letters to two of
Rossetti's most important patrons, Leonard Rowe Valpy and William Graham,
are also a serious loss for the additional light they would cast both on the
artist's business acumen, not always precisely evident in the incoming
correspondence, and on the compositional history of the pictures in the
two collections. The letters to Valpy may still exist, but a decade of searching and telephone calls to every Valpy in the British Isles has produced no
leads; those to Graham were probably destroyed in the fire that destroyed
Mells Park, the home of Graham's daughter, Lady Horner, in 1917. Of
course, the lacunae do not all relate to in-depth correspondence: dozens
of letters that have not been discovered are mentioned in Rossetti's correspondence; and the Angeli-Dennis Papers contain incoming letters from
130 correspondents who do not appear as recipients in the edition. Still,
the number of located letters in the new edition will far exceed the total
published in Doughty/Wahl's edition and the four separate collections
published since then.

While I determined at the outset to distance myself as far as possible
from Doughty/Wahl's edition, comparisons are inevitable and potentially
invidious. Leaving aside the omission of over 3,500 letters and the absence
of an index, which for a quarter century has been the bane of Rossetti and
Victorian scholars, the four volumes of the Doughty/Wahl edition constitute an editorial mare's nest, containing every possible kind of error save
forgeries: mistranscriptions ('Boyd' for 'Boyce,' leading to a redundant
note on the death of Alice Boyd's brother, Spencer, on 1 February 1865
[2:537]); misdatings (often by several years), misidentifications of recipients and of manuscript locations, and misprints; duplication of identical
letters in different volumes, a decade apart; and misidentification of recipients. Because the editors tended to print from published sources, even

when manuscripts existed, the edition contains a plethora of unacknowledged fragments and conflations, especially for the letters to Hall Caine, William Bell Scott, and Frederic Shields, which they printed in their respective memoirs. Most of these, including postscripts attached to the wrong letter, have now been restored. The annotations, often perfunctory, misinformed, and almost always pedantic, can on occasion, be humorous, such as the substitution of '*Yawned* on each other' for 'Fawned' in a note on 'Nuptial Sleep' (2:740); but any joy the reader might take in these discoveries is vitiated by the confusion created by the factual inaccuracies of the editors.

Two examples, from literally hundreds, must suffice to indicate the misleading nature of so many of their annotations. In an 1879 letter to Watts-Dunton (79.36 in my edition; D/W 2022), Rossetti refers to the *Illuminated Magazine*, which he designates by the unambiguous abbreviation, '*Illum: Mag.*.' In glossing this reference, Oswald Doughty, overlooking the obvious, resorts to an abstruse and pseudo-erudite explanation that distorts the meaning of the letter:

'(Illuminato Magna?)': 'Probably a half-remembrance from childhood of Gabriele Rossetti's eccentric Dantesque studies including his belief that he had discovered *the great secret – the Mysterium Magnum.*'

The second example is more far-reaching. D/W's letter 504 is a brief note to Jane Morris dated only 'Sunday Night,' which Doughty dates 5 July 1863. The full text of the letter reads:

My dear Janey,
    The photographer is coming at 11 on Wednesday. So I'll expect you as early as you can manage. Love to all at the Hole.
    Ever yours,
    D.G. Rossetti

The editorial note provides only a perfunctory identification of the photographer:

The Rev. C.L. Dodgson (1832-98), 'Lewis Carroll,' author of *Alice's Adventures in Wonderland* (much admired by D.G.R.), Oxford Don and amateur photographer.

Amusingly, both the date and the note are incorrect; the editors have

conflated two photographic sessions by two different photographers two
years apart, the first on 5 to 9 October 1863, when Lewis Carroll took a series
of family and other photographs in the back garden at Cheyne Walk; the
second, in June 1865, when John R. Parsons shot the portraits of Jane
Morris arranged by Rossetti, again in the back garden at Cheyne Walk.

The editors' misidentification of the 'photographer' had a unique, and
what must surely be the most unusual, impact ever made by any annotation
in any edition, for it completely misled the Pulitzer Prize poet Richard
Howard, who, in his *Untitled Subjects* (1969), paraphrased this letter in his
dramatic monologue on Jane Morris entitled 'A Pre-Raphaelite Ending,
London 1915.' In Howard's poem, Jane, on the eve of death (she actually
died in 1914), is going through her letters with her daughter, May, when
she comes across the photographs for which Rossetti posed her:

> Take care with the ones
> on top, they are photographs.
> Read out what is scrawled there: 'Dearest Janey,
> Dodgson will be here tomorrow at noon,
> do come as early as you can manage.'
> They have no backing
> and break like dead leaves.
> Often Gabriel painted
> from these when he could not see me. He said
> Mr. Dodgson knew what to leave out. Give
> that one to me. No, it does not matter.
> I want to hear you
> say the words aloud.

Foreshortening the episode, Howard then conflates this letter with another to Jane, written on 4 February 1870, published in Bryson's edition
but not included in D/W, which he also paraphrases rather than quotes:

> Absence can never make me
> so far from you again as your presence did
> for years. Yet no one seems alive now –
> the places empty of you are empty
> of all life.

It was probably Rossetti's dated letter to his mother of 30 September
(63.90; D/W 510), which also begins 'the photographer ... is coming' but

specifies Lewis Carroll, that led Doughty/Wahl to misdate the letter 5 July 1863 and place it before the one to his mother. In all, an interesting example of art imitating, not life, but faulty scholarship.

When I reviewed the Doughty/Wahl edition, I remember wondering how the editors could be as insensitive to their subject as the errors in the dating and annotations suggested or so unaware of Rossetti's biographical connections as not to be alerted by huge gaps in the correspondence. Doughty, after all, had edited T. J. Wise's manuscripts of Rossetti's letters to his publisher, F.S. Ellis, in 1928, and twenty years later published his major study of the poet-artist, which is still the standard biography. It was only when I gained access to the archive of the edition and examined the correspondence exchanged between the editors and Dan Davin of the Clarendon Press, that I began to understand how so many of the lapses occurred. The summary that follows is provided as a moral exemplum for future editors.

The publication history of the edition revealed in the archive, which extends over nearly twenty years, is a bizarre comedy of errors, involving a complete breakdown in communication, that Dan Davin described as an 'editorial limbo ... far worse than Dante's.' The correspondence also provides a perfect paradigm of the pitfalls of collaboration, especially when the disparity in age and status is as great as that between Doughty and Wahl. In 1949, when Mrs Angeli, before leaving for Italy, gave John Robert Wahl permission to edit Rossetti's letters, he agreed to share with her a portion of the royalties. He was still a doctoral student at Balliol when he signed the publication contract with the Clarendon Press on 20 December 1950. Doughty, his former professor at Capetown, was in 1951 negotiating with Constable, through Michael Sadleir, to publish a selected edition of Rossetti's letters when Wahl invited him to join him as co-editor, without mentioning the shared royalties. A curmudgeon by disposition, Doughty was 60 at this time and nearing the end of his academic career; Wahl was only embarking on his, and editing the letters was not his first priority.

The extent of their consultation on editorial principles is uncertain, but one of their initial decisions, on how to share the work, was destined to wreck the edition. Ideally, they should have worked together, but because mutual commitments precluded their doing so, they determined to divide the task, each taking responsibility for a chronological portion of Rossetti's epistolary life, from 1835 to '82. However, instead of basing the division on either a key date or an educated estimate of the total number of letters likely to be involved, they decided to quarter Rossetti's life, each taking alternating quarters: Wahl was responsible for the years from 1835-1862 and 1871-6 (Vols. 1 & 3), Doughty for 1863-70 and 1877-82 (Vols. 2 & 4). From this point, the collaboration became an unmitigated disaster. Doughty, anxious to beat the final deadline, beavered away and submitted his complete letter texts and annotations well before Wahl, distracted by other projects, even commenced his editing. He did not complete his D.Phil at Oxford until 1954 and then spent an indeterminable period in the United States on a Commonwealth Fellowship, during which he had a serious altercation with the 'doyen terrible' of Rossetti collectors, Janet Camp Troxell of New Haven, by whom, I may tell you, parenthetically, I was some years later conned into cataloguing her collection for a possible sale to UBC after she had already succumbed to the charms of Dudley Johnson and decided her papers would go to Princeton. In 1958, Wahl accepted a chair at the University of the Orange Free State in Blumfontaine and returned to South Africa. In the same year, he also sent the Press a portion of the letters for the first volume, but the final instalment was not received until January 1961.

In the intervening years, Doughty, already disillusioned with Wahl and impatient of his dilatoriness by the mid-'50s, became increasingly frustrated at not seeing his work in print, though he knew full well that because the letters were not contiguous, they could not be published. Under relentless pressure from Doughty, Davin reluctantly agreed in late 1956 to set his volumes in galley proofs, a decision Doughty later admitted was the greatest mistake of his publishing career. When told early in 1959 that Wahl had informed the Press his work would be completed by 15 June, Doughty responded, 'Did he say what year?' After a meeting with Wahl in Capetown in February 1960, Doughty refused to correspond directly with him again, and letters between the two had to go through Oxford, though both editors were in South Africa, a few hundred miles apart.

In November 1961, the Press began printing the first two volumes; a month later, Wahl finally forwarded the final portion of Volume 3, nearly six years after Doughty's volumes had been set in galleys. Meanwhile, it had become clear that hundreds of letters had been missed out, and in November 1959, Davin drafted a memo stating that 'We must remember not to make any suggestion in the title or publicity that this is a complete edition.' By August 1962, it was clear that a supplementary volume would be required.

As time dragged on, the correspondence between Doughty and Davin became increasingly invidious. Exasperated by Wahl's extended procrastination, by Davin's unwillingness to publish his volumes, and, subsequently by the four-year hiatus between the printing of the first two volumes and their publication in December 1965, Doughty made repeated threats to withdraw his materials and on more than one occasion tendered his resignation. He also repeatedly threatened litigation, and later even put in his will that if he died before the publication of the first two volumes, then scheduled for 31 May 1964, all his materials would be withdrawn. In November 1964, he wrote Davin that he was involved in a 'veritable race with death.' Over the question of the index and a proposed fifth volume, Doughty became apoplectic, arguing that it was not the responsibility of editors to do their own indexing. When Wahl suggested in March 1965 that he would index his volume and, for a fee of £50 against the advance to Mrs Angeli, Doughty's as well, Doughty withdrew, forcing Davin to seek a legal interpretation. Since he had not been privy to Wahl's arrangements with Mrs Angeli, Doughty categorically refused to share his royalties, which had been seriously eroded in any event by the expenses to the Press caused by the delay. After this episode, Doughty refused to correspond with the Press and would only deal with the Vice Chancellor, K.C. Wheare, to whom, on 5 August 1965, he sent a sixteen-page summary of the whole fiasco.

The first two volumes were published on 16 December 1965 with a dust-jacket announcement that the next two volumes would contain an index. In late 1965, Wahl offered to edit a fifth volume, containing a brief section of additional letters, a chronological list of contents, arranged by correspondent, and an index. In Doughty's penultimate letter to Davin, whom he had never met, he refused either to participate in or to allow the publication of a fifth volume and threatened to bring an action against Wahl if he attempted it. Although Davin rejected Wahl's offer, the dust-jacket of the second two volumes, which appeared in 1967, announced a fifth volume, with additional letters and an index. Of course, no fifth volume and no index ever appeared. When Wahl, on 5 April 1970, killed his wife, who was dying of cancer, and drove his car off a jetty, Jon Stallworthy, then visiting the South African branch of OUP, sent a clipping announcing Wahl's death to Davin. The last entry in the file is Davin's endorsement: 'This means no index ...' When I came on the scene in 1973, Doughty was 83; his response to the announcement of a new edition I leave to your imagination.

VI

While the edition of Rossetti's letters has occupied me for nearly two decades, it would be disingenuous to suggest that these years have been devoted exclusively to the letters. Other activities – personal, administrative, editorial, and academic – have also occupied my time and attention, such as the editing of *JPRAS*, which in 1991 I passed to Professor Julie Codell of Arizona State University, who has now, after issuing six numbers, passed it back to Canada into the capable hands of the present editor, David Latham. The watching brief I mentioned at the outset of this address has become increasingly difficult to maintain as interest in the Pre-Raphaelites has accelerated around the world at an alarming pace. In France and Germany, where there has always been sporadic interest in the Pre-Raphaelites, books continue to appear occasionally, such as Jacques de Langlade's *Rossetti* (1985), the monumental historical and aesthetic studies of Wolfgang Lottes (1985) and Lothar Hönnighausen (1971; reworked in English 1988); or the valuable, albeit less ambitious, anthology, *Die Präraffaelliten*, edited by Gisela Hönnighausen (1992); but the most furious activity over the past decade has been in Italy and Japan. Whereas Italian interest in the Pre-Raphaelites is doubtless grounded, in part at least, in nationalistic ties, especially with the Rossettis, the fascination of the Japanese with the movement, which has a long tradition, reflects their preoccupation with all aspects of design – which also attracted the Pre-Raphaelites to Japanese art in the nineteenth century – with all aspects of the exotic, and with Western art and literature in general. Some idea of the extent of the influence of the Pre-Raphaelites in Japan can be gleaned from Eriko Yamiguchi's checklist of exhibition catalogues and special issues of journals devoted to them in the Fall 1994 number of *JPRS*, a prolegomenon to the extended bibliographical overview she has in preparation.

In Britain, two new societies have been formed in the past four years: the Pre-Raphaelite Society, launched in Birmingham in 1991, publishes a periodic *Review*; and the Rossetti Society, begun in Birchington on Sea in the following year, now issues a periodic *Newsletter*. When its founder, Dr. Henry Campbell, was asked 'why start a Rossetti Society in Birchington?,' he is reported to have responded, 'We have the body.' Neither of these essentially parochial journals promises to be of as much interest to the Pre-Raphaelite scholar as *The Journal of the William Morris Society*; but the societies deserve support, and their publications are not devoid of interest, both for the printed texts of lectures presented at meetings and for the reports they contain of Pre-Raphaelite activities and events that might otherwise be missed. Of far greater interest, however, is the recently organized Ruskin Programme and the Ruskin Collection, under the aegis of Lancaster University, at Brantwood, in the Lake District, which will house on permanent loan the unrivalled collection of Ruskin and Ruskiniana formerly in the Bembridge School on the Isle of Wight, amassed by John Howard

Whitehouse and curated by James Dearden, who will continue to edit the *Ruskin Newsletter*.

It is not possible in the time remaining to list, let alone discuss, the symposia, exhibitions, and book-length publications on the Pre-Raphaelites that have appeared in the last seven years. The products of the Elizabeth Siddal and Christina Rossetti feminist factories alone would occupy several pages. Of the dozen or so new books that have appeared since 1987, the new biographies of Ford Madox Brown and Holman Hunt are especially welcome additions, though many, I suspect, would quibble with Anne Clark Amor's title claim for Holman Hunt as the only 'True' Pre-Raphaelite. Roger Peattie's edition of William Michael Rossetti's letters is an exemplary scholarly achievement, as are the successive publications and exhibition catalogues by Susan Casteras, the Director of the Yale Center for British Art, and the numerous exhibitions of Burne-Jones and the Pre-Raphaelites in England, France, and Japan curated by John Christian. Singular among feminist studies of the movement is Jan Marsh and Pamela Nunn's *Women Artists of the Pre-Raphaelite Movement* (1989), which makes accessible biographical and critical material and assessments on the unjustly ignored women artists of the period, many of whom have until now been largely anonymous. Equally singular, but located at the opposite pole occupied by the fanatical fringe of feminism is Lynne Pearce's *Woman/Image/Text: Readings in Pre-Raphaelite Art and Literature* (1992), a self-indulgent, misanthropic, and narcissistic attack on the Pre-Raphaelite artists and poets that, purporting to be interdisciplinary, actually employs hermeneutical tactics that locate meaning in the 'silent margins' of the pictures and poems she examines rather than in the actual verbal and visual texts; in brief, a crude application of the theoretic excesses of a methodology, which, as I noted in reviewing the book for *Essays in Criticism* (1993), 'subverts the credibility of legitimate feminist criticism.' Alicia Faxon's *Dante Gabriel Rossetti* (1989), with its dozens of coloured reproductions, has no competitors as the most scrumptious book on the Pre-Raphaelites ever issued. While it does not quite replace Marillier, it is a valuable survey that draws on modern scholarship to trace both Rossetti's development as an artist and the critical and personal influences that shaped his art.

That the Pre-Raphaelite fad, launched by the Hippies in the '60s and entrenched by the Tate retrospective in 1984, is alive and flourishing is confirmed by the spate of new publications, annual calendars, posters, and diaries and the proliferation of coffee-table and picture non-books and the reprints of standard works on the movement. Pre-Raphaelite works are reproduced on mugs, plates, trays, wall-hangings, and other bric-a-brac sold in Museum shops; and Halcyon Days has issued a pretty, pricey, and petite enamelled 'Pre-Raphaelite Box' at £160, with miniscule reproductions of six works by Millais, Hughes, Hunt, Brown, Burne-Jones, and Morris around the edge, Rossetti's *Bower Meadow* on the top, and a thumb-nail history of the movement on the inside lid. The range has now been broadened to include Pre-Raphaelite music, with the publication of Stephanie Sobey-Jones's cassette, *Pre-Raphaelitism: Nature and Imagination*, a series of ten songs composed around individual sculptures, such as Munro's *Lover's Walk*, for the 1991 *Pre-Raphaelite Sculpture* exhibition, organized by Joanna Barnes and accompanied by an invaluable catalogue edited by her and Benedict Read.

That the more bizarre side of the movement still has its appeal is clear from the segment on Rossetti and Elizabeth Siddal, in Ripley's *Believe it or Not* TV series, menacingly narrated by Jack Palance; by the availability of Ken Russell's puerile *Dante's Inferno* on video for $19.95 through Barnes & Noble, advertised a few months ago on the Internet; and in the garish bookjacket design by Denise Satter for Harold Bloom's Modern Critical Views volume, *The Pre-Raphaelite Poets* (1986), a primitively naturalistic adaptation of *The Bower Meadow*, to which has been added a caricature of Rossetti shovelling earth into a grave marked by a headstone. This cover depicts, according to the dust-jacket blurb, 'the characteristic emblems of the Pre-Raphaelite Brotherhood ... gathered together in a composite image of this school of poets and painters, who advanced yet another supposed return to nature, but meant by nature a hard-edged phantasmagoria.'

Those of you who have followed the several continental and Japanese exhibitions of the Pre-Raphaelites will have encountered the art conglomerates known enigmatically as 'Pre-Raphaelites Inc.' and the 'Pre-Raphaelite Trust.' But you may be unaware that even vanity publishers are now attempting to join the Pre-Raphaelite parade: I was recently given a presentation copy of the first (and only) book published by 'The Pre-Raphaelite Press': 'a biography,' and I quote, 'of the shorthand inventor, educator, publisher and humanitarian, whose achievements enriched the lives of millions' – John Robert Gregg, written and published by the self-anointed, and again I quote, 'leading authority on the work of the Pre-Raphaelite painter, Arthur Hughes.' I had hoped in retirement, having completed the letters and the supplement to the *Bibliocritical Study*, to write a biography of William Bell Scott and to edit the unpublished diaries of William Michael Rossetti, which will soon be available as 'A Preservation Microfilming Project of the University of British Columbia Library.' What's a poor bibliographer to do with such a melange?

But those projects must now stand down in my list of research priorities and may, alas, never be accomplished. I was just Casaubon's age, when I embarked on the new edition of Rossetti's letters, which over the years has taken on something of the nature of his 'Key to All Mythologies.' While prescience in these matters is denied us, I do not this evening anticipate having to recruit my own Dorothea Brooke to devote the remainder of *her* life to the completion of my *magnum opus*. This is, after all, a retrospective, not a swan song; nor, I should like to believe, a 'LAST HURRAH!'

NOTES

1 The text of this paper is slightly revised from the keynote dinner address presented at the Armstrong Browning Library International 'Pre-Raphaelites and Their Circle' Conference at Baylor University in Waco, Texas, on 21 April 1994. Little did I know on the evening of its delivery that within the year the 'Godfather of the PRB Mafia' (as Mark Samuels Lasner labelled/libelled me in his presentation inscription to my copy of the catalogue of his collection, *A Private Library*) would marry the Belle of Baylor, the ABL's Librarian for twenty-two years, from 1972 to 1994, Betty Ann Coley. We were wed in Vancouver on 16 January 1995 and plan to collaborate on a number of projects, including a study of Browning and the Pre-Raphaelites. The first stipulation of our prenuptial agreement, however, was a binding guarantee that, while, in stealing her from the ABL, I may have played Browning to her Elizabeth Barrett or Capponsacchi to her Pompilia, she would never be expected to play Dorothea to my Casaubon and be saddled with the completion of *The Letters of Dante Gabriel Rossetti*! [Editor's note: This keynote address was first published in *The Journal of Pre-Raphaelite Studies*, ns 4 (Spring 1995): 7-28.]

2 Editor's note: The first two volumes of *The Correspondence of Dante Gabriel Rossetti*, published by D.S. Brewer, appeared in July 2002, three years after William E. Fredeman's death on 14 July 1999.

12

A CHECKLIST OF PUBLICATIONS BY WILLIAM E. FREDEMAN

David Latham

A. BOOKS, MONOGRAPHS, AND SEPARATE PUBLICATIONS

A1. *Pre-Raphaelitism: A Bibliocritical Study.* Cambridge, MA: Harvard UP, 1965. xxvi, 327 pp.

A2. *A Pre-Raphaelite Gazette: The Penkill Letters of Arthur Hughes to William Bell Scott and Alice Boyd, 1886-97.* Manchester: John Rylands Library, 1967. 89 pp. [Reprinted from two articles, Part 1 and Part 2, in *Bulletin of the John Rylands Library,* 49 (Spring 1967): 323-62; 50 (Autumn 1967): 34-82.]

A3. *Prelude to the Last Decade: Dante Gabriel Rossetti in the Summer of 1872.* Manchester: John Rylands Library, 1971. 104 pp. [Reprinted from two articles, Part 1 and Part 2, in *Bulletin of the John Rylands Library,* 53 (Autumn 1970): 75-121; 53 (Spring 1971): 272-328.]

A4. *The P.R.B. Journal: William Michael Rossetti's Diary of the Pre-Raphaelite Brotherhood, 1849-1853, together with other Pre-Raphaelite Documents.* Oxford: Clarendon, 1975. xxviii, 282 pp.

A5. *An Issue Devoted to the Work of William Morris.* Ed. William E. Fredeman. Special issue of *Victorian Poetry,* 13 (Fall/Winter 1975): i-xxx, 1-191 + 38 illus.

A6. *The Letters of Pictor Ignotus: William Bell Scott's Correspondence with Alice Boyd,*

1859-1884. Manchester: John Rylands Library, 1976. 93 pp. [Reprinted from two articles, Part 1 and Part 2, in *Bulletin of the John Rylands Library,* 58 (Autumn 1975): 66-111; 58 (Spring 1976): 306-52.]

A7. *Centennial Essays on Dante Gabriel Rossetti.* Ed. William E. Fredeman. Special issue of *Victorian Poetry,* 20 (Autumn/Winter 1982): 1-247 + 46 illus.

A8. *Victorian Novelists After 1885.* Ed. William E. Fredeman and Ira B. Nadel. *Dictionary of Literary Biography.* Vol. 18. Detroit: Gale, 1983. ix, 392 pp.

A9. *Victorian Novelists Before 1885.* Ed. William E. Fredeman and Ira B. Nadel. *Dictionary of Literary Biography.* Vol. 21. Detroit: Gale, 1983. xi, 417 pp.

A10. *Victorian Poets Before 1850.* Ed. William E. Fredeman and Ira B. Nadel. *Dictionary of Literary Biography.* Vol. 32. Detroit: Gale, 1984. xv, 417 pp.

A11. *Victorian Poets After 1850.* Ed. William E. Fredeman and Ira B. Nadel. *Dictionary of Literary Biography.* Vol. 35. Detroit: Gale, 1985. xiii, 437 pp.

A12. *The Victorian Muse: Selected Criticism and Parody of the Period.* Ed. William E. Fredeman, Ira Nadel, and John Stasny. 39-volume reprint series. New York: Garland, 1985-86. Two volumes – one a collection of the Biographical introductions to A.H. Miles's *Poets and Poetry of the Century,* the other a collection of Prefaces to Victorian editions – include introductions by Fredeman.

A13. *Centennial of Queen Victoria's Golden Jubilee.* Ed. William E. Fredeman. Special issue of *Victorian Poetry,* 25 (Autumn/Winter 1987): 1-242.

A14. *The Rossetti Cabinet: A Portfolio of Drawings by Dante Gabriel Rossetti.* Ed. William E. Fredeman. Special issue of *Journal of Pre-Raphaelite and Aesthetic Studies,* 2 (Fall 1989): xi, 17 pp. +113 illus. Reprinted. Stroud: Ian Hodgkins, 1991.

A15. *The Correspondence of Dante Gabriel Rossetti. The Formative Years: 1835-1862.* Ed. William E. Fredeman. Vol. I: 1835-1854; Vol. II: 1855-1862. Cambridge: D.S. Brewer, 2002. lxii, 402 pp.; 634 pp.
Forthcoming: *The Chelsea Years: 1863-1872.* 3 vols. *The Last Decade: 1873-1882.* 4 vols. Ed. William E. Fredeman. Cambridge: D.S. Brewer.

B. CHAPTERS IN BOOKS, INTRODUCTIONS, ETC.

B1. 'The Pre-Raphaelites.' In *The Victorian Poets: A Guide to Research.* Ed. Frederic Faverty. 2nd ed. Cambridge, MA: Harvard UP, 1968. 251-316.

B2. 'Coventry Patmore,' 'Dante Gabriel Rossetti,' 'Christina Rossetti,' and 'William Morris.' In *New Cambridge Bibliography of English Literature.* Vol. 3. Ed. George Watson. Cambridge: Cambridge UP, 1969. 486-9, 490-5, 496-500, and 563-71.

B3. 'Introduction.' *Books from the Libraries of Christina, Dante Gabriel, and William Michael Rossetti.* London: Bertram Rota, 1973. [A bookseller's catalogue.]

B4. 'Rossetti's "The Blessed Damozel": A Problem in Literary History and Textual Criticism.' In *English Studies Today.* 5th ser. Papers Read at the Eighth Conference of the International Association of University Professors of English Held at Istanbul, August 1971. Ed. Spencer Tonguc. Istanbul, 1973. 239-69.

B5. 'A Key Poem of the Pre-Raphaelite Movement: W.M. Rossetti's "Mrs. Holmes Grey."' In *Nineteenth-Century Literary Perspectives: Essays in Honor of Lionel Stevenson.* Ed. Clyde de L. Ryals. Durham, NC: Duke UP, 1974. 149-59.

B6. '"From Insult to Protect": The Pre-Raphaelites and the Biographical Fallacy.' In *Sources for Reinterpretation: The Use of Nineteenth-Century Literary Documents: Essays in Honor of C.L. Cline.* Austin: Department of English and Humanities Research Center, U of Texas at Austin, 1975. 57-80.

B7. Introduction and Index of Provincial Imprints. In *Victorian Poetry, 1850-1900.* Dorking: C.C. Kohler, 1980. [A bookseller's catalogue.]

B8. — and Jane C. Fredeman. "Introduction." *Stuart Ramsay Tompkins: The Secret War, 1914-1918.* Victoria, B.C.: Morriss, 1981.

B9. 'One Word More: On Tennyson's Dramatic Monologues.' In *Studies in Tennyson.* Ed. Hallam Tennyson. London: Macmillan, 1981. 169-85.

B10. 'On the Importance of Manuscripts in Editing.' Public Workshop on Editorial Principles and Procedures. Ottawa: CEECT [Carleton University], 1983. 19-34.

B11. 'Oliver Madox Brown.' *Victorian Novelists Before 1885. Dictionary of Literary Biography.* Vol. 21. Detroit: Gale, 1983. 68-73.

B12. 'William Bell Scott.' *Victorian Poets Before 1850. Dictionary of Literary Biography.* Vol. 32. Detroit: Gale, 1984. 235-48.

B13. 'Introduction.' *A Bookman's Catalogue: The Norman Colbeck Collection of Nineteenth-Century and Edwardian Poetry and Belles Lettres.* Vancouver: U of British Columbia P, 1987. xxiii-xxxli.

B14. 'The Last Idyll: Dozing in Avalon' with an Appendix: 'The Laureate and the King: An Iconographic Survey of Arthurian Subjects in Victorian Art.' In *The Passing of Arthur: New Essays in Arthurian Tradition.* Ed. Christopher Baswell and William Sharpe. New York: Garland, 1988. 264-306 + 9 illus.

B15. 'Pictures at an Exhibition: Late Victorian and Modern Perspectives on the Pre-Raphaelites.' In *Victorian Connections: Essays in Honor of Cecil Y. Lang.* Ed. Jerome J. McGann. Charlottesville: UP of Virginia, 1989. 179-99.

C. ARTICLES AND REVIEW ARTICLES

C1. 'The Road to Freedom.' *U.B.C. Chronicle,* 13 (Summer 1959): 14-16. [Analysis of social disorder in the southern U.S.]

C2. 'Earle Birney: Poet.' *British Columbia Library Quarterly,* 23 (January 1960): 8-15. Rpt. in *Earle Birney.* Critical Views on Canadian Writers. Ed. Bruce Nesbitt. Toronto: McGraw-Hill Ryerson, 1974. 107-14.

C3. 'Pre-Raphaelites in Caricature: "The Choice of Paris: An Idyll" by Florence Claxton.' *Burlington Magazine,* 102 (December 1960): 523-29.

C4. 'D.G. Rossetti's *Early Italian Poets.*' *Book Collector,* 10 (Summer 1961): 193-8.

C5. 'D.G. Rossetti and T.J. Wise.' *Times Literary Supplement*, 19 May 1961: 309.

C6. 'Rossetti's Impromptu Portraits of Tennyson Reading "Maud."' *Burlington Magazine*, 105 (March 1963): 117-18.

C7. 'William Morris & His Circle: A Selective Bibliography of Publications, 1960-1962.' *Journal of the William Morris Society*, 1 (Summer 1964): 23-33.

C8. Review of *Christina Rossetti*, by Lona Mosk Packer and *The Rossetti-Macmillan Letters*. *Victorian Studies*, 8 (September 1964): 71-8.

C9. 'Rossetti's "In Memoriam": An Elegiac Reading of *The House of Life*.' *Bulletin of the John Rylands Library*, 47 (March 1965): 298-341.

C10. 'William Morris & His Circle: A Selective Bibliography of Publications, 1963-1965.' *Journal of the William Morris Society*, 2 (Spring 1966): 13-26.

C11. 'William Morris' Funeral.' *Journal of the William Morris Society*, 2 (Spring 1966): 28-35.

C12. 'Rossetti's Letters.' Review of *Letters of Dante Gabriel Rossetti*, ed. Oswald Doughty and J.R. Wahl. Vols. 1-2. *Malahat Review*, no.1 (January 1967): 134-41; Review of Vols. 3-4. *Malahat Review*, no. 6 (April 1968): 115-26. Revised in *Victorian Studies*, 12 (September 1968): 104-8.

C13. '"A Sign Betwixt the Meadow and the Cloud": The Ironic Apotheosis of Tennyson's "St. Simeon Stylites."' *University of Toronto Quarterly*, 38 (October 1968): 69-83.

C14. 'Pre-Raphaelite Novelist Manqué: Oliver Madox Brown.' *Bulletin of the John Rylands Library*, 51 (Autumn 1968): 27-72.

C15. 'The Bibliographical Significance of a Publisher's Archive: The Macmillan Papers.' *Studies in Bibliography*, 23 (1970): 183-91.

C16. — and Leonid M. Arinshtein. 'William Michael Rossetti's "Democratic Sonnets."' *Victorian Studies*, 14 (March 1971): 241-74.

C17. '"The Sphere of Common Duties": The Domestic Solution in Tennyson's Poetry.' *Bulletin of the John Rylands Library*, 54 (Spring 1972): 357-83.

C18. Review of *The Germ: A Pre-Raphaelite Little Magazine,* by Robert Stahr Hosmon. *Victorian Poetry,* 10 (Spring 1972): 87-94.

C19. 'Impediments and Motives: Biography as Unfair Sport.' Review of *Rossetti and the Fair Lady,* by David Sonstroem. *Modern Philology,* 70 (November 1972): 149-54.

C20. 'The Pre-Raphaelites' [Guide to the Year's Work]. *Victorian Poetry,* 12 (Spring 1974): 77-99.

C21. 'Emily Faithfull and the Victoria Press: An Experiment in Sociological Bibliography.' *The Library,* 5th ser., 29 (June 1974): 139-64.

C22. 'William Morris: "What may he not yet do?"' *Victorian Poetry,* 13 (Fall/ Winter 1975): xix-xx.

C23. 'D.G. Rossetti's "The Death of Topsy."' Ed. William E. Fredeman and Jack Lindsay. *Victorian Poetry,* 13 (Fall/Winter 1975): 177-9.

C24. Review of *The Waterloo Directory of Victorian Periodicals, 1824-1900: Phase 1,* ed. Michael Wolff, J.S. North, and Dorothy Deering. *English Studies in Canada,* 4 (Summer 1978): 238-46.

C25. '"Fundamental Brainwork": The Correspondence between Dante Gabriel Rossetti and Thomas Hall Caine.' *AUMLA* [*Journal of the Australasian Universities Language and Literature Association*], 52 (November 1979): 209-31.

C26. 'Roy Daniells: 1902-1979.' *Proceedings of the Royal Society of Canada,* 4th ser., 17 (1979): 77-79. Rpt. as Part 2 of 'The Canadian Scholar: Roy Daniells.' *English Studies in Canada,* 5 (Winter 1979): ix-xi. [Obituary. Parts 1 and 2 by Northrop Frye and Laurenda Daniells.]

C27. '"What Is Wrong with Rossetti?": A Centenary Reassessment.' *Victorian Poetry,* 20 (Autumn/Winter 1982): xv-xxviii.

C28. 'A Rossetti Gallery: Twenty Unpublished Rossetti Drawings.' *Victorian Poetry,* 20 (Autumn/Winter 1982): 161-86.

C29. 'A Shadow of Dante: Rossetti in the Final Years: Extracts from W.M.

Rossetti's Unpublished Diaries, 1876-1882.' *Victorian Poetry*, 20 (Autumn/ Winter 1982): 217-45.

C30. Review of *In Memoriam*, ed. Susan Shatto and Miriam Shaw. *The Library*, 6 (October 1984): 306-16.

C31. 'New Directions in English Studies.' *Transactions of the Royal Society of Canada*, 4th ser., 22 (1984): 227-32. Rpt. in *English Studies Today and Tomorrow*. A Symposium of Academy II of the Royal Society of Canada, University of Guelph, 30 May 1984. *Proceedings of the Royal Society of Canada* (1984): 3-8.

C32. 'The Story of a Lie: A Sequel to *A Sequel*.' Review of *A Sequel to an Enquiry into the Nature of Certain Nineteenth Century Pamphlets*, ed. Nicolas Barker and John Collins. *Review*, 7 (1985): 259-96.

C33. 'Thomas Bird Mosher and the Literature of Rapture: A Chapter in the History of American Publishing.' *Papers of the Bibliographical Society of Canada*, 26 (1987): 27-66. Revised in *Thomas Bird Mosher: Pirate Prince of Publishers*, by Philip R. Bishop. New Castle, DE, and London: Oak Knoll Press and British Library, 1998. 5-33.

C34. 'William Michael Rossetti and the Wise-Forman Conspiracy: A Footnote to *A Sequel*.' *Book Collector*, 36 (Spring 1987): 55-71.

C35. '"Visionary Vanities": Leaves from the Pre-Raphaelite Apocrypha.' *The Journal of Pre-Raphaelite & Aesthetic Studies*, 1 (Fall 1987):1-14.

C36. '"England Our Home, Victoria Our Queen."' *Victorian Poetry*, 25 (Autumn/Winter 1987): 1-8.

C37. 'A Charivari for Queen Butterfly: *Punch* on Queen Victoria.' *Victorian Poetry*, 25 (Autumn/Winter 1987): 47-73.

C38. '"She Wrought Her People Lasting Good": A Commemorative Exhibition in Colour of Artifacts Associated with Queen Victoria.' *Victorian Poetry*, 25 (Autumn/Winter 1987): 223-41.

C39. 'Pre-Raphaelitism Revisited: or, Dr. Frankenstein Reprograms the Monster.' *The Journal of Pre-Raphaelite & Aesthetic Studies*, 1 (Spring 1988): 4-11.

C40. 'The Pre-Raphaelite Literary Art of Dante Gabriel Rossetti.' *The Journal of Pre-Raphaelite & Aesthetic Studies*, 1 (Fall 1988): 55-74.

C41. 'Thomas J. Wise's Last Word on the Reading *Sonnets.' Book Collector*, 37 (Autumn 1988): 422-3.

C42. 'Two Uncollected Bibliographers: Simon Harcourt Nowell-Smith and Michael Trevanion of Erewhon.' *Book Collector*, 38 (Winter 1989): 464-82.

C43. Review of *The Collected Letters of William Morris*. Vol. 2, ed. Norman Kelvin. *Modern Philology*, 87 (November 1989): 200-5.

C44. 'Tennyson and His Bibliographers.' Review of *The Poems of Tennyson*, 2nd edition, ed. Christopher Ricks; and of *The Letters of Alfred, Lord Tennyson*, vols. 1 & 2, ed. Cecil Lang and Edgar Shannon. *Review*, 12 (1990): 1-36.

C45. Review of *The Contributors' Index to the Dictionary of National Biography, 1885-1901*, by Gillian Fenwick. *Papers of the Bibliographical Society of Canada*, 30 (Spring 1992): 78-81.

C46. 'An Embedded Text in the Tennyson Canon: The "Deathsong for the Ghouls" in *The Ancient Sage.' Tennyson Research Bulletin*, 6 (November 1992): 20-33.

C47. 'Silent Margins.' Review of *Woman/Image/Text: Readings in Pre-Raphaelite Art and Literature*, by Lynne Pearce. *Essays in Criticism*, 43 (April 1993): 157-65.

C48. 'The Great Pre-Raphaelite Paper Chase: A Retrospective.' *Journal of Pre-Raphaelite Studies*, ns 4 (Spring 1995): 7-28.

C49. 'Pre-Raphaelites in America.' Review of *Visions of Love and Life: Pre-Raphaelite Art* exhibition. *Journal of Pre-Raphaelite Studies*, ns 4 (Spring 1995): 107-11.

C50. '"Woodman, Spare That Block": The Published, Unpublished, and Projected Illustrations and Book Designs of Dante Gabriel Rossetti.' *Journal of Pre-Raphaelite Studies*, ns 5 (Spring 1996): 7-41.

C51. 'Wise and the Trial Book Fallacy: Review Essay.' *English Literature in Transition*, 40 (1997): 437-47.

C52. 'Scholarly Resources: The Pre-Raphaelites in Canada.' *Journal of Pre-Raphaelite Studies*, ns 6/7 (Fall/Spring 1997/98): 191-216. Rpt. in *Scarlet Hunters: Pre-Raphaelitism in Canada*. Ed. David Latham. Toronto: Archives of Canadian Art, 1998. 191-216.

C53. 'The Search for Arthur Hughes: A Review Article.' Review of *Arthur Hughes: His Life and Works: A Catalogue Raisonné*, by Leonard Roberts. *Journal of Pre-Raphaelite Studies*, ns 7 (Fall 1998): 97-105.

Contributors

Carolyn Hares-Stryker is the McCoy Professor of English and director of the Honors program at Marietta College, Ohio. She edited *The Pre-Raphaelites: An Anthology of Writings* (1996) and is currently working on the editorial team completing the multi-volume *Correspondence of Dante Gabriel Rossetti.*

Lorraine Janzen Kooistra is Associate Professor of English at Nipissing University, Ontario. She is the author of *The Artist as Critic: Bitextuality in Fin-de-Siècle Illustrated Books* (1995) and *Christina Rossetti and Illustration: A Publishing History* (2002), and co-editor with Mary Arseneau and Antony H. Harrison of *The Culture of Christina Rossetti: Female Poetics and Victorian Contexts* (1999).

David Latham teaches English at York University and edits *The Journal of Pre-Raphaelite Studies.* His recent books include an edition of William Morris's *Poems by the Way* (1994), *Magic Lies: The Art of W.O. Mitchell,* edited with Sheila Latham (1997), and *Scarlet Hunters: Pre-Raphaelitism in Canada* (1998).

Allan Life is Associate Professor of English and Associate Professor of Asian Studies (adjunct) at the University of North Carolina. He worked as an undergraduate research assistant for William E. Fredeman, and later wrote his disssertation under Fredeman's direction. He is currently completing a book on the twelfth-century relief panels in the Nataraja temple in Chidambaram, India.

Jerome McGann is the John Stewart Bryan University Professor at the University of Virginia and Adjunct Professor at Royal Holloway College,

University of London. His latest books are *Dante Gabriel Rossetti and the Game that Must Be Lost* (2000), *Radiant Textuality: Literature after the World Wide Web* (2001), and *Byron and Romanticism* (2002), as well as the ongoing *Complete Writings and Pictures of Dante Gabriel Rossetti. A Hypermedia Research Archive.* [http://jefferson.village.virginia.edu: 1828/archive.html]

J. Hillis Miller is Distinguished Research Professor of English and Comparative Literature at the University of California, Irvine. The author of many books and articles on nineteenth- and twentieth-century English and American literature and on literary theory, his most recent include *Reading Narrative* (1998), *Black Holes*, with Manuel Asensi (1999), *Others* (2001), *Speech Acts in Literature* (2002), and *On Literature* (2002).

Ira B. Nadel is Professor of English at the University of British Columbia and a Fellow of the Royal Society of Canada. His most recent books include *Various Positions: A Life of Leonard Cohen* (1996), *The Cambridge Companion to Ezra Pound* (1999), and *Double Act: A Life of Tom Stoppard* (2002).

Roger Peattie is Professor of English (Emeritus) at the University of Calgary. In addition to his articles on various Pre-Raphaelite subjects, he is the editor of the *Selected Letters of William Michael Rossetti* (1990) and an editor on the team completing the multi-volume *Correspondence of Dante Gabriel Rossetti*.

E. Warwick Slinn is Professor of English at Massey University, New Zealand. The author of *Browning and the Fictions of Identity* (1982) and *The Discourse of Self in Victorian Poetry* (1991), he is currently completing a book on the politics of performative language, *Victorian Poetry as Cultural Critique*, scheduled for publication in 2003.

Bibliography

Ackroyd, Peter. *Dressing Up: Transvestism and Drag: The History of an Obsession.* London: Thames and Hudson, 1979.

Ali, Muhsin Jassim. *Scheherazade in England: A Study of Nineteenth-Century English Criticism of the 'Arabian Nights.'* Washington: Three Continents P, 1981.

Allen, Dennis. 'Young England: Muscular Christianity and the Politics of the Body in "Tom Brown's School Days."' *Muscular Christianity: Embodying the Victorian Age.* Ed. Donald E. Hall. Cambridge: Cambridge UP, 1994. 114-32.

Allen, Roger. *The Arabic Literary Heritage.* Cambridge: Cambridge UP, 1998.

Archer, Mildred, and Ronald Lightbown. *India Observed: India as Viewed by British Artists: 1760-1860.* London: Victoria and Albert Museum, 1982.

Amor, Anne Clark. *William Holman Hunt: The True Pre-Raphaelite.* London: Constable, 1989.

Armstrong, Isobel. *Victorian Poetry: Poetry, Poetics and Politics.* London: Routledge, 1993.

Arnheim, Rudolf. *The Power of the Center: A Study of Composition in the Visual Arts: The New Version.* Berkeley: U of California P, 1988.

Auerbach, Nina, and U.C. Knoepflmacher, eds. 'A Trio of Antifantasies: Speaking Likenesses.' *Forbidden Journeys: Fairy Tales and Fantasies by Victorian Women Writers.* Chicago: U of Chicago P, 1992. 317-23.

Avery, Gillian. 'George MacDonald and the Victorian Fairy Tale.' *The Golden Thread.* Ed. William Raeper. Edinburgh: Edinburgh UP, 1990. 126-39.

Battiscombe, Georgina. *Christina Rossetti: A Divided Life.* London: Constable, 1981.

Baudrillard, Jean. *Seduction.* Trans. Brian Singer. New York: St. Martin's, 1990.

Beardsley, Aubrey. *Best Works of Aubrey Beardsley.* New York: Dover, 1990.

— *The Collected Drawings of Aubrey Beardsley.* With an Appreciation by Arthur Symons. Ed. Bruce S. Harris. NY: Bounty Books, [1967].

— *The Early Work of Aubrey Beardsley.* With a Prefatory Note by H.C. Marillier. New York: Dover, 1967.

— *The Letters of Aubrey Beardsley.* Ed. Henry Maas, J.L. Duncan, and W.G. Good. Rutherford, NJ: Fairleigh Dickinson UP, 1970.

— *The Story of Venus and Tannhäuser or 'Under the Hill.'* Ed. Robert Oresko. London: St. Martin's, 1974.

Bettelheim, Bruno. *The Uses of Enchantment: The Meaning and Importance of Fairy Tales.* New York: Knopf, 1977.

Bishop, Philip R. *Thomas Bird Mosher: Pirate Prince of Publishers.* Newcastle, DE, and London: Oak Knoll and British Library, 1998.

Bornand, Odette, ed. *Diary of William Michael Rossetti: 1870-1873.* Oxford: Clarendon, 1977.

Branson, Major L.H. *Indian Conjuring.* London: Routledge, [1922].

Brierley, Harry. *Transvestism: A Handbook with Case Studies for Psychologists, Psychiatrists and Counsellors.* Oxford: Pergamon Press, 1979.

[Buchanan, Robert]. 'The Fleshly School of Poetry.' *Contemporary Review,* 18 (October 1871): 334-50.

Bullen, J.B. *The Pre-Raphaelite Body: Fear and Desire in Painting, Poetry, and Criticism.* Oxford: Clarendon, 1998.

Butler, Judith. *Gender Trouble: Feminism and the Subversion of Identity.* London: Routledge, 1990.

Caracciolo, Peter L. 'Introduction.' *The 'Arabian Nights' in English Literature.* Ed. Peter L. Caracciolo. New York: St. Martin's, 1988. 1-80.

Carpenter, Edward. *Love's Coming-of-Age.* London: Methuen, 1914.

Casteras, Susan. '"The Utmost Possible Variety in Our Combination": An Overview of The Pre-Raphaelite Circle as Book Illustrators.' *Pocket Cathedrals: Pre-Raphaelite Illustration.* New Haven: Yale Center for British Art, 1991. 1-43.

Castle, Terry. *Masquerade and Civilization: The Carnivalesque in Eighteenth-Century English Culture and Fiction.* Stanford: Stanford UP, 1986.

Cavalcanti, Guido. *Rime, a cura di Letterio Cassata.* Anzio: De Rubeis, 1993.

— *Rime di Guido Cavalcanti edite ed inedite.* Ed. Antonio Cicciaporci. Firenze: Niccolo Carli, 1813.

Carman, Bliss. *Bliss Carman's Poems.* Toronto: McClelland & Stewart, 1929.

Charles, Edna K. *Christina Rossetti: Critical Perspectives, 1862-1982.* London: Associated UP, 1985.

Chorley, H.F. Review of *The Defence of Guenevere, and Other Poems. Athenaeum,* 3 April 1858: 427-8.

Cockerell, Sydney. *The Best of Friends: Further Letters of Sydney Cockerell.* Ed. Viola Meynell. London: Rupert Hart-Davis, 1956.

Coleridge, Samuel Taylor. *Collected Works of Samuel Taylor Coleridge.* Vol. 14. Princeton: Princeton UP, 1990.

Conners, John R. '"A Moment's Monument": Time in *The House of Life.' *The Journal of Pre-Raphaelite Studies*, 2 (May 1982): 20-34.

[Cox, Edward William]. Review of *The Germ*. *The Critic*, 15 February 1850: 94-5.

Cowan, Leslie. 'A Study of the Painting of Arthur Hughes.' Diss. U of Edinburgh, 1973.

Crane, Walter. *Claims of Decorative Art*. London: Lawrence and Bullen, 1892.

— *Ideals in Art: Papers, Theoretical, Practical, Critical.* London: George Bell, 1905.

Curle, Richard. *Caravansary and Conversation: Memories of Places and Persons*. New York: Frederick A. Stokes, 1937.

Dalziel, George. *The Brothers Dalziel: A Record of Fifty Years' Work in Conjunction with Many of the Most Distinguished Artists of the Period 1840-1890*. London: Methuen, 1901.

Dante Alighieri. *Vita Nuova, a cura di Domenico de Robertis*. Milano, Napoli: Riccardo Ricchiardi, 1980.

— *Dante Alighieri: Opera Minore di Dante*. Ed. Pietro Fraticelli. 3 vols. Firenze: Leopold Allegrini & G. Mazzoni, 1834-39.

Davis, Richard H. *Ritual in an Oscillating Universe: Worshiping Siva in Medieval India*. Princeton: Princeton UP, 1991.

De Beauvoir, Simone. *The Second Sex*. Trans. H.M. Parshley. New York: Vintage Books, 1989.

De Girlami Cheney, Liana. 'Locks, Tresses, and Manes in Pre-Raphaelite Painting.' *Pre-Raphaelitism and Medievalism in the Arts*. Lewiston, NY: Mellen, 1992. 59-191.

Deleuze, Gilles, and Félix Guattari. *Anti-Oedipus: Capitalism and Schizophrenia*. Minneapolis: U of Minnesota P, 1983.

Dellamora, Richard. *Masculine Desire: The Sexual Politics of Victorian Aestheticism*. Chapel Hill: U of North Carolina P, 1990.

— 'Traversing the Feminine in Oscar Wilde's *Salomé*.' *Victorian Sages and Cultural Discourse: Renegotiating Gender and Power*. Ed. Thaïs E. Morgan. New Brunswick, NJ: Rutgers UP, 1990. 246-64.

Derrida, Jacques. 'Envois.' *La carte postale*. Paris: Aubier-Flammarion, 1980; *The Post Card*. Trans. Alan Bass. Chicago: U of Chicago P, 1987.

— 'Télépathie.' *Furor* 2 (February 1981): 5-41. Rpt. in *Psyché: Inventions de l'autre*. Paris: Galilée, 1987, 237-70; 'Telepathy.' Trans. Nicholas Royle. *Oxford Literary Review*, 10, nos. 1-2 (1988): 3-41.

Dickens, Charles. 'Frauds on the Fairies.' *Household Words*, 8 (October 1853): 97.

— 'Old Lamps for new Ones.' *Household Words*, 15 June 1850, 12-14.

Dijkstra, Bram. *Idols of Perversity: Fantasies of Feminine Evil in Fin-de-Siecle Culture*. Oxford: Oxford UP, 1986.

Docter, Richard F. *Transvestites and Transsexuals: Toward a Theory of Cross-Gender Behaviour*. London: Plenum Press, 1988.

Doniger, Wendy. *The Implied Spider: Politics and Theology in Myth.* New York: Columbia UP, 1998.

— *Splitting the Difference: Gender and Myth in Ancient Greece and India.* Chicago: U of Chicago P, 1999.

Doshi, Saryu. 'Attire and Ornaments.' *Shivaji and Facets of Maratha Culture.* Ed. Saryu Doshi. Bombay: Marg, 1982. 166-72.

Dowling, Linda. 'The Decadent and the New Woman in the 1890s.' *Nineteenth-Century Fiction,* 33 (March 1979): 434-53.

Dulcken, H.W., ed. *Dalziels' Illustrated Arabian Nights' Entertainments.* London: Ward, Lock, and Tyler, [1865].

Dundes, Alan, ed. *Cinderella: A Folklore Casebook.* New York: Garland, 1982.

Easton, Malcolm. *Aubrey and the Dying Lady: A Beardsley Riddle.* London: Secker & Warburg, 1972.

Elliott, Bridget. 'Aubrey Beardsley as Performer: *Fin-de-Siècle* or *Entr'acte?*' *Aubrey Beardsley: Sixty Selected Drawings.* Ed. Bridget Elliott. London: Academy Editions, 1995.

— 'New and Not so "New Women" on the London Stage: Aubrey Beardsley's *Yellow Book* Images of Mrs. Patrick Campbell and Réjane.' *Victorian Studies,* 31 (Autumn 1987): 33-57.

Ellis, Havelock. 'Sexual Inversion.' *Studies in the Psychology of Sex.* Vol. I. New York: Random House, 1915.

Ellmann, Richard. *Oscar Wilde.* London: Hamish Hamilton, 1987.

Faxon, Alicia Craig. *Dante Gabriel Rossetti.* New York: Abbeville Press, 1989.

Fletcher, Ian. *Aubrey Beardsley.* Boston: Twayne, 1987.

Flint, Kate. 'Arthur Hughes as Illustrator for Children.' *Children and Their Books: A Celebration of the Work of Iona and Peter Opie.* Eds. Gillian Avery and Julia Briggs. Oxford: Clarendon, 1989. 201-20.

Fischlin, Daniel. 'The Performance Context of the English Lute Song, 1596-1622.' *Performance on Lute, Guitar, and Vihuela: Historical Practice and Modern Interpretation.* Ed. Victor Anand Coelho. Cambridge: Cambridge UP, 1997. 47-71.

Foucault, Michel. *The History of Sexuality.* Trans. Robert Hurley. Vol. I. New York: Vintage Books, 1990.

Fredeman, William E. 'Correspondence of Dante Gabriel Rossetti.' Unpublished Prospectus.

— '"England Our Home, Victoria Our Queen."' *Victorian Poetry,* 25 (Autumn/Winter 1987): 1-8.

— 'A Pre-Raphaelite Gazette: The Penkill Letters of Arthur Hughes to William Bell Scott and Alice Boyd.' *John Rylands Library Bulletin,* 50 (Autumn 1967): 34-82.

— *Pre-Raphaelitism: A Bibliocritical Study.* Cambridge: Harvard UP, 1965.

— Review of *The Germ: A Pre-Raphaelite Little Magazine*, by Robert Stahr Hosmon. *Victorian Poetry*, 10 (Spring 1972): 87-94.

— Review of *In Memoriam*, ed. Susan Shatto and Miriam Shaw. *The Library*, 6 (October 1984): 306-16.

— 'Rossetti's "In Memoriam": An Elegiac Reading of *The House of Life*.' *Bulletin of the John Rylands Library*, 47 (March 1965): 298-341.

— 'Rossetti's Letters.' Review of *Letters of Dante Gabriel Rossetti*, ed. Oswald Doughty and J.R. Wahl. Vols. 1-2. *Malahat Review*, no.1 (January 1967): 134-41; Vols. 3-4. *Malahat Review*, no. 6 (April 1968): 115-26. Revised in *Victorian Studies*, 12 (September 1968): 104-8.

— 'Silent Margins.' Review of *Woman/Image/Text: Readings in Pre-Raphaelite Art and Literature*, by Lynne Pearce. *Essays in Criticism*, 43 (April 1993): 157-65.

— 'Tennyson and His Bibliographers.' Review of *The Poems of Tennyson*, 2nd edition, ed. Christopher Ricks; and of *The Letters of Alfred, Lord Tennyson*, vols. 1 & 2, ed. Cecil Lang and Edgar Shannon. *Review*, 12 (1990): 1-36.

Frye, Northrop. 'Varieties of Literary Utopias.' In *The Stubborn Structure*. London: Methuen, 1970. 109-34.

Galland, Antoine. *Les Mille et Une Nuits*. Ed. Gaston Picard. 2 vols. Paris: Garnier, 1960.

Garber, Marjorie. *Vested Interests: Cross-Dressing and Cultural Anxiety*. London: Routledge, 1992.

Gardner, Joseph H. 'Michelangelo's Sweetness, Coleridge's Flycatchers, Ligeia's Eyes, and the Failure of Art in *The House of Life*.' *Journal of Pre-Raphaelite Studies*, ns 4 (Spring 1995): 67-74.

Garnett, Richard. Review of *The Defence of Guenevere, and Other Poems*. *Literary Gazette*, 6 March 1858, 226-7.

Gaunt, William. *The Pre-Raphaelite Tragedy*. London: Cape, 1942.

Gosse, Edmund. Rossetti. *Sunday Times*, 6 May 1928, 8.

Granger, John. 'The Critique of the Mirror in Rossetti's *The House of Life*.' *Journal of Pre-Raphaelite Studies*, 4 (May 1984): 1-16.

Hackford, Terry Reece. 'Fantastic Visions: British Illustration of the *Arabian Nights*.' *The Aesthetics of Fantasy Literature and Art*. Ed. Roger C. Schlobin. Notre Dame: U of Notre Dame P, 1982. 143-75.

Hall, Donald, ed. *Muscular Christianity: Embodying the Victorian Age*. Cambridge: Cambridge UP, 1994.

Hanft, Lila. 'The Politics of Maternal Ambivalence in Christina Rossetti's *Sing-Song*.' *Victorian Literature and Culture*, 19 (1991): 213-32.

Harriosn, Martin, and Bill Waters. *Burne-Jones*. London: Barrie & Jenkins, 1973.

Harwood, Ian. *A Brief History of the Lute*. Richmond: Lute Society, 1975.

Heaney, Seamus. *Electric Light*. London: Faber, 2001.

Heyd, Milly. *Aubrey Beardsley: Symbol, Mask and Self-Irony*. New York: Peter Lang, 1986.

Heifetz, Hank, trans. *The Origin of the Young God: Kalidasa's 'Kumarasambhava.'* Berkeley: U of California P, 1985.

Hobbs, Steven. 'Mr. Pollitt's Bookplate.' *Book Collector*, 36 (Winter 1987): 518-30.

Hogarth, Paul. *Artists on Horseback: The Old West in Illustrated Journalism: 1857-1900*. New York: Watson-Guptill, 1972.

— *Arthur Boyd Houghton: Introduction and Check-list of the Artist's Work*. London: Victoria and Albert Museum, 1975.

— *Arthur Boyd Houghton*. London: Fraser, 1981.

Hönnighausen, Gisela. *Die Präaraffaeliten. Dichtung, Malerei, Asthetik, Rezeption. herausgegeben und übersetzt.* Stuttgart: Reclam, 1992.

Hönnighausen, Lothar. *The Symbolist Tradition in English Literature: A Study of Pre-Raphaelitism and fin de siécle.* Cambridge: Cambridge UP, 1988.

Houghton, A[rthur] B[oyd]. *Home Thoughts and Home Scenes*. London: Routledge, 1865.

Houghton, Walter E., and G. Robert Stange, eds. *Victorian Poetry and Poetics*. 2nd ed. Boston: Houghton Mifflin, 1968.

Housman, Laurence. *Arthur Boyd Houghton: A Selection from his Work in Black and White*. London: Kegan Paul, 1896.

— 'Pre-Raphaelitism in Art and Poetry.' *Essays by Divers Hands (Transactions of the Royal Society of Literature, n.s. XII)*. London: Oxford UP, 1933, 1-29. Rpt. in *Journal of Pre-Raphaelite Studies*, ns 10 (Spring 2001): 9-26.

Howard, Richard. *Untitled Subjects*. New York: Athenaeum, 1969.

'How to Court the "Advanced Woman."' *The Idler*, 6 (1895): 192-211.

Hueffer, Ford Madox. *Memories and Impressions: A Study in Atmospheres*. New York: Harper, 1911.

Hughes, Thomas. *Tom Brown's School Days*. Illus. by Arthur Hughes. London: Macmillan, 1882.

Hunt, Violet. *The Wife of Rossetti*. London: John Lane, 1932.

Hunt, W. Holman. *Pre-Raphaelitism and the Pre-Raphaelite Brotherhood*. London: Macmillan, 1905.

Irwin, Robert. *The Arabian Nights: A Companion*. London: John Lane, 1994.

James, Henry. *The Wings of the Dove*. Rpt of New York edition of 1907-09. Fairfield: New Jersey: Augustus M. Kelley, 1976. *The Wings of the Dove* are vols. 19 and 20 of this edition, but are identified on the title pages as vols. 1 and 2 of the novel.

Johnson, Samuel. *Rasselas and Other Tales*. Vol. 16. Ed. Gwin J. Kolb. New Haven: Yale UP, 1990.

Keightley, Thomas. *The Fairy Mythology*. 2nd ed. London: Bell, 1878.

Kent, David. Sequence and Meaning in Christina Rossetti s *Verses*. *Victorian Poetry*, 17 (Autumn 1979): 259-64.

Kittler, Friedrich. *Essays: Literature, Media, Information Systems.* Ed. John Johnston. Amsterdam: G+B Arts International, 1997.

Kooistra, Lorraine Janzen. *The Artist as Critic: Bitextuality in Fin-de-Siècle Illustrated Books.* Aldershot: Scolar Press, 1995.

— 'Beardsley's Reading of Malory's Morte Darthur: Images of a Decadent World.' *Mosaic,* 23 (March 1990): 55-72.

— 'The Dialogue of Image and Text in Christina Rossetti's *Sing-Song.*' *Victoria Poetry,* 37 (Winter 1999): 465-91.

— 'The Jael Who Led the Hosts to Victory: Christina Rossetti and Pre-Raphaelite Book-Making.' *Journal of Pre-Raphaelite Studies,* ns 8 (Spring 1999): 50-68.

Lacan, Jacques. 'The Meaning of the Phallus.' *Feminine Sexuality: Jacques Lacan and the école freudienne.* Ed. Juliet Mitchell and Jacqueline Rose. Trans. Jacqueline Rose. New York: W.W. Norton, 1985. 74-85.

Landow, George P. 'And the World Became Strange: Realms of Literary Fantasy.' *Fantastic Illustration and Design in Britain, 1850-1930.* Ed. Diana L. Johnson. Providence, RI: Museum of Art, Rhode Island School of Design, 1979. 28-43.

Lane, Edward William, ed. and trans. *'The Thousand and One Nights,' commonly called, in England, 'The Arabian Nights' Entertainments.'* 3 vols. London: Knight, 1839-1841.

Lang, Cecil, ed. *The Pre-Raphaelites and Their Circle.* Chicago: U of Chicago P, 1975.

Langenfeld, Robert, ed. *Reconsidering Aubrey Beardsley. With an Annotated Secondary Bibliography by Nicholas Salerno.* Ann Arbor, MI: UMI Research Press, 1989.

Langlade, Jacques de. *Dante Gabriel Rossetti.* Paris: Mazarine, 1985.

Lanigan, Dennis. 'William E. Fredeman, 1928-1999.' *Journal of Pre-Raphaelite Studies,* ns 8 (Fall 1999): 5-8.

Lasner, Mark Samuels. *A Selective Checklist of the Published Work of Aubrey Beardsley.* Boston: Thomas G. Boss Fine Books, 1995.

Leavy, Barbara Fass. *In Search of the Swan Maiden: A Narrative on Folklore and Genre.* New York: New York UP, 1994.

LeMire, Eugene, ed. *The Unpublished Lectures of William Morris.* Detroit: Wayne State UP, 1969.

Life, Allan R. '"That Unfortunate Young Man Morten."' *Bulletin of the John Rylands Library,* 55 (Spring 1973): 369-402.

Lottes, Wolfgang. *Wie ein goldener Traum. die Rezeption des Mittelalters in der Kunst der Präraffaeliten.* Munich: Fink, 1985.

MacCarthy, Fiona. *William Morris: A Life for Our Time.* London: Faber, 1994.

MacDonald, George. *At the Back of the North Wind.* Illus. by Arthur Hughes. London: Strahan, 1870. Rpt. Whitethorn, CA: Johannesen, 1992.

— 'The Imagination: Its Function and Its Culture.' *A Dish of Orts.* London: Edwin Dalton, 1908.

— *The Princess and the Goblin.* Illus. by Arthur Hughes. London: Strahan, 1871. Rpt. New York: Alfred A. Knopf, 1993.

— *Unspoken Sermons.* Series 1. London: Strahan, 1868.

MacFall, Haldane. *Aubrey Beardsley: The Man and his Work.* London: John Lane at the Bodley Head, 1928.

Mackail, J.W. *The Life of William Morris.* London: Longmans, 1899.

Mahdi, Muhsin. *The Thousand and One Nights.* Leiden: Brill, 1995.

Malory, Sir Thomas. *Morte d'Arthur.* Illus. by Aubrey Beardsley. London: J.M. Dent, 1893-4.

Malti-Douglas, Fedwa. *Woman's Body, Woman's Word: Gender and Discourse in Arabo-Islamic Writing.* Princeton, NJ: Princeton UP, 1991.

Mancoff, Debra N. *The Arthurian Revival in Victorian Art.* New York: Garland, 1990.

— *The Return of King Arthur: The Legend through Victorian Eyes.* New York: Harry N. Abrams, 1995.

Marcus, Jane. 'Salomé: The Jewish Princess was a New Woman.' *Art and Anger: Reading Like a Woman.* Columbus: Ohio UP. 3-19.

Marcuse, Herbert. *One Dimensional Man: Studies in the Ideology of Advanced Industrial Society.* Boston: Beacon, 1965.

Marsh, Jan. *Christina Rossetti: A Literary Biography.* London: Jonathan Cape, 1994.

McGann, Jerome. '"A Thing to Mind": The Materialist Aesthetic of William Morris.' *Huntington Library Quarterly,* 55 (Winter 1992): 55-74.

— 'Dante Gabriel Rossetti and the Betrayal of Truth.' *Victorian Poetry,* 26 (1988): 339-61.

— *Dante Gabriel Rossetti and the Game That Must Be Lost.* New Haven: Yale UP, 2000.

McInnis, Maurice. 'Allegorizing on Their Own Hooks: The Book Illustrations of Dante Gabriel Rossetti and Arthur Hughes.' *Pocket Cathedrals: Pre-Raphaelite Book Illustration.* Ed. Susan Casteras. New Haven: Yale Center for British Art, 1991. 67-79.

McSweeney, Kerry. *Supreme Attachments: Studies in Victorian Love Poetry.* Aldershot: Ashgate, 1998.

Mitchell, Scott. 'D.G. Rossetti's *The House of Life:* Allegory, Symbolism and Courtly Love.' *The Journal of Pre-Raphaelite Studies,* 6 (November 1985): 47-54.

Mitterwallner, Gritli v. 'Evolution of the *Linga.*' *Discourses on Siva.* Ed. Michael W. Meister. Philadelphia: U of Pennsylvania P, 1984, 12-31.

Morgan, Charles. *The House of Macmillan (1843-1943).* London: Macmillan, 1944.

Morris, William. 'Address at the Twelfth Annual Meeting, 3 July 1889' [SPAB Report]. In *William Morris: Artist, Writer, Socialist.* Ed. May Morris. 2 vols. Oxford: Basil Blackwell, 1936, 1:146-7.

— 'Address on the Collection of Paintings of the Pre-Raphaelite School.' In *William Morris: Artist, Writer, Socialist.* Ed. May Morris. 2: 300-12.

— *The Collected Letters of William Morris.* Ed. Norman Kelvin. 4 vols. Princeton: Princeton UP, 1984-96.

— *The Collected Works of William Morris.* Ed. May Morris. 24 vols. London: Longmans, Green, 1910-15.

— 'How I Became a Socialist.' In *News from Nowhere and Other Writings.* Ed. Clive Wilmer. Harmondsworth: Penguin, 1993. 379-83.

— *The Ideal Book: Essays and Lectures on the Arts of the Book.* Ed. William S. Peterson. Berkeley: U of California P, 1982.

— 'Preface.' *The Nature of Gothic* by John Ruskin. Hammersmith: Kelmscott Press, 1892. In *News from Nowhere and Other Writings.* Ed. Clive Wilmer. Harmondsworth: Penguin, 1993. 365-9.

— 'Some Hints on Pattern-Designing.' In *News from Nowhere and Other Writings.* Ed. Clive Wilmer. Harmondsworth: Penguin, 1993. 255-83.

— 'Textiles.' In *Arts and Crafts Essays by Members of the Arts and Crafts Exhibition Society.* London: Longmans Green, 1893. 22-38.

— *The Unpublished Lectures of William Morris.* Ed. Eugene LeMire. Detroit: Wayne State UP, 1969.

— *William Morris: Artist, Writer, Socialist.* Ed. May Morris. 2 vols. Oxford: Basil Blackwell, 1936.

Moss, Anita. 'Sacred and Secular Visions of Imagination and Reality in Nineteenth-Century British Fantasy for Children.' *Webs and Wardrobes: Humanist and Religious World Views in Children's Literature.* Eds. Joseph O'Beirne Milner and Lucy Floyd Morcock Milner. Lanham, Maryland: U P of America, 1987. 65-78.

Mottahedeh, Roy P. 'Aja'ib in *The Thousand and One Nights.*' *'The Thousand and One Nights' in Arabic literature and society.* Ed. Richard G. Hovannisian et al. Cambridge: Cambridge UP, 1997. 29-39.

O'Flaherty, Wendy Doniger. *Women, Androgynes, and Other Mythical Beasts.* Chicago: U of Chicago P, 1980.

Packer, Lona Mosk. *Christina Rossetti.* Berkeley: U of California P, 1963.

Panofsky, Erwin. *Early Netherlandish Painting.* 2 vols. Cambridge: Harvard UP, 1953.

Parkin-Gounelas, Ruth. '"Speaking Likenesses" – And "Differences": The Prose Fantasies of Christina Rossetti.' *Victorian Literature and Culture,* 23 (1995): 147-57.

Pater, Walter. 'Dante Gabriel Rossetti.' In *Appreciations with an Essay on Style.* London: Macmillan, 1915.

— 'Poems by William Morris.' *Westminster Review,* 90 (October 1868): 300-12.

— *The Renaissance: Studies in Art and Poetry.* The 1893 Text. Ed. Donald L. Hill. Berkeley: U of California P, 1980.

Peattie, Roger. W.M. Rossetti as Reluctant Biographer: The Genesis of *Dante Gabriel Rossetti: His Family Letters, With a Memoir.*' *Nineteenth-Century Prose,* 22 (Spring 1995): 54-62.

Pennington, John. 'Muscular Spirituality in MacDonald's Curdie Books.' *Muscu lar Christianity: Embodying the Victorian Age.* Ed. Donald E. Hall. Cambridge: Cambridge UP, 1994. 133-49.

Pollock, Griselda. 'Woman as Sign: Psychoanalytic Readings.' *Vision and Difference: Femininity, Feminism, and the Histories of Art.* London and New York: Methuen, 1988.

Pound, Ezra. A *Draft of XXX Cantos.* Paris: Hours Press, 1930.

— *Umbra: The early poems of Ezra Pound.* London: Elkin Mathews, 1920.

Prettejohn, Elizabeth. *Rossetti and His Circle.* New York: Stewart, Tabori & Chang, 1997.

Proctor, Ellen A. *A Brief Memoir of Christina G. Rossetti.* London: SPCK, 1895.

Psomiades, Kathy Alexis. *Beauty's Body: Femininity and Representation in British Aestheticism.* Stanford, Calif: Stanford, 1997.

'Publisher of Minor Poets: A Chat with Mr. John Lane.' *The Sketch* [Supplement], 4 December 1895: 6.

Reade, Brian. *Aubrey Beardsley.* Intro. by John Rothenstein. New York: Viking, 1967.

— *Beardsley Re-Mounted.* London: Eighteen Nineties Society, 1989.

Rees, Joan. *The Poetry of Dante Gabriel Rossetti: Modes of Self-Expression.* Cambridge: Cambridge UP, 1981.

Reid, Forrest. *Illustrators of the Eighteen Sixties: An Illustrated Survey of the Work of 58 British Artists.* London: Faber & Gwyer, 1928.

Review of *The Defence of Guenevere, and Other Poems. Tablet,* 19 (April 1858): 266.

Review of *The Defence of Guenevere, and Other Poems. Saturday Review,* 20 November 1858, 506-7.

Reynolds, Joshua. *Discourses on Art.* Ed. Robert R. Wark. San Marino, CA: Huntington Library, 1959.

Riede, David G. *Dante Gabriel Rossetti Revisited.* New York: Twayne, 1992.

Rickels, Laurence. *Aberrations of Mourning.* Detroit: Wayne State UP, 1988.

— 'Kafka and Freud on the Telephone.' *Modern Austrian Literature: Journal of the International Arthur Schnitzler Association,* 22: 3/4 (1989): 211-25.

Rivière, Joan. 'Womanliness as a Masquerade.' *Formations of Fantasy.* Ed. Victor Burgin et al. London: Methuen, 1986. 35-44.

Ronell, Avital. *The Telephone Book.* Lincoln: U of Nebraska P, 1989.

'Rossetti and the Rest..' *Times Literary Supplement,* 23 September 1965, 836.

Rossetti, Christina. *Family Letters.* Ed. W.M. Rossetti. London: Brown, Langham, 1908.

— *Maude: A Story for Girls.* Ed. W.M. Rossetti. London: James Bowden, 1897.

— *New Poems.* Ed. W.M. Rossetti. London: Macmillan, 1896.

— *Poems.* Golden Treasury Series. Ed. W.M. Rossetti. London: Macmillan, 1904.

— *Poetical Works, with Memoir.* Ed. W.M. Rossetti. London: Macmillan, 1904.

— *The Rossetti-Macmillan Letters.* Ed. Lona Mosk Packer. Los Angeles: U of California P, 1963.

— *Sing-Song.* Illus. by Arthur Hughes. London: Routledge, 1872.

— 'Speaking Likenesses.' Illus. by Arthur Hughes. *Forbidden Journeys: Fairy Tales and Fantasies by Victorian Women Writers.* Eds. Nina Auerbach and U.C. Knoepflmacher. Chicago:U of Chicago P, 1992.

Rossetti, Dante Gabriel. *The Early Italian Poets.* London: Smith, Elder, 1861.

— *The Complete Writings and Pictures of Dante Gabriel Rossetti. A Hypermedia Research Archive.* Ed. Jerome McGann. First instalment of four, released June 2000. [http:// jefferson.village.virginia.edu: 1828/archive.html]

— *Letters of Dante Gabriel Rossetti.* Ed. Oswald Doughty and John Robert Wahl. 4 vols. Oxford: Clarendon, 1965-67.

— *The Works of Dante Gabriel Rossetti.* Ed. William Michael Rossetti. London: Ellis, 1911.

Rossetti, Olivia. *The Christina Rossetti Birthday Book.* London: Macmillan, 1896.

Rossetti, William Michael. *Dante Gabriel Rossetti as Designer and Writer.* London: Cassell, 1889.

— *The Germ, Being a Facsimile Reprint.* London: Stock, 1901.

— *The P.R.B. Journal: W.M. Rossetti s Diary of the Pre-Raphaelite Brotherhood, 1849-1853.* Ed. William E. Fredeman. Oxford: Clarendon, 1975.

— *The Pre-Raphaelites and Their World: From Some Reminiscences of W.M. Rossetti.* Intro. and Epilogue by Angela Thirlwell. London: Folio Society, 1995.

— ed. *Rossetti Papers: 1862-1870.* London: Sands, 1903.

— *Ruskin: Rossetti: Pre-Raphaelitism.* London: George Allen, 1899.

— *Selected Letters of W.M. Rossetti.* Ed. Roger Peattie. University Park: Pennsylvania State UP, 1990.

— *Some Reminiscences.* 2 vols. London: Brown, Langham, 1906.

Rothenstein, William. *Men and Memories.* 3 vols. London: Faber & Faber, 1931-39.

Ruskin, John. *The Works of John Ruskin.* Ed. E.T. Cook and Alexander Wedderburn. London: G. Allen, Green, 1903-12.

S., G.U. 'The Finding of the Saviour in the Temple: Notes on Mr. Holman Hunt's Picture.' *Once a Week,* 14 July 1860, 64-66.

Said, Edward W. *Orientalism.* New York: Vintage, 1994.

Sallis, Eva. *Sheherazade through the Looking Glass: The Metamorphosis of the 'Thousand and One Nights.'* Richmond: Curzon, 1999.

Schmidgall, Gary. *The Stranger Wilde: Interpreting Oscar.* New York: Dutton, 1994.

Sharp, William. *Dante Gabriel Rossetti: A Record and a Study.* London: Macmillan, 1882.

Shiloah, Amnon. *Music in the World of Islam: A Socio-cultural Study.* Detroit: Wayne State UP, 1995.

Showalter, Elaine. *Sexual Anarchy: Gender and Culture at the Fin de Siècle.* New York: Viking, 1990.

Sigman, Joseph. 'The Diamond in the Ashes: A Jungian Reading of the "Princess" Books.' *For the Childlike: George MacDonald's Fantasies for Children.* Ed. Roderick McGillis. Metuchen, NJ, & London: Children's Literature Association and Scarecrow Press, 1992. 183-94.

Siegel, Lee. *Net of Magic: Wonders and Deceptions in India.* Chicago: U of Chicago P, 1991.

Sketchley. R.E.D. 'The Art of J. W. Waterhouse, R.A.' *The Art Journal* (Christmas 1909): 1-31.

Smith, Lesley. 'Old Wine in New Bottles: Aspects of Prophecy in George MacDonald's *At the Back of the North Wind.*' *For the Childlike: George MacDonald's Fantasies for Children.* Ed. Roderick McGillis. Metuchen, N.J., & London: Children's Literature Association and Scarecrow Press, 1992. 161-68.

Smulders, Sharon. *Christina Rossetti Revisited.* New York: Twayne, 1996.

Smythe, A. Egerton. *The Balance of Life: A Biographical Sketch of Mackenzie Bell.* London: Curlew Press, nd.

Snodgrass, Chris. *Aubrey Beardsley: Dandy of the Grotesque.* Oxford: Oxford UP, 1995.

— 'Decadent Mythmaking: Arthur Symons on Aubrey Beardsley and Salome.' *Victorian Poetry,* 28 (Autumn/Winter 1990): 61-109.

— 'Decadent Parodies: Aubrey Beardsley's Caricature of Meaning.' *Fin de Siècle/ Fin du Globe: Fears and Fantasies of the Late Nineteenth Century.* Ed. John Stokes. London: Macmillan, 1992. 178-209.

Spector, Stephen J. 'Rossetti's Self-Destroying "Moment's Monument": "Silent Noon."' *Victorian Poetry,* 14 (Spring 1976): 54-58.

Spender, Stephen. 'The Pre-Raphaelite Literary Painters.' *New Writing and Daylight* 6 (1945): 123-31. Rpt. in *Journal of Pre-Raphaelite Studies,* ns 10 (Spring 2001): 27-34.

Stasny, John. 'In Memoriam: William E. "Dick" Fredeman, July 19, 1928-July 15, 1999.' *Victorian Poetry,* 37 (Spring 1999): iii-iv.

'The Sterner Sex!' *Punch,* 26 September 1891, 147.

Sterling, John. Review of *Poems* (1842). *Quarterly Review,* 70 (September 1842): 400.

Stirling, A.M. *William De Morgan and his Wife.* London: Thornton Butterfield, 1922.

Stephens, Frederic George. *W.H. Hunt and His Works: A Memoir of the Artist's Life, with Descriptions of His Pictures.* London: Nisbet, 1860.

Strabo. *Geography.* Trans. Horace Leonard Jones. 8 vols. Cambridge: Harvard UP, 1932.

Sullivan, Edmund J. 'Arthur Boyd Houghton,' pts. 1 ('An Artists' Artist') and 2. *The Print Collector's Quarterly,* 10 (February 1923): 94-122; 10 (April 1923): 124-48.

Swinburne, Algernon. Rev. of *Fleurs du mal* by Charles Baudelaire. *Spectator,* 6 September 1862, 998-1000.

Symons, Arthur. 'The Decadent Movement in Literature.' *Harper's New Monthly Magazine*, 87 (November 1893): 858-67. Rpt. in *Dramatis Personae*. Indianapolis: Bobbs-Merrill, 1923.

— 'The Decay of Craftsmanship in England.' *Weekly Critical Review* [Paris], 19 and 26 March 1903: 5-6; 17-18. Rpt. in *Studies in the Seven Arts*. London: Constable, 1906.

Symons, A.J.A. 'An Unacknowledged Movement in Fine Printing: The Typography of the Eighteen-Nineties.' *The Fleuron: A Journal of Typography*, 7 (1930): 83-119.

Talamini, John T. *Boys Will Be Girls: The Hidden World of the Heterosexual Male Transvestite*. Washington: UP of America, 1982.

Tennyson, Alfred Lord. *The Poems*. Ed. Christopher Ricks. 3 vols. London: Longman, 1987.

Thompson, E.P. *William Morris: Romantic to Revolutionary*. London: Lawrence and Wishart, 1955. Revised London: Merlin, 1977.

Townsend, Rev. Geo. Fyler, ed. *The Arabian Nights' Entertainments*. London: Warne, [1865].

Trevelyan, Raleigh. *A Pre-Raphaelite Circle*. London: Chatto & Windus, 1978.

Tucker, Herbert F. 'Of Monuments and Moments: Spacetime in Nineteenth-Century Poetry.' *Modern Language Quarterly*, 58 (September 1997): 269-97.

Turner, Victor. *The Forest of Symbols: Aspects of Ndembu Ritual*. Ithaca: Cornell UP, 1967.

[Tupper, John Lucas]. 'The Subject in Art. No. II.' *The Germ: Art and Poetry*, No. 3 (March 1850): 118-25.

Waugh, Evelyn. *Rossetti: His Life and Works*. London: Duckworth, 1928.

Weintraub, Stephen. *Aubrey Beardsley: Imp of the Perverse*. University Park: Pennsylvania State UP, 1976.

— *Four Rossettis: A Victorian Biography*. London: W.H. Allen, 1978.

Whalley, Joyce Irene, and Tessa Rose Chester, eds. *A History of Children's Book Illustration*. London: John Murray, 1988.

Wildman, Stephen. 'Arthur Hughes: 1823-1915.' *Arthur Hughes: His Life and Work*. Ed. Leonard Roberts. Suffolk: Antique Collectors' Club, 1997. 11-47.

Wilde, Oscar. 'The Decay of Lying.' *The Complete Works of Oscar Wilde*. Intro. by Vyvyan Holland. London and Glasgow: Collins, 1988. 970-92.

— *Decorative Art in America: A Lecture by Oscar Wilde*. Ed. R.B. Glaenzer. New York: Brentano's, 1906.

— *The Letters of Oscar Wilde*. Ed Rupert Hart-Davis. London: Rupert Hart-Davis, 1962.

— *Salome*. London: Elkin Mathews and John Lane, 1894.

Wilson, Simon. *Beardsley*. Oxford: Phaidon, 1983.

Williams, Raymond. *Keywords. A Vocabulary of Culture and Society*. London: Croom Helm, 1976.

Whistler, J.A.M. http://www2.iinet.com/art/artists/major/w/whistler. htm.

Yeats, W.B. *Autobiographies: Reveries over Childhood and Youth and The Trembling Veil.* London: Macmillan, 1926.

— *Collected Letters of W.B. Yeats.* Ed. John Kelly. Oxford: Clarendon, 1986.

Zatlin, Linda Gertner. *Aubrey Beardsley and Victorian Sexual Politics.* Ed Dennis Farr. Oxford: Clarendon, 1990.

— 'Drawing Conclusions: Beardsley and Biography.' *biography,* 15 (Spring 1992): 111-39.

Zimmer, Heinrich. *Myths and Symbols in Indian Art and Civilization.* Ed. Joseph George MacDonald, Oscar Wilde, and L. Frank Baum.' *Fairy Tales and the Art of Subversion: The Classical Genre for Children and the Process of Civilization.* New York: Routledge, 1988. 97-133.

Zipes, Jack. 'Inverting and Subverting the World with Hope: The Fairy Tales of George MacDonald, Oscar Wilde, and L. Frank Baum.' *Fairy Tales and the Art of Subversion: The Classical Genre for Children and the Process of Civilization.* New York: Routledge, 1988. 97-133.

Index

Ackroyd, Peter 180, 190-1, 192
Anderson, Hans Christian 159
Angeli, Helen Rossetti 8, 218-20, 222, 229
Armstrong, Isobel 63, 68, 69
Arnold, Matthew 69
Auerbach, Nina 106
Avery, Gillian 94

Barry, Charles 13
Battiscombe, Georgina 77
Baudillard, Jean 54
Beardsley, Aubrey 24, 31, 132-3, 177-95
Beardsley, Mabel 179-80
Bell, Mackenzie 72-3, 77-80
Bennett, Mary 216
Bettleheim, Bruno 153, 161-2
Blake, William 86, 204
Boehm, Sir Joseph 207
Boyce, George Price 215
Boyd, Alice 8, 107, 212-13, 220, 225
Brown, Ford Madox 8, 13, 25, 33, 100, 107, 146, 233, 234
Brown, Lucy Madox 72

Brown, Oliver 9
Browning, Elizabeth Barrett 28, 69
Browning, Robert 18, 23, 43
Bruccoli, Matthew 223
Bryan, Alfred 193
Bryson, John 216
Buchanan, Robert 58, 204
Bullen, J.B. 97
Burne-Jones, Edward 5, 24, 25, 33, 185-6, 214, 233, 234
Burne-Jones, Georgiana 91
Butler, Judith 184
Byron, George Gordon 37, 51

Caine, Hall 226
Carman, Bliss 22
Carpenter, Edward 192
Carpenter, William 147
Carroll, Lewis 112, 227-8
Castle, Terry 188
Cavalcanti, Guido 37, 54
Cayley, Charles 71-2, 73, 79
Cheney, Liana de Girlami 96
Cockerell, Sydney 87
Colbeck, Norman 9, 223-4

Coleridge, Samuel T. 25
Coley, Betty Ann 235
Collinson, James 79
Colvin, Sidney 106
Conners, John 61, 65
Cornelius, Peter von 13
Crane, Walter vii

da Vinci, Leonardo 183
Daltry, Roger 2
Dalziel Brothers 146-50
Dante Alighieri 21, 27, 36-7, 38, 39, 40,
    41, 54
Davin, Dan 229
Davis, Richard H. 175
de Beauvoir, Simone 183
De Morgan, Evelyn Pickering 91
de Pougey, Liane 182
Dearden, James 232
Deleuze, Gilles 60
Dellamora, Richard 180, 183
Dennis, Edward 218
Dennis, Imogin 218, 222
Dent, J.M. 132-3, 186
Derrida, Jacques 136-8, 140
Dickens, Charles 3, 92-3
Dijkstra, Bram 97
Disraeli, Benjamin 103-4
Doniger, Wendy 168
Doughty, Oswald 198-9, 225-31
Dowling, Linda 191
Dryden, John 154
Dulcken, H.W. 148-9, 163

Easton, Malcolm 180
Elliott, Bridget 179
Ellis, F.S. 107
Ellis, Havelock 192
Evans, Frederick 73

Faxon, Alicia Craig 233
Fazio degli Uberti 55-6, 61
Flint, Kate 93, 96, 112
Ford, George 207
Fraser, F.A. 107
Fredeman, William E. vii, ix, 2, 6-13,
    27, 32-3, 57, 60, 87, 135, 145, 197-210
Froissart, John 5
Frost, Robert 6
Frye, Northrop 122
Fuller, Loie 182

Gainsborough, Thomas 14
Galland, Antoine 149, 155, 158-60,
    171, 173, 174
Gardner, Joseph H. 66
Garnett, Olivia 73
Garnett, Richard 74
Gaunt, William 213
Gautier, Théophile 189-90, 192
Gere, John 216
Golffing, Francis 204
Gosse, Edmund 77, 85-6
Graham, William 226
Granger, John 66, 68
Grimm Brothers 162
Guattari, Felix 60
Guilbert, Yvette 182

Hall, Donald 101
Hamilton, Walter 204
Hares-Stryker, Carolyn 30
Heaney, Seamus 119
Heimann, Adolph and Amelia 74
Horne, R.H. 204
Hosmon, Robert 198
Houghton, Arthur Boyd 31, 145-75
Housman, Laurence 14, 31, 117, 145-
    6, 157

Howard, Richard 228
Hueffer [Ford], Ford Madox 2, 74
Hughes, Arthur 8, 9, 30-1, 91-118, 212,
    221, 234
Hughes, Thomas 91, 93, 100-5
Hunt, Violet 18
Hunt, William Holman 13-14, 16, 33,
    96, 233, 234

James, Henry 16, 141-2
John, Elton 2
Johnson, Samuel 21

Kant, Immanuel 22
Keats, John 23, 145, 156, 204
Kent, David A. 87
Kittler, Frederich 137
Knoepflmachar, U.C. 106
Kooistra, Lorraine Janzen 31-2, 107-8

Lacan, Jacques 183-4
Landow, George 185, 204
Lane, Edward 148-9
Lane, John 179, 191
Lang, Cecil 8, 10, 11, 12-13, 212, 216,
    201
Latham, David 29-30, 204, 232
Leathart, James 9, 222-3
Life, Allan 31, 222
Love, Courtney 2

MacColl, D.S. 91
MacDonald, George 30, 91-100, 105,
    117
Mackail, J.W. 132
Macmillan, Alexander 111-12
Macmillan, Frederick 76
Macmillan, George 75
Malory, Thomas 16, 25, 185

Mancoff, Debra N. 185
Mander, Lady 217
Marcuse, Herbert 127
Marsh, Jan 71, 108, 114, 115, 233
Marx, Karl 36
Maurice, F.D. 100-1
McAmmond, Ron 205
McCartney, Paul 2
McGann, Jerome viii, 3, 27-8, 60, 65,
    68, 127, 207
McInnis, Mauri 96, 110
McSweeney, Kerry 69
Millais, John Everett 3, 13-14, 15, 18,
    33, 96, 147, 234
Miller, J. Hillis 30
Milnes, A.H. 204
Mitchell, Scott 68
Morris, Jane 8, 16, 47-8, 222, 227-8
Morris, William 2, 4-5, 15, 16, 18-19,
    20, 21, 22, 23, 25, 26, 30, 31, 33, 87,
    119-33, 156, 221, 234
Mosher, Thomas B. 6, 208
Moss, Anita 94
Munro, Alexander 101, 234
Munroe, Marilyn 208
Murray, Charles Fairfax 73
Myers, F.W.H. 97

Nadel, Ira B. 32

Packer, Lona Mosk 77, 221
Page, Jimmy 2
Palgrave, Francis 204
Parsons, John R. 228
Pater, Walter vii, 4, 16, 18-19, 20-1, 22,
    23, 180, 183
Pearce, Lynne 202, 233
Peattie, Roger 28-9, 33, 233
Poe, Edgar A. 19

Polidori, John 9, 74
Pollitt, Herbert 179, 181-2
Pope, Alexander 36
Pound, Ezra 1, 27, 35, 39
Poynter, Edward John 147
Prettejohn, Elizabeth 97
Prinsep, Val 33
Proctor, Ellen A. 77
Psomiades, Kathy Alexis 97
Pugin, Augustus 13

Raffalovich, Andre 183
Raphael 14
Reade, Brian 179-80, 194
Rees, Joan 69
Reid, Forrest 95
Reynolds, Joshua 14, 16
Rickels, Laurence 137
Ricks, Christopher 200-1, 207
Riede, David 60, 65, 68
Rimsky-Korsakov 153
Rivière, Joan 183
Robertson, W. Graham 180
Ronnell, Avital 137
Rosenberg, John D. 207
Rossetti, Christina 17-18, 22, 28-9, 31, 69, 71-90, 91, 105-16, 219, 221
Rossetti, Dante Gabriel viii, 2, 3, 8, 11, 12, 13, 16, 17, 18, 19-21, 24, 27-8, 33, 36-69, 71, 76, 83, 84, 86, 96, 100-1, 106, 107, 145, 158, 204-7, 212, 214, 219, 220, 222, 225-31, 234-5
Rossetti, Gabriele 74
Rossetti, Maria 71, 73
Rossetti, William Michael viii, 8, 11, 12, 14, 16, 17, 21, 28-9, 31, 32, 69, 71-90, 107, 147, 203, 218-19, 234
Rothenstein, William 87
Ruskin, John 10, 12, 14-15, 16, 18, 25, 26, 30, 92, 100, 106, 121-2, 226, 232, 226, 232, 199

Said, Edward 148
Sanders, T.C. 101
Sandys, Frederick 221
Schor, Naomi 202
Scott, William Bell 8, 212-13, 220, 227, 234
Shakespeare, William 21
Shannon, Edgar F. 201
Shatto, Susan 199-200
Shaw, Marion 199-200
Shelley, Percy Bysshe 46, 86, 204
Shields, Frederic 226, 227
Showalter, Elaine 191
Siddal, Elizabeth viii, 17-18, 25, 47-8, 206, 234
Simeon, Sir John 7
Sketchley, R.E.D. 16
Slinn, E. Warwick 27-8
Smithers, Leonard 177-8, 181
Smulders, Sharon 108
Solomon, Simeon 33
Spector, Stephen J. 61, 69
Stanhope, Roddam Spencer 33
Stasny, John 6-7, 204
Stephens, Frederic G. 17
Sterling, John 25
Stevenson, Lionel 207
Stuart-Stubbs, Basil 8
Surtees, Virginia 216, 225
Swinburne, Algernon 18, 23, 24, 30, 33, 71, 72, 106, 140-3, 221, 204
Symons, Arthur 1

Tenniel, John 112, 147
Tennyson, Alfred 5, 7, 19, 23, 25, 199-201

Thirkell, Angela 87
Thompson, E.P. 120
Traill, H.D. 77
Troxell, Janet Camp 230
Tupper, John Lucas 4
Turner, Victor 169

Ulrichs, K.H. 192

Valpy, Leonard Rowe 226
Van Gogh, Vincent 146
Van der Weyden, Roger 102
Victoria, Queen 208

Wahl, John Robert 198-9, 225-31
Walker, Emery 83
Warner, Malcolm 11, 211
Waterhouse, John 96
Watson, Lacon 84-5
Watts, George F. 18

Watts-Dunton, Theodore 71, 73, 76
Waugh, Evelyn 16-17
Whistler, James A.M. 24, 30, 140-3
Whitman, Walt 86, 220
Wilde, Oscar 1, 24, 186, 189, 191, 193
Wildman, Stephen 91, 100, 105, 113
Williams, Raymond 25-6, 126
Willison, Ian 218
Wise, Thomas J. 73, 218, 229
Woodward, John 216
Woolner, Thomas 18
Wordsworth, Willliam 51, 94

Yamaguchi, Eriko 232
Yeats, W.B. 1, 18

Zatlin, Linda 181, 193, 194
Zimmer, Heinrich 175
Zipes, Zack 98-9